Shanghai and the Edges of Empires

Shanghai and
the Edges of Empires

Meng Yue

University of Minnesota Press

Minneapolis · London

Copyright 2006 by the Regents of the University of Minnesota

Published by the University of Minnesota Press
111 Third Avenue South, Suite 290
Minneapolis, MN 55401-2520
http://www.upress.umn.edu

Library of Congress Cataloging-in-Publication Data

Yue, Meng.
   Shanghai and the edges of empires / Meng Yue.
     p.   cm.
   Includes bibliographical references and index.
   ISBN-13: 978-0-8166-4412-4 (hc)
   ISBN-10: 0-8166-4412-8 (hc)
   ISBN-13: 978-0-8166-4413-1 (pb)
   ISBN-10: 0-8166-4413-6 (pb)
   1. Shanghai (China)—Civilization—19th century. 2. Shanghai (China)—Civilization—20th century. I. Title.
   DS796.S25Y8   2006
   951'.132033—dc22
                                 2005037318

Printed in the United States of America on acid-free paper

The University of Minnesota is an equal-opportunity educator and employer.

12 11 10 09   10 9 8 7 6 5 4 3 2

Contents

INTRODUCTION

The Border of Histories

Between "Overlapping Territories"

SHANGHAI!
Shanghai, the sixth city of the World!
Shanghai, the Paris of the East!
Shanghai, the New York of the West!

With this geographic metaphor, a 1935 English tour book, *All about Shanghai*, announced the city's cosmopolitan status to potential visitors from around the world. The metaphor's inspiration lies in its bold statement that a "world city," usually thought to exist only in the heart of the modern West, had emerged on the landscape of the East: in China. The vivid image made Shanghai an exciting reflection of Paris or New York in Asia. A non-Western cosmopolitanism, though not yet well known, clearly asserted itself through the metaphor. But this bold metaphorical claim also elicited deep ambivalence. Calling Shanghai a "Paris of the East" was an incredible geographic misnomer. It actually reaffirmed the globe's imaginary, yet untouchable, "border" between East and West. Calling Shanghai a "New York of the West" perceived Shanghai's position in Asia in much the same way Japan's was at that point in history. But political leaders had conferred "Western" status on Japan, claiming that it, not Shanghai, was the center of Asia (Tanaka 1993). Shanghai did not have a coherent subjectivity or a national identity, nor was it anywhere close to being a national state, as Japan was. These geographic misnomers raise about Shanghai a question that can be asked about few comparable cities: What does it mean to be a city so prominently doubly located, or doubly dislocated, in the world?

The question is not merely rhetorical, considering that any interpretation of the metaphor is impossible without invoking a specific picture, a theory, or a historical narrative of the world that establishes China's relevance. Even in Shanghai's current status, one can clearly see the persistence of its imagined dual character: As the city doubles its past fame and builds its future grandeur, it signals, from different perspectives, either the triumph of China, a noncapitalist country, in the capitalist global economy, or the victory of the global economy over a noncapitalist China, or, paradoxically, both. In this sense, the metaphorical transposition of Shanghai becomes a checkpoint on which different world pictures or contested geopolitics are tested. It is clear that if Shanghai provides an exciting site where these geopolitical agencies act out their parts, then it is the cultural, political, and historical configurations of the globe, rather than the location of the city, that needs to be mapped out.

To better illustrate the theoretical and historical implications embedded in these geopolitics, I would like to imagine what I envision a number of contemporary theorists and historians would have to say in a conversation on mapping Shanghai (imagined, because any misrepresentations of their theories will be my errors). Starting with the most obvious question, I would like to ask, for example, where a leading thinker in geopolitics, such as Immanuel Wallerstein, would find Shanghai in terms of the "world system." Perhaps he would argue that the capitalist world system, by transporting new resources and laborers from the periphery to the core, used the city as an outpost of expansion and thus gave it prominence in relation to the vast peripheries of the rest of China (Wallerstein 1989).[1]

One should also be able to envisage another pair of thinkers, a Michael Hardt and an Antonio Negri (Hardt and Negri 2000) considering Shanghai as one of the nodes on the mesh of the "empire of capital" spreading throughout the globe. In the same context, the city would also be a node on the global network of "the multitude," contesting capital from every site. In their theory, Shanghai's prominence might not relate to the "periphery," since capital does not reside in any "center" but flows without a border.

Another geopolitical thinker, Andre Gunder Frank (1998), however, would strongly object to these two visions. He would place Shanghai within an arguably long-established Asian-oriented world economy, or a "global economy of the Asian age," to which the West was only a latecomer.[2]

The economic historians Hamashita Takeshi and Kawakatsu Heita (1991) may not agree with Frank's one-world theory, but they would probably also like to bring the Asian world-trade system to the fore, based upon the tributary systems of the Ming and the Qing dynasties prior to the late nineteenth century.[3] Peter Perdue, by exploring the cross-continental expansion of the Qing Empire, would argue that what Wallerstein takes as the periphery (central Asia) of the capitalist world system was actually the domain of the Qing Empire (2005).

I would assume that for Frank, Hamashita and Kawakatsu, and Perdue, Shanghai's ascent to prominence was not so much a result of the West's expansion but the outcome of the internal rotation of the Asian world system. In this sense, the metaphor of "the New York of the West" may serve to confirm not only the accepted status of New York but also the unrecognized vitality of the Asian world nexus.

Without having to identify this Asian world system with the capitalist system, as Frank did, many urban historians would be willing to materialize the driving force of the Asian world trade in a cross-regional network of port cities. Historians of southern Asia have long demonstrated that Macao, Malacca, Indonesia, and the Malay Archipelago formed a world trading zone between East Asia, the Arabian Peninsula, and Africa.[4] Cities and ports along this trading zone—Malacca, Macao, Guangzhou, and sporadically Quanzhou and Ningbo—remained the central nexus of trade and cultural exchange between Europe and Asia during the Qing era (Liang Jiabin 1960).[5] Important Chinese cities, including Yangzhou, Suzhou, Nanjing, and Shanghai, like Guangzhou, hosted the customs installations of the Qing Empire before the Opium War (1840) (Liang Jiabin 1937, 19–36). Shanghai, as Linda C. Johnson has demonstrated, had had a customs office superior to that of Suzhou since 1730 (1995, 155–75). It was also the most important internal trading port of the Qing Empire after 1760 and opened foreign trade via the "southern and northern oceans" prior to the nineteenth century (ibid).[6] Since Shanghai's volume of shipping was comparable to that of London in the 1830s, it would be hard not to see how effectively the Qing state's inland and maritime regions meshed with Manchuria, Korea, Japan, and Southeast Asia without the "help" of the Opium War.

Even though Wallerstein's theory of a capitalist world system still holds (Wallerstein 1999; Arrighi 1999),[7] further inquiries are being made to explore the distinction and correlation between the history of capitalism and the history of noncapitalist development or an alternative history of development. To mention just a few, Xu Baoqiang's inquiry (2001) into the actual practice of a free market, rationality, and private property suggests the need to differentiate between "oppressive capitalism" and "alternative," "liberating capitalism," which, in terms of its cultural and social institutions, is closer to a "socialist ideal." Richard von Glahn's study of the circulation of silver in late-imperial China puts in focus the social and cultural uses of "money" in late-imperial China and calls into question our conception of capital as a sheer economic unit (von Glahn 1996; Flynn, Giraldez, and von Glahn 2003). Pomeranz's comparative study of the world's core economic zones demystifies the conventional story that the "rest" fail when the "West" rises (2000, 2002). With these new frontiers, our imagined conversation is bound to move on to debates over the issues of the cultural, social, and historical formations that were noncapitalist but not unsuccessful.

Indeed, rethinking "the rest" this way has already characterized theories aimed at "provincializing Europe" (Chakrabarty 2000), approaches that were strategically "China-centric" (Cohen 1984), analyses that looked at China's sustained unity in a positive rather than a negative light (Wong 1997), and research that found that China's most recent pursuit of political change originated in the dialectical dynamics within Neo-Confucianism from before contact with the West (Elman 1990). Resituating this China back into the world has further changed the way the world is envisioned. The eighteenth century did not see so much an "irresistible" expansion of the British Empire but rather its confrontation and contestation by the external, noncapitalist, more flexible, and cogent Qing Empire (Hevia 1995, 2004; Liu 2004; Perdue 2005). The world's economic cores grew into "great divergence" not because the core in Western Europe was more progressive but because it accidentally came in contact with and unfairly cashed in on agricultural resources in the Americas and slave labor from Africa (Pomeranz 2000). This trend of rethinking the history of China on its own terms is balanced by efforts to rescue the "subhistories" from a national framework and to explore how collaborators with Japanese colonialism and imperialism helped reconstruct Asia as a region (Duara 1995, 2003).

With the capitalist world system and its critique on the one hand and the history of China as other than a failure of capitalism on the other, the cultural identity of Shanghai is found somewhere between semi-colonialism and cosmopolitanism. On the one hand, having success-fully undone the paradigm of "Western impact, Chinese response," schol-ars have refurbished Shanghai as a modern metropolis that was not necessarily derived from the West and yet was more cosmopolitan than the West. It has been shown that Shanghai has long been an important center of global fashion and consumption, an urban nucleus of "cosmo-politan chic" (Lee 1999). It has also been a center for art deco and new architectural experiments (Abbas 2000), a last resort of diasporic com-munities (Ristaino 2001), and the possessor of a specific cosmopolitan culture that was dissimilar to the typical Western notion of culture but was not necessarily "Eastern." The essence of these studies suggests, to some extent, that "cosmopolitanism . . . is not a circle created by culture diffused from a center"; rather, "centers are everywhere and circumfer-ences nowhere" (Breckenridge 2002). This non-Western cosmopoli-tanism, together with multiple modernity (Wittrock 2000), alternative modernity (Gandelsonas 2002), and contested globalization (Appadurai 2002), has presented us with a polycentric, culturally specific, and site-based world.

On the other hand, potential challenges from Marxist and postcolonial perspectives also seem to be valid. Arif Dirlik (2001) may have argued against these presentations, suggesting that the cultural hybridity and multiplicity that many found in Shanghai are internal to imperialist strategies. Lu Hanchao (1999, 13) may have urged us to turn to a "more realistic picture" of the city and to look at the everyday practices of the urbanities who enjoyed little of the modern facilities available in Shang-hai. Shih (2001) has explored the complexity of Shanghai modernity in the condition of semicoloniality by showing how cosmopolitanism at the global level displaced the political and cultural task of anticolonial-ism at the local level (30–40). The question of whether Shanghai is a cosmopolitan or a semicolonial site, like many of the other imagined debates I have just addressed, opens the way to more discussion.

Nevertheless, my imagined conversation has exposed what was em-bedded in the opening metaphor: that Shanghai is located in different worlds because different worlds meet in Shanghai. In addition to the so-called Asian global economy and the capitalist world system, there was the Japanese Empire, which created its own Orient in Asia (Tanaka 1993), as well as what is called "cultural China," which was more imperial, cosmological, or cosmopolitan than is expressed in the phrase "native Chinese" (Tu Weiming 1999). There were also cultures and communities of Shanghailanders, imperialists, (semi)colonizers, diasporans, and foreign sojourners. If these cannot define what Shanghai was in the early twentieth century, they can define what the city was not. Shanghai was definitely more than an Asian counterpart to a cosmopolitan European metropolis, since it was not at the heartland of capitalism but, rather, at its periphery or frontier. Yet Shanghai was more than a colonial city, since the partial Chinese sovereignty secured fragmented dominations and multiple subject positions (Shih 2001), and the elites and underclasses were better prepared to voice themselves than were "subalterns" (Hershatter 1993). Shanghai was also more than a Third World city depleted by imperialism, since it sprouted from a developed economic core zone where science and technology were known (Elman 1984, 79–83) and where cities and the urban public in general were more developed and commercialized than scholars at first anticipated (Rowe 1984, 15). Shanghai, in short, was not merely a site that housed different worlds; rather, it was a result of their meetings and interactions.

I suggest that the overlay of these "worlds" in Shanghai can be assessed in what Edward Said would have called "overlapping territories," a term he used to emphasize that the culture of the United States was actually formed by *two* parts (not one): the literature of the colonized and that of the colonizer (Said 1994, xxv). The concept of "overlapping territories" is related to another concept of Said's, "contrapuntal histories," which depicts the way the cultures of the colonized and the Third World formed active, visible counterzones and counterhistories from those that derive from within First World culture (ibid). To transfer these concepts to the context of Shanghai, I take the liberty of expanding the meaning and multiplying the number of "territories" so that the term serves to refer to regions, cultures, subcultures, sociopolitical units, and different sovereignties that pertained to city life. The most important of the "overlapping territories" referred to in this book include, among many, two or more types of empires and two or more types of histories. The types of empires represented by the Qing Empire and imperialism,[8] though comparable, were dissimilar and were facing different types of internal crises and conflicts.

A related point is that if we think of "territories" in temporal terms, they became overlaid histories. Conceivably, agents in these histories varied from emperors to rebels, members of the bourgeois to members of the peasantry. It was the territory they claimed for themselves and the histories they made that overlaid in Shanghai, "contrapuntally" or not. The possible interactions and convergences between capitalist and noncapitalist histories would also therefore be part of the unsolved mystery of Shanghai. I use the somewhat awkward expression "non-capitalist histories" as a strategic phrase that aims not at defining cultural histories but at freeing histories from definitions. The phrase, therefore, opens itself to what can be called "de-capitalist histories," alternative histories of development or what Xu Baoqiang would call alternative capitalist histories.[9] The ambiguity of locating Shanghai, therefore, calls for an exploration or a characterization of the mysterious relationship between these territories or histories. And, of course, to answer this call is the pursuit of this book, even though the book covers merely a small slice of the cultural and historical Shanghai.

The Route of the Qing Empire: Catastrophes and "Change"

The urban historiography of China is one area where the mythology of the rise of "the West" and the failure of "the rest" is most effectively disputed. William Skinner's (1977) survey of imperial cities further demystifies the uniformity of "Chinese cities" as administrative units and the "walled city" as the sole space of urban activity (Xu Yinong 2000, 165). William T. Rowe has shown the comparability and differences between the long-distance trade, occupational community, and urban "public" of nineteenth-century Chinese cities and those of the cities of early modern Europe (Rowe 1984, 1989). Others have explored the interplay of tradition and modernity that changed the role of cities (Esherick 2000). At the turn of the millennium, Shanghai studies have been liberated from the old paradigms that point to the West, the imagined ultimate center of power in the world, as the true hero or true villain in China's historical change.[10] Instead, Shanghai studies have focused our attention on the city's history as an important international port since the fourteenth century (Johnson 1995), on the migration and coinage of the underclass as an "ethnicity" (Honig 1992), on trade organizations and their cross-regional networks (Goodman 1995), and on the city's underground world (Martin 1996). These studies have also drawn our attention to the birth of Shanghai's police system (Wakeman 1995), the dangerous impact of prostitution (Hershatter 1997), and the anatomy of its growing neighborhoods (Lu Hanchao 1999).[11]

The constant attention that old Shanghai attracts from the world, however, makes one question apparent: What was unique about Shanghai that conferred such historic and ideological prominence on it? Shanghai was not the only treaty port forced to open to European trade after the Opium War, nor was it the only treaty port that lay along the coast of China, nor was it the only trading site to house international communities. Shanghai was not the city with the longest history in China's world trade or the one with a history of cosmopolitan culture. For centuries Guangzhou was the most important connection among continental China, Europe, Africa, and Southeast Asia, and it remained active in the Asia-America China trade after the Opium War (Metropolitan Museum of Art 1941; Lee and Philadelphia Museum of Art 1984). Wasn't Guangzhou a worthy competitor to Shanghai in the late nineteenth century? And why was Shanghai the only city referred to as "the Paris of the East"?

I maintain that while scholarship on Chinese cities widens our vision of an alternative history of development, it also raises questions concerning change, if not progress, in such a history. The question "Why Shanghai?" is actually embedded in such an inquiry of change. The implications of this inquiry are most evident if it is examined in terms of culture rather than of economic history.

Some concrete examples of the radical cultural shift help illustrate the issue: From 1782 to 1844, when the first three volumes of *Chouren zhuan*, or *Biographies of Mathematicians and Astronomers*, were compiled, the 204 most respected contemporary scientific and technological experts were concentrated primarily in the major cities of the south. These people traveled a lot from city to city, but one can roughly state that among these cities, Yangzhou, before its decline, contained about one-fifth of these talented individuals, including the top experts in I-ching studies, renowned visiting officials, mathematicians, musicians, and self-taught astronomers. Suzhou and Guangzhou, with some overlaps with other cities, each was home to one-fifth of these intellectuals, including Ruan Yuan, the compiler, and others from the Yue Hai Tiang Academy. Hangzhou and Changzhou comprised at least a quarter of the total, including those famous for teaching in the renowned private academies of Jiangnan. Shanghai, then merely a county, was home to only one local mathematician and had few scientific societies, formal or informal, to host intellectuals from out of town.

As another example: During the same period, the late imperial period, the Jiangnan cities and Guangzhou were the publishing and learning centers of China. The Jiangnan cities Yangzhou, Hangzhou, and Suzhou housed the cultural resources of *Wen yuan ge siku quanshu* (The Complete Collection of the Four Treasuries) as well as many famous private book collections (Ding Shen 1957; Guy 1987; Elman 1984). Several hundred public and private academies dotted the urban and suburban landscapes of these cities. The publishing and reprinting of research papers and classics were both prestigious and thriving businesses in the cities (Woodside 1994, 458–92). Up to the mid-nineteenth century, Suzhou had over 100 printing presses, some of them having a history stretching back more than 300 years (Zhang Xiumin 1989, 589). Other cities in the south, such as Hangzhou and Guangzhou, each had a few dozen (590). Shanghai, a town a night's travel away from Suzhou, had only a few printers, a couple of academies, and some book collectors.

Still another example: As commercial centers, these cities were also the focal points of entertainment and theaters. Hundreds of opera troupes from all regions flocked in and out of these cities. Suzhou alone hosted several dozen opera houses (Gu Gongxie [1785] 1917, 40–41). In Yangzhou, where musical scores for plays and operas were compiled by order of the Emperor Qianlong, any merchant's family could be a patron to a couple of opera troupes performing new plays in different local styles. During the same period, however, Shanghai only had a few theaters, of which only one troupe was known to offer a couple new plays (Ying Baoshi and Yu Yue [1872] 1975; Gu Duhuang 1987, 34–41).

Why did these early cosmopolitan centers not last into the late nineteenth century? And why were they surpassed in prominence and grandeur by Shanghai, previously a minor town?

I would suggest that an unprecedented geographic shift of culture and society within the Qing Empire during the nineteenth century was part of Shanghai's rise to the joint frontier of "world systems." This shift of the dominant culture and society from the Jiangnan Grand Canal–based and river-based Jiangnan urban centers to the sea route–based cities took place between the 1820s and the second decade of the twentieth century. In this era, the eighteenth-century Grand Canal–based urban centers of the Qing dynasty declined, and their cultural and social vitality migrated to the coastal port of Shanghai. The causes of this shift can be traced back to the Qing state's policies for dealing with damage to the Grand Canal during the early nineteenth century and to the turmoil of the Taiping Rebellion, which swept across the entire southern half of China. Just as one cannot think of Shanghai without considering the expansion of the imperialist empires, so would the rise of the city be equally inconceivable without the dramatic historical shift of the Jiangnan cultural center toward the shore.

To understand this shift, one needs to take a closer look at the location of the urban centers of the Qing Empire in the eighteenth century. The urban network of cultural centers in the Qing Empire was not identical to the urban network of commerce and trade. The urban nexus of commerce and trade had been concentrated along the Grand Canal and the inland water system that was the backbone of the empire's south-north transportation until the first two decades of the nineteenth century (Hoshi Ayao 1969; Leonard 1996, 1–39, 78–133). These trade cities formed a cross-regional and far-reaching network, connecting the southern and southeastern Asian sea routes with the inland river-and-canal-based system of the Qing Empire on the continent. Starting from Guangzhou, then the location of the headquarters of the Hong merchants, the East India Companies, and the Thirteen Foreign Factories, the network reached conveniently north to China's most prosperous region, Jiangnan, where Suzhou, Hangzhou, and Nanjing are located. It then connected Yangzhou and Zhenjiang to northern China via the river systems and the Grand Canal. To the west the network connected the middle and upper Yangtze cities of Hankou and Jingzhou. To the east, via Shanghai and Quanzhou, it linked Japan and Taiwan; and to the south, it went to southern ocean ports frequented by both European and non-European ships. On this map, however, only a few heartland cities—Suzhou, Nanjing, Hangzhou, Yangzhou, and Guangzhou—enjoyed the glory of urban cultural centers in the vast territory of the Qing Empire. They housed transdynastic cultured communities that were familiar with classicism (Mote 1973, 33–65; Elman 1984), salt-merchant classes who were apt at turning appropriated literati tastes into court hobbies (Mayer-Fong 2003), and mathematical and astronomical experts seeking transdynastic connections in translated sciences. These cities were where the centers of culture congregated—a thriving treasure house of high-ranking literati, well-versed official-merchants, academies, rare books, knowledge, expertise, technology, arts and crafts, gardens and architects, antiques, imported goods, royal gifts, fashions and styles, medicine, and recipes (Fang Hao 1953–1954). Although Shanghai had already proved to be an indispensable part of the commercial urban network by the mid-nineteenth century, its culture was still relatively provincial.

The shift of culture and society from these canal-based cities to the coastal city of Shanghai, and that city's subsequent development, was largely generated by varying international conditions and unprecedented internal crises, as well as efforts at recovery from those crises. Two catastrophes, which took place during the nineteenth century, help explain why Yangzhou and Suzhou stopped being centers of cultural traffic and why, by the late nineteenth century, they were replaced by Shanghai.

The first catastrophe was the socioeconomic changes of the early nineteenth century caused by the Qing state's reluctance to repair the flooded Grand Canal and its decision to temporarily use sea routes instead (Leonard 1996, 51–77). This created difficulties in the south-north transportation of grain and salt, which had customarily been transported via the Grand Canal. The state also changed its policy on the salt monopoly and restricted the income of salt merchants.[12] The result was the decline of their political and economic status, which precipitated the decline of Yangzhou as a transit center at the hub of empire-wide trade. When the Grand Canal ceased to be the main route between the south and the north, literati and merchants alike shifted their business and civil examination itineraries to include stops in Shanghai. As a result, Shanghai rose on the debris of Yangzhou's ruin.

The second catastrophe was the Taiping Rebellion (1851–1864), which took over large areas of southern China. It almost ended the Qing dynasty, and it brought about the fatal decline of the Jiangnan urban centers. Lasting more than a decade and making a huge impact on the political, social, and cultural systems in a vast area of southern and southeastern China, the rebellion was the final blow in a crisis that had been waiting even in the prosperous era of the "high Qing." Population pressures on the land, polarization of wealth and property, bureaucratic problems, and depression had all appeared by the mid-nineteenth century, drawing to a close a long era of "development" in the Qing dynasty (Kuhn 1980, 37–38).

The rebellion created a decisive and permanent change in Jiangnan, whose urban centers of Hangzhou, Suzhou, and Yangzhou were devastated by the rebels and the Qing army. Shanghai was hurt only briefly and in minor ways by the war because of its rather unsatisfactory military position and because of its foreign settlements. But Suzhou and Hangzhou were traumatized during the war. In 1862, after a long siege, Suzhou and Hangzhou, the last and most central cities of Jiangnan, fell into the hands of the Taiping. After another three-month siege, the Qing army took back the cities but once again turned the urban areas into killing fields. In that year, Shanghai saw more than 50,000 refugees flock to the International Settlement, almost tripling the population of 1850 (Yu Xingmin 1991, 8–23). Wealthier members of Jiangnan society, gentry and merchants alike, were uprooted; they found it hard to rise from the ruins even after the war and returned to Shanghai with money and skills. Meanwhile, the government's "restoration" policies put more weight on controlling social and cultural activities than on encouraging creativity (I will discuss this point in detail below). As a result, the number of migrants into the International Settlement increased to 90,000 by 1865 and to 171,950 by 1890 (Zou Yiren 1980). Events that caused the decline and fall of Yangzhou and Suzhou meant a new beginning for Shanghai.

The Taiping Rebellion and the devastation of Jiangnan urban society caused unique and complicated patterns of migration to Shanghai (Lu Hanchao 1999, 8–12). In terms of culture and society, these migrations formed historical trajectories to reconstruct the displaced urbanism of the previous cluster of urban sites. Military leaders from the northwestern provinces of Hunan and Anhui, for example, who emphasized practical technology, replaced civil scholar-officials in the political and cultural arena of the coastal province of Jiangsu. Scholars of evidential studies and classical learning who were uprooted from Jiangnan cities came in contact with translated knowledge and either used it or fought it for cultural authority. For safety reasons as well as for expansion, missionaries of various Christian churches moved from their traditional stations in the Anhui, Fujian, Guangdong, and Zhejiang provinces to Shanghai, where they joined the lay Chinese and foreign communities and began to mix their religious mission with scientific translation, as well as with international politics. Jiangnan entrepreneurs came to compete with Guangdong and "southeast ocean" merchants and with Western businessmen. Popular theater, which had previously lacked consistent venues for its performances, established itself in Shanghai and created the most prosperous avenues in the International Settlement (chapter 4). High-class and lowbrow consumers from Guangzhou and Jiangnan displayed their centuries-old disparate tastes in interior decoration as well as in the culture of commodities.

The significance of the Taiping Rebellion in causing a geographic shift of urban society breaks the "natural" course of development of Shanghai and makes the city's "rise" as a cultural center a paradoxical outcome of the catastrophes of the Qing Empire. It reveals the large-scale crisis that preconditioned "the Paris of the East" and, ironically, the "origin" of "Chinese modernity." Like any rebellion, the Taiping Rebellion in the end repeated the vital conflict between the redistribution system of the dynasty and the basic survival needs of all members of society. But it hit the systemic weak spot of the Qing hard when it ruined Jiangnan, the economic and cultural heartland of the Qing Empire, and pressed on to the border of the Yellow River. The great shift of culture and society from Jiangnan to the coast turned the Qing Empire inside out, and its core became the periphery, even the frontier, of defense. One outcome of this process was that every element that gave rise to Shanghai indicated every disruption the empire had experienced. As a cultural center, Shanghai was neither a product of sheer Western modernity nor a result of pure Asian capitalism. Its birth as a modern metropolis embodied the crisis-driven historical trajectory of the Qing after the eighteenth century.

Beyond "the West and the Rest": Imperialism and the Unruly

By mapping Shanghai as a result of the catastrophic inside-out-turn of the Qing Empire, I by no means intend to minimize the role of imperialists, modernity, or even "the West." That would be to deny a series of key factors that influenced modern Chinese history, such as modern warfare, unequal treaties, extraterritoriality, the craze for electricity, significant new ways of using industry, labor, the sciences, and technology, and the global politics that have dominated mankind for at least two centuries. The purpose here, rather, is to shed new light on Western influence on Shanghai and the imperialist dominance of China. Many scholars have noted the complicit relationship between Chinese society and imperialism, yet the historical reason for that complicity has been explored in the context of the controllers rather than from the side of the controlled or, in my opinion, of the uncontrollable. Without denying that the imperialist encroachment on China had crucially conditioned the rise of Shanghai, I contend that the paradoxical turn of the Qing Empire gave rise to various unruly cultural and political practices that were far more active than mere "resistance" and that were, in fact, capable of generating an impact upon and influencing the relationship between China and imperialism.

The uncontrollable cultural and social practice I am talking about, rather than being a product of imperialism or semicolonialism, has its own cultural logic embedded in China's late-imperial history. This logic was manifested, for example, in the unfolding of Neo-Confucianism (Daoxue) itself. As Benjamin Elman (1984, 26) shows, the Song and Ming Neo-Confucian thinkers invented a metaphysical and cosmological system of thought that centered on the moral philosophy that was allegedly handed down directly from the ancient saints and sage-kings. Although the Qing rulers enshrined this system, Neo-Confucian scholars discovered a contradiction between the claimed true teaching of the ancient saints and evidence from alternative texts. This contradiction, though internal to Neo-Confucianism, generated a powerful undercurrent in the eighteenth century that led to the negation of the system itself. To be more specific: By the late seventeenth century, the philologist Yan Ruoju (1636–1704), in an attempt to resume the interrupted conversation with antiquity, found that some parts of the key Confucian classic, *The Book of History*, were a forgery. Intending to establish Confucius's true meaning, their evidential studies of the classics nonetheless "advanced the front of objectivity and the cause of disbelief" of Neo-Confucianism itself (ibid., 30–32).

Scholars of the New Text school, having given up their search for authentic classics from the time of Confucius, emphasized the importance of alternative texts derived from a later period, especially the *Gongyang Commentary*, which supported the picture of Confucius as a charismatic visionary rather than as a distinguished teacher (Elman 1984, 23). In doing so, they recovered a long-forgotten political movement between the crowned sage-kings and an "uncrowned king" in his own right (ibid). Moreover, the eighteenth-century scholar Dai Zhen's (1724–1777) interpretation of the works of Mencius resuscitated a forgotten justification of the right to revolt and the power of people as opposition to the ruler (ibid., 17–18). His interpretation undermined the orthodoxy of the Qing ideology that theorized the human world and the cosmos as a uniform polity with no internal contradictions (Brokaw 1994, 257–91). In short, by the eighteenth century, the classical origin upon which the orthodox cultural system had been established had split. A gap thus revealed differences and contradictions between the ideal nondiscriminative cosmos and its textualization and materialization in ways characteristic of fragmentation.

This unexpected loss of the unified, genuine, harmonious political and cultural cosmos of the sage-kings was to Neo-Confucianism what deconstruction was to the Western philosophical lineage, except the former had a more significant impact on social and political spaces. It subverted the classical textuality that had functioned as a state apparatus. It destabilized the meaningfulness of civil service examinations. It challenged the centrality of moral order in cultural reproduction and opened unexplored, alternative fields in classicism, such as the sciences, astronomy, medicine, and mathematics.

The subversive power of the absence of a unified or authentic origin was most intensively embodied by the Taiping Rebellion. Its leader, Hong Xiuquan, who had failed the civil service examination several times, claimed he had received heavenly visions and that Christ, instead of the ancient Chinese saints, had assigned to him the mission to build a heavenly kingdom on earth. The fact that this political visionary, among other things, mobilized hundreds of thousands of people indicates how intense the need was to replace and renovate the origin of the political cosmos. What was initiated by the discovery of the irreparable split in that origin was the subversive historical process itself, a process that constantly negates its own base. What Nietzsche described as modernity was quite suitable here: After the death of God, human beings began to sway toward X from the center of the world.

But what made the cultural practice "unruly" was not merely its subversion of Neo-Confucian orthodoxy but its political quest for ways of renewing the ideal of polity, the universal public, and the ultimate goal of human society that had once been attributed to the ancient saints and sages. This quest for the ideal polity and human society urged Hong Liangji (1746–1809), a prominent New Text school philologist, to challenge the misuse of the public for personal interests (Elman 1984). It caused Gong Zizhen (1792–1841), a renowned New Text scholar, to admit the decay of the Qing Empire and to realize the need for a revitalization of the culture and the Tao. It triggered the desire of Kang Youwei (1858–1927), Tan

Sitong (1865–1898), and other thinkers, to establish a universal framework for human society in the world, while at the same time radically eliminating all the heritage, hierarchy, and borders of culture. This was an ongoing search, for each answer contained its own negation and proliferation. Kang Youwei posited compassion as the ultimate origin of an ideal order; Tan Sitong found that benevolence, or *ren*, served, instead of conservative, sage ways, revolution and nihilism. Whereas Sun Yatsan established "people" as the final goal for political regimes, Mao Zedong redefined "people" in terms of classes and masses. Radical changes, revolution, and the quest for an ultimate public community and unsurpassable public culture were the results of the momentum begun by the unfulfilled quest to renew the ultimate political and cultural ideal.

It is in this sense that the evisceration of the Qing urban culture I have been talking about was not merely geographical and societal but also cultural and political. Wang Liping's work (1997, 2000) has revealed one side of this inside-out-turn by showing how the tightened political control over Hangzhou after the Taiping Rebellion transformed the city from the front line of culture and knowledge into a conservative site of "tradition." The growth of Shanghai into a cultural center represented the other side of this inside-out-turn, which led to the final stage of the cultural, social, and political *de-centric* process of the Qing Empire. The de-centric process set in motion the constant pursuit of the new: Constant revolution became the symptom of culture; Huang Zunxian's (1848–1905) vernacular poetry was replaced by Liang Qichao's (1873–1929) poetry revolution. What to Liang was a revolution was outmoded to the New Culturalists who sought to replace the entire base, including the language of cultural heritage. Yet such a movement itself was criticized and criticized itself in the decade that followed, giving way to left-wing literature. Rather than self-colonization, what first appeared here was a centuries-old process of self-deconstruction—deconstructing in order to be constructive, denying the self in order to set a path along which the culture would be renewed.

I attempt to show how this centrifugal or unruly dynamic vigorously intervened between the imperialist economics and the cultural invasion—these interactions brought about Shanghai. To those who pursued the ultimate political ideal, the presence of the West brought forth both a new form of domination and the chance for outsourcing. It generated a two-way circulation that was typical of Shanghai culture prior to the 1930s. While the imperialists and colonialists launched cultural projects inside and outside China, aiming at domination and colonization, the unruly practices of politics and culture within the Qing Empire also brought in from Japan and the West political ideals and cultural imaginations that would eventually be subversive to the imperialists. The imperialist infiltration was often countered by the outsourcing practice of the radical and unruly Chinese intellectuals, students, youth, and workers. Without a consideration of the contradictions between imperialist domination and the unruly practices de-centered from the Qing, our understanding of Shanghai would be incomplete.

Several levels of interaction need to be reviewed in this new light. Many have noticed the way interaction between control and incomplete control manifested itself at the local and social level. The "cooperative and competitive" intra-imperialist relationship featured, in Shih's words, an informal, fragmented, layered, and multiple domination of China (2001, 15–21). The chaotic situation of Shanghai, on the other hand, was due not only to a lack of control but also to an influx of the uncontrollable both from abroad and from the interior. The incomplete semicolonial domination, for example, was partly due to the influx to Shanghai of such illegitimate social players as fugitives from justice, former bandits, and prostitutes, as well as to the lifestyles and cultural behaviors that moved to Shanghai at the time. What can be called the unruly at the social level included an uninvited influx of rebels, illicit figures, and outlaws from all over the world. Among Shanghailanders were wanted criminals, businesses that had fled lawsuits in their homelands, diasporans, and White Russians. The influx of illicit figures also included those who were involved with the Taipings and those who practiced the banned businesses of "urban vice" (Wakeman 1996), prostitution and amoral practices in the theater and entertainment world. Even though Shanghai's police force, laws, and prisons were among the best in China, they could not get rid of these illicit activities (Wakeman 1996). Along with the "urban vice" figures and the prostitutes were the political dissidents and, later, the political radicals who were not only opponents of the Chinese government but also enemies of capitalism and imperialism abroad.

What can be called "the unruly" did not limit itself to the illicit but also appeared in legal and political forms. Interactions between the Qing court or the Guomindang (GMD, or Nationalist Party) government and the British and Japanese states were not necessarily confrontational but were more often collaborative, so the rebellious, radical practices that had been nurtured within China extended to the imperialists. Socially and politically speaking, these unruly forces not only overthrew the Qing dynasty and proclaimed the 1911 Revolution; they were also involved in multiple anti-imperialist activities, such as public lectures, large-scale meetings and gatherings, the mobilization of boycotts of U.S. and Japanese goods, the organization of demonstrations that blocked the streets, and lawsuits against local authorities for violating the property rights of native-place associations (groups or organizations of fellow villagers and people who come from the same place) (Goodman 1995). They also organized riots, student demonstrations, and, most prominently, the May Fourth movement by workers across the spectrum of society. In a few decades these activities turned Shanghai into the first harbor of revolution, where workers' movements were mobilized (Perry 1993) and strikes were held against imperialism, before the bloody beginning of the Nanjing period (1927–1937).

What can be called the unruly also manifested itself in the cultural interventions with imperialists. One sees in Shanghai the confrontation of two imagined Wests, a radical and rebellious West versus a cosmopolitan and imperialist West.[13] In the era prior to the Nanjing period, the radical West not only was juxtaposed to but also contested the imperialist West. Shanghai also manifested a need to separate the "world" of capitalism from the minor world. Literature translated from Western languages, for example, might not be from the dominant West—America, Britain, France, and Germany—but from other Western countries, such as Greece, Scotland, and Poland. The world of capitalism was represented by the powers that became involved in World War I; the minor world was formed by India, Egypt, Africa, Poland, Turkey, Korea, and Vietnam, an imagined international community of which China was a part (Karl 2002).

Cultural and political relations between China and Japan embodied this contradictory circulation in similar ways. While the Japanese state turned Shanghai into its trading port and poured into inland China with commodities, military forces, and modern cultural authorities, Chinese youth brought home from Japan critical sentiments, revolutionary political theories, and radical nationalism. The Qing court had hoped that Chinese students studying in Japan would bring back knowledge of science and technology; the Japanese government, on the other hand, directed at Chinese students a "colonial" education whose nucleus was a docile Confucianism (Judge 2001). However, as I will show in chapter 4, Chinese students abroad had a radical effect on the Shanghai-Tokyo connection.

One important overlapping territory in Shanghai was that between the imperialists and the unruly. Unlike Yangzhou and Suzhou, Shanghai did not, by any means, represent the inner order of the empire. Unlike Wallerstein's "cosmopolitan core" paradigm, represented by Western Europe, the city-empire relationship between Shanghai and the Qing was a twisted one. Whereas cities in the "cosmopolitan core" were nurtured by the frontier with the power of the imperialist empires, Shanghai grew with the weakening of the Qing Empire. Unlike Calcutta or Mexico City, prior to the 1930s, Shanghai did not confirm the dominance of imperialist or colonialist or any order. Shanghai carried within its birth a peripheral element, a subversive, rebellious spirit that was ungovernable by either the Qing Empire or the imperialist regime. It turned the city into a haven for outlaws, as well as a cradle of anarchists, anti-Qing revolutionaries, early Chinese Communists, radical journalists, and strikers and demonstrators against imperialism. This unruly Shanghai and its history was buried, or at least diminished, by the Shanghai of the 1930s, when the GMD successfully cracked down on the workers' movements, jailed and murdered activists, killed demonstrating students, arrested writers and artists, solicited all the unstructured economic and social elements, and pacified the city with blood, terror, and guns. Only then did a docile, regulated, and commodified urbanity come to cover the demonic, chaotic, and carnival urbanity and eventually to embellish the image of Shanghai.

On the Border of Overlapping Histories

From the historical contexts of the catastrophe and the unruly, I now return to the thesis of overlapping territory and overlapping histories for conceptual and methodological concerns. One question immediately meets the eye: Where is the border of overlapping histories? Similarly, how does one address the relationship between the overlapped histories—are they to be conceived in terms of collaboration or of contestation, of juxtaposition or of one being subsumed in the other?

Theoretical efforts have been made to envision the coexistence of multiple histories. As did Said (mentioned earlier), Fredric Jameson, among

others, maintained that noncapitalist and capitalist histories form concentric circles. Precapitalist histories can be considered the core (Jameson
1987). This image of history is already different from the classical Marxist
notion of historical progress in which a more advanced phase of history
replaces a less advanced one. Here, in Jameson's vision, other histories
exist within the history of capitalism not only as fragmented residues
but also as unities. Their interactions must be brought about by critical
interpretation.

From a slightly different perspective, postcolonial critic Dipesh Chakrabarty has noted differences and interactions between "two histories
of capital": first, the better-known history of Western capitalism that
developed into the capitalist mode of production, European modernity,
and imperialism, which he calls "History 1" of capital; and, second, the
histories of the colonized and the Third World that have developed forms
of capital, commodity, and labor yet do not take capitalism as their tele-
ological goal (2000, 47–71). These histories he calls "History 2s" of capital. The "two histories of capital" differ between "being" and "becoming."
History 1 is the "being" of capital, that is, it embodies the logic of capital.
History 2s, as a stage of "becoming" (62), refer to "a process of deferral
internal to the being (logic) of capital" (65). History 1 is hegemonic,
translating the difference of History 2s into the master narrative of capitalism. History 2s are inherent in capital and yet "interrupt and punctu-
ate the run of capital's own logic" (64). In History 2s resides the "social
formation" that was "not yet conquered," "unconquered," or simply "unconquerable" by Western capitalism (64–65). In History 2s there were
also differences that are simply "untranslatable" into the master narrative code of capitalist history.

Although "the unconquerable" and "untranslatable" that Chakrabarty
talked about resonates in interesting ways with "the unruly" that I have
tried to convey, I cannot help but be distracted by his quick subsuming
of History 2s into a "history of capital." It seems that his critical work is
ready to draw connections between "subaltern history" and the "history of capital" rather than between subaltern and noncapital histories
in the Third World. In his theorization of the "outside," for example,
Chakrabarty described "something that attached to the category of 'capital' itself," something that "conforms to the temporal code within which
capital comes into being" even as it violates that code, something "we
are able to see only because we can think/theorize capital, but that also

reminds us that other temporalities, other forms of worlding, coexist and are possible" (95). While this theorization is sophisticated and enlightening, its reasoning does not go beyond the paradigm of "capital and its other," a binary logic in which "the other" is not conceivable without capital. At one point Chakrabarty even declined those possible noncapitalist histories as "stories" that "are predicated on imagining a space that is external to capital" (2000, 95) and therefore excluded them from speculation.

As someone who studies Chinese culture and history, where the presence of capitalism has only been relatively recent and fragmented, I feel the urge to reverse the paradigm so that the history of capital can be imagined only because we think of noncapitalist histories. In other words, instead of studying cultures and histories in China merely as "the other" of capital, one should take the history of capital as "the other" of most Third World histories. After all, it was the history of capital and capitalism that was the "provincial" and the anomalous, instead of the universal, in the total of human histories on a world scale, as Chakrabarty's own title, *Provincializing Europe*, suggests.

Thus I intend to enlarge and transfer what to Marx and Chakrabarty were "the unconquerable" to "the unruly" as an attempt to move from a capital-based analysis of subaltern history toward a socially, culturally, and politically based discussion of noncapitalist histories. By making this move, I am by no means suggesting that a vague term such as "the unruly" covers anything near the "essence" of noncapitalist history. State and governance, despite "the unruly," often play equal or more important roles in formulating noncapitalist histories. I am arguing, however, that in China during the period I am covering, "the unruly" is a possible place to farm out the origin of the historical "outside." Such an "outside" is not identical to the "other" of capitalism, such as Communist socialism. Rather, it lies beyond the history of capital and its binary opposition. The term "the unruly" indicates not only elusiveness but also the transformability and randomness of these "outside" practices. To an extent, the unruly can be thought of as a warehouse where was stored the impetus that "interrupted" the run of capital's logic, modified and rejected the regime of colonialism, and actually brought forward an alternative picture about nations and the world. What is known as Communist socialism was an after-the-fact deformation of this impetus, if not an error.

Just as capitalism and imperialism can and do encompass all sorts of cultural and political practices, "the unruly" can also refer to linguistics, ideology, sentiment, text, performance, cultural production, and so on. Since this volume aims to provide a cultural history of Shanghai, cultural practices, instead of site, place, facade, and space, will become the primary unit of analysis. Henri Lefebvre's vision of a modern city as a "product of social practices" (1991, 36) has clarified this point succinctly. The city, including its material aspects, is the historical *consequence* of specific actions conducted by definite social actors (classes). As a *product*, the city is not decipherable without reconstructing the entire process of social practices that brought it forth. Of course, for Lefebvre, it was the political practice of industrial capitalism as well as the bourgeois class strategies of structuring space, living, and the culture of everyday life that spawned the modern city (1995, 63–85). In the case of Shanghai, a product of two histories, the code for deciphering the city lies in the interrelation between capitalist and imperialist cultural politics on the one hand, and the sociocultural practices of "the unruly" on the other.

But how do we address their relationship, exactly? Are they related as "contrapuntal histories," as Said said, or, to borrow from Jameson, are they somewhat "concentric"? To address the question, I return to Chakrabarty's concept of "translational histories." Like Jameson and Said, Chakrabarty also emphasized the role of critical interpretation in rescuing the work of History 2 from the oppressive control of the capitalist regime. To bring cultural difference into theorization, Chakrabarty specifically defined this critical interpretation, a task of *translation*. As he pointed out, the cultural hegemony of History 1 over History 2 embodied itself in the very fact that the experience of History 2s in the Third World was constantly translated into the master narrative of History 1. A historian's job is to (re)translate and retrieve what has been translated into the universal language of History 1 and insert it into the experiences and vocabularies of History 2s. Thus, for example, if the master narrative translated the life-world and the divine in Indian life into a universal sociology, the historian's task is to translate them back (2000, 73–83). Retranslation, in this sense, brings us one step forward from Said and Jameson's phrases and is itself a process of cultural decolonization (that is, emancipating morality, ideology, and culture from the control of the West [Duara 2004, 2]). Retranslation may not be the only

way, but it is certainly a workable way, to uncover as well as to participate in the histories of noncaptial.

I intend to further elaborate on (re)translation—not as a historian's
strategy but as a practice by which the "unconquerable" interacted with
imperialist cultural politics. To do so, I extend Chakrabarty's concept
from a method of historiography to a historical process itself and claim
that retranslation as a cultural practice has made a historical difference.
My take on retranslation in a sense departs from the linguistic paradigm since I do not assume that the target language, the language to be
retranslated into, is a ready-made signifying system. Rather, one retrieves
from the master code the right, the conventions, and the freedom to use
terms and expressions of one's own. My take on retranslation, therefore,
prioritizes the *situational* social cultural relationships built among the
original translator (or the colonizer), the original receiver/listener (the
colonized), the retranslator (the critic of colonialism), and the possible
new audience/participants (others colonized and critics). I argue that
the cultural exchange across the border of histories took place through
these relationships. Whereas for Jameson and Chakrabarty a noncapitalist or subaltern history is to be uncovered via retrospective interpretation, such retranslation formed a fair amount of the cultural practices
that brought about Shanghai. In retranslation the unconquered was ac-
tivated and entered the multiparty history again. The consequence of
retranslation was not simply a restoration of the terminology of the
colonized; rather, it was a de-systemization and multiplication of social
and cultural relationships at the cross of the empires. Retranslations of
this sort were themselves unruly and by the first decade of the twentieth
century had turned Shanghai into a contradiction to the capitalist
dream city.

The Arrangement of the Book

Since this volume unfolds in a nonlinear manner, I will provide a general view of the chapters here. Chapters 1 and 2, which form part I of
this book, share the theme of knowledge and cultural reproduction in
the dual contexts of the continuing development of the practical learning of the Qing Empire on the one hand, and the translated knowledge
of science, technology, and humanity on the other. The two enterprises
discussed in part I, the experimental Jiangnan Arsenal and the business

that later became the nation's leading publisher, the Commercial Press, together witnessed several transitions that unfolded as the Jiangnan urban centers declined. Among these were the Taiping Rebellion, the Sino-Japanese War (1894), the New Policy (1902), and the New Culture movement (1917) after World War I. Two practices, the specific use of the Neo-Confucian term "investigation of things" *(gezhi)* and a broader way of compiling printed knowledge *(bianyi),* manifest the unruly in the form of providing undefinable, unrationalizable science and technology.

Chapters 3 and 4 of part II switch to an uncontrollable aspect of cosmopolitanism that manifested itself at the historical nexus of entertainment, consumption, and the sense of community. Chapter 3 introduces, from the connections between city and popular theaters, the comparability between an urban culture characterized by *fanhua* (prosperity) or *yin* (decadence) and the cosmopolitan entertainment culture of the West. Rampant *yin* defied the meaning of prosperity and order and became the creative agent of Shanghai's bustling theater zone. Chapter 4 focuses on the way agents of noncapitalist history, starting with the boycott movement of 1905, subverted the colonial relationship between the world "community" of overseas Chinese, African Americans, and Filipinos on the one hand and the world community of "superior" nations on the other.

Part III of this book deals with the construction of exotic and cosmopolitan urban spectacles represented by the "estates" of different entrepreneurs, from the late eighteenth to the early twentieth centuries. The chapters show the way the world order was retranslated in the constructed European gardens and cosmopolitan spaces earlier in the urban center of Yangzhou and later in Shanghai. The chapters also present the change of these urban spaces, during the Qing Republic transition, from the Zhang Garden (1882) to the Great World (1917). In this change the embodiment of the desire for a reversed expansion from Asia to the Old and New World was transformed into a display of a somewhat chaotic fantasy of the coexistence of all cultures and all nations in "one world." I should emphasize that each of the three parts traces the transformation of urban culture, and each unfolds along a similar period of time, from approximately the second half of the nineteenth century to the early twentieth century.

PART I
Cosmic and Semiotic Centers of Knowledge

ONE

The Shifting Locations of the Translation of Science

The Qing Empire in the middle decades of the nineteenth century saw the cultural centers of its heartland—cultural centers that had adorned the economic cores of China with magnificent and sophisticated urbanism—transferred to the tiny treaty port of Shanghai. When I say "transfer" I mean both physical relocation and the thematic transformation of social and cultural practices. As one of the few cities in the southern half of China that was not involved in a prolonged civil war after 1860, Shanghai became the primary refuge for those who had built the previous cultural centers and for their knowledge of mathematics and astronomy, for the philological "investigation of things" intertwined with translated scientific and technological methods, for classical and popular book cultures and publishing enterprises, for prestigious scholarship, and for countless literary and vernacular writings. Yet the word "refuge" does not completely describe Shanghai because the relocation of political elites and of the urban knowledge society also reinvented the city. Some brought with them to Shanghai political and military experiences of the internal frontier of the Qing Empire—experiences that fostered the visions and networks of the dynasty's last group of dominating elite. Others brought cutting-edge talents in the sciences and prestigious training in philology—talents and training that drove home a century-old cultural endeavor of unraveling the prevailing Neo-Confucian orthodoxy. Still others pursued their unfulfilled dreams of a freer society and became elements of change in the new space. The question of what their practices were, naturally, is the subject of this and the following chapter—"naturally" in part because without these practices, there would hardly have been an elite society or any cultural activities sizable enough to make Shanghai a cultural center.

Let us begin with a return to 1860, to the days when Suzhou and Hangzhou, the key cities of commerce, culture, and transportation, became the war zone in the conflict between the Qing army and the Taiping rebels. The social and cultural impact on urban history of the fall of Suzhou and Hangzhou is hard to estimate even today. It meant, for example, the devastation of the empire's urban sites for academies, book markets, printing shops, young-literati clubs, study societies, poetry circles, and dinner-table gatherings of scientific figures. It meant the dispersion of most private collections of rare books and art pieces, collections that had been put together by generations of literati families; the burning and loss of many publishing houses, some of which had been famous for several hundred years; the termination of books in process; the cessation of scholarship; and the interruption of the learning process.

What is more directly related to this chapter is that it caused the death of central figures in the scientific culture that had spread beyond the curriculum of civil service examinations (Elman 1984, 284–96). In Hangzhou, colleagues and students of the renowned mathematician Xiang Mingda (1789–1860) committed suicide when Taipings broke into the city (Luo Shilin 1962, 767–70). In Suzhou, the death of Dai Xu (1806–1860), the major author of mathematics and philology, caused a long delay in the publication of his last book on classical mathematics (Zhu Kebao [1844] 1962, 795), as did the death of Xu Youren (1800–1860), the governor of the Jiangsu Province who was also a leading figure in the Jiangnan circle of mathematicians and astronomers of the time (ibid., 782–85). The activities of Dai Xu's small circle of friends with similar interests in math, the classics, I-ching studies, and other branches of science and technology ended (ibid., 789–97), as did the gatherings that Xu Youren had initiated for the culture of *chouren* ("men of math," a term that then referred to those who had achievements in any scientific or technological field) and their book sharing and conversations on topics related to astronomy, medicine, clockworks, and the principles of triangles. In short, the fall of Suzhou and Hangzhou in 1860 marked the collapse of a long and prominent scientific culture that had been a lively core of city life.

The fall of Suzhou and Hangzhou meant that the scientific thinkers and men of letters who survived the civil war carried on their practices when they took refuge in, or later immigrated to, Shanghai. In this forced travel, they met people from all over the country with or without similar cultural interests; they browsed books that had stopped being circulated elsewhere during the war; and they toured the port and foreign shops. For the mathematician Li Shanlan (1810–1882) and the philologist Wang Tao (1828–1897), the miserable experience of fleeing to Shanghai during the Taiping Rebellion gave them an unexpected chance to get to know the missionaries who had also recently moved to Shanghai from other cities. Together with Alexander Wylie (1815–1887), they launched collaborative translations of recent developments in science. Going to Shanghai enabled Xu Shou (1818–1884), a minor figure from a small town, to meet and chat with a young mathematician, Hua Hengfang (1830–1902), who would later become a lifelong friend and his colleague in studying the properties of lenses and perhaps steam engines and the principles of physics. Their visit to Li Shanlan let them cross a mental border into a collection of current books on scientific and technological topics. The book *Bowu xinbian*, in which the missionary Benjamin Hobson outlined the principle of the steam engine, inspired Xu Shou and Hua Hengfang so much that they lost no time in applying the principle to their successful attempt to build the first steamship in China (Wright 1997, 35–70; Wang Zhaochun 1991, 356–57).

The fall of Suzhou and Hangzhou also meant the end of the political careers of four high-ranking men in a network of commerce-oriented administrative officials: He Guiqing, the governor-general of Jiangsu and Zhejiang; Wang Youling, the former governor of Jiangsu; Xue Huan, the governor of Jiangsu; and Wu Xu, the Shanghai *taotai* (intendant of circuit). They were blamed for having lost the Jiangnan military base as well as the two heartland cities to the enemy of the dynasty, and they were removed from office. This marked a dramatic replacement of one type of political elite by another at the provincial and regional level of the Qing Empire. These four officials were characterized by their networking skills, their ability to mobilize resources, and their interests in antiques, painting, calligraphy, classics, and other cultural commodities valued by the Jiangnan urban society. But militarily they were slow and inept. Governor-General He Guiqing was skilled in the timely provision of grain and taxes for military emergence, but he had no experience in training an army or in fighting the Taipings. Former governor Wang Youling might have been experienced in administration, but his lack of military ability led to the loss of the Jiangnan military base to the rebels. His replacement, Xue Huan, did not make any big mistakes in his political career, but it was said that he focused too much on purchasing expensive calligraphies even in wartime. Such a cultured, well-networked, resourceful, and yet somewhat slow and corrupt officialdom had long occupied the most prominent cultural centers until the fall of Suzhou. In this sense, the fall of Suzhou and Hangzhou marked the end of a political order and of the dominance of one type of political elite in the heartland cities of the Qing Empire.

In addition, the fall of Suzhou and Hangzhou meant the introduction of new political and cultural leadership in Jiangnan, leadership that would carry what was left in Jiangnan toward Shanghai. Those who came to the rescue of Suzhou and Hangzhou were military leaders who were just emerging from the battlefields of the civil war in the region west of Jiangnan. Zeng Guofan (1811–1872), later known as the "savior of the dynasty," who had just been appointed acting governor-general of Jiangsu, Anhui, and Jiangxi because of the crucial battles his Xiang militia had won against the Taipings in Anhui, was ordered to send troops to Jiangnan. Li Hongzhang (1823–1901), later known internationally as China's "number one figure" but at the moment merely a member of Zeng's secretariat (Kuo Ting-yee and Kwang-Ching Liu 1963, 1:390), was appointed the new governor of Jiangsu and was to lead the Huai army, which he had personally trained, to the garrison at Jiangnan. Having won the honor of academians of the Hanlin Academy in the capital, they began serious political pursuits by devoting themselves to what seemed to be low and supplemental activities: militia training in their home provinces, Anhui and Hunan. Because of the collapse of the military regime, the Green Banner system during the Taiping Rebellion, the previously temporary militia, usually called up only as needed, became a necessary army that was active locally and transregionally and was hence a flexible mediating force between local entities and the center as well as between different types of powers. The experience of leading such forces gave Zeng and Li the skills to deal with practical problems at all levels of the Qing system. These included finding ways to handle relations with the Green Banners, hunting for resources from other provinces, securing tax revenues, strengthening bureaucratic efficiency, recruiting able people from personal contacts, and mediating the Han Learning–Song Learning rivalry among the educated elite.[1] In a sense, Zeng Guofan and Li Hongzhang rose to the apex of power because they had taken the geographic, bureaucratic, and cultural sidelines of the Qing system. They were to carry out the task of rescuing Suzhou and Hangzhou from Shanghai, hence the urban shift from the heartland to the shore.[2]

At the allegorical level, the fall of Suzhou and Hangzhou meant that the storyline of Shanghai's rise was heading "back to the future" some-what—to be more specific, back to the future of "the sidelines." At first, Shanghai was not so much a replacement for Suzhou as a compensation or "supplement" to it. To the imperial court as well as to the new political elites, who were also the future leaders of the Foreign Affairs movement, Shanghai was merely a tool serving to help restore the central cities; its development was a side product of the push toward the recovery of the main route. Yet perhaps it was exactly the social practices of Shanghai as a tool, as a side culture, that produced Shanghai—"produced" in Lefebvre's (1991, 3–67) sense that a city is a result rather than a site of social prac-tices. This and the following chapter deal with two cases of those prac-tices out of which a cultural Shanghai—based upon certain bodies of books and knowledge, certain words and vocabularies, certain cultural markets and learned circles—was produced.

Transplanting the Empire's Heart to the Shore

On April 6, 1862, Li Hongzhang and 500 soldiers from the Huai army, on board five British ships rented by the Jiangnan gentry for 180,000 taels of silver, left Anqing and headed east for Shanghai to complete the mission of rescuing the fallen cities of Jiangnan (Ying Baoshi and Yu Yue [1872] 1975, 11:38–39). All sorts of people came to Shanghai, but this was a parade that turned the pages of urban history in the most obvious way. Li and the Huai army brought with them not only soldiers but also people and institutions that later became the core of the Foreign Affairs movement, which is now seen as the first step toward a top-down mod-ernization. In less than a decade, what Li brought with him turned into a growing network of a new generation of intellectuals and administra-tors—who had gathered around Zeng and Li from all over the country—flexible institutions nurtured by the militia system, several arsenals that had already begun producing modern weaponries, and technological experts and translators of modern sciences who very much inherited the *chouren* tradition. They in turn attracted missionaries, who had moved to Shanghai only recently from Ningbo and other places, and hired technicians from abroad. These, I shall add, implanted the first sizable urban society of knowledge in Shanghai. But more than that, while Li Hongzhang's Huai army and the Western army (European soldiers who formed an army in Shanghai) collaborated in the successful defeat of the Taipings, they did so at the expense of unraveling important rules of the Qing system. This presented an ambivalent picture of the future for Shanghai.

The ad hoc institutions of Li Hongzhang and the Huai army were unconventional structures that would later have a double-edged impact on the Qing system. Militia-related ad hoc institutions served the needs of the army where and when the existing local and central bureaucratic systems did not work during the Taiping era (Kuhn 1980). Zeng Guofan's Xiang militia alone had bureaus of taxation, a salt business, and army supplies, plus an arsenal, a translation bureau, and a printing press (Zhu Dongan 1994, 17–126). The headquarters of Li Hongzhang and the Huai army had similar subsidiary bureaus, the most prominent being the Jiangnan Arsenal (founded in 1867), a translation bureau, and a printing press founded under the name of the Shanghai Polytechnic Institute. The Jiangnan Arsenal combined the equipment and manpower of two existing gunneries from Shanghai and Suzhou and Thomas Hunt and Company (Wei Yungong [1904] 1969, 195–205; Xia Dongyuan 1992, 75), and it was augmented by imported machines and technical experts from China and abroad (Rong Hong [1909] 1961, 90–93; Du Shiran, Lin Qingyuan, and Guo Jinbin 1991) (Figure 1). The Shanghai Polytechnic Institute's project of translating works of Western science and technology turned out to be the largest project of that kind in the entire late imperial era. The staff from these ad hoc institutions, recruited from many places, native and foreign, formed an increasing circle of unofficial or subofficial but practical men as Li Hongzhang's headquarters moved to the shore.

Zeng Guofan's and Li Hongzhang's *mufu* (secretariats) perhaps best embodied the ambivalent nature of the new type of political and cultural group they were staffing from all over the empire. The secretariats of Zeng and Li were made up of efficient, able men, with or without a degree, who were recruited from all over the country for their variety of abilities. Unlike in the conventional way of recruiting officials through civil service examinations, "capability" was the only criterion for recruitment. Some of those who worked and trained in Zeng's (and later Li's)

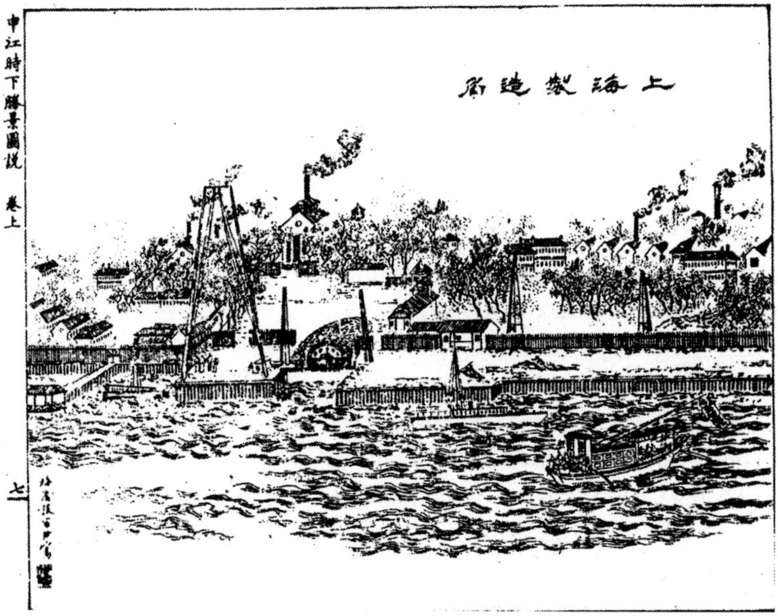

Figure 1. Drawing of the Jiangnan Arsenal. From Mei-hua-an-zhu, *Shenjiang shengjing tushuo* [Pictures and textual explanations of the spectacles at the Shen River], reprinted in *Minsu congshu*, comp. Guoli Beijing daxue Zhongguo minsu xuehui (Beijing: N.p., 1912), 7.

ad hoc institutions turned into a new generation of officials who were influential in the political arena until the end of the Qing dynasty. Quite a number of important figures in the top-down modernization—such as Zuo Zongtang, who later became the governor of Zhejiang; Xue Fucheng (1838–1894), who later became ambassador to several European countries (United Kingdom, France, Italy, and Belgium) and America; and Li Hongzhang himself—had this background (Xue Fucheng 1966, 163–72). Administrators of these ad hoc bureaus such as Ding Richang, Liu Kunyi, and Guo Baiyin proved to be the key officials in the Foreign Affairs institutes. Others recruited by the ad hoc institutions were more controversial, even radical. Feng Guifen (1809–1874), the author of the influential *Jiaobinlu kangyi*, in which he proposed a systematic reform in taxation, civil service examination, currency exchange, curriculums of learning, and official participation in spreading technological knowledge, was a respected guest at the secretariat of Li Hongzhang's Shanghai headquarters. Wang Tao, a more contentious figure who had written to suggest that the Taipings take over Shanghai, was later invited by Li to be the president of the Shanghai Polytechnic Institute (Cohen 1973). Such a *mufu* of elites, intended to correct the systematic errors of the Qing society, formed the social and cultural core for a future restoration of the Qing order.

Another odd group who joined Zeng's and Li's enterprises were the missionaries, who held a specific vision of China's future and who sought to update themselves with the new possibilities for rapport between religion and science. As the "transmitters" of science and technology themselves, the missionaries and the foreign sojourners who participated in the task of scientific translation were struggling at the crossroads of another set of major and minor histories. Participation by missionaries in the dissemination of science and technology can be traced back to the Ming dynasty, when this task was an inseparable part of spreading Christianity. Being absorbed into the Jiangnan Arsenal's large project of translating nonreligious scientific and technological works, the missionaries obviously shifted their roles in spreading Christianity. Post–Civil War industrialization in the United States not only stimulated a scientific culture in higher education but also provided Methodist missionaries in China with a new ideal of Christian science—a scientific education that was compatible with the nonmissionary schools.[3] The foreign translators—in particular the Methodist missionary Young J. Allen (1836–1907) and the British sojourner John Fryer (1829–1928), who worked in the Jiangnan Arsenal—were influenced by this new wave of scientific modernity as well as by the ideal of Christian scientists. They actively shared the ideal of this new wave of scientific culture in Christianity by acting as agents of "enlightenment" for scientific education in China. Fryer, in particular, actively engaged in soliciting scientific books from Europe and the United States for translation, in organizing the Chinese scientific book depot, and in compiling a popular science journal (Wright 1996, 1–16). The price of doing so, however, was the ironic situation in which they found themselves: As agents of scientific culture in China, they did not possess any scientific authority because they lacked training and expertise.[4]

Finally, the ad hoc practices of the Jiangnan Arsenal and the Shanghai Polytechnic Institute were not possible without the reemergence of a science-oriented circle and their ideal of scientific culture. The most representative figures in this circle were Xu Shou, Hua Hengfang, Xu Jianyin (1845–1901), Jia Buwei, and others who worked in the Jiangnan

Arsenal and the translation bureau. I call their role in the Jiangnan Arsenal a reemergence because their life stories—self-taught experts in math, physics, chemistry, and manufacture—as well as their cultural ideal echoed that of the *chouren,* whose practice can be traced back to the eighteenth-century cities.

I would like to elaborate a bit more on the term "*chouren.*" It originally referred to a "man of math," an official title, in *Kaogong ji* in the *Rites of Zhou.* In the late eighteenth century the term came to refer to a specific sociocultural category made up of those who mastered specialized knowledge, especially knowledge in science, crafts, and technology.[5] The four volumes of *Biographies of Mathematicians and Astronomers* (Chouren zhuan, hereafter *Biographies),* compiled by Ruan Yuan (1764–1849), a well-known official and mathematician, and his friends and colleagues between 1799 and 1844, evidenced the activities of a loosely defined *chouren* community.[6] During this time the *chouren* category was reinvented in the urban sites of Yangzhou, Suzhou, Hangzhou, and Guangzhou, where the rich productions of scholarship and of the learned had expanded beyond the orthodox curriculum and the quotas of the civil service examinations.[7] Wealthy salt merchants, private academies, family teaching genealogies, and friendship groups in these cities formed the institutional bases for non-degree-oriented mathematical and astronomical studies (Ho Ping-t'i 1954, 130–68; Woodside 1989, 158–84; Elman 1990; and Horng Wann-sheng 1993).

Here *chouren* scholarship referred to an open spectrum of learning established through a translative relationship between different systems of knowledge. It had expanded its fields from mathematics and astronomy to include philology, optics, technology, physics, chemistry, and manufacturing. *Chouren* also became an imagined cosmopolitan scientific community. Among the lives and works of 437 men and women recorded in *Biographies,* 53 were non-Chinese, ranging from Aristotle to Newton and later thinkers.[8] Expertise and specialized knowledge were no longer solely linked to social status, the professions, and specific localities;[9] rather, they had come to form an independent, hybrid, and international field of culture exceeding the limits of regional borders, schools of thought, the hierarchy of status, gender distinctions, nationalities, and languages. Together with alternative curriculums, informal paths of communication, clubs and friendship groups, book exchanges, and the publication of new manuscripts, the *chouren* culture marked the minor urban society of knowledge until the eve of the Taiping Rebellion (Elman 1984, 2000; Horng Wann-sheng 1993).[10]

The self-taught Jiangnan technological masters solicited by the Jiangnan Arsenal were clearly successors in spirit to the eighteenth-century cultural archetype of the *chouren,* even though their family genealogies could not be traced back to the Zhou dynasty. Like Xiang Mingda and many other better-known members of the *chouren* circle in late-eighteenth-century Jiangnan, Xu Shou failed the civil service examinations several times and eventually gave up the thought of a civil service career (Yang Mo 1910). Yet the fact that he was up-to-date on the thinking in physics and other sciences that was in circulation in Jiangnan at the time tells how widespread *chouren* learning was even during the civil war.[11] Coming to the Jiangnan Arsenal, Xu Shou hoped to see what the compilers of *Chouren zhuan* would have liked to see, that "the studies of sciences prevail[ed] the land of China" (Yang Mo 1910). Hua Hengfang, on the other hand, was as devoted to compiling and republishing the *chouren* works lost in the civil war as he was committed to translating new works in the Jiangnan Arsenal.[12] What differed in their practice was the opportunity to carry the eighteenth-century ideal of scientific culture forward into the official program of the Qing state.

With the compound practices of a specific official group, controversial cultural figures, missionaries, amateur scientists, and *chourens,* an urban society of knowledge and learning was embedded in Shanghai, and it had an impact. Activities related to the Shanghai Polytechnic Institute and the Jiangnan Arsenal became national and international news in the following decades: Not only was the translation project the largest in the Qing dynasty, but the books also became a "must see" for anyone who traveled to the civil service examinations in the capital by way of Shanghai. As for the Arsenal, by the 1880s it already had thousands of workers, a dozen foreign technicians, and hundreds of machines and was thus a pioneer modern enterprise in Asia at the time.[13] It was not unknown to its contemporaries in the West that even by the eve of the Sino-Japanese War in 1894, the Jiangnan Arsenal's technology and manufacture was still in the lead in many aspects.[14]

Although the ad hoc or "tool" practice surrounding the Arsenal made Shanghai visible, it also brought to the fore its own ironical and dialectic dynamic. It is not entirely surprising that the ironical energy—embodied by controversial figures, alternative learnings, off-curriculum texts, and a nondegree criterion for recruiting—would generate a cultural practice that, in the end, might not necessarily serve the best interests of the political order of the Qing Empire. The ad hoc practice or the tool society might outgrow the cultural and political framework that had originally been determined for them.

"The Great Divide Not": Uncontrolled Mediations of Knowledge

What was at the core of this ad hoc practice from a cultural perspective? If Zeng Guofan and Li Hongzhang had planned the restoration of the Qing cultural order, then the ad hoc practice was everything but order-building. The imperialist discourse on knowledge and translation advanced the hierarchy of the civilized over the primitive and discriminated against the non-Western, but the ad hoc practice denied any ranking or ladder of cultures and knowledge systems. I maintain that a *chouren*-related principle, belief in the internal translatability of knowledge systems (despite the possible external untranslatability), had set off the cultural practice of an unrestrained mediation of learning in the Jiangnan Arsenal circle, which in turn set the tone for the development of a serious and vernacular scientific culture specific to Shanghai prior to 1894.[15] This section and the next attempt to show, from different perspectives, that this cosmological ideal, and its practice, turned Shanghai at this moment of history into an agent of *uncontrolled* mediation of all sorts of knowledge.

There are at least two keys to the understanding of this practice: (1) the ambiguity of *gezhi* learning as a practice of science and technology in the Jiangnan Arsenal, and (2) the implications of *tong* or *tongfa* as an internal principle of the translatability of all knowledge, even of the possibility of knowing itself.

Gezhi, "investigation of things," or *gezhi xue*, "the study of the investigation of things," best characterized the scientific and technological learning practiced at the Jiangnan Arsenal, and as such it invites us to replay the history of knowledge to the history of the city. Although other officials and missionaries preferred the terms "*suanxue*," "mathematical learning," or "*bowu*," "wide understanding of things," to refer to science and technology,[16] the Jiangnan Arsenal circle of officials, intellectuals, and translators deliberately conceived of *gezhi* as a category encompassing both Chinese and Western, both literary and hands-on science and technology.[17] The couplets that Feng Guifen and Li Hongzhang wrote to celebrate the joining of the Shanghai Foreign Language School (Shanghai guangfangyan guan, established 1863) with the Arsenal both bore the horizontal inscription *Gezhi tang* (The Hall of the Investigation of Things) for the academy hall (*Wanguo gongbao* [1876] 1992, 739). The Polytechnic Institute was known in Chinese as Gezhi shuyuan, its planned syllabus was *gezhi xinxue tigang*, "an outline of new learning,"[18] its Science Primer Series was known in Chinese as *Gezhi qimeng*, the scientific book depot was *gezhi shushi*, and finally, men of science and technology were called *gezhi jia*.[19] The Jiangnan Arsenal circle was the first post-Taiping group to bring *gezhi*, the practice of science and technology, to Shanghai.[20]

The term "*gezhi*" was originally coined in the commentary to the *Daxue* (Grand Learning) by the Neo-Confucian philosopher Zhu Xi (1130–1200) and was lent, as history unfolded, to different parties as a term referring to science and technology. The word originally meant to grasp the single unchangeable universal principle through observing different things.[21] In the context I am dealing with, Ruan Yuan and other *chouren* scholars in the eighteenth century seemed not to favor this term so much, since its Neo-Confucian connotation tended to block the more creative and more subversive pursuits of knowledge.[22] The missionaries, on the other hand, seemed to appropriate this epistemological term because of the seeming closeness between Neo-Confucianism's usage of the universal principle and the missionaries' ideal of God in relation to science.[23] In the more secular and more popular practices of urban society, however, *gezhi* silently drifted away from both Neo-Confucian and Christian connotations.[24] On the late-imperial book market, *gezhi* became a cultural practice of mastering the material world. A popular Ming collection, *Gezhi congshu* (Collectanea of the Investigation of Things), for example, juxtaposes topics ranging from agriculture, technology, and astronomy to painting skills and the aesthetics of teapots and porcelain.[25] Till the mid-Qing period, in a much less commercialized *Gezhi jingyuan* compiled by Chen Yuanlong, *gezhi* meant the investigation of "things" in both physical and mythical worlds as well as other objects of the philological studies. By the time of the Jiangnan Arsenal, the term "*gezhi*" officially referred to the translation of science and technology, without necessarily implying any connection to Christianity (Wang Hui 1996, 21–82).[26]

An updated practice initiated among the missionaries and the officials of the Jiangnan Arsenal, *gezhi* was something similar to the *chouren* spirit, embracing modern technology in the city of Shanghai through secularizing missionary translations. Under the category of *gezhi*, a body of unprecedented knowledge and practice, that of science, particularly technology in the industrial age, was installed in the system of knowledge production (Wright 1997, 35–70). Adrian Bennett's study shows that the first thirty-four volumes collaboratively translated by Xu Shou, John Fryer, Hua Hengfang, and others between 1871 and 1880 were heavily oriented toward manufacturing and military sciences, including gunnery, fleet maneuvering, fortifications, coastal defense, Gatling gun drill instructions, manufacture of gunpowder, iron manufacture, boring and blasting, principles of steam engines, metallurgy, lithography, and coal mining (Bennett 1967, 33–40). The translations emphasized natural sciences next most heavily. However, as Bennett's study also shows, during 1880–1885, among the seventy-eight books translated, forty-three (55 percent) were in the natural sciences, nineteen (26 percent) were in applied science, and only four (5 percent) were in military or naval sciences (Bennett 1967, 37). Textbooks for students both within and outside the Arsenal, such as the books in the Science Primer Series (1879–1880) for beginners, were also published. These included seven translations on astronomy, physics, chemistry, geography, and mechanical engineering.

But the translators also provided the field of *gezhi* with all sorts of other knowledge, so much that the historically ambiguous, all-inclusive character of the vernacular version of *gezhi* practice was carried into the modern moment of the Foreign Affairs movement. Besides hard science and technology, the category *gezhi* opened into areas that would be considered nonmodern, even nonscientific. While translating Western books, the circle of the Jiangnan Arsenal also collected and published recent works of the *chouren*, such as that of Dai Xu, which were more philological than scientific to, say, a manufacturing engineer.[27] Hua Hengfang's *Xing suxuan suanxue bitan* too was based upon the interpretation of concepts that can be traced to "premodern" texts. The translated Western books also included books on topics that were "cultural," such as the world expositions held in the United States, factory management, and moving pictures, as well as the impression of an armament factory. At the book depots of the Polytechnic Institute, John Fryer often put books on art, history, and law on display under the category of *gezhi*. In a preface to a translated scientific article on physics published in the *Journal of Sciences and Industry*, the translator even made the up-to-date comment that "science *(gezhi)* is the evidential scholarship *(shixue)* of the West" (*Gezhi huibian* 5, no. 1 [1890]: 2–3). Having clearly assigned the scientific part of the *gezhi* learning to the West, he nevertheless thought it was knowledge similar, comparable, to evidential studies. All this seems to suggest that for the Jiangnan Arsenal circle, books of modern science were translated, not to be divided from nonsciences but, rather, to be mixed with them. The modern science included in the *gezhi* was nondivided or nondividable from nonsciences and the nonmodern.

Although this ambiguous, nondivided feature of the *gezhi* practice can be easily identified as an imperfection from a Western-centered view of "modern science" (Reardon-Anderson 1991), it was indeed a positive enterprise seen from the perspective of the *chouren* learning, and it was also a conscious, albeit ad hoc, cultural practice of science and technology at the Jiangnan Arsenal. To the scientists at the Arsenal, the very task of translation was not so much transmission as the establishment of connections or translatability, if not commensurability, between Chinese and Western scientific systems as well as between the old and the new knowledge.[28] Their most often quoted rule of translation, as written in the *Huazi mingming* (Chinese Nomenclature) section of the first book translated, *Huaxue jianyuan* (Wells's Principles and Applications of Chemistry), by David A. Wells (1871), was that the translator's job was not only to find Chinese words for Western meanings but also "to match Western concepts with existing Chinese concepts" (Wright 1997, 35–70). The translators were fully aware of the fact that their imagined readers were not blank minds but carriers of existing knowledge that had a long history to trace; thus they chose the nomenclature that best expressed the existing mathematical, medical, chemical, and astronomical information. The instance often referred to was the case of chemistry, a discipline said to have been "unknown" to the Chinese before the 1920s. The translators used extant Chinese terms for two-thirds of the sixty-four elements, and for the remaining elements they invented new nomenclature using preestablished ways of creating Chinese characters (ibid., 35–70). Similarly, in mathematics they also used many already-existing key concepts, such as nonillion *(mi)*, as well as nomenclature derived from the existing math system, such as *tian di ren*. In this practice of *gezhi*, therefore, translated science marked not so much the beginning of a field but a completion, a perfection, of preexisting knowledge. *Gezhi* had thus existed all the time as a diachronic dimension, and it had always encompassed more than one system.

But questions naturally arise. What makes the translatability between different knowledge systems legitimate? Why not separate the practice of science and technology from that of other disciplines? Was there any scientific justification for this type of nondivided translation? To look for the answers to these questions, we need to turn to the second crucial key to the practice of the Jiangnan Arsenal, *tong*, "to understand" or "oneness," or *tongfa*, "universal understanding."

For the *chouren* scientists in the Jiangnan Arsenal, the legitimacy of pursuing translatability as well as of nondivided knowledge was internal to the nature of knowing itself. Hua Hengfang's use of the words "*tong*" or "*tongfa*," which stood for the innate connection and translatability of all kinds of knowledge, reveals this internal principle. Hua Hengfang, while explaining the necessity of translating algebra in the translator's preface (1873) to *Daishu shu* (Algebra) by John Wallis (1616–1703), described this *tongfa* in different mathematical systems. He began with examples of how mathematics was used in everyday life—comparing, buying and selling, bargaining—but he ended with the innate reason for all different systems of knowledge.

> If each individual problem is to be solved by a different mathematical method (*shu*), then methods will become numerous and redundant, yet there still will not be enough to solve new problems. A better way of solving problems is to find an all-applicable principle (*tongfa*) that can handle various situations. It was to find the all-applicable rule that can solve different mathematical problems that gave the reason (*yu*) the Chinese discovered the *tianyuan* system and Westerners invented algebra. (Hua Hengfang [1873] 1896, 1–2)

There is no doubt that to Hua Hengfang, Western algebra and Chinese *tianyuan* were equivalent systems and that the translation was an exchange carried out in both directions, between Western language/concepts and Chinese, and between past and present. But I suggest that this simple passage contains a more important message. It confirms the internal nondivided nature of human knowledge, including the sciences. For Hua Hengfang, what defined the equivalency between *tianyuan* and algebra was the internal need or reason (*yu*) for an all-applicable principle, a need shared by the two systems, a need that surpassed the difference in their applications. To push his argument further, one may say that to him the external differences shaped by languages, nomenclatures, regions, and cultures did not split this internal reason of knowledge. Even if algebra was a better system, it was still equivalent to *tianyuan* because they were internally of one human endeavor: They came into being for that one reason and served that one goal of knowing and handling different situations. What is implied here is the internal *oneness* or internal exchangeability of knowledge practices that were diverted by regions and cultures. This oneness does not confirm sameness or homogeneity, since it exists only when differences (things) are relevant. This implied internal oneness of different practices of sciences, which was at the core of the term "*tong*" (a term that was by no means the invention of Hua Hengfang), legitimated and justified the translatability that the Jiangnan Arsenal circle saw existing between different knowledge systems.

How did the "internal oneness" justify itself? This question points to the very philosophical and historical core of the terms "*tong*" and "*tongfa*," where the cosmological ideal of all things, including the human mind, provides the very possibility of knowing and handling the natural and the manmade world. The word "*tong*" as a signifier of the cosmological imagination had a long history and a variety of usages. Here I will limit my explanation to the most relevant use of the term by mathematicians and astronomers themselves. Take *Wuli xiaoshi* (The Small Knowledge of the Principle of Things), a well-known work by the late-Ming astronomer and alchemist Fang Yizhi (1611–1671), for example. Fang Yizhi explained the work of the material world and the possibility of human knowledge by elaborating on the internal connections among *wu* (things, that is, concrete forms of materiality), the *Tao* (the nature or the principle of the cosmos), and the *xin* (the human mind). Fang Yizhi restated the Taoist cosmological idea that all things, including the human mind and mechanics, are manifestations of the Tao, the principle of the cosmos (Fang Yizhi 1983, 867–944). Based on this vision, he established a cosmological theory of knowledge that granted the human mind as a witness of the internal oneness of all things, therefore as the agent of knowing. According to Fang Yizhi, the human mind was the only "thing" that could relay (or *tong*) all things *(wanwu)*, know their origins, and master their works *(zhi qi yuan, jin qi xing)* (Fang Yizhi, 1983, 744–45). This is because, as he indicated, the mind communicates with things not on a physical level but at an even deeper level of creativity or energy—

of which the pattern of movement was the cosmic Tao. To elaborate further, "things" are works of the changing pattern of the energy. As works they are different, but as products of creativity they are nondividable. It is possible for the human mind to know and to relay all things exactly because they are diverse works of the cosmological principle.

Partially informed by this cosmological ideal, *tong*, or knowing-all, was the practicing principle of astronomers and mathematicians from the eighteenth century on, except that their practice was heavily influenced with philological studies. As Hu Minghui's work shows, the cultural ideal of the eighteenth century was to be a *tongru*, or an all-knowing Confucian (Hu Minghui 2002). Without explicitly being a Taoist term, "knowing-all" nonetheless included three connected dimensions of knowledge: that of the cosmos, that of the earth, and that of human beings. The *tongru* ideal therefore valued both the erudite in Confucian classics and the mastery of the translatability of scientific knowledge. Leading mathematicians and astronomers of the eighteenth century, such as Dai Zhen and Ruan Yuan, took as their task the possible translations between Chinese learning and Western learning and engaged literately in translating between Western concepts and terms from classical Chinese. Looking ahead from Fang Yizhi's time, one can say that these attempts at establishing connections between knowledge systems added to the cosmological vision of human knowledge with applicable tools and methodologies. Hua Hengfang was only one of those who carried this ongoing, century-old *chouren* practice into a new moment, into the practice of science and technology in the Jiangnan Arsenal.

This pursuit of translatability and a great union of science and technology set up an alternative cultural ideal to that of modern science. Bruno Latour has characterized the fatal dilemma of modern science as being part of the purification process that was the result of the "great divide"—dividing nature from culture, reason from emotion, sciences from humanity, abstract from concrete, universal from cultural, and hence pure knowledge from impure (1993, 97–98). The "great divide" characterized the conceptual logic of modern science in the West, even though the pure knowledge had never been true in practice, and therefore Latour concluded that the modern actually "has never been" (46–48). Comparatively, what we see here in the case of the *gezhi* was a practice that seemed to have followed an opposite logic. The *tongfa*, or the all-applicable principle Hua Hengfang talked about, the internal cause for both algebra and the *tianyuan* system, was inevitably inseparable from concrete historically and culturally defined conditions. *Tongfa* emphasizes the transferability or translatability between different knowledge systems rather than the homogeneity or universality of knowledge. It assumed one origin for different practices of knowledge rather than one singular system of knowledge. In this way, *tongfa* embodied an ideal about modern science or about all knowledge: According to this ideal, the pursuit of knowledge should be the pursuit of a heterogeneous whole, of which any division defined by languages, cultures, or politics is superficial.

Uncontrollable Proliferation of Textualities

This cultural practice of *tongfa*, I argue, was crucial to Shanghai's development from a city to be used as a tool in the restoration of the Jiangnan cities into a crucible of the Foreign Affairs movement. The key point here is not that the practice established commensurability between knowledge systems but that the practice connected, juxtaposed, and valorized different knowledge systems to the extent that terminologies proliferated in an uncontrollable manner. This uncontrollable proliferation brought forth mixtures of different types of textuality or textualities. The very uncontrolled, open, and somewhat chaotically proliferating textuality of knowledge instituted the movement of the urban society of the learned from the Jiangnan cities to Shanghai.

The practice of universal translatability, or of "the great uniting," once it was brought to the fore by the post-*chouren* circle of the Jiangnan Arsenal, opened up a public space where the new textuality and new semiology of knowledge created the infrastructures for the heterogeneous exercise of vernacular sciences. The "great uniting" as a recurring principle of cultural translation resonated among many literati from near and far and was informed by their interactions with the official projections of cultural politics. An example can be found in the 1889 essay contests held by the Polytechnic Institute, in which Li Hongzhang left the translatability between "*gezhi* systems" in Chinese and Western contexts an open question.[29] "More than a few dozen theories about *gezhi* have appeared since the day of the 'Great Learning,'" the question went. "Are they similar to present learning in the West? From the time of Aristotle in ancient Greece to Bacon in Britain, the *gezhi* learning changed tremendously. It has become more refined since Bacon's time, and in the present day, Darwin and Spencer have developed their theories to an even further extent. Can you explain these changes?" (Wang Tao 1886–1893, 4:1). The question itself set up a binary opposition between Chinese and Western learning, as most of the official discourse about knowledge did at the time. But to that division the four top essayists argued only superficially. The first-prize winner, Jiang Tongyin, maintained that the Western sciences were advanced in dealing with the physical world whereas the Chinese were advanced *gezhi* in dealing with metaphysics.[30] The second-place essayist, Wang Zuocai, believed that *gezhi* was practiced differently because Chinese scholars tended to preserve the old whereas Western scientists sought to replace the old. Yet none of the four winners believed absolute differences existed between the systems. Rather, all of them, with amazingly rich evidence, saw culture-specific learning as mutually translatable, as supplementary, as having different emphases, and as therefore being mutually helpful (Wang Tao 1886–1893, 4:1–18). The fourth-place essayist, Zhong Tianwei from Guangdong, went so far in making this point that his answer challenged the very Chinese-Western binary implied by the question itself. He used rich evidence to prove that, since many scientific fields did not originate in the West, Western science was itself a culturally mixed historical product. It was through borrowing from other cultures that Western scientists built their systematic knowledge, and it was only later that the true non-Western origins of science were concealed (Wang Tao 1886–1893, 4:15–18). The scope of this argument reached far beyond the official vision of cultural differences based upon binary oppositions, such as the one crystallized in Zhang Zhidong's well-known formula of Chinese learning as "the essence" and Western learning as "the application." Beneath the solid surface of an official division between Chinese learning and Western learning, the boundaries of knowledge systems began to be blurred and transgressed. What the cultural institution of the annual essay contest in Shanghai brought to the fore was the dialectics, the dynamics of the ordered imperial and imperialist framework of knowledge translation and the actual practices that kept breaking the order. This made the city the center of attention among post-Taiping intellectual society.

The dialectic dynamics of translation yielded great fruits in the textual and semiotic arenas of the urban cultural life of the educated groups, but these fruits were contradictory. On the one hand, the educated society that can be traced back to Suzhou was transformed through the reconstruction of the semiology (learning, languages) in the practice of translation. On the other hand, this transformation tended to be out of bounds, as the translation between knowledge systems dismissed boundaries, even rules. It became something close to an endless proliferation of terminologies. To observe the emergence of this contradictory, and somewhat uncontrollable, proliferated textuality, I will make a close reading of the way Xue Fucheng, another important figure in the Foreign Affairs movement and a diplomat sent to Britain and the United States, translated between different sign systems of knowledge. In his preface to the *Scientific and Industrial Magazine* in 1890, Xue gave an authoritative interpretation of various branches of science. This preface sought not only to combine new and existing knowledge but also to reduce the social and cultural gap between the bookish and the practical:

> The learning of *gezhi* established the foundation of social order in China and led the way to wealth in the West. This was not because the practices were different . . . but because the ancient Confucians tended to be ashamed of pursuing interests, whereas the Western people tended to glorify creation, abundance, and competition. . . . Since the loss of the book *Donggong*, those who master the arts of manufacture refused to spread the skills and held their ability to themselves. Those bookish scholars, on the other hand, looked down upon the arts and crafts. As I have examined it, the learning of manufacturing is to measure the weight and the speed of things and to manufacture products—this is the technique of working wood, metal, and stone. The learning of chemistry is to analyze materials and apply them in different quantities in order to generate new things—this is the job of mathematicians and mining experts. The learning of steam engines is to change water to power by fire—which is the principle of manufacturing things with steam boilers. The study of light (optics) is to use glass lenses to control focus—which means the art of lenses and mirrors. The learning of electricity is to understand such phenomena as a magnet attracting a needle or a piece of amber picking up a seed. The learning of geometry is to know the reason why one takes a foot-long measure, every day halves it, and yet it will not be exhausted even in 10,000 lifetimes. (Xue Fucheng 1890, 1)

An internal fissure has already been revealed. As a diplomat who was looking to strengthen the Qing state, Xue Fucheng, following Zeng Guofan and Li Hongzhang, took *gezhi,* or the practice of science and technology—which could yield strong weapons—as the foundation of order. At the same time, he could not help but note the way this practice fragmented into different, isolated practices of the bookish (philological) and the practical, the classical and the translated. Obviously he had the insight that to change the semiotic circulation of useful, technological, and scientific knowledge among different groups of people could actually change the society of the learned and the skilled. He therefore devoted the second half of the passage to an effort to amend the fragmentation by bringing together translated and classical categories of disciplines. The effort was delivered in a style used by *chouren* scholars of earlier decades.[31] Typical of this style, his idiomatic definition of physics and chemistry returns to the key classical texts: in philological studies, to works such as *Kaogong ji* (Records of Technology); in the study of light, to the *Huai nan zi* (Master Huainan) or *Huai nan zi gujin zhu* (Classical and Contemporary Interpretations of Master Huainan); in electricity, to the *Bencao gangmu* (or *Materia Medica*). Whether or not the connections he established make any "scientific" sense is beyond the interest of this book; what deserves our attention is the way this discourse reshuffles different semiologics that were organic to the educated groups. Xue Fucheng, in a sense, extended what Hua Hengfang and Xu Shou characterized as *tongfa* into a larger realm of culture and society, by enforcing possible textual and semiotic exchanges between the Chinese and the Western, the translated and the original, the philological and the practical, without setting up a rate or a mean.

But exactly because of this, the attempt is self-contradictory. Its aim was to order and organize different knowledge systems, but its method avoids order and shies away from building any hierarchy and from setting up any boundaries. By making open connections between the philological and the translated branches of knowledge, Xue unintentionally used a free-associative translative way of changing social and cultural orders. This contradiction between the intention or the goal and the method, I maintain, was not a personal issue of Xue's. It reflected the dialectical dynamic between a controlled, official, political usage of science and technology and an uncontrolled or uncontrollable proliferation of vernacular science and technology. Xue's very literate, bookish, and allusive explanation of science not only throws light on the scope of the reading of a prestigious member of the elite but also reflects the disordered way in which signs and themes circulated in the print markets to which he had been exposed. To an extent, Xue's preface was the product of the ongoing exercise in uncontrolled translatability. That is, we can take a glimpse at an unordered proliferation of *gezhi* practice through a close reading of his preface.

At least three sets of signs circulated in two types of book markets or book consumers, in addition to that of the translated Western texts, signs that appeared in the preface. The three groups were related to (1) the word for technology, (2) light and optics, and (3) the rhetoric used to describe the studies of electricity. The three types of print markets, in which two overlapping groups of readers were involved, were characterized by, first, the boom in reprinting classics and works of evidential studies that followed a philological tradition; second, the print market for new knowledge beyond the philological tradition; and the third, the intermittent popular market for *xiaoshi,* or "small knowledge," of all sorts of menus and recipes. All these print markets saw revival during the post-Taiping period.

Xue's description of manufacturing technology, which was dubbed *kaogong,* was itself the result of a particular type of semiotic production of knowledge typical of the eighteenth- and nineteenth-century philological tradition. The fact that Xue borrowed sentences from the *Kaogong ji* (namely, "the technique of working wood, metal, and stone") to define the nature of manufacturing reflects the reemerging popularity of ancient texts among his readers. Philological studies in the eighteenth and early nineteenth centuries had already produced several famous works on the topic, including *Kaogong ji tu* (Diagrams of the Records of Technology) written by the compiler of *Siku quanshu,* Dai Zhen, *Kaogong chuangwu xiaoji* (A Minor Record of Technology and Manufacturing), by Cheng Yaotian (1725–1814), and *Zhouli zhengyi* (The Authentic Meanings of the Rites of Zhou), by Sun Yirang (1848–1908). The dispersion of the imperial collection of classics in Jiangnan, the Wenyuange collection of the *Four Treasures,* during the Taiping era stimulated a boom in the market for reprints of the classics (Reed 2004) as well as in the circulation of books of evidential scholarship, including the ones mentioned above. Those who amassed the main collectanea compiled during and after the Taiping Rebellion were proud to have collected and reprinted the works of philologists and Jiangnan mathematicians.[32] In this trend of reprinting and recollecting, *kaogong* became a known, fashionable topic even for those who did not have a chance to read the scholarly works. Actually, different types of texts and various authors found chances to publicize themselves through their use of the word "*kaogong*." The translation of the second volume of the *Aid Book to Engineering Enterprises Abroad*, by Ewing Matheson, for example, used the word "*kaogong*" in its Chinese title, *Kaogong jiyao* (Bennett 1967, 93).[33] Xue Fucheng's preface displays just one more popular use of the word or the topic. In this sense his expression was an artifact of the growing and popularized philological print market.

To contextualize the group of signs about optics and lenses in Xue's passage, namely, the *yangsui* (lenses and mirrors made to light a fire) and the "study of light" (optics), one is led to a fresh motif in the nonphilological study of things popular in another regional print market. They appeared in *Jingjing lingchi* (Fascination with Lenses and Mirrors), by Zheng Fuguang (b. 1780), at Guangzhou. This synthetic work (written around 1835 and published in 1847) explores the principles of optics and lenses. In 1873, another Guangdong mathematician, Zou Boqi, published a work on optics entitled *Geshu bu* (Supplemental Treatises on Optics). Zhu Kebao, the author of the 1886 edition of *Biographies*, drew from both of these works and proclaimed the hands-on methodology of *geshu* (methods of optics) as the principle of *yangjian* (mirrors and lenses) (Zhu Kebao [1844] 1962, 810–15).[34] Later, one of the top essays of the 1889 essay contest held by the Polytechnic Institute tied "*guangxue*" (a translated term for "optics") with "*yangsui*" (the mirror that lights a fire), a philological term that traced back to classical texts (Wang Tao 1886–93, 4:5a–6b). Xue Fucheng adapted all the already-established connections between the classical philological term "*yuangsui*" and more recent works of optics. His wording reflected the ongoing fusion of the philological and the experimental, the translated and the classical practices.

To turn to the third example, Xue Fucheng's phrase "*cishi yinzhen, hubo shijie*" ("such phenomena as a magnet attracting a needle and a piece of amber picking up a seed") followed the popular usage of *Materia Medica* in the vernacular print market of *xiaoshi*, "small knowledge." As far as content goes, the circulation of small knowledge can be traced back to *Bowu zhi*, written by Zhang Hua during the Han dynasty. This type of book contains wide-ranging entries on useful recipes and methods: "Lighting up the *ai* grass that has stored for three years, one gets liquid lead from the burning grass, and this has been proved to be true," or "Mixing the *hufen* powder, chalk, with water and spreading the mixture on the beard can prevent the facial hair from turning white" (Zhang

Hua 1983, 576). After the Taiping Rebellion, the publication of recipe books and menus *(zhinan)*, travelogues and travel notes *(biji)*, and popular encyclopedias *(wanbao)* also entered a new era, and its unsystematic themes were extended to include geography, medicine, chemistry, and agriculture. Marked by its lowbrow rhetorical style and everyday topics, this particular practice of vernacular science found itself outside both the *chouren* tradition and the translated sciences. The phrase Xue used to describe the origin of electricity was a cliché that the popular books would copy from *Material Medica* to establish their own "scientific" legitimacy. As a cliché, it followed the opening sentence in Zhou Liujing's *Qunwu qizhi* (The Wonderful Making of Things, 1940), a late-Ming text full of popular recipes solving problems of everyday life, modeled after Fang Yizhi's *Wuli xiaoshi*.[35] Considering that a prestigious philologist would warn against the use of a lowbrow cliché, Xue Fucheng's use of it inevitably resonated with the vernacular sciences in ways beyond his own control. The fact that a philological quotation of *Materia Medica* was indistinguishable from a popular cliché tells how quickly, and uncontrollably, the vernacular practice of sciences had expanded.

Aiming at establishing the order of modern scientific disciplines, Xue Fucheng's preface ironically showcased the emergence of a new, proliferated textuality of translational scientific knowledge, brought forth by the coexistence and the fusion of practices that were originally staggered and separated in the late-imperial cultural hierarchy—practices of modern science and technology in industry and weaponry, of philology, of the *chouren* studies overlapped with it, of missionary translations and "Christian sciences," of the everyday application of "small knowledge." A dialectical turn took place in the translation of modern science. The translation of Western sciences, although a long-repressed desire for those interested literati, was uninvited and was, rather, forced upon the Qing as an ad hoc practice both by the internal crisis and by the imperialist warfare. For both the Qing state and the imperialists, modern science and technology signified power, strength, wealth, and control. But in the ad hoc practice in the Arsenal, the pursuit of strength and control through translation created the freedom to make the maximum connections among differences, multiplicity, and cultural and historical specificities. These free associations of different practices turned translated science into a heterogeneous field of knowledge expanding in an unsystematic, disorderly manner. From this perspective, Shanghai was a

Suzhou reborn—in the sense that it liberated Suzhou from its unfulfilled, oppressed, and ruptured cultural dreams. Shanghai was also a Suzhou turned modern—modern in the sense that the practice of science and technology for order building was, self-contradictorily, dissolving the order.

When "the Western" Became "the New"

The Sino-Japanese War of 1894, however, interrupted this disorderly proliferation of "sciences." A complex cultural and political effect of the war was the domination of *xixue* (Western learning) and *kexue* (science via the lexicon of Japan) over the cultural order of the urban society. This reorganization replaced the *gezhi* practice with a cultural hierarchy of Chinese and Western learning, with the latter taking the superior position. These changes overcoded what used to be the mixed practice of *gezhi* studies with Western modernity.

The Sino-Japanese War led both conservative officials, such as Weng Tonghe (1830–1904) and Zhang Zhidong (1837–1909), and reformists, such as Liang Qichao as well as his intellectual colleagues, to react to the imperial crisis in cultural terms. Although they spoke from very different perspectives, both factions spoke for the binary, even hierarchy, of Chinese versus Western learning. Theorists of the conservative group at court sought to link "Chinese learning" to imperial authority, so they never fully accepted the broad concept of *gezhi*. Zhang Zhidong, the student of an influential figure at court, Weng Tonghe, had devoted himself to renewing a cultural genealogy in order to strengthen the authority of the newly invested Emperor Guangxu (Zhongguo shixue hui 1995).[36] Unlike the Jiangnan Arsenal translators, who tended to break down the boundaries between systems, Zhang assiduously reproduced the Chinese learning versus Western learning dualism. In his *Shumu dawen* (Annotated Bibliography of Books, 1874), he perpetuated the distinction between genealogies of Chinese and Western knowledge that had originated during the Kangxi reign (1662–1722), even though for many Jiangnan mathematicians "Chinese" and "Western" learning were actually commensurate. For instance, he pointedly divided mathematicians as well as mathematical texts into two rival camps, those who were thought to do mathematics the "Chinese way" and those who were thought to do mathematics the "Western way," while putting those who did not fit the division into a third category of "conducting both ways"

(Zhang Zhidong [1898] 1963, 3831–67).[37] When Zhang himself obtained higher office in the early 1890s, the once-obscure binary category of Chinese learning *(zhongxue)* versus Western learning *(xixue)* was popularized again by the reprinting of his work *Quanxue pian* (Persuasion of Learning). There, Zhang rearranged a binary opposition in which the content of "Chinese learning was the essence" whereas the content of "Western learning was function" *("zhongxue wei ti, Xixue wei yong")* (Zhang Zhidong [1874] 1963, 6:3831–67). Thus, he reduced science and technology from a possible cultural field with multiple identities to a small tool in the specialized toolbox of Western learning.

Replacing *gezhi* with *xixue* was also one of the most remarkable cultural victories of reform-minded groups led by Kang Youwei and Liang Qichao, who promoted *Xixue* as a means of building a new, Western-style, political system following the Sino-Japanese War. Liang Qichao's famous *Xixue shumubiao* (Bibliography of Western Learning, 1896) contains 355 titles, of which no fewer than 165 had been published by the Jiangnan Arsenal. Those 165 titles comprised almost all the publications of the Arsenal. But while *gezhi* in the Arsenal environment had referred to a wide range of scientific and technological knowledge (including social sciences), in Liang's bibliography it was utterly separated from learning and reduced to a very technical term. Liang divided all the listed books into three types or volumes: Western learning, Western politics, and miscellany. *Gezhi* appeared only as one of the five categories in the miscellany volume, *gezhi zong,* and that category included only eleven titles (Liang Qichao 1896, 14a–15b). In another place, Liang indicated that *gezhi* was no more than the study of physical things *(xing er xia zhi xue)* (Liang Qichao 1936, 4, 11:3–14). Indeed, whereas the Arsenal community had sublimated *gezhi,* Liang trivialized it.

Minimizing the term "*gezhi*," Liang attached to the same body of knowledge a cultural identity as well as a political role model for government. He introduced this role model for government by reorganizing the translated texts into a category called "the Western art of government" *(xizheng).* Liang declared that the Arsenal and other official presses had done poorly in translating works on political science and government, so poorly that there was "almost no complete translation of a single book on agriculture, governmental systems, or education" (Liang Qichao 1896, Part I, 3a). Yet, looking at the books he listed under the "art of government," one sees that the category was not dramatically different from what the Jiangnan Arsenal circle meant by *gezhi:* Under "the art of government" Liang included 55 volumes on military technology and military history, 38 on manufacturing, 7 on agriculture and textiles, 9 on mining, 25 on the histories of Western countries, 1 on the German political system, 7 on the European educational system, 13 on international law and legal systems in European countries, and 4 on commerce. Not only did the content of *xizheng* overlap with *gezhi*, but the publishing agencies also overlapped: Among the 169 volumes Liang grouped together under the rubric of the "Western arts of government," 101 were translated and published by the Jiangnan Arsenal (Liang Qichao 1896, Part II, 7a–13b).

The fact that different political factions in China were all involved in creating a totalistic Western learning after the Sino-Japanese War reflected an actual need to establish "China" as an organic whole out of a rather loosely knit political and cultural system. The political factions, of course, conflicted on what kind of totality it should be: whether a China that could dominate relations with modern European nations, as the conservative politician Zhang Zhidong would have hoped, or a China that was materially and politically the equal of the European nation-states, as the reformists Liang Qichao and Tan Sitong had dreamed. This political battle over a totalistic China was bound to rule out the mediating realm of *gezhi*, even though it was "modern" and open to knowledge from both "China" and the "West." This overwriting of *gezhi* with *xixue* hardened the symbolic tie between scientific subjects and the West. If *gezhi* was a loosely perceived vague field opening to social subjects engaged in diverse practices, *xixue* was promoted by the reformists as a learning that belonged to the West only, thus a field to which no practices currently extant in China could make any contribution.

The learned society in Shanghai began to be pulled apart over this rewriting of the cultural category of *gezhi* with that of *xixue*, though a change in lexicon gave definitions to the political lines with which the educated groups identified. The Sino-Japanese War denied or erased, at least at the ideological and psychological levels, any possible scientific and technological achievements prior to 1894. Those who were politically frustrated with court policies and who sought reform and social change now found themselves with no choice but to identify with Liang Qichao in promoting Western learning. Compared with the conservative formulations of Zhang Zhidong, Liang's concept of Western science, although totalistic, functioned as a mirror image of a future culture of Chinese elite, an elite culture that would get rid of all the unsuccessful cultural elements from prior to the Sino-Japanese War. But in lining up with Liang, one confirmed the Western ownership of science and technology that was part of the psychological and ideological impact of the Sino-Japanese War. This silent confirmation transformed the self-expression of the educated groups. Take the circulation of *xixue* among the literati as an example. A study society in Hubei, Zhixue hui (Society of Chemistry), put the books in the *Series of the Western Art of Government* compiled by Liang Qichao side by side with the earlier works of Jiangnan mathematicians and published them in a collection entitled *Xixue fuqiang congshu* (Books of Western Learning, Wealth, and Power) (Zhang Yinhuan 1897, 1–2). In a casual but striking way, the title recast works by Jiangnan mathematicians as *Xixue*, even though the name of their society, Zhixue, was an older term without cultural identity. Obviously, Western learning became the symbolism that the avant-garde and nonconservative political groups sought to confirm.

Ironically, this division between Chinese and Western learning cut the Western learning off from its previous life in Suzhou, Hangzhou, or other Jiangnan cities. Shanghai, as the crucible of possibility for translations, was overcoded into something else: the primary site of transmission for the cultural and scientific West. Western learning, as the new coding system for the practices of science, erased semiotic traces of the *chouren* learning of the eighteenth century or *gezhi* learning of the nineteenth century. Moreover, in 1902, the dichotomy between Western and Chinese learning was further changed into opposition between the "new learning" and the old.[38] The binary between the new and the old did not fully dispose of the cultural identity of the Chinese and the West as they had intended; in fact, it enhanced their hierarchical relation instead. The urban society of Shanghai was now both "Western" and "new"—the latter was actually made identical with the former.

The interrupted pursuit of translatability in the field of science and technology did not mean the death of the spirit of translatability, nor did it ensure the disappearance of counterpractices to the imperialist knowledge in other cultural arenas. This thought leads us to the next chapter, where we will see that the practice of translatability and retranslatability was evidenced in another area of urban culture, where philology and the word were at the center.

TWO

Semiotic Modernity:
The Politics of Philology and Compilation

Several rupturing events took place in China around the turn of the twentieth century: the Sino-Japanese War of 1894, the Hundred Day Reform of 1898, the Qing state's New Policy of 1902, and the influx of new ideas brought from Japan by Chinese dissidents and students. These events had a tremendous cultural effect, the emergence of what one may call "semiotic modernity," that is, the modernity of semiotics and words. Because of the convenient affinity between the Japanese and Chinese written languages, modern concepts, vocabularies, texts, and graphics flooded China's printed world during this period by way of Meiji Japan, making a semiotic impact upon the urban society of knowledge.[1] In 1897, the thinker Liang Qichao was still using the binary opposition between Western learning and Chinese learning to promote reform, but just a few years later, scholar Xu Weize had begun to stress the need to invent the category of *dongxue*—Japanese learning—for the new crop of books (1902). Within a few years following the publication of the New Policy, translations of foreign history, philosophy, politics, and scientific books numbered in the thousands (David Wang 1997; Feng Ziyou 1965; Zhang Yuying [1941] 1953, 140–83). The number of translations of Western works retranslated from Japanese now equaled the number of existing translations made directly from Western languages (Tarumoto Teruo 2002; Ah Ying 1957). The transnational print culture as well as cross-cultural textuality, which Leo Lee identified as the basis of the "Shanghai Modern" of the 1930s (1999, 120–49), find their precedent at this very moment, when "textual transactions" took place not only across the boundary between Chinese and European languages but also across the boundary between Chinese and Japanese. The difference is that whereas the textual transactions of the later period supported a modernity of genres and styles, the earlier semiotic transaction of vocabularies generated a modernity of words.

To observe the semiotic change of the urban print culture challenges the existing conceptual connection between the birth of the print industry and urban modernity. Jürgen Habermas (1989) and Benedict Anderson (1983) long ago analyzed, in their own ways, the profound and complex connections between the cultural industry of printing and the rise of modern society, whether in the form of a "public sphere" or an imagined national community. An urban historian may further argue that the birth of the print industry was crucial to the rise of modern cities such as London and New York as it brought newsstands, bookstores, and readers in coffee shops to the everyday life of urban society. Although all these arguments are well-founded, conceptually they confirm only one moment of historical change, namely, the industrial moment. Industrial technology did influence the print culture of Shanghai from the 1870s on,[2] but its overall effect remained limited. Indeed, in China's long history of bookstores, literary societies, and urban print culture, political and cultural factors often contributed to change in more fundamental ways than print did. The semiotic moment of modernity discussed here represented another change of this sort. It brought to the fore a *surplus,* if not redundant, moment of modernity, a moment characterized by massive semiotic exchanges and vocabulary transactions rather than by the infrastructural transmission of technology.

The semiotic moment was even more epochal in the rise of Shanghai than the "industrial moment," since it initiated the chapter in which translated (and retranslated) Western concepts and Japanese texts became the everyday exercise of learned urban society. As such, it reveals a sociopolitical dimension of "disharmonious overlap" that is inaccessible from the industrial moment of urban history, that is, the "disharmonious overlap" between a cultural practice that leads toward the unraveling of Qing orthodoxy and a practice that adds to the hegemonic symbolic order of the modern West via Japan. In this circumstance, the incorporation of Meiji words into modern Chinese risked becoming a colonial practice, *unless* it brought with it the retranslation of hegemony embedded in Meiji semiotics back into antihegemonic forms.[3]

The antihegemonic retranslation of these imported words enjoins us to view print culture and the publishing enterprise as management of the imported semiotic modernity. It presents us, therefore, with the questions of who were to be the managers of translation and retranslation, and into what semiotic system the imported languages were retranslated. Exploring these questions will lead us directly to the heart of the transition of the urban cultural practice from a post-Suzhou stage to the Shanghai moment.

This chapter takes the first few decades of the Commercial Press (founded in 1897) as the showcase of this transition in urban cultural practice. As a publishing enterprise, the Commercial Press participated in semiotic modernity specifically through the modes of translation and retranslation, namely, by interpreting, compiling, editing, redefining, typesetting, and publishing. These activities mobilized multiple layers of actors with specific tools from the dislocated but ongoing Jiangnan networks of philologists, reform-minded scholars, and entrepreneurs providing popular printed material. A cultural principle manifested itself through the Commercial Press's effort to connect to the modern in diverse ways or, to put it differently, to preserve semiotic and textual diversity as much as it could in the face of universal modernity. This principle is best observed through the process of *bianyi* (compilation and translation, at the face value of the word; translingual compilation, or "trans-compilation"), a specific cultural procedure of combining and restructuring words and texts that was commonly seen in the urban culture prior to the mid-1920s. The successful application of this principle, I shall argue, brought to Shanghai competitive semiotic managers who turned semiotic modernity into a semiotic interaction with the potential to defy modern hegemony.

Print Workers, Activist Philologists, and Trans-Compilation

One day in February 1897, four young men pooled their personal savings and opened a small printing press on a corner of Jiangxi Street in Shanghai. Nothing looked especially momentous in their opening event: Western-style print institutions in Shanghai such as Shenbao Press (founded in 1872) and Dianshizhai shuju (founded in 1874) had been enjoying success for two decades. Like other small businesses, the new press started with individual, small-scale jobs such as printing business brochures. Their assets were not outstanding, merely consisting of some manual printers and three narrow workrooms, plus several years of professional experience as print workers. This small press seemed likely to become one those unknown shops that barely survived or quickly went out of business for lack of economic or intellectual resources. The name of this little printing shop was the Commercial Press.[4]

Starting from that small street-corner shop, the Commercial Press was able to achieve a dominant position in the nation's publishing culture within a few years. It solicited many of the most prominent scholars and educators of the time as professional editors in a way that no official or foreign press had done before. It enlarged its capital by 250 percent per year during its first eight years, and it increased sales by about 100 percent per year during its first six years (Zhuang Yu 1931, 46–47; Tarumoto Teruo 1979, 300–339; 1988, 1–48).[5] By 1901 it owned the most advanced technology and printing facilities in Shanghai, and by 1902 its textbooks for primary education were the envy of the official presses. During the "boom period" of journal publishing around 1911, the staff already had several years of experience publishing journals for groups of readers ranging from intellectuals to women and children. By the eve of the New Culture movement (1917), the Commercial Press had become a large, multifaceted institution that cut across several sociocultural layers by connecting printing factories, circulation networks, editorial headquarters, an affiliated library, and several primary and professional schools. Its technology and technological inventions surpassed those of other presses, and its publications took the lead in almost every aspect of print culture, ranging from preliminary textbooks, collections of rare classics, fiction series, translated literary works, encyclopedias, and technical manuals. Not surprisingly, the Commercial Press played a crucial role in constructing modern fields of cultural studies in China such as the social sciences and the humanities. It placed Shanghai right at the center of the transformation of China's book culture.

What brought the Commercial Press to success as it maneuvered the semiotic moment of book publication? I propose that the collaboration of two distinct founding groups, that is, the industrial printing entrepreneurs and the philologist activists (if one may call them so) and their shared practice of *bianyi,* or trans-compilation, hold the answer. The industrial printing entrepreneurs were of humble origins, having labored as migrant workers in Shanghai. The philologist editors came from the prestigious scholarly circles of the Jiangnan region and were actively involved in social and cultural reform movements. The two groups would hardly have had the chance to meet and share an activity had there not occurred the geographic movement of urban centers from Jiangnan to the shore that I described in the introduction and chapter 1. The convergence of these individuals demonstrated the reshuffling of a migrated urban society as well as that of its core practices of publishing and philology at the beginning of the twentieth century.

The personal histories of the founders of the Commercial Press were typical of the first and second generations of migrant laborers who came to Shanghai from inland cities and nearby regions in the country. Two of the four founders, Bao Xian'en (d. 1910) and Bao Xianchang (d. 1929), were brothers and natives of Ningbo. Their father died early, and the three brothers and two sisters in the family depended on a meager income from their mother's labor in order to survive. An elder sister who worked at service jobs in Shanghai enrolled in a newly opened Presbyterian school, the Lowrie Institute (Qingxin), and luckily became a staff member of the school after graduation (Zhang Xichen 1987, 102–24).[6] With her income, the Bao family moved from Ningbo to Shanghai, and the three brothers were all educated at Lowrie. The main leader of the press, Xia Ruifang (1871–1914) moved to Shanghai at the age of twelve from the countryside of Qingpu County and enrolled in the Lowrie Institute on the recommendation of an American priest for whom his mother worked as a servant.[7] There he was befriended by his fellow villager Gao Fengchi and by two of the Bao brothers. The four friends all became print workers after graduation: Xia and Bao Xian'en did typesetting for the *China Gazette*, sponsored by the *North China Herald*; Bao Xianchang and Gao Fengchi worked for the American Mission Press. Xia and Bao Xian'en grew tired of the working environment at the *North China Herald* and decided to establish their own printing shop (Zhuang Yu 1931, 46–47; 1987b, 6–8). They gathered an initial fund of 3,750 yuan by issuing stock.[8] Yet their long-term friendship and mutual loyalty extended far beyond money relations: The four founders of the press not only remained good friends and business partners but also became each other's relatives. The Bao brothers' younger sister married Xia Ruifang, and Gao Fengchi's daughter married the son of one of the Bao brothers (Zhang Xichen 1987, 102–24) (Figure 2).

Young and energetic, the founders of the Commercial Press expanded their infrastructure through hard work and pure luck. In the first couple

Figure 2. Portraits of the founders of the Commercial Press. Top, Xia Ruifan;
bottom, Yin Youmo; left, Bao Xianchang; right, Bao Xian'en. From Zhuang Yu
and He Shengding, comps., *Zuijin sanshiwu nian zhi Zhungguo jiaoyu* [Education
in China in the past thirty-five years] (Shanghai: Commercial Press, 1931),
unnumbered page.

of years the press printed whatever was at hand, ranging from small orders for foreign merchants and missionary organizations to larger orders involving printing the Bible for the Presbyterian Church; from a reprint of a popular collection, *Tongjian jilian*,[9] to serious journals such as *Waijiao bao* (Journal of Foreign Relations).[10] Meanwhile, Xia Ruifang and his colleagues had the good fortune to seize two business opportunities that were crucial to the future of the press: First, through networking, they purchased a secondhand Japanese factory in 1900, Shubun Shokan, which allowed the press to build up its technical and mechanical base at a low cost (Nakamura Tadayuki 1989, 51–64). Second, the press gained the financial and technical cooperation of the Japanese investors of Kinkodo Press in 1903 (ibid.). The Japanese shareholders, according to Tarumoto Teruo, had been charged with bribery in a lawsuit in Japan, which had greatly damaged their reputation in Japanese publishing circles (1979, 300–339). The partnership was based upon a mutual investment of 20,000 yuan, split equally between the two presses, with Kindoko supplying technical support and the Commercial Press offering management.[11] Lasting until 1914, this collaboration expanded the financial as well as technological assets of the press (Chang Zhou 1992, 642–55; Tarumoto Teruo 1979, 300–339).

The specific practice that led to the press's success, even at this early stage, can be translated as "trans-compilation," *bianyi* in Chinese. *Bianyi* refers to prepublication work done by compilers, translators, and editors. In the Chinese system, the editor, or *biancuan*, performed a much more crucial role than his European counterparts. A *biancuan* was himself an expert and scholar in the books he compiled for publication and was thus a powerful figure in controlling cultural production and reproduction. Derived from "*biancuan*," the word "*bianyi*" is formed with two parts: "*bian*" means to compile and to edit for publication, or someone who had the status of a *bianxiu* (secretary) in the Hanlin Academy; "*yi*" simply means to translate or to interpret from a foreign language. *Bianyi*, or trans-compilation, was a common practice during the Foreign Affairs period if not earlier. Departments of translation and compilation characterized Foreign Affairs institutions such as the Jiangnan Arsenal, the Fuzhou Dockyard, and the Nanyang Academy, to name just a few.

Because of the cultural status of Xia Ruifang and his friends, the *bianyi* practice appeared in the early days of the press in the case of a type of self-instructional publication, practical books that would enable a reader to do translations him- or herself. The press's first few publications tended to be instructional books such as language aids, foreign-language dictionaries, and textbooks about world geography. As Xia Ruifang and his friends were graduates of a missionary school, it is not surprising that the press's *bianyi* activities started with the retranslation of missionary dictionaries and textbooks for Chinese readers. For instance, a phonetic English-Chinese dictionary was retranslated into a true bilingual format. The phonetic form of the dictionary carried no Chinese characters and was useful only to missionaries familiar with romanization. By adding Chinese characters and short explanations entry by entry, the press transformed the dictionary into a bilingual book, thus making it useful for Chinese readers. Similarly, the press's first hit, *Huaying chujie*, was an English-Chinese textbook based on a revision by Xie Honglai, a student of A. Pierson Parker, of *English Primer*, a textbook used in colonial schools in India and then missionary schools in China (Chang Zhou 1992, 650–51). *English Primer* was written in English only. By adding Chinese translations as well as line-by-line explanations,[12] the press made the book bilingual, thus turning it into a book for self-study at home. *Huaying chujie* and *Huaying jinjie* (Basic and Advanced English) were immensely popular: The first volume sold out in a week, and the two books continued to be popular for decades to come. So was the largest bilingual English-Chinese dictionary published by the press, which comprised "120,000 words and phrases with translations, pronunciations, definitions and illustrations" (Shangwu yingshuguan 1899, title page) and which was so welcomed that "almost everyone in the learned circles owned a copy" (Yen Huiqing 1974). The success of this trans-compilation was no secret: It inserted into colonial textbooks and missionary dictionaries a different user, perhaps a counter-user, of language and knowledge.[13]

The necessity of dealing with Japanese texts provided the entrepreneurs with a chance to strengthen their press by soliciting top scholars and intellectuals to participate in their projects of rewriting imported knowledge. The beginning of the twentieth century saw many "translations" that were actually paraphrases, interpretations, expansions, or contractions. The Commercial Press pushed this practice in the direction of rewriting and then institutionalized the practice by establishing the largest ever *bianyisuo*, or translation and editorial department. In 1900, the unexpected unpopularity of the Japanese books brought Xia

Ruifang to consult Zhang Yuanji (1867–1959), then the dean of the translation bureau at Nanyang Academy, with whom the press had done business before. Xia Ruifang learned that Japanese textbooks had to be rewritten in a form more useful and relevant for Chinese readers (Jiang Weiqiao [1935] 1957, 138–45; Zhuang Yu 1987a, 62–72). Xia immediately made *rewriting* the main task of publication, but rewriters were inevitably either hard to find or already occupied with other tasks. Seeing that good translators or rewriters were such a crucial element in the publishing world, Xia Ruifang decided to establish his own editorial institution, a *bianyisuo*, which would gather a band of the best editors available (Bao Tianxiao 1990). Private presses in Shanghai at the time, following the example of the Shenbao Press, had all invited one or two Hanlin academians to take charge of their publications.[14] Yet few had seen the necessity, even in the official institutions of the Foreign Affairs movement, to have their own team of rewriters. With Xia Ruifang's vision of establishing a *bianyisuo*, the Commercial Press began to transform from a publisher of bilingual self-study books into a producer of bicultural knowledge. I shall return to the issue of rewriting shortly.

With the founding of the *bianyisuo* in 1902, the press brought into its history the second crucial group, the "activist philologists," as editors and compilers.[15] A generation born immediately after the Taiping Rebellion, these editors shared at least two characteristics: their scholarly training in philology as well as "new learning" on the one hand, and on the other hand, their political and social pursuit of radical social and political change. Trained in highly prestigious and specialized fields of knowledge ranging across philology, history, botany, medicine, and cataloguing, these editors' research work is of high scholarly value even today—Meng Sen (1868–1938) and Xu Ke (1869–1928), the chief editors of the press's intellectual journal *Dongfang zazhi* (Eastern Miscellany), were the best examples. All editors were also promoters of the new knowledge, particularly on the topics of politics, economy, technology, and philosophy from Western and Japanese sources. Meanwhile, the "activist" aspect of the lives of these compilers added a social and political dimension to their mastery of philological and new knowledge. They dreamed of changing society and the governmental system. Therefore, before they came to work at the Commercial Press, they had already devoted themselves to such activities as organizing politically oriented societies and study groups, writing to the authorities or to the public about the need for change, initiating reform projects, building new-style schools, and participating in a variety of social and cultural movements, such as anti-foot-binding and women's education. As with the late-imperial philologists, education and learning were internal to their political pursuit of social and cultural changes—indeed, philological studies of the Qing had always been the symbolic acts through which the learned groups, centralized in Jiangnan cities, had interacted politically with the Qing court (Elman 1984). Unlike the pursuits of the late-imperial philologists, theirs were much more public and easier to put into action.

The director of the editorial institute, Zhang Yuanji, for example, was a "radical" ex-official who had extraordinary expertise in philology. The descendant of a high-ranking branch of the Zhang family from Haiyan County (Wang Shaozeng 1984, 1–67),[16] Zhang Yuanji had a superb knowledge of the classics, mastered English and international affairs (Mao Dun 1987, 140–47),[17] and shared the political ideals of such fellow Han-lin academians as Wang Kangnian (1860–1911) and Cai Yuanpei (1868–1940), who pursued systematic reform in government and society. Working as a secretary for the Bureau of International Relations, he amassed modern knowledge specializing in railways, schools, mineral manufacture, and shipbuilding before 1898. He participated in the 1898 Reform by suggesting that the Emperor Guangxu restructure the bureaucracy. He also devoted himself to supervising the Tungyi xuetang (School of Science and Art), which aimed at teaching contemporary skills and practical knowledge. When the 1897 Reform was crushed, Zhang was found guilty of manipulating the emperor and was permanently barred from holding any official position. He came to Shanghai to work at Nanyang Public Academy. Even there, he opened new frontiers of social and cultural change by taking charge of publishing influential works such as Yan Fu's translation of the work of Adam Smith.

Similarly radical figures include Gao Fengqian (1869–1936), Jiang Weiqiao (1873–1958), and Zhuang Yu (1868–1930), as well as Du Yaquan (1873–1933). Gao Fengqian, the first chair of the Language and Literature Department and the second director of the Translation and Editorial Department of the press (1916–1921), came from a family of high literary fame in the Tongcheng writing style, in Fujian Province. Besides being a poetic and decorative writer, Gao was a pioneer promoter of cultural change, and he wrote to the then radical journal *Shiwu bao* (Journal of Current Affairs) calling on the public to oppose the practice of such symbolic rituals as kneeling and *koutou*. Two figures, Jiang Weiqiao and Zhuang Yu, bring us even closer to the heart of the philological activists, since they came from the home of the New Text school of Confucianism, Chaozhou. Having been in Japan, Jiang Weiqiao shared the radical anti-Qing sentiments of the Chinese students in Tokyo. To engage in social change, he joined the Chinese Educational Society (Zhongguo jiaoyu hui), founded by Cai Yuanpei, and became the president of Patriotic Women's School (Aiguo nuxiao), founded by the association. Zhuang Yu, a grandson of the famous New Text scholar Zhuang Dajiu,[18] was another active figure in social and cultural reforms carried out by organizations such as the Anti-Foot-Binding Society (Tianzu hui), the Sports Club (Tiyu hui), and the Private School Reform Club (Sishu gailiang hui), as well as the Society of Evolution (Renyan she), which took the notion of evolution to mean radical changes (Zhuang Shi 1987, 73–75). Du Yaquan, a native of Shaoxing, believed in changing society with "useful" knowledge, so much so that he quit the prestigious Chongwen Academy and taught himself mathematics, medicine, chemistry, and other sciences (Zhang Xichen 1987, 112–13). Actively promoting the new scientific education, he founded the Yaquan Study Club (Yaquan xuegaun, 1900–1902), the Studio of Vernacular Education (Putongxue shushi), the scientific journal *Yaquan zazhi*,[19] and the Public School of Shaoxing City (Yuejun gongxue) (Yuan Hanqing 1987, 83–85).

What these compilers brought to the press was a unique political and intellectual vision for change, plus a much-needed authority over the competing crosscurrents of "knowledge" taking place across China at the time. The publications of the press quickly reflected this. From 1902 onward, the publications of the Commercial Press extended the work of *bianyi* to the publication of books written on much larger issues in the fields of politics, economics, law, science, sociology, and philosophy in more cultured and scholarly forms such as collectanea, encyclopedias, and series, as well as systematic textbooks. The small collectanea of seven books published by the early Commercial Press, *Diguo congshu* (Imperial Collectanea), for example, contained six translations from Japanese ranging across law, citizens' rights, Egyptian history, Japanese political history, and military subjects (Shangwu yinshuguan 1981, 56).[20] Within ten years, the press was publishing a few categories of books: (1) five dictionaries and tool books, from Chinese-English and Chinese-German dictionaries to glossaries of physics and chemistry terminology; (2) seven large-set book series, including twenty-four volumes of documents from the Russo-Japanese War, eighty volumes of complete translations of Japanese law, and thirty-two volumes of records of the Chinese delegations to various countries; (3) a dozen translations and original works in philosophy, sociology, politics, religion, ethics, and history; and (4) six influential intellectual and literary journals. The press's most significant publications at this time included, to name just a few, Yan Fu's translations of works by Herbert Spencer, Montesquieu, and T. H. Huxley, a complete edition of the Japanese legal code, Ma Jianzhong's (1844–1900) contemporary scholarship on Chinese linguistics, twenty-one volumes of translated novels, and the influential journals *Eastern Miscellany, Jiaoyu zazhi* (Journal of Education), *Qingnan zazhi* (Youth), and *Xiaoshuo yuebao* (Fiction Monthly) (Figure 3).

The press's many different types of trans-compilations created a position for its philological activists in the cultural role of compilers, and conversely, the philological activists, having become compilers, redefined the role of compilers. The press's projects in translation and compilation expanded to such a degree that by the middle of the second decade of the twentieth century, the editorial department had increased from just a few people to more than a hundred (Zhuang Yu 1987a, 62–72). Partly because of the specific character of the press's compilers, trans-compilation became a primary means of controlling and promoting transnational cultural exchange in the fields of literature, philosophy, education, and in the creation of encyclopedias at the moment of semiotic modernity. By assigning itself such a cultural task, the press influenced other publishing enterprises, including its competitor, Zhonghua shuju (China Press, founded 1912). It gave Shanghai the leading role in the change of China's book culture.

Textbooks and Rare Books: Inbound and Outbound

Two seemingly contrasting projects, the compilation of introductory textbooks and the collection and reproduction of rare classics, demonstrate the compilers' way of engaging directly with the semiotic moment of modernity. As is well known, after the Sino-Japanese War the Meiji state established cultural programs that served to construct Japanese domination of the cultures of East Asia. Policy makers of the Meiji state proclaimed that Japanese culture and education would be modern, while at the same time they sought to exercise cultural authority over

Figure 3. The Commercial Press. From Zhuang Yu and He Shengding, comps., *Zuijin sanshiwu nian zhi Zhungguo jiaoyu* [Education in China in the past thirty-five years] (Shanghai: Commercial Press, 1931), unnumbered page.

traditional Asian culture. As a result, traditional and conservative curriculums were designed for other Asian students (Judge 2001, 765–803), yet cultural resources and treasures were shipped, through market or nonmarket means, from China to the museums and libraries of Japan. Japan's imperialist schema assigned the culture of China a position of backwardness or traditionalism but without any of the authority due to that traditionalism. The compilers at the Commercial Press engaged the situation through translation and compilation by inducing inbound streams of new educational concepts and competing outbound streams of cultural treasures. They countered the global circulation of literature with publication, instead of with the resistance or silence often encountered in a colonial situation.

The new textbook project made the press the agent of China's modern elementary education during the first years of the twentieth century. The compilation itself was launched in 1902, when the Qing state put the New Policy into practice. Because compulsory education for 90 percent of the population was one explanation for Japan's rapid success in modernization, the reforming Qing state put forth a similar educational initiative by launching school reforms and publishing *School Regulations*. Similar to that of Japan, the compulsory education pursued by the Qing state reflected the change in the focus of education from *xue* (learning, study, cultivation) to *jiaoyu* (pedagogy, education, schooling). But unlike in Japan, where the schools and textbooks formed a united front in compulsory education, in China the schools and textbooks followed two separate trends. Although the compulsory education through the Qing state schools was basically an institutional failure, the textbooks, as a means to carry out social and cultural change, became a hit in the world of textuality, accessible to most of the educated. Not only did the compilation of textbooks as a nonstate practice provide the blueprint for modern education in a more progressive manner than did the policies of the Qing state (Guomin zhengfu jiaoyubu [1935] 1953, 219–53), but it also carried a message of the "rise of the social" as a revolutionary force challenging the state.

The Commercial Press distinguished itself from the ongoing trend of textbook compilation by providing overall guidelines for the new primary education. The leading textbooks compilers of the time, such as the Nanyang Academy and the Three-Grade School of Wuxi City (Wuxi sandeng xuetang), emphasized "understanding" (instead of mere memorization) and accessibility to children (Jiang Weiqiao [1935] 1957, 138–45).[21] The Commercial Press's compilers also established the concept of "beginners" who had almost none of the literacy prerequisite for a primary education. Students entering most primary schools at the time, including the two schools mentioned above, had achieved a certain level of literacy, from their families or through *sishu* (private lessons). The school regulation published in "Zouding chudeng xiaoxue zhangcheng" (Official Regulation of Primary Schools), not surprisingly, required the primary schools to allot twelve hours per week to the study of the classics (Zhang Shunian 1991, 48). To lower the entry level to make schooling accessible to illiterate beginners, the Commercial Press's compilers eliminated the lessons in classical Chinese and oriented the textbooks toward child beginners with a lower literacy level than that of actual school students. For example, they set up a rule that in order to be easy enough for illiterate children, the characters used in introductory textbooks should be restricted to a certain number of strokes. Characters used in the first volume, for example, were limited to six strokes, and the maximum number of strokes for first-year students was set at fifteen (Jiang Weiqiao [1935] 1957, 142). The text of every lesson in the first two volumes was discussed among the compilers in a seminar. Debates over easier and more common words sometimes lasted for hours until they had reached a resolution (Gao Hanqing 1992, 1–13). The process of compilation was a rational procedure that redefined primary education: An ideal subject for study in the reformed education was expected to grow and eventually to become a future subject of modern knowledge.

The concept of a neutral, universal beginner evoked the idea of a single, universal type of school. Starting from the beginner, the New Elementary Textbooks series laid out a very systematic educational arrangement. It structured, in printed form, different sorts of schools by providing simultaneity in the school calendar, regularity in the length and content of each lesson, and consistent standards for the presentation of writing, reading, and homework assignments. New Elementary Textbooks required, for example, a space between complete sentences in all textbooks, a picture below the text of each lesson, and at least one repetitive use of new vocabulary items in the later lessons (Zhuang Yu 1987a, 62–72). New Elementary Textbooks were also characterized by a set of teaching guides with pedagogical keys and consistent, identical student notebooks for homework (ibid.). The curriculum of the New Elementary Textbooks was a highly organized pedagogical design. The press's Japanese partner, the Kinkodo Press, then the largest publisher of textbooks in Japan, might have greatly inspired the compilers (Tarumoto Teruo 1979, 300–339). The New Elementary Textbooks were divided into a beginning level and an advanced level, corresponding respectively to the new school structure of elementary and junior high schools. By reducing the emphasis on classical literature, the beginning-level New Elementary Textbooks created room for calculation, mathematics, and calculation using the abacus in addition to elementary Chinese and "self-cultivation."[22] The advanced elementary textbooks continued five of the original subjects at a higher level while adding four new classes: history, geography, agriculture, and commerce.[23] The middle-school textbooks, following this pattern, expanded the sciences into eleven subdivisions, including zoology, botany, geology, physics, chemistry, algebra, biology, and geometry, while adding English, calligraphy, and other subjects to the curriculum. Schooling, in this vision of education, meant acquiring knowledge in all of these subjects gradually and systematically.

In Japan, the state was the agent of compulsory education, but in China the state school for new education was almost a failure. It was the compilers of textbooks who performed the role of educational reformer. In other words, the blueprint of a school system provided by the Commercial Press, although partly borrowed from Japan, carried out a symbolic act that was quite different from the role of modern Japanese schools. A close study of the word "*jiaoyu*" (education), widespread both in Japan and China, will explain the difference.

Jiaoyu had been a central concern as well as a main practice of reformist intellectuals, including compilers at the press such as Zhuang Yu, Jiang Weiqiao, Gao Mengdan, and Zhang Yuanji, since 1897. The kanji characters of "*jiaoyu*" can be retranslated back into the Chinese context with at least two distinct ramifications: (1) *jiao* or *jiaohua*, "to teach" and "to transform," and (2) *yu* or *yucai*, "to cultivate able and moral members" so as to restaff the state offices. Since in the Qing era, government bureaus were still staffed by the learned members of society, *jiaoyu*, or implicitly, "to teach and to change" and "to cultivate so as to restaff the government," carried out a revolutionary quest to reform the state system. The Education Association of China (founded in 1902), an organization whose name—Zhongguo jiaoyu hui—contained the word "*jiaoyu*," especially embodied this quest in its early stage.

Whereas an older generation of reformers, such as Kang Youwei, had sought to change China within the framework of the imperial system, namely, by following the political model of Japan and Britain, the members of the Chinese Educational Society saw the Qing state as the object of reform. The most active members were leading anti-Manchu intellectuals such as Zhang Binglin and revolutionary activists such as Cai Yuanpei. The official journal of the association, *Subao* (Paper of Jiangsu), published bold attacks on the Qing state as well as articles proclaiming political change, for instance, Zou Rong's well-known piece "Revolutionary Army" ("Geming jun," 1903). Leading compilers at the press, Jiang Weiqiao, Cai Yuanpei, Zhuang Yu, and Zhang Yuanji, were members of the Educational Association of China.

The organizational interpretation of *jiaoyu*, being so close to "revolution" or radical change, also characterized their social and cultural reforms mentioned earlier, such as open schools and anti-foot-binding. In this context, their devotion to textbook compilation was meant to be a devotion to revolution in a specific form: to teach and to change, as well as to cultivate future staffs of the state and society. It is only ironic that this retranslation of *jiaoyu* into the Chinese context reversed the political meaning of the word: Whereas *jiaoyu* in Japan was a state means of penetrating society and molding modern citizens, in China the work of the textbook compilers turned *jiaoyu* into a symbolic act of revolution, an act to end the imperial system of China.

Perhaps it was the symbolic meaning of *jiaoyu* that forced the Qing state to follow in the steps of the presses concerning "the social" in schooling and education. In 1906, the Bureau of Learning (Xuebu) confirmed 102 varieties of textbook edited by different publishing institutions as national standard textbooks for a five-year term of primary school education. Of the 106 varieties, 85, that is, 80 percent of the books listed, were edited and published by nonofficial presses. The Commercial Press itself contributed 54 types of books to the standard list (Li Zezhang 1931, 259–78).[24] Entrusted with more than 50 percent of all the national standard textbooks, the Commercial Press was ideally positioned to promulgate its vision of education—a vision that extended beyond education per se to include a blueprint for radical change. The "rise of the social"? Perhaps. The "rise of the radical," for sure.

Beside promoting the new and the basic as means of political reform, the compilers also engaged in preserving the old and prestigious to defend against both commodification and imperialist plunder of rare cultural objects. This aspect of the press's practice turns our attention to a paradoxical situation in which the industrial means of commodification devalued books of classics on the domestic market while, at the same time, valuable classics were the targets of imperialist hunting.

During the last two decades of the nineteenth century, lithographic printers had become the main presses to reproduce classics, which they were able to do in smaller sizes and at cheaper prices.[25] The ease with which these volumes could be stored and carried, the whiteness of the paper, and the beauty of the printed characters became their principal attractions. The authenticity of the books, which used to be the cultural criterion guaranteed by the expert work of compilers, was sidestepped. The philologists of the press could not help but note that "classics sold in the market were not to be trusted" as reference books and that it was safer to buy classics "from private book collectors" who at least knew about books (Zhang Yuanji [1911] 1981, 1–7). To them, the classics circulated in the domestic market were devalued to a great extent.

Meanwhile, as imperialism developed its cultural dimension in the late nineteenth century, rare Chinese cultural objects, including copies of classic texts, became the object of looting, not only as profitable treasures but as evidence of the cultural authority of the colonizers (Hevia 2004, 1–18). As the looting of Beijing around 1900 demonstrated, precious cultural objects such as paintings and copies of classic texts replaced tea and even money, becoming new targets of imperialist possession (Hevia 1999, 192–213). Of those robbers who were known as "scholars," the most notorious were Paul Pelliot (1878–1945) and Sir Aurel Stein (1862–1943), who took thousands of pieces of precious art and prints, including a rare set of the Buddhist canon.

International capital also stimulated the outbound flow of precious cultural objects from China. In 1906 the Commercial Press found itself in competition with domestic and international buyers for the well-known *Bisonglou* rare-book collection of the Lu family in Jiangnan. The collection was eventually sold to a Japanese buyer for 250,000 taels of silver, a price three times what the Commercial Press could offer (Zhang Shunian 1991, 60).[26]

The collection (or looting) of rare cultural objects and the establishment of "authentic" authority over Chinese civilization not only defined the imperialist "English lessons" (Hevia 2004, 75–118) but also characterized Japan's self-proclaimed cultural leadership in Asia. After the Sino-Japanese War, the draining of rare cultural items in China became even more devastating. As the son of a book collector and as a classical scholar, Zhang Yuanji, the dean of the compilation department of the Commercial Press, "felt unspeakable agony" at seeing the seemingly inevitable outward flow of classical books (Zhang Yuanji [1911] 1981, 1–7), and he pushed the press into taking action to stop this outward flow and to compete with those buying up national treasures. At his suggestion, the press launched several projects to collect, edit, and reprint rare classics, investing money to purchase the private collections. The first purchase was made in 1904 from the private collection of *Rongjing zhushi zhai* (The Furnace Studio of Classics and History) of the book collector Xu Shulan (Zhang Yuanji 1951). These books, fifty shelves of them, became the first collection of the press's reading room (Zhang Shunian 1991, 53). Beside Xu's collection, the press also purchased the collections of the Jiangs from Changzhou, the *Qinhan shiyin zhai* (The Studio of Ten Seals of the Qin and the Han) collection, and of the Gus from Fengshui, the *Souwen zhai* (Studio of Detailed Information) collection, and later, Miao Quansun's (1844–1919) collection *Yifengtang* (The Pavilion of Art and Style) from Jiangyin (Zhang Yuanji 1992, 21–22). All these books were shelved in the press's reading room, which soon became a library—formally named Hanfen lou in 1909.

Without the necessary capital to prevent the flight of rare classics, Zhang and his friends also promoted the alternative circulation of both rare books and books in general. This alternative circulation used two main strategies. The first pooled the resources of buyers of rare classics so that small amounts of private capital became large, competitive, and public. Combined investments were especially useful for building the necessary holdings in public or semipublic libraries. Zhang asked many people, officials as well as collectors, to purchase rare classics whenever they could. He also promoted collective support to increase the holdings of libraries. The press's Hanfen lou collection became the first public library in Shanghai, the Dongfang tushuguan (Eastern Library, opened 1926) (Dongfang tushuguan 1933, 1–19). This combination of small amounts of capital to build library holdings was an effective resistance to the predations of international capital.

The second strategy for resisting the outbound flow of classics was to reproduce rare books so that they were not rare. The press's publishing projects worked to interfere with the export of rare books. The press maximized the compilation value of rare books (the value of the philological work of the editors) by collecting, editing, and organizing them to counter the surplus value of the original rare book. In 1911 Zhang introduced the idea of selecting the best editions of individual books from different private collections and reproducing them in the form of collectanea. Although as reproductions the books did not share the authentic aesthetic value of the originals, the collectanea put together the best individual volumes one could find from different sources, thus acquiring a compilation value on its own. The works compiled in *Bai na ben ershisi shi* (Twenty-Four Histories from Selected Editions), for example, were selected, borrowed, and proofread by Zhang Yuanji and other compilers over the years. Each individual volume was a reproduction of its best extant edition. By bringing together precious texts from separate collections into a coherent whole, the value of *Bai na ben ershisi shi* exceeded in important ways that of the more diffuse contents of the originals. Here, it was the work of the compiler—that is, selecting and borrowing—instead of the wallet of international buyers that created the use value and the surplus value of the set. These values were invented to oppose and to interdict the outbound flow of rare classics.

To achieve the task of countering the outbound flow of classics, the press's compilers took not only philological action but also the social action of establishing reciprocal relationships with the private collectors in Jiangnan and other regions. The press's *Sibu congkan* (Library of Chinese Classical, Historical, Philosophical, and Literary Works) was compiled on the basis of this reciprocal network. The project started in 1910 and publication began in 1920 with the aim of reproducing all the best editions to be found in private collections and libraries within the country and beyond. To carry out this project, Zhang Yuanji persuaded as many private collectors as possible to lend the press their books as a favor. The press's reproduction would return the favor, since it would increase the reputation of the original.

The first printing of *Sibu* alone contained 349 sets of works in good editions that had been selected and borrowed from eighteen public and private owners (Wang Yunwu 1973, 102–3). Besides the press's own collection, the most important contribution to this first printing came from the Miao Quansun collection and the collection *Tieqin tongjian lou* (The Pavilion of Iron Harp and Bronze Sword), owned by one of the four best-known book collectors of the time, Qu Liangshi (1873–1940) (Qu Fengqi 1987, 324–27). In order to keep the original calligraphy and reduce mistakes in typesetting, the press used photographic reprint technology and reproduced the texts on site at Qu's house (Qu Fengqi 1987, 324–27). The rest of the collectors contributed rare classics from older sites of book culture in Zhejiang and Jiangsu, particularly from the cities of Changshu, Wuxi, and Yaiyan. To a certain extent, these projects of resisting the outbound flow of classics mobilized Jiangnan's older, favor-based book culture to retranslate the capital-based international circulation.

Because of the careful work in compilation and the preciousness of the editions selected, the collectanea themselves became collectible. Even in Japan, their publication was praised as the fourth-largest publication of fine editions in history, comparable to the *Yongle dadian* (The Yongle Classics), the *Four Treasures*, and the *Gujin tushu qicheng* (The Complete Collection of Books and Illustrations from the Past and the Present) (Wang Yunwu 1973, 98–104). With the publication of *Sibu congkan* and another rare book series, *Xu guyi congshu* (The Sequel to Obscure Books of the Past), the press, to some extent, created an alternative to the way rare books and good editions of classics circulated in the international arena. Not only did the larger-scale circulation of good reprint editions compensate for the dearth of copies of the classics caused by the outward flow, but this circulation also preserved the subjective space, if not the actual property, of an alternative history beyond the reach of imperialist modernity.

The Practice of Countersemiology

Another important issue the philological activists had to deal with was the potential hegemony of imported modern semiotics. The triumph of Meiji vocabulary in the semiotic field of China brought the world closer to educated Chinese in a much faster way through the affinity of the written languages. From a philological perspective, the flood of Meiji vocabulary introduced a different history of modernity, a history that sometimes erased what had already been modern, translated, and in practice. I have discussed the way "*gezhi*," a missionary translation of "science and technology" was replaced by "*kexue*," a Japanese kanji term referring to the same concept. Similarly, "*quanti*," which had been used by Benjamin Hobson in his translation with Chen Xiuting of *Treatise of Anatomy (Quanti xinlun)* in 1851, was later replaced by "*jiepou*," a kanji-based term for "anatomy"; "*delufeng*," a rendering of "telephone" in the Shanghai dialect, was replaced by the kanji "*dianhua*"; "*saizhenhui*," a missionary term for "world fairs," was replaced by the kanji-based "*bolanhui*"; "*gezheng*," a missionary translation of "surgery," was replaced by the Japanese-originated "*waike*"; the Chinese term "*cangshulou*" was replaced by "*tushuguan*," a kanji-based term for "library." The Meiji vocabulary's kanji characters also brought in distorted applications of classical Chinese words, but the applications were accepted without clarification. "*Juti*," for example, was a Japanese translation of the European term "concrete," but it originally meant "basically ready" in classical Chinese. To an extent, the parts of "modern Chinese" that were "loan words" returning from Japan, to use Lydia Liu's ingenious metaphor (1995), brought with them a different history of the modern, a history different from what had already existed in China.

Philology became the tool the press's compilers used to interact with an imported modern history that threatened to achieve possible hegemony. Lydia Liu and other scholars have long pointed out that the same discourse generated different, even contested (though conjoined), translingual practices in China and the West (Liu 1995). The Commercial Press's compilers went translingual too, juxtaposing Chinese and English or other languages in the same book, and their publishing projects strove to preserve the difference in history of the words. After 1902 the philological activists of the press immediately involved them in the unprecedented endeavor of publishing encyclopedic dictionaries. In 1908 the press published *Xin zi dian* (New Chinese Dictionary), then *Ciyuan* (The Encyclopedic Chinese Dictionary, 1908–1915); in another few years it published *Botanical Nomenclature*, or *Zhiwuxue da cidian* (1908–1917), and *Nomenclature of Zoology*, or *Dongwuxue da cidian*, as additions to the already-published glossaries of physics and chemistry terminology. These encyclopedic dictionaries functioned in opposition to the complete "takeover" of Meiji word usage and terminology by preserving, in philological ways, alternative histories of universal concepts and negotiating space for what was about to turn into "local knowledge."

The compilations of two projects, *Ciyuan* and *Botanical Nomenclature*, best illustrate this principle. In many ways, *Ciyuan* was compiled to tackle the interruption of the ongoing history of words. Unlike foreign-language dictionaries published by the press, *Ciyuan* was compiled to document the historical definitions of the words it included. Its preface explains why the history and documentation of words claimed so much attention in this moment of history:

> In recent years new terms and new affairs have flooded into China. People from less-informed backgrounds find it hard to understand what "new learning" is about because of terms that are incomprehensible. Those who had classical knowledge often ended up giving up on new learning. On the other hand, those who went to study abroad did not understand what had already existed in their homeland when they returned. We therefore published this dictionary to indicate the history of and changes in the meanings of words, in the hopes of bridging that gap. (Lufei Erkui 1992, 158–62)

Obviously, the "gap" had to do with the rupture between "what had already existed" and the "terms" used in "new learning," a majority of which were Meiji words. By calling it a "gap," the compilers indicated the existence of two ongoing histories or two ongoing present moments: the ongoing use of the words in the new tide of translation at the turn of the century and the ongoing use of words from before. To bridge the gap meant to connect, and to interact between, the two practices or the two histories.

Ciyuan relied on philological work to establish the histories of each meaning. In other words, it focused on the classical origins of current words. Each word or phrase was an entry. Each entry was arranged and indexed by the number of strokes in the first character. The format of the entries was laid out in a philological pattern; that is, each entry was the result of research into the textual origin(s) and chronological usage of the word. First came the word itself, followed by a short explanation of its original meaning(s) and its variations in later historical moments. When there were multiple meanings of words, they were made into subentries marked by numbers. Each subentry contained a quotation from an original text to attest to the usage. The reader was informed of the title of the text, the name of the author, and the date (that is, the name of the dynasty). The following is a partial translation of one entry:

> [Minzhu] The leader/ruler of the people. Used to refer to emperors or officials. The *Duofang* section of *Shangshu:* "Because Heaven knew that there was a need for a leader of the people at the time, it bestowed its mandate on Chengtang (the king)." "The biography of Zhong Limu of the Wu kingdom" in *The Three Kingdoms:* "I am the head of the people; therefore, I should show the law to all under heaven." (Shangwu yinshuguan 1979, 1703)

What we see here is the documented history of the word, a methodology derived from the philological and evidential studies that had been practiced among Jiangnan literati since the rise of the New Text school for learning the classics in the eighteenth century.

The methodology of philology, having helped challenge the authenticity of Neo-Confucian orthodoxy in the eighteenth century, now became a critical tool in undermining the singularity of Meiji modernity represented by words. We have known that philology as a methodology, though originally adopted to trace the genealogy of the classics to their very origins, undercut the imagined genealogy of Neo-Confucianism and gave rise to new cultural and scientific interest in the classics during the eighteenth century (Elman 1984). It is not surprising that at the beginning of the twentieth century, this methodology served to re-historicize a modern vocabulary. "*Minzhu*" as a modern vocabulary item was first constructed by the missionaries as "people ruling," as opposed to "*junzhu*," or "emperor ruling." Meiji vocabulary adapted the missionary use and turned "*minzhu*" into a noun meaning "democracy." By re-historicizing the original meaning of the word as "emperor" or "ruler," *Ciyuan* reveals the missionaries' as well as the Meiji actors' manipulations of the signifying system. In fact, Liang Qichao as well as Yan Fu's translation of "democracy" as "*qunzhi*," "rule by the many," had an origin that was closer to the spirit of "democracy." *Ciyuan* helped make it obvious that the replacement of "*qunzhi*" by the kanji term "*minzhu*" was not a logical progression of modern Chinese but instead a crucial stopping of it. The philological method provided a way to engage with semiotic modernity since it uncovered how the history of a word as well as the history of a translation could be interrupted and changed dramatically by the semiotic effect of the Sino-Japanese War.

Compilation as a form engagement with the hegemony of semiotic modernity becomes more evident if we turn to another significant scholarly contribution by the press, the compilation *Botanical Nomenclature*. If *Ciyuan* was a project of historicizing words, *Botanical Nomenclature*, one of the first scientific encyclopedias to appear at the turn of the century, seems to have aimed at searching for the roots of the names of plants—to such a degree, in fact, that it broke down a seemingly universal botanical knowledge to display polycentric origins of that knowledge. Unlike *Ciyuan, Botanical Nomenclature* was tied to a specific field of "modern science." It was laid out as a trilingual dictionary of botanical terms (Chinese, Latin, and Japanese), containing mostly the Chinese names of plants and grasses whose Latin names—literally "proper names" *(xueming)*—had been assigned by that time. The compilation was started in 1908 under the leadership of Du Yaquan, and another twelve Chinese scholars also contributed.[27] After ten years of hard collaborative work, the final product was striking. It consisted of 1,700 pages and 4,170 entries with brief introductions and definitions of the plants. It also included over 1,000 pictures and three major indices: the Western languages index, which was mainly Latin, English, and German; the index of Japanese terms; and the index of Chinese terms.

The compilers devoted so much time and energy to work on botanical nomenclature because they took botany as a crucial field with which to engage semiotic modernity. Nomenclature, or terminology, was itself a sign of "natural science" in the field of botany. In a Western context, the names of plants bore very specific significance that could be traced back at least to Carolus Linnaeus (1707–1778), an eighteenth-century Swedish theologian who sought to use the studies of plants to reveal the order of Creation (Eriksson 1983, 63–109; Lindroth 1983, 1–62). Linnaeus studied thousands of plants from all over the world and (re)named them in accord with a distinct system, using Latin terms. His influential rule was that to avoid confusion, each plant could have only one proper name, and that proper name would be a Latin one. He further divided plants into species and gave to each species a binomial name, "a name consisting of a generic name-word plus a descriptive epithet, both of Latin form" (Gledhill 1989, 11). As a result, his taxonomy of botany was a non-vernacular language (in the sense of system and structure) that assumed the preexistence of all its parts and words, whether they were present or not. Thus, one could not study one plant without knowing the entire system. As Foucault summarized this principle in another context, here "nature" was the product of naming: "Nature is posited only through the grid of denominations" and was "visible only when wholly spanned by language" (Foucault 1970, 160).

Not until the late nineteenth century did Linnaeus's invention become a universal practice of botany, when it was globally institutionalized as a result of European expansion and colonization. From 1866 to the end of the nineteenth century, several proposals had been made to the International Botanical Congress held in European cities concerning the use of Latin in naming plants based upon the original models provided by Linnaeus (Lindroth 1983, 28). In 1905 the International Botanical Congress held in Vienna, which was attended by several hundred delegates from different European countries, declared Latin nomenclature and Linnaean categorization the universal nomenclature and the universal system of categorization for botany (Briquet 1935). By this moment in history, plants had been shipped from all over the non-Western world — including India, China, Africa, and Latin America — to European botanical gardens, museums, and laboratories (Brockway 1979; Bretschneider [1892] 1962). Collecting plants and making them into specimens were physical procedures of possessing these biological resources, while naming and knowing the plants — systematizing and talking about them — were crucial symbolic acts toward "having" them in the European colonial empire. This knowing/having complex, which came along with European colonialism, partly explains why botanical nomenclature became "universal" among European nations at this moment of history and why naming plants changed so smoothly from a theological matter into a matter of science.[28]

But while the European system of botany claimed universality, other histories and naming systems were evolving outside the West. In a Chinese context, the naming of plants was related, on the one hand, to the philosophical problem of coherence between *ming* (name) and *shi* (object) and, on the other, to the organization of such human-centric concerns as medicine, edibility, and harm/benefit to the human body. That is why, according to Yamada Keiji, *Materia Medica* contained different systems of classification (Yamada Keiji 1995, 3–42). First was the hierarchy of upper, middle, and lower categories *(shangpin, zhongpin, xiapin),* which was abstracted from an ancient record of plants, *Shennong bencao jing* (The Classic of the God of Agriculture), which ranked all plants in terms of their positive or negative effects on human beings; second was the cosmological classification embodied in the several *bu* (or *gang,* "realms") such as water, fire, earth, metal and stone, grass, grain, vegetable, fruits, woods, fabrics, insects, fish, crustaceans, birds, animals, and humans. Yamada Keiji showed that it was the practical classification based upon harm or benefit to the human body, rather than the more abstract cosmology of the five elements, that was most fully developed in *Materia Medica.*

This multiple classification actually contained a binomial system quite similar to that of Linnaeus, except it was more open as a system. The multiple classifications displayed in *Materia Medica* even invited discussions of culture, life habits, and poetry in the descriptions of plants as the study of plant names further developed in the nineteenth century. *Zhiwu mingshi tukao* (An Evidential Study of Plant Names, with Pictures; Wu Qijun [1848] 1960), juxtaposed a close examination of names and objects on the one hand with prose and poetic writings on the other.[29] The author Wu Qijun (1789–1847) closely followed the practical classification embodied in *Materia Medica,* but at the same time he extended the medical use of plants to culture, politics, and livelihood. It would be hard to find commensurability between such a system rooted in actual practice and the artificially constructed system of Linnaeus.

While the declaration of a universal system by European scientists had its methodological validity, it also worked to establish the hegemony of European modernity over the rest of the world. In practical terms, it meant that plants collected from areas where non-Indo-European languages were spoken could not be recognized through or be recorded by their native languages. Unaware of this, Cai Yuanpei, then president of the Educational Bureau of the new Republic, hoped that botany was one field where the Chinese practice could be updated into a science, once it was equipped with modern nomenclature and a more refined classification (1918, 1–2). Gist Gee, a missionary botanist and a teacher at the Dongwu University, also believed that since "many large (Chinese) herbaria have been collected and deposited in the museums of the West," and since the specialists there had started to work on the "systematic side" of the flora, what was left to be done in China was "the assignment and promulgation of Chinese equivalents for the already-known Latin names" (1918, 1–2). This high vision immediately faced the challenge of how to translate universal botanical knowledge without giving up Chinese practice entirely. Assigning "Chinese equivalents for the already-known Latin names" faced the predicament of whether to preserve the information that found no equivalent in the already-known system of Latin names. Du Yaquan, the chief compiler of *Botanical Nomenclature*, put the problem very clearly:

> When we were compiling textbooks for primary and middle schools, we borrowed contents from both Western language works and Japanese works. However, whenever we came across a plant name in Western works, we encountered extreme difficulties because no trace of Chinese names was presented anywhere. We used to look to Japanese sources for Chinese names that had been identified with Latin names, but recent Japanese scholarship had given up the task of listing Chinese names and merely listed Japanese transliterations of the Latin name. It was from this moment on we began to put together notes about those Chinese and Japanese names that had been already identified with the Latin names. These notes served at the beginning as a functional reference for our translation. (Du Yaquan 1918, 1–2)

Du Yaquan and his colleagues could have taken the Japanese way, namely, to simply transliterate the Latin pronunciation and omit the Chinese names of the plants. This would quickly transmit Western knowledge into China and remove the technical barriers blocking Chinese students from obtaining information from other languages. But, obviously, for the humble purpose of keeping the Chinese names and related information, Du Yaquan and his colleagues approached the translation the hard way. Starting from the scattered notes on the names of the plants, Du Yaquan and other compilers of *Botanic Nomenclature* embarked on a much longer research quest than they might have expected. At the end of this journey, the dictionary preserved a useful index to a body of knowledge stored in *Materia Medica* and other Chinese works that existed beyond the hegemonic system of modern botany.

Taking a look inside the *Botanical Nomenclature*, instead of the mere Chinese equivalents to Latin names that Gist Gee desired, one finds trans-compiled encyclopedic entries as the fruits of evidential studies. Not only can one find a plant's name(s)—that is, its Latin name as well as its Japanese names and all its Chinese names known at the time— but one could also read a brief but informative Chinese documentation of the plant, arranged in chronological order. Each listing gave information in five categories: (1) the Linnaean and Andersonian classification of the plant's class, genus, and family; (2) the sexes of flowers, another characteristic of the Linnaean system; (3) naturalists' morphological description of shape, color, and taste according to their identification; (4) the Li Shizhen–style morphological description of the plant's uses as medicine and food; and (5) very brief philological accounts of the original Chinese text(s) that recorded the shape, the nature, and the names of the plant, sometimes even including very short quotations. The following example is a medium-length entry in the *Nomenclature* demonstrating most of the features listed above:

> *Roudoukou* (Mussel bean fruit): *Myristica fragrans, Houtt, nekoubukou.* Myristica fragrans class, *Myristica fragrans* genus, evergreen. Thirty *chi* in height. Long oval-shaped leaf with pointed end. Single-sex flowers. Mussel fruit. There is a red false skin inside the skin mussel of the fruit, which wraps the case of the seed. The case is hard and contains a seed inside. The red false skin and the seed are both fragrant and can be used as spices. They can also be used as medicine for digestive and other disorders. Recently, *roudoukou* has been widely planted in India, Brazil, and Xiwangfeng. The [Chinese] name of the plant can be found in the Kaibao edition of *Materia Medica*.[30] A vernacular name of the plant is *rouguo* (meat fruit). Another name is *jiajule*. According to Kou Zongli,[31] "Mussel bean fruit is named to distinguish it from grass bean fruit (*caodoukou*)." (Du Yaquan et al., 1918, 413)

In this entry, the classes of the plant, the sex of the flower, and the naturalistic description of the plant according to visual details and selected parts are typical of botanical nomenclature books written in Western or Japanese languages. But the entry also contains several characteristics that can only be attributed to the tradition of *Materia Medica*. For example, the entry records the geographical places where the plant was growing (in addition to a strictly biological description of its environment). It provides specifics for the plant's use in food and medicine—specifics that had been documented in *Materia Medica* and other texts. It indicates the vernacular names of the plant in Chinese as well as the titles of and quotations from documents where the plant was recorded, given in chronological order. In this way, *Botanical Nomenclature* rescued the Chinese documentation of herbal knowledge, as well as the minor cultural history stored there, from beneath the "scientific" surface of a "universal" botanical system conveyed in Latin.

In the project of recovering non-European knowledge of plants, entries, rather than "system(s)," became the focus of knowledge for the trans-compilers of *Botanical Nomenclature*. In other words, what *Botanical Nomenclature* seems to have given up was the "systematic" side of modern botany as well as that of *Materia Medica*. If one compares *Botanical Nomenclature* with a similar work in Japanese, Makino Tomitaro's well-received *Nihon shokubutsu zukan* (A Dictionary, with Pictures, of Japanese Plants) ([1925] 1926), this particular preference becomes quite obvious. *Nihon shokubutsu zukan* is organized entirely according to the classification system of botanical science, without including any names or accounts in Chinese or kanji, not to mention the Chinese system of categorizations. The Commercial Press's *Botanical Nomenclature*, on the other hand, never used any system of classifications as a principle for organizing the dictionary's contents, even though it gives the classes and the genera of plants in individual entries.

Yet the lack of a botanical system does not mean *Botanical Nomenclature* does not have an order. The compilers indexed everything in alphabetical order as well as by the number of strokes in a plant's name. This order of the index was in fact a philological order, or an encyclopedic order. If, in another context, the alphabetical order of the Diderot's *Encyclopédie* was found to be a "massacre" of categories,[32] then the alphabetical and stroke order in *Botanical Nomenclature*, too, might have well served to dissolve all kinds of classification, whether that of *Materia Medica* or that of Linnaeus and Anderson. Perhaps I should add that *Botanical Nomenclature* worked not so much as a symbolic "great massacre" of the hegemonic systems as it succeeded in a "great rescue" of minor knowledge that was endangered by the hegemony of botanical names. In *Botanical Nomenclature*, rid of organizational categories, individual entries were sites of refuge where minor knowledge, minor practices in the use of the plants, and the minor cultural history of plants remained active. Entries provided a knowledge production alternative to institutionalized "modern science."

It is worth noting that the Chinese names of plants not only marked a "Chinese" history of plant studies but also recorded a long history of cultural exchange between China and other places. Take again the *roudoukou* entry as an example. The entry shows us that the Chinese names of this plant are actually taken from multiple languages. *Jiajule* (a name for the seeds of *Myristica fragrans Houtt*), the other name of *roudoukou*, was a transliteration of the plant's name in Xiongnu, a central Asian language, and was recorded in the *Shennong bencao jing* before it appeared in *Materia Medica*. This name had actually circulated in China ever since the beginning of sea trade (Hu Guochen et al. 1992, 670). In another entry, the Chinese proper name *buguzhi* and the vernacular names *poguzhi* or *pooguzh* for the plant *Psoralea corylifolia* L. are all transliterations of the same central Asian term. As Cai Jingfeng (1985) found, *Materia Medica* recorded at least sixty or so plants whose names were transliterations from central Asian, European, Arabic, and Indian languages (200–224). *Botanical Nomenclature* documented the cultural and historical origins of these terms and recorded the names from this earlier documentation. In doing so, *Botanical Nomenclature* positioned itself at the intersections between Western botanical sciences and the branches of knowledge from China, the Middle East, and India. Transcompilation here became an enterprise of retranslating a singular modernity into multiple positions of minor histories. Where the urban society of *Nihon shokubutsu zukan* found itself identical to a Western urban society, the readers' community of *Botanical Nomenclature* positioned itself at the crossroads of the major and the minor histories where Shanghai was characterized.

Conclusion

The collaboration between the print entrepreneurs and the activist philologists marked a particular, though exceptional, way in which a core portion of the post-Suzhou urban society of the learned was reconstructed in Shanghai. The early history of the Commercial Press presents a history of publishing that cannot be understood thoroughly in the paradigm of "cultural industry." Here, the philological work of trans-compilation carried out a cultural politics that was in fact countering the development of an imperialist and colonialist industrial production of Chinese classics (or knowledge about Chinese classics). The Commercial Press, I suggest, gave us a chance to observe the unfolding and continuation of publishing enterprises in a noncapital cultural history. In this history, cultural expertise, the skills of the literati, family learning, and exchanges of favors for prestige were equally powerful cultural-political means. With the language tools, textbooks, encyclopedic dictionaries, and trilingual nomenclatures of the Commercial Press, the urban society of the learned in Shanghai took the lead in retranslating, recodifying, and rewriting imported modern semiology at the beginning of the twentieth century. With this retranslating or recodifying, the popular compilers had an influence upon the educational and the book-ish, the philological met the scientific and the industrial, and the minor histories of knowledge diversified European and Japanese universality. The cultural tasks conducted here were no longer of the same sort as those of the Restoration. Rather, they belonged to a reborn practice of philology and compilation. The importance and the uniqueness of the cultural tasks of this sort transformed Shanghai from a post-Taiping refuge into a cradle of the new urban culture. Not until after 1917, when the younger, more radical group of students and intellectuals around the *New Youth* and Beijing University launched attacks on *Eastern Miscellany* and the Commercial Press, did the front line of radical culture move from Shanghai to Beijing (Huters 1999, 261–78). More specifically, not until after the mid-1920s, when the activist philologists volunteered to hand the leadership of the press to an even "newer" group of elites, represented by Hu Shi and Wang Yunwu, who had experiences of studying abroad, did the early but more creative stage of the press's history come to an end.

PART II
The Carnival and the Radical

THREE

Urban Festivity as a Disruptive History

Having discussed the historical transformation of urban society from Suzhou to Shanghai I now turn to focus on another type of urban culture practice, what can be called "urban festivity," during the same historical transition.

The mere mention of Broadway in New York, the West End of London, central Paris, Sunset Boulevard in Los Angeles, or Shanghai's Nanjing Road provokes images not only of glamour and success but of an opulent culture of urban festivity. In Shanghai, that culture involved the energy generated by a concentration of such urban settings as restaurants, hotels, theaters, shops, teahouses, and singsong places, filled of course with milling crowds of businessmen, travelers, theatergoers, sightseers, small shopkeepers, "country bumpkins," rich ladies, prostitutes, and pickpockets. Yet "urban festivity" was deprived of its own history with the coming of the modern era. For Henri Lefebvre, industrial capitalism had turned the city from a site of "unproductive festivity" to a product of production (1995, 65–84). Unproductive festivity, in this context, bears a heavy, outmoded, medieval, even feudal, tenor (67–69). For Walter Benjamin (1999), the festive districts thrived in the modern city only to mark the rise of the culture of consumption governed by the pleasurable dream-logic of capitalism, which exacerbated the alienation of laborers from their own being. In both perspectives, these pleasure centers did not create a buoyant, carefree atmosphere for the urban inhabitants but gave rise to an alienated "lonely crowd" (Riesman, Denney, and Glazer 1950, 373) or transformed an engaged and critical citizenry into an apathetic "society of spectacle" (Debord 1970), depriving human society of its liveliness and leaving little more than a collection of "rootless cosmopolites" (Spengler 1969, 65).

This section of the book, however, has to do with the question derived thereby: Is there an urban festivity that is neither the embodiment of the dream-logic of commodification nor the byword of an out-of-date medieval energy? The chapters in this section seek to picture an urban festivity whose development went beyond political control, as well as beyond the division between medieval and modern, preindustrial and industrial. This unique practice of urban festivity, I argue, itself carried out a political ideal opposed to the world of capitalist modernity.

We can catch a glimpse of the way "unproductive festivity" prevailed in premodern and modern Chinese cities by noting a few statistics about theaters. By the end of the eighteenth century, before any standard "modern city" was present in China, the number of entertainment teahouse theaters in the capital of Jiangsu Province, Suzhou, amounted to several dozen (Gu Gongxie [1785] 1917, 40–41).[1] By the turn of the nineteenth century, another Jiangnan city, Nanjing, was host to over 100 professional opera troupes (Gu Duhuang 1987, 81–82). Adding Yangzhou to the list, the total number of troupes was at least several hundred (Gong Zizhen 1920).

The rise of these festive institutions was not coextensive with the coming of modernity, the expansion of world capitalism, or the spread of commercial culture from a cosmopolitan center to the Third World. Nor did their fall match the schedule of medieval progressing to modern. By the beginning of the twentieth century, theatrical life in China, like that of China's growing commodity culture, had swept the city of Shanghai, where the number of theaters grew by the hundreds not because of the development of industrial capitalism in the treaty port but because of the devastation of the cities of Jiangnan.[2] Contrary to the widely accepted idea that Shanghai was the cradle of modern urban culture in China, the city acted less as the origin of new theater centers and commercial culture and more as a refuge or a receiver for theaters and commerce that had long existed in other parts of the country. The "unproductive festivity" was the mark of both the nonmodern and the modern cities, so much that modernity seemed to have made no difference to the festivity itself.

My emphasis here goes beyond the point that China, a so-called Third World country, actually had its own version of "modernity" or its own moment of modernity. On this point there have already been refined arguments. Arjun Appadurai, for example, has argued that the social life of commodities comprises differing commodity and noncommodity phases in different social economic fabrics (1986, 14). John Frow has further pointed out that the moment of decommodification becomes imaginable when commodities circulate beyond the capitalist border and embody noncapitalist social relationships (1997). My argument differs from theirs in that I look not at "modernity at large" (to borrow a phrase from Appadurai) but at urban festivity as a primary drive of the urban history of noncapital (if not nonmodern). The important point is that urban festivity was carried out by forces other than capital, commodity, and production and therefore protected the city from being commodified or being produced. My central thesis is that the history of social unrest, and perhaps of noncapitalist forms of consumption, was equally crucial to the development of urban festivity of the modern city. This urban festivity, in a sense, embodied a community of everybody formed by fate or by volunteerism.

Fanhua: Festive Urbanism and Cosmic Cycle

The wide circulation of the term "*fanhua*" (prosperity), which was often used to describe prosperous urban culture as well as theater centers during the nineteenth century, reveals a potential minor history of urban festivity. Almost a cliché, "*fanhua*" is among the terms most frequently used to describe the prosperous, lively, and "cosmopolitan" quality of urban culture, of which "hanging out," singing, and theatergoing formed important parts. The word "*fanhua,*" as we see in well-documented encyclopedia dictionaries such as *Hanyu da cidian* (Chinese Dictionary), literally refers to several different ideas, ranging from beautiful flamboyant young figures, material bountifulness, extravaganza, and material luxury, to lavish consumption of wine, pleasure, songs, and dances.[3] Historically speaking, *fanhua* was particularly important in imagining the city as a center of circulation of people, cultures, goods, and activities. A city of *fanhua* would have "merchants flocking in like clouds" *(shanggu yunji),* with trade and commerce depicted in phrases such as "a thousand ships wait to sail" with cargoes *(qianfang jingfa).* The word "*fanhua*" refers to extravagant materiality, whether this is represented by clothing, silk and textile patterns, exotic and decorative goods, or the rare scene of human activity represented in the phrase "extravagant wagon-tops loom with the dawn."[4] Together with this concentration of retailers and goods were the forms of entertainment and travel pleasures—as in the description of a city that "echoed with the melodies of river songs."[5] *Fanhua* was associated with spatial concepts of "musical miles," "pavilion miles," and "manufacturing areas." In its long history of usage, the word became nearly synonymous with the southeastern cities, Yangzhou and Suzhou, known since ancient times for their luxurious goods, thriving businesses, songs, flutes, and the beautiful residences constructed for concubines.

The factors that create such a center of *fanhua* consistently contain what can be called "cosmopolitan" principles. Within the Chinese conception of a prosperous society, this cosmopolitan dimension contains two layers, the physical or worldly layer and the cosmos layer. An eighteenth-century painting by Xu Yang entitled *Gusu fanhua tu* (Prosperous Suzhou; in Xu Yang and Liaoning sheng bowuguan [1757] 1988), also titled *Shengshi zisheng tu* (Life Thrives in the Prosperous Age), represented this cosmopolitan imagination well by establishing an aesthetic connection between a prosperous city and the entire human world. Suzhou was, as the painting depicts, in every sense a typical Jiangnan city: fluid, busy, gregarious, full of life and diversity (Figure 4). It was a street-oriented city: The doors and windows of shops, businesses, stores, bars, restaurants, teahouses, and theaters all opened onto the street. Many small business families made the lower part of their houses into shops and stores and kept the upper parts as their residences. In other cases, they simply built their shops and their residences next to each other. Walking on the street or going in and out of the shops was a significant pastime for all classes (Xu Yinong 2000, 153–58). Teahouses served as gathering places, casual settings where friends could enjoy popular music. Open spaces in front of the city temple and around the city gate were sites of public events, including festival performances and gatherings of circus and traveling troupes. At restaurants and theaters, everyone, even the rich and powerful, shared the same smells, noises, and enjoyments. Private gardens functioned as economic resources and hosted salon gatherings featuring poetry, drinking, calligraphy, concerts, arts, antiques, books,

Figure 4. A section from *Gusu fanhua tu* (Prosperous Suzhou). From Xu Yang and Liaoning sheng bowuguan, *Qing Xu Yang Gusu fanhua tu* [Xu Yang's painting *Prosperous Suzhou*] (Hong Kong: Shangwu yinshuguan, [1757] 1988), unnumbered page.

sciences, and learning (Clunas 1996).[6] In *Gusu fanhua tu,* the artist presented the street-oriented city in a "cosmopolitan" vision. The city is painted as boundless, open, inclusive—one city containing all the cities of the empire and manifesting its material bountifulness. To be "cosmopolitan" meant that all under heaven are next to one another.

The "cosmos" layer becomes apparent when we turn to the temporal dimension of the painting—another level of meaning reflected in the title *Shengshi zisheng tu* (Life Thrives in the Prosperous Age.) The two key words here, "*sheng*" (life) and "*shi*" (age), are derived from the "law of the cosmos" in the Chinese philosophical thinking of the day. The interpretation of different *ages* started with the Han dynasty philosopher Dong Zhongshu, whose *History of Spring and Autumn* proposed a theory of Three Ages connecting political and institutional history with the principles underlying the transformation of the universe.[7] The Three Ages became a particular focal point of debate among eighteenth- and nineteenth-century scholars and intellectuals, with *shengshi* becoming a loaded cliché that referred to a final, perfect, and ideal state in which the human world was in perfect harmony with the movement of the cosmos

(Gong Zizhen 1961, 41–47). This final age was set against two others: the early stage of human history, the *luanshi* (chaotic age), and the *shengping zhishi* (progressive age), which achieved peace and order but not prosperity. To human eyes, these different ages were the products of the movements of the cosmos, human hearts, and material and life worlds, as well as of the morality of the ruler or political system. In the prosperous age, these different components stood in supporting and compensating relationships, whereas in the chaotic age they were in conflict.

At the political level, *shengshi zisheng* was a rhetorical device used to praise the Qianlong reign for generating the harmonious energy expressed in thriving trades, bountiful goods, and many enjoyments. It was even used at times as a rhetorical convention to conceal a crisis of overpopulation.[8] It also helped to frame the phenomenon of *fanhua*— the circulation of people, goods, enjoyments, and activities in and out of the city—within an enchanted world where material bountifulness was the outward reflection of the work of the cosmos. In the painting by Xu Yang, Suzhou was thus not necessarily ruled by the logic of com- modities—the alienating power preventing laborers and consumers from seeing surplus value and the way it constructed social relations. In the artist's representation, the city was animated by a different logic: one of livelihood within the cosmological cycle. It was the cosmological dimension of *fanhua* that connected two seemingly different phenom- ena: material prosperity on the one hand and cosmopolitan human vitality on the other.[9] In this vision, morality and political order were inseparable from prosperity and consumption. Despite its beauty and allure, however, *fanhua* also conveyed the sense that this bounty was a temporary state of material being, a fantastic and ephemeral stage of life.

The boundary of *fanhua* can be understood by considering two closely related terms: "*shehua*" (luxury, waste, excessive consumption) and "*yin*" (eroticism, decadence, chaos). *Shehua* and *yin* represented the flip side of *fanhua*—the external, physical violation of the principle of cosmos *(shehua)* and the moral or internal transgression of social and political order *(yin)*. *Shehua* refers to a consumptive behavior, also a form of *fanhua*, that abuses universal vitality in physical terms. Epitomized by a compulsive consumption or uncontrollable pursuit of wealth and goods, it was usually interpreted as violating the law of the universe by violently vandalizing the bounty offered by the cosmos, *bao tie tienwu,* and trans- gressing the give-and-take balance between nature and humanity. This transgression took place when people use materiality to lay bare their desire rather than seeking knowledge of the true nature of human needs.

The concept of *yin* indicated a disorder in the realm of the human heart. In contemporary usage, the word "*yin*" refers to the erotic and therefore to spiritual decadence, but the term covered a much wider range of moral and political meanings before the twentieth century. Although seemingly unrelated now, *yin* was at the time I am concerned with conceptualized as a *fanhua* that had transgressed its moral, psychological, and political boundaries. Encyclopedia explanations show that the word "*yin*" referred to pleasure, desire, and desire-fulfilling actions that have transgressed their limits. In time, *yin* came to be interpreted as overindulgence, even stagnation *(danzhi)*, disorder *(buci)*, excess or opulence *(lan, guo)*, an anomaly in the universal and social order *(shici)*, a violation of principles and structure *(qin)*, and moral and political unruliness *(can, fang, zong)*. At the core, *yin* was a state of mind that had become corrupted and types of behavior that did not fit harmoniously with the ruler and the movement of universal vitality. Compared with *shehua* (impulsive consumption), *yin* indicates a cultural anomaly that has the potential to grow "chaotic." Here, consumption or desire-fulfilling behavior leads to a ruleless and anarchical—as opposed to emancipating—energy of disorder.

The concept of *yin* brings to the fore an important dimension stunted in the Marxian analysis of the logic of commodities: the unruliness of the human heart. In the Marxian concept of the commodity, the human heart does not participate actively in the mode of production; it is mostly captivated and alienated. Arjun Appadurai (1986) and others have shown how the human heart is capable of repealing the course of commodification. The concept of *yin*, too, implies that when consumption exceeds its natural and political limits, it leads to a crisis in the logic of consumption itself. What is at stake here is therefore not a moment of alienation but a moment of liminality (or reversability) of the human heart. This liminality threatens political catastrophe because the human heart operates beyond sociopolitical visibility—as a force that is mostly unknown yet looming—and at times has the potential to overturn the entire social and political order.

The above relationship is illustrated in Figures 5 and 6. *Fanhua*, or a prosperous era with flourishing energy, comes into being when the cosmos, human hearts, "life," material bountifulness, and the sociopolitical

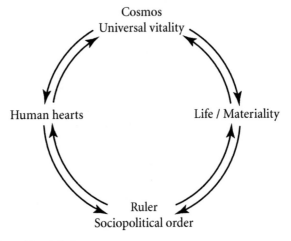

Figure 5. *Shengshi* and *fanhua.*

order are in good communication and remain within their proper limits and in harmonious relations (Figure 5). But *fanhua* becomes *yin* when human hearts become uncooperative with the sociopolitical order. *Fanhua* is also transformed into *shehua,* in which the give-and-take relations between consumption and the cosmos's offerings become unbalanced. *Shehua* and yin, in connected ways, lead to a "chaotic era" (Figure 6).

As the relations among *fanhua, shehua,* and *yin* reveal here, the logic of the commodity can have very different dimensions and proceed through different stages, each of which left traces in the urban commercial culture of China. One can discern the coexistence and overlapping of two different logics of commercial culture and cosmopolitanism. The first is the dream logic of pleasure-seeking, which deprived material culture of human participation and created the "society of spectacle" as embodied by *shehua.* Alongside this was a second dimension, where human involvement overflowed the sociopolitical order, as embodied by *yin.* The driving force behind the rise of new urban centers was compound: Both bourgeois commercial culture and its flip side played important roles in the transference of the center of culture from Yangzhou and Suzhou to Shanghai during the nineteenth and early twentieth centuries. In the following section, I focus on the cosmopolitan theatrical centers of Yangzhou and Suzhou in the late eighteenth and early nineteenth centuries. I then trace the moment of *yin* during the mid-

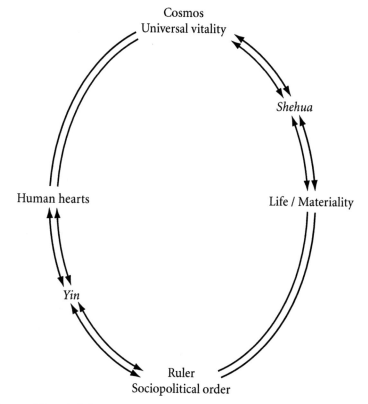

Figure 6. *Yin* and *shehua*.

nineteenth century. Finally, I discuss how *yin* as a liminal force can be used to analyze the rise of the theatrical district of Shanghai and to map an alternative morality and justice in this newly fashioned way of staging the world.

The Cosmopolitan Culture of the Canal-Based Cities

Theater activity as a form of *fanhua* spread along the north-south canal system and from there into the west-east river systems during the late eighteenth century, nourishing the urban cultures of both prosperous and less-prosperous cities. In the eighteenth century, theatrical spectacles were much more common in the canal-based cities than in Beijing. An eighteenth-century scholar-official, Gu Gongxie, observed in Suzhou a scene of urban cultural life comparable, in my eyes, to that of modern cities. He records that troupes, which used to perform on large boats in the rivers, began to build their theaters on land in Suzhou during the Qianlong era (1736–1795). Their example gave rise to theater-building in many other cities (Gu Gongxie [1875] 1917, 40–41). As a result, theatrical activities became a much more important and visible part of the cultural life of many cities:

> Large numbers of merchants flocked to the Jinlu (Suzhou) like birds. Banquets were held constantly and operas were performed every day at several dozen theaters, and these provided a living for at least tens of thousands of common people. (Gu Gongxie [1875] 1917, 40)

Flocks of merchants, banquets, performances, and dozens of theaters performing daily indicate that Suzhou had the prominent visibility, central location, and sizable crowds that characterize a "modern" urban scene. The key elements in this description of Suzhou correspond to the concept of *fanhua* as represented in the painting by Xu Yang we considered earlier. Prosperity here is not represented as a miraculous or sublime materiality; the description focuses, rather, on the extraordinary frequency of human contacts—the coming together, the large gatherings, and flocking audiences and troupes. It is cosmopolitan in the sense that everything exists together, with the transcendental meaning of the cosmos only in the background.

Fanhua as the density and variety of human cultural activity found its best exemplar in the theater world of Yangzhou. Its location at the intersection of the Grand Canal and the Yangtze River—between north and south on the one hand and between west and east on the other hand—made the city a junction of several provinces and regions and thus the best location for a coming together of theaters. As the location of the headquarters of the Salt Administration of five provinces along the Yangtze, Yangzhou had the "largest aggregate capital possessed by any single commercial or industrial group in the empire" (Ho Ping-ti 1954, 130–68). The city's culture had been inundated by literati, writers, artists, and laborers traveling along the north-south and west-east corridors of China even before the city was transformed into an imperial urban center at the hands of the salt merchants (Mayer-Fong 2003).

The city took its role as cultural repository seriously at its imperial moment in the seventeenth and eighteenth centuries. A bureau for compiling opera scripts and scores was founded, and six experts were assigned the task.[10] After four years of work they were able to assemble a huge collection of plays entitled *Chuhai* (The Ocean of Operas), including 1,013 scripts dating as far back as the Yuan dynasty (Li Dou [1795] 1984, 108–16). Opera collections and studies became an important element of the print market.[11] The emperor's frequent visits to Yangzhou not only publicly displayed royal power but also highlighted the city's material extravagance, splendid ceremonies, pleasures, and theatrical spectacles. Known for being fond of literature and music, the Emperor Qianlong was able to find a wide variety of operatic performances in the city when he stopped there during his southern tour (Xu Ke 1917, "Xunxing lei"). In addition to its magnificent gardens and refined scholars (Ho Ping-ti 1954; Chen Congzhou 1983), the city boasted a large variety of traveling and seasonal performers in addition to the permanent opera troupes, actors, and actresses supported by city patrons (Lu Eting 1995; Mackerras 1972). A large opera troupe patronized by a salt merchant could have well over 100 actors (Lu Eting 1995, 117).

Yangzhou was a "cosmopolitan" center of theater activities in that it was an ideal meeting ground for different regional operas sponsored by wealthy patrons, such as the salt merchants who sought to develop cultural ties with the court (Mackerras 1971, 67–78). No other city was so well positioned geographically and socially for coexistence with, and exchanges among, a variety of regional theatrical genres. Colin Mackerras has noted that there were at least four types of occasions for theatrical performance in Yangzhou: the grand dramas, or *daxi*, performed for official occasions; the Kunqu and regional theaters that salt merchants prepared for the amusement of the emperor and gatherings of literati; private performances at informal gatherings; and popular local and regional theaters that played seasonally on "straw stages" *(caotai xi)* for audiences of the lower strata (Mackerras 1972, 60–65). These various types of theater were marked by differing musical systems, dialects, and performing styles. Almost every kind of theater had a regional identity, with specific attributes marking its place of origin.[12] As Li Dou noted, there were quite a number of contemporary regional music styles gathered in Yangzhou. These included Kunqu operas from the Suzhou and Wu regions; the *jingqiang* musical system from northern China; the *qinqiang*, a musical system originating in Shanxi (northwest); the *gaoqiang*, a musical system from Yiyang (northwest); the *lo-lo qiang* from Huguang (southwest); the *erhuang* from Anching (west), and the *bangzi* from Jurong (northeast) (Li Dou [1795] 1984, 125). Performances took place in different or multiple dialects. Although the dialects of specific troupes were distinct, individual actors often performed in a variety of dialects, ranging from Chu or Hunan and Hubei dialects, Qi or Shandong dialect, Jingqiang or Mandarin, to *tuyu,* or Yangzhou native dialects, which varied from county to county (Li Dou [1795] 1984, 126–27).

This gathering of regional theaters in Yangzhou resulted in a well-defined "vernacular" theater, or flower *(hua)* drama, as it was later named, that came to be seen as distinct from classical theater, Kunqu opera or elegant *(ya)* drama. Kunqu opera from the Wu area had a relatively longer history and had become refined as the musical system associated with the cultural life of the literati, with scripts and musical scores written down and performed with little change across regions. By contrast, during the seventeenth and eighteenth centuries vernacular theaters thrived in different regions but performances were put on without fixed scripts or musical scores. This more fluid and open style was known as *luantan,* "performing without fixed scores." Vernacular theaters made such an impact on urban life that they generated long-lasting discussions about the values and imagined hierarchy of the *ya* and *hua* genres.

It is outside the purview of this book to follow the details of those discussions, but I would like to draw attention to the "cosmopolitan" side of these vernacular theaters—despite their remote locations and the long distances troupes traveled between performances. Tanaka Issei, a respected scholar of Chinese opera, has given us a sense of nearby and remote by pointing out that Kunqu opera was "urban" because its sophisticated melodies were more suitable for an indoor environment, whereas local and regional operas were more practical for market towns or village performances (1987, 143–60). Jiao Xun (1763–1820), a famous scholar and mathematician of the eighteenth century, disliked the "complicated" tones of Wu opera and praised the local performance of northern-style operas for their preservation of the simple, direct musical tradition of Yuan drama, which was influenced by the musical style of the northern nomads (Jiao Xun 1959–1960, 8:1–8).[13] Li Dou observed that local theater had excellent actors who could vividly imitate "clumsy men and women, greedy merchants, and slang from the provinces of Hunan and Shandong" ([1795] 1984, 126–27). Another form of vernacular performance was called *huagu xi* (flower drum). This form did not come from any specific local community; it focused not on the delicate and beautiful sounds of language but on vivid plots, dialogue, and body language, and it was performed in a wide variety of local dialects. All these distinctions of tone and dialect were marks of the variety of places and peoples who mingled in the city.

The remoteness of these regional theaters and the distances the troupes traveled become clear if we look at the talented actors of regional operas that Jiang Chun (1720–1789), a leading salt merchant dwelling in Yangzhou, collected into the troupe he patronized. Jiang Chun was "the most colorful head merchant during the second half of the 18th century" (Ho Ping-ti 1954, 160; Lu Eting 1995, 231–44; Li Dou [1795] 1984, 104; Mackerras 1971, 77). The fourth-generation descendant of a salt-trading family, Jiang was a brilliant artist, a famous poet, and an expert in music (Li Dou [1795] 1984, 261–62). His multiple talents and his close relationship to the court made him a fan of Kunqu opera and an expert in regional dramas and local performances in and around Yangzhou. He patronized many actors and organized them into two troupes, a Kunqu opera troupe called Virtuous Music (Deyin ban) and a troupe formed with actors from different regional theaters, Spring Stage (Chuntai ban) (Li Dou [1795] 1984, 127). In his description, the troupes of Kunqu opera were also called *ya* (elegant) troupes, and troupes and operas from other regions were called *hua* (flower) troupes.[14] The actors of Spring Stage were recruited from different parts of the country and could usually perform in more than one local genre or dialect. The chief female-role actors, Yang Baguan and Hao Tianxiu, natives of Suzhou and Anching, respectively, performed in the combined styles of the local (Kunqu), northern *(jing)*, and northwestern *(qin)* dramas (Li Dou [1795] 1984, 127). A chief male-role actor, Liu Ba, originally from the southeast coast, Guangdong, spoke Mandarin in Spring Stage and gradually broadened the scale of performing arts associated with the role as well as the spectrum of audiences (Li Dou [1795] 1984, 126–27). Nicknamed "Spirit of Opera," a local Yangzhou actor, Fan Da, was known for his performance of the play *Sifan*, which started with the Kunqu style from Nanjing, followed successively by a melody from the north, *bangzi;* a tune from the southwest, *lo-lo;* a piece in another musical style from the northwest, *yiyang;* and a piece in a singing style from the north, *erhuang.* Xie Shouzi and Lu San'guan preserved folk theatrical arts, either by vividly acting as a female flower drum singer with a "sad sweet voice that touches the souls of audience," or by mixing the essence of the flower drum play with the *jing* (northern) and the *qin* (northwestern) music systems (Li Dou [1795] 1984, 126–27). These are just a few examples.

The *fanhua,* or the cosmopolitan culture of Yangzhou, at this time embodied itself in the unprecedented gathering together of regional and local operas from all over the country: from the northwestern provinces of Shanxi, Shaanxi, and Sichuan; from the Wu dialect region of Suzhou and Hangzhou; from the capital, Beijing; from nearby provinces such as Anhui, Hunan, and Zhejiang; and from the remote southeast region of Guangdong. The coexistence of this wide assortment of styles and skills turned the city into a crucible of new genres and new plays. The *fanhua* of Yangzhou, in this sense, was a result of the long-distance exchanges of musical systems, dialectics, repertoires, acting and singing styles, and individual creative talent.

Yangzhou's *fanhua,* however, rapidly disappeared from the public scene during the first half of the nineteenth century because of a vigorous backlash at the end of the eighteenth century. The chaotic flux that had earned the city fame as a cosmopolitan center now made it a site of *yin*—of decadence and decay. There were two immediate causes for this redefinition. First, Jiang Chun, the most important salt-merchant sponsor of the theater, was arrested for economic corruption after a legal suit by the state against a large group of salt merchants from Yangzhou. Although his prison term was short, Jiang Chun, like many other salt merchants, was stripped of the social status and cultural resources he had accumulated over the years.

The second and perhaps more important factor in the decline of Yangzhou's *fanhua* was the state ban on vernacular theater as a legitimate form of cultural activity in the city. In 1797 the Qing state issued a ban on all types of regional and local theaters falling in the category of flower theater or *luantan,* and sanctioned only Kunqu—elegant opera. The ban labeled regional and local vernacular theaters as "erotic and decadent plays" *(yinmi xiqu)* and prohibited their performance on the grounds of their "corruptive" influence on the human heart (Jiangsu sheng bowuguan 1959, 295–97). Yangzhou's *luantan* troupes were ordered to disperse and return to their homes (Jiangsu sheng bowuguan 1959, 296; Mackerras 1971, 67–68). *Yin* or *yinxi* (erotic theater) had become a cliché in the state's official lexicon referring to something that was sexually arousing but morally and spiritually corruptive and decadent.

I will return to the concept of *yin* in more detail in the following section; it is sufficient here to see that both *fanhua* and *yin* were actually based upon the same type(s) of cultural and historical practices within the theater world. In fact, the same attributes that had made a city famous for being *fanhua*, or "cosmopolitan," now came to be seen as evidence of its corruption, decadence, and decay. If *fanhua* encompassed the material world and human spirit come to their full flower, *yin* was these same qualities' exceeding their natural boundaries and spinning out of control.

These two events in the post-Qianlong era led local theaters to look away from Yangzhou and other big cities and toward local patrons in the countryside and in smaller towns before flocking to Shanghai. This shift had a long-term impact, eventually driving all the local troupes from the city to the countryside and heavily damaging urban culture in Yangzhou, whose vibrancy depended on the stimulation and cross-fertilization of input from different regions. Damage to Yangzhou's cultural vitality became permanent after the devastating floods of the 1820s, which destroyed a large sector of the Grand Canal, and particularly after the state changed its salt-management policy in the early nineteenth century. In 1832 the state started to abandon professional salt business managers, thus taking away their semiofficial status. The salt merchants were still able to patronize opera troupes, but they completely lost their authority and leadership in the cultural domain. Nor could they continue to define the city of Yangzhou as the heart of the cultural activity and exchange within the empire.

Both *fanhua* and *yin* withered when Yangzhou stopped being the center of imperial transportation and the salt merchants stopped being captains of the empire's culture. But *yin*, as the object of the ban, continued to spread into the countryside before it was urbanized again in the next urban center, Shanghai. The shift of urban culture from inland cities such as Yangzhou and Suzhou toward the coastal city of Shanghai was characterized by the swing from *fanhua* to *yin*, from controlled, orderly prosperity to excessive, disorderly, even unruly cultural activities.

Yin as a Subcultural Arena: Championing Nineteenth-Century Jiangnan

Yin contained two kinds of cultural vices, with different potentials for social and political unrest. The first was the potential for human hearts and society at large to come under the influence of limitless desires, particularly sexual desire and things associated with it. A primary danger here was the way *yin* theater could destabilize sexuality and gender roles. A second form of cultural vice was the increasing presence of zealots in the militant martial arts, who were potentially rebellious and unruly in the social and political realms. Young villagers, for instance, became interested in group martial-arts practice, sometimes going so far as to form informal organizations and clubs. These activities had little to do with the sexual dangers of *yin*, yet they were often targeted when the government banned *yin* books and *yin* operas. The true danger of both vices, from the state's perspective, lay in their ability to disturb the gender order and familial and communal structures, and ultimately to undermine political authority.

Wu Yun, a nineteenth-century gentryman from Guangdong, explained how these two types of *yin* violated the cosmic order in different but complementary ways. He found that women audiences influenced by *yin* operas lost their desire to be virtuous wives and obedient daughters and that teachers and students lost their sense of their social roles while watching erotic performances in the theater (Wu Yun [1869] 1969, 11a); second, and more damaging, such popular novels as *Shuihu* (Outlaws of the Marsh) and the operas derived from it staged "all the pleasure and excitement of being thieves, murderers, and other criminals without staging their punishments" (Wu Yun [1869] 1969, 10b). Here, his use of the term "*yin*" brought together two quite different realms of culture: One belongs to the literary tradition of the love story and the other to the martial arts, which involved both literary imagination and actual practices and exercises. Although referring to different pastimes, these two genres of culture were united in their violation of social norms. In this sense, *yin* was the threatening underside of cosmopolitanism.

The 1797 ban, though aimed at categorically eliminating *yin* vernacular theaters, failed to prevent these theaters from thriving and traveling throughout the nineteenth century in smaller towns as well as in the countryside around big cities. The Lixia River region near Yangzhou was one such place where mid-nineteenth-century salt merchants preserved theatrical vitality as private patrons. Many actors who had trained in the flower genres switched to Kunqu after the ban, and this ironically accelerated the exchange between Kunqu and local genres, generating new genres instead of choking off the flower theater. Troupes performing in different styles exchanged and therefore enlarged their repertoires.[15] Parts of the earlier flower drama repertoire of Yangzhou were absorbed by the *yi* music system popular in Jiangnan cities such as Shaoxing, Jiaxing, Hangzhou, and Suzhou. When the Kunqu style further absorbed the *yi* system, its repertoire was renewed too. A play entitled *Dazhai fan*, for example, a flower drama originally known through performances during the eighteenth century by Spring Stage in Yangzhou (Li Dou [1795] 1984, 126), was performed in the nineteenth century in different locations by traveling troupes such as the Shaoxing-based Kunyi xiao ruizhin ban (The Xiao Rui Troupe of the *Kunqu* and the *Yi* Styles) and the Suzhou-based Wenwu quanfu ban (The Civil and Martial Complete Good Fortune Troupe) (Gu Duhuang 1987, 129).

New local theaters continued to emerge throughout the nineteenth century. These included the development of Hui opera (troupes organized by Anhui merchants), northern Jiangsu local dramas *(xianghuo xi)*, southern Jiangsu local genre plays *(duizi xi)*, and theatrical genres derived from chanting the precious scrolls *(baojuan)*. These genres originated from self-entertainment and religious activities, as well as from different kinds of flower drum and puppet shows. Their development into theatrical forms produced great benefits for the mixed performances in small towns, country markets, and villages during the nineteenth century (ZGXQZBWH 1992, 131–35, 124–27).

The "erotic" and "decadent" vernacular performances thus exceeded and defied cultural categorization rather than disappearing as a cultural category. These types of theater, which managed to evade cultural categorization, became socially ungovernable, as evidenced during the decades of the Taiping Rebellion, when theater was one of the most flourishing cultural activities in the country. The tumultuous decades of the Taiping Rebellion did not eliminate theatrical activity; rather, the upheaval encouraged it. The Taiping leaders held opera performances, which they shared with local communities, whenever they conquered a city or a town held by the Qing army. The Small Swords, a branch of the Taiping Rebellion, for example, organized theatrical performances while occupying Shanghai and protected the temple theaters in Shanghai before they had to leave the city to the Qing soldiers (Shanghai shehui kexueyuan 1958). The culturally sophisticated Taiping leaders attracted both literati and traveling actors. The Taiping leader Chen Yucheng, for example, patronized an opera troupe named Tongchun (Common Spring Stage). He was able to solicit brilliant Jiangnan actors as well as talented

teenage actors into the troupe. The already well known actors from Jiangnan and other regions acted as teachers for these teenage performers
(Li Hongchun 1982, 44–50). The teachers and students of the Tongchun
troupe were mostly actors for male roles: those who later were known
as "the three Qis" of Jiangnan theater, Meng Qi, Ren Qi, and Zhang
Qi; those who later became renowned martial-arts actors, such as Xia
Kuizhang (1824–1893), Wang Hongshou (1848–1924), and their contemporaries Xiong Wentong, Li Chunlai, Li Yanqing, and Zheng Chang-
tai; those who later became *xiaosheng* actors, such as Li Yuanlong
and Liu Tingyu; those who later became well-known *hualian* (painted
face) actors, such as Liu Jiqing and Li Chunlai; and those who later became comic actors, including Yang Mingyu, Han Zhonghe, and Zhou
Laikui.

The student actors in the Tongchun troupe not only had to learn
operatic arts and to perform for the army, but they also had to do military exercises, travel wherever the army went, act as guards, and even
participate in fighting. After each Taiping victory, Chen Yucheng would
call for the Tongchun troupe to perform operas for the troops based
upon the fights they had just experienced (Li Hongchun 1982, 44, 46).
After the fall of the Taipings, the Tongchun members continued to
travel and perform as a troupe for some time before they disbanded.
Immediately after they disbanded, however, they came to Shanghai to
perform as individual actors and to organize their own theaters. Xiong
Wentong, for example, founded the Jing'ui Theater (1870) and the Tianbao Theater (1899), and Li Chunlai was the manager of the Tongle and
other theaters founded later (ZGXQZBWH 1990, 635). The Taiping-
related performances later became an important source for the southern-
style Beijing opera that marked the theatrical identity of Shanghai. I
shall return to this point when I discuss the social and cultural formation
of Shanghai-style Beijing opera in the fourth section of this chapter.

Their category-free, ungovernable vitality made the popular theaters
a potential threat to the social and political order of the Qing state.
Once the Taiping Rebellion was put down, "decadent" theater became
one of the primary cultural targets for state regulation. The cultural
policy toward vernacular culture as a whole during the Tongzhi Restoration (1861–1874) in the Jiangnan region was representative of this effort.
For recently empowered politicians, who were mostly imported from
other regions, the goal was to restructure Jiangnan culture rather than

to restore it to its prewar condition. In 1867 the newly appointed governor of Jiangsu, Ding Richang, issued three bans on popular culture: What he called *yin*—decadent and unruly—stories and lyrics were to be to banned and burned; building or repairing theaters either inside or outside the city was prohibited; and women were forbidden to go to teahouse theaters (Ding Yusheng, 1868a, 1868b, 1868c). Ding was a politician of the statecraft school entrusted with many tasks by Zeng Guofan and Li Hongzhang, whom I discussed in chapter 1, and his ban on *yin* popular theaters went hand in hand with a program of giving public moral lectures based on the Sacred Edict of the Qing emperors.

Seeking to correct the decadent lifestyle of Jiangsu society, Ding created a long list of books and stories to be banned. The list included 148 titles, among which 112 were popular lyrics and 36 were stories. Many of these had been popular in both the elite Kunqu opera and popular genres such as *tanci* for more than a century, since the Ming dynasty. "Leifeng Pagoda" from *Baishe zhuan* (The White Snake) and sections of *Xixiang ji* (Stories of the West Chamber), because of their scenes of martial arts and of love, were typical of the banned lyrics (Ding Richang 1877, 46–53). Operas based on *Shuihu* and martial-arts operas such as *Lu mudan* were also banned as *yin* works. As a cultural and political project meant to restore order, Ding's ban ironically deprived Jiangnan of the cultural privilege that had been embodied in its highly literate Kunqu operas and *tanci* or southern *ci* lyrics, not to mention the rich martial-arts motifs of the region's popular culture.

This ban on *yin* cultural materials reveals the political underside of the "cosmopolitan." The list of banned books and plays was made up mostly of love stories and other works with sexual implications. But in Ding's notice to the public, we find something more than just a concern for public morality. As the notice makes clear, the cosmopolitan became decadent not only because of its threat to morality but also because it had grown to be politically rebellious. Ding's notice explains why:

> Recently booksellers have sought to make a profit through reprinting vulgar stories and lyrics, so much that almost every household owns a set, each person owns a volume. These books originated from those frivolous youngsters who mistook sentiment for style, and those militant countrymen who thought wantonness was bravery. Ordinary people could not tell the difference, and they therefore viewed rebellious behavior as normal. (Ding Yusheng 1868a, 14a)

In other words, society decayed when people "mistook sentiment for style" and lost the ability to distinguish cultural order from chaos. Decadence, the downside of cosmopolitan society, was the disintegration of cultural norms and moral values into a state of chaos—a society that was ungovernable and hence rebellious. And when people took the rebellious as normal, the results were political subversion, even if this was not immediately evident. As Ding pointed out, "Stories and lyrics were quite likely to have silently caused the war and turmoil we just experienced" (ibid.). Ding obviously viewed *yin* decadence as a political stance, a central component of the Taiping Rebellion and hence equivalent to political animosity toward the state.[16] He therefore asked local officials not only to concern themselves with the increasing rate of robberies and other crimes but also to place special importance on combating the downward slide of customs and ideas that were negatively influencing the minds and actions of the populace.

As part of this campaign, Ding sought to eliminate the social institutions that had given rise to the decadent/rebellious influence of *yin* theater. Heavy punishments were imposed for offering space for the performance of *yin* theater: "No one is allowed to establish theaters for commercial and enjoyment purposes either inside or outside the city, as before the war. If people are found rebuilding theaters and organizing actors to perform, the theater will be confiscated whether the construction is finished or not. The instigator will be strictly punished" (Ding Yusheng 1868b, 25a–25b). Ding's edicts revealed the underlying meaning of *yin*—a decadence unfolding into disruptiveness (*huo* or *luan*). From its original meaning centered on private sexual morals, *yin* had come to embody political and social issues of grave importance to the state. As the flip side of cosmopolitism, it came to represent political rebellion and the disintegration of society into a state in which it was ungovernable.

Perhaps because of the overlap between cosmopolitan urban culture and the "decadent culture" of the eighteenth and nineteenth centuries, it was hard to eliminate *yin* cultural elements without eliminating cosmopolitan culture itself. In the latter half of the nineteenth century, Yangzhou could no longer recapture its status as an important center of urban culture because of the dismemberment of its elite class. Other cities, such as Hangzhou and Suzhou, trapped inside the war zone during the Taiping Rebellion were having a hard time recovering. The ban on *yin* theaters issued during the Restoration, like the one in the 1790s, ruined the chances of Suzhou becoming a center for mixed popular urban theater by isolating it from the flows and concentrations of popular culture. As a provincial capital, Suzhou had a chance to reconstruct its long tradition of vernacular culture. Yet it was closely watched by the provincial government to prevent any influx of popular theater. Even in the 1880s, when Beijing opera had dominated the stage in both the capital and Shanghai for more than a decade, it was still difficult to schedule performances in downtown Suzhou. A troupe from Shanghai performing at the city temple theater in Suzhou was ordered to stop its performance and return to Shanghai because it was violating a state ban. As the Kunqu opera scholar Gu Duhuang observed, from 1867 to 1875 at least four or five Kunqu troupes were reorganized, but flower troupes were not seen in Suzhou before the 1890s. Between 1895 and 1918, popular martial-drama actors *(wuban)* of Kunqu and *yi* styles from Shaoxing, after having performed in Suzhou,[17] joined with Suzhou civil drama *(wenxi)* actors and performed in a combined troupe called Wenwu quanfu ban (The Civil and Martial Complete Good Fortune Troupe).[18] Yet they won their fame mostly by traveling to Jiaxing, Hangzhou, Huzhou, and small market towns and villages instead of staying in Suzhou (Gu Duhuang 1987, 107–49).[19]

The Qing state's efforts to maintain cultural and political control of vernacular theater successfully prevented Yangzhou and Suzhou from regaining their status as urban centers, but they were unable to prevent Shanghai's rise as a new center of vernacular theater. The pressure the state put on major Jiangnan cities pushed a large body of theatrical activities into the countryside and, most importantly, to Shanghai. There was a massive influx of what could be considered *yin* opera troupes to Shanghai during the latter half of the nineteenth century. The number of Shanghai opera theaters, including teahouses *(chayuan)* and opera theaters *(xiguan)* increased rapidly, from two in 1863 to forty-one in 1880 to more than a hundred by 1900 (ZGXQZBWH 1990, 667). Troupes and individual actors and actresses also went to perform at private social occasions *(tanghui)* as well as at occasions sponsored by native-place and professional associations in Shanghai. The accumulation of different theaters from a variety of regions eventually turned Shanghai into a new urban center of cosmopolitan theatrical culture.

This is not the same as saying that the political "system" of the International Settlement was democratic enough to encourage the free development of theatrical culture. The International Settlement did not invite or nurture the influx of vernacular theaters. Therefore, even though it had been established in Shanghai in 1842, theaters did not begin to thrive there until the 1860s. Much more important were the social changes wrought by the Taiping Rebellion and the Qing state's cultural policy of Restoration. As we shall see in the next section, thriving "decadent" vernacular theaters were a central force in transforming Shanghai into a cosmopolitan city.

The flow of theatrical activity from Jiangnan to Shanghai was sudden, carrying with it many of the cosmopolitan features that had once characterized Yangzhou. The flow had started during the Taiping Rebellion, when the city served as a refuge for the opera troupes of Suzhou.[20] Sanyayuan, which was founded in 1842 by the Gu clan, was the only theater in Shanghai before the Taiping Rebellion (He Ma and Zheng Yimei 1956, 2–3), but the city received more than 100 Kunqu opera performers escaping from the war zone around Suzhou. These were mainly gathered into two troupes, which performed in Shanghai for the duration of the turmoil (Jiangsu sheng bowuguan 1959, 3–40, 306).[21] The movement of theaters multiplied after the Taiping Rebellion, and Shanghai experienced an even greater influx of theaters. By the early 1870s,

> There were altogether more than thirty big and small theaters in the foreign settlement. Among them, some were for actors to perform, some for actresses, and some for both actors and actresses. The most famous among the civil troupes were Jumei xuan and Sanyayuan. The most prominent among the martial troupes were those that performed at Dan'gui and Mantingfang Theaters. (Huang Maocai [1898] 1984, 559)[22]

From 1870 to the beginning of the twentieth century, Shanghai saw the rise and fall of over 100 opera theaters (Xue Liyong 1996, 119).[23] Both the number of theaters and the number of genres performed increased rapidly. Regional and local theaters performed in different dialects, and theatrical traditions appeared in Shanghai in a way echoing the growth of theater in Yangzhou during the late eighteenth century. By 1885 Shanghai had gathered most of the mature genres from Jiangnan. After the turn of the century, more local dramas—developed in remote areas during the late nineteenth century—could travel far enough to appear in Shanghai. Shanghai thus was turned into the afterlife of Yangzhou festivity.

A list of regional folk genres gathered in Shanghai by the turn of the twentieth century gives us a quick view of the cosmopolitan feature of the urban festivity. Besides the Kunqu opera popular in Shanghai from the mid-nineteenth century onward, the city also saw, in chronological order, the Hui opera troupes, which enriched themselves with other styles and established theaters in Shanghai in the 1860s; the Beijing opera troupes, which entered Shanghai around 1867; Guangdong opera (Yueju), which established theaters in Shanghai in the 1860s; the Tanhuang operas from Suzhou, which also appeared in Shanghai in the 1860s; the Maoer female theater from Yangzhou, staged in Shanghai no later than the 1870s; the flower drum that had originated in the villages near Shanghai entered the city as the Shen opera in 1914; Ningbo opera, or Yong ju, which originated around the 1830s and spread to Shanghai in the 1890s; the martial drama of the countryside of Shaoxing, which matured in Shanghai in the first decade of the twentieth century; the Changzhou civil opera from southern Jiangnan, which was spread to Shanghai around 1909 (ZGXQZBWH 1992, 157–65; 124–28; 1990, 666–67); the Yangzhou and northern Jiangsu opera, or Weiyang opera, a generic combination of flower drum with northern style folk music, which expanded into Hangzhou and Shanghai around 1910; the north-western operas known as Huai opera, a variation of shaman ceremonial performance, which was first staged in Shanghai in 1912 (Deng Xiaoqiu 1996, 181–93); the Xi opera developed in the Wuxi and Taicang regions, which was first performed in Shanghai in 1912; the Zhejiang opera known as Yue ju, which was first performed in Shanghai around 1917; and Hebei opera or Ping ju, known as the folk genre *bengbeng xi* in Hebei province, which was first staged in Shanghai prior to the 1920s. The city became the intersection of remote and distant theaters and the bearer of the cosmopolitan spirit.

A historical irony revealed itself here: In Yangzhou and Suzhou, what used to be *fanhua*, or cosmopolitan, was redefined as *yin*, or decadent. The influx of these *yin* theaters into Shanghai, however, contributed greatly to rise of the *fanhua* of the city. This is not to say that the rise of Shanghai against Suzhou and Yangzhou was a repetition of the *yin* forces in these cities. On traveling to Shanghai, the creativity and ungovern-ability of vernacular regional theaters, which the official discourse had tried to envelop and ban as "erotic" and "decadent" culture, rewrote the meaning of urban festivity. As we shall see in the following sections, Shanghai vernacular theaters developed and broadened social and cultural meanings of decadence and further developed the cosmopolitan spirit of the histories of noncapital.

Semi-Illicit, Seductive, and Liminal: Fourth Avenue in Shanghai

The influx of vernacular *fanhua*—the cosmopolitan spirit embodied by the gathering together of remote, sometimes unruly cultures—established the cultural status of Shanghai's "foreign miles" *(shili yangchang)*. The phrase "foreign miles" referred to Shanghai's International Settlement, often imagined as the origin of the modern city of Shanghai. The way this origin is imagined conceals many aspects of the actual history of the city by replacing "cosmopolitan" with "foreign" or "Western." The cosmopolitan culture of Shanghai was more than simply a reaction to "Western impact" or a mere continuation of the culture of Yangzhou; it was the result of the influx of all sorts of goods and cultures, including theaters from remote areas. Theaters in particular brought to Shanghai an exciting but chaotic, even disruptive, street life and urban crowds. The disruptive nature of *yin* theaters created a peripheral, even liminal, social and cultural space—a space that in other cities would not have been possible. The building up of two well-known streets—Baoshan Street (a street south of present-day Fuzhou Road) and Fourth Avenue (present-day Fuzhou Road)—materialized this space. From the 1860s to the 1890s, these two streets took turns earning Shanghai fame as the center of *fanhua* culture by representing the "bustling cores" *(renao zhiqu)* of the city, as many travelogues would call them.[24] Unlike Suzhou or Broadway in New York, the bustling cores in Shanghai were both attractive and disturbing. The disorder of post-Taiping China was reflected in a theatergoing culture that transgressed traditional social and institutional boundaries. As the streets filled with theaters, Baoshan Street and Fourth Avenue came to occupy central positions in the nineteenth-century cosmopolitanism of Shanghai before the more famous Nanjing Road, an international capital of consumption for a later period, became the city's center.

Among the many cosmopolitan sites of Shanghai in the 1860s and 1870s—the Bund, the Race Ring, the Banks, for example—the theater streets were the most prominent in the travel writings of the time. In these writings, Baoshan Street, the street where the first Beijing opera theaters were founded, was one of the most spectacular urban spaces in the city. The first two theaters, Mantingfang Theater and Dan'gui Theater, were founded in 1867, and by the 1870s Baoshan Street already hosted six well-known teahouse theaters specializing in different opera genres, as well as several other casual performing sites. I will turn to these theaters in greater detail later. For the moment I will note that these theaters were central to turning the street into the center of activities in the urban scene of the northern district of Shanghai. In 1867 the descriptions of Baoshan Street were already quite spectacular. In the popular *zhuzhici* (bamboo branches) poems of the time, Baoshan Street was praised in a variety of fresh and invigorating metaphors. The road was described as a boundless "flow of spring" ("Baoshan jietou si haichun" [Spring is like the sea flowing on Baoshan Street]) (Ge Yuanxu [1876] 1989, 53). Other contemporary writings refer to it variously as the "thumb" *(jubi)* of the bustling northern area of Shanghai (Huang Xiexun [1883] 1984, 127), as a "gigantic money pit," as "the nightless city" (Chi Zhizheng [1891] 1989, 157), and as a place where people "strove to keep it running" (Ge Yuanxu [1876] 1989, 49). Going to the theaters on Baoshan Street was listed in contemporary travelogues as first among the "top ten attractions" of northern Shanghai *(hushang shijing)* (Wang Tao [1875] 1989, 112–13).[25] Even the names of specific theaters were written into the poetry: "going to Dan'gui Theater" *(guiyuan guanju),* for instance. The spectacle of Baoshan Street won Shanghai fame as an urban center.

The notion of spectacle I am using here does not necessarily refer to material opulence such as the size or magnificence of the architecture, as is often the case in descriptions of modern Western cities. Rather, it was the heat and density of activity that was at the core of the spectacle. This density corresponded to the frequency of performances. As attested in the *Shenbao* advertisements of playbills from 1872, most of the theaters offered both daytime and evening shows daily, except on the anniversaries of the deaths of former Qing emperors and empresses.[26] Each theater had several shows a day, performed by different stars and troupes (Clark 1894, 1).[27] On April 1, 1876, for example, Dan'gui Theater offered nine shows during the day and nine in the evening (*Shenbao,* April 1876, 1). Performances lasted from early afternoon until 1:00 am, if not later.[28]

Moreover, programs changed every day. In April 1876, the Dan'gui Theater presented 108 shows every six-day week, and only two plays were performed twice in any week.[29]

The density of activity was also related to the size of the audiences. The streams of theatergoers in Shanghai must have been very impressive: They filled theaters no matter what hour of the day, what day of the week. Chi Zhizheng, a calligrapher who lived in Shanghai from 1879 to 1891, described a striking scene:

> The show was on every weekday and it was particularly crowded every Saturday night.... When the clock struck eight, the performances started. The audiences filled the space with waves of hundreds of thousands of heads, like flocks of ants and numerous buzzing bees. (Chi Zhizheng [1891] 1989 156–57)

The audiences in this description themselves formed a somewhat horrifying, grotesque spectacle for the author. Chi Zhizheng was by no means the first to spot the spectacle of human density on the Baoshan Street. Huang Xiexun, a member of the Jiangnan literati who had been residing in Shanghai since the 1860s, noted that the opening of the first theaters on Baoshan Street in 1867 was already a landscape in which the "men and women of the city dressed up and went for the event, like numerous ants scurrying towards a piece of meat" (Huang Xiexun [1883] 1984, 116). The concentration of theatergoers and theaters presented an unprecedented, somewhat absurd scene. It is not hard to remember that the Qing state, as Tanaka Isseii suggested, had forbidden theaters because of their power of *juzhong*—amassing an immense crowd in the middle of the city. This concentration of people was threatening because of its power to influence and mobilize the human heart and human action. This might partially explain the demonic overtones one perceives in these descriptions. These demonic features, however, did not stop the authors themselves from enjoying the theaters as well as the theatrical culture that Baoshan Street had to offer.

In the early 1880s the theaters on Baoshan Street moved to Fourth Avenue, a parallel street where modern conveniences such as electricity and running water were available and transportation was accessible. In the 1880s and 1890s Fourth Avenue became what Baoshan Street had been in the 1860s and 1870s, but with electric lights. Its fame and milling crowds began when the first Beijing opera theater, Dan'gui Theater, rebuilt itself on Fourth Avenue after a short period of closure for the then infamous Yang Yuelou lawsuit.[30] By 1884, when Huang Xiexun published his Shanghai travelogue, the theater street had already become the number-one urban spectacle with electricity. For Huang, the street scene of Fourth Avenue in the electric light was comparable to a fantasy:

> When the day is over and the light is on, vehicles and carriages begin to arrive at the theaters. All you see and hear are beautiful profiles and fragrant clothes on the stage. Wonderful melodies and dances keep your eyes busy and lead you into a world of fairy tales. Then the night is deep and the moon afar, yet the latecomers from "green mansion" still flow into the theater like pieces of perfumed smoke and silken clouds. It is indeed a fragrant city of eternal brightness, a huge den of melting gold. ([1883] 1984, 116)

In his travelogue, published a few years later, the calligrapher Chi Zhizheng urged his readers to go and visit the theaters in Shanghai because they "were (and still are) the best theaters under heaven" (Chi Zhizheng [1891] 1989, 156–57). He repeated the above description by Huang Xiexun, adding here and there details using rhetoric reminiscent of fairy tales:

> Some performances were specially made with light and fire, and over 2,000 candles were used to make this light. Even the ancient phrase "flaming trees and silver flowers" could not describe this bright and beautiful scene. Then the night was deep and the moon afar, yet the latecomers from "green mansion" still flowed in like pieces of perfumed smoke and silken clouds. It was indeed a fragrant city of eternal brightness, a magnificent parade of the world of troupes. These were the theaters of Shanghai. One must go and enjoy oneself. ([1891] 1989, 156)

The mixture of entertainment and commercial life on Baoshan Street and Fourth Avenue became the symbol of urbanity in Shanghai. Theaters, shops, and restaurants built and rebuilt against each other. Chinese and foreign stores and shops also helped attract theaters and theatergoers, and the theaters in turn invited more shops, teahouses, and restaurants. By 1877 Baoshan Street housed at least seven highly profitable theaters, mixed among eleven stores owned by foreign companies and nine Chinese-owned stores (Ge Yuanxu [1876] 1989, 79–80, 84). These included opium shops, drugstores, foreign goods stores, silk stores, and restaurants from Suzhou and Hangzhou. The number and variety of shops and theaters had already surpassed the thirteen foreign stores on Nanjing Road, which had a much greater international reputation.

By the late 1880s and 1890s Baoshan Street and Fourth Avenue together had attracted twenty-eight teahouse theaters (sixteen on Fourth Avenue, twelve on Baoshan Street), a few dozen singsong theaters, and numerous shops, restaurants, foreign goods stores, brothels, and opium shops (Chen Wuwo [1928] 1997, 10–11; Ge Yuanxu [1876] 1989, 79–80). This was the greatest concentration of theaters and teahouse theaters of any two neighboring streets in the entire British Settlement and Shanghai in general.[31]

A street of all kinds of theaters was a new form of cultural density and diversity that attracted a variety of human activities and thus created a new form of urban environment, full of light, sound, and movement. In the early 1890s the theatergoing scene in the International Settlement struck the newly appointed British customs officer, John D. Clark (1842–?) so deeply that it occupied the beginning ten pages of his book about Shanghai (Clark 1894, 1–10). What Clark's description of his visits to Jin'gui Theater on Fourth Avenue gives us is a detailed picture of theatergoing, despite its uncomplimentary tone:

> The theater is a large square building, standing off from the side of the street, and the approach to it is by a broad alley, the two-storied shops and tea-houses on either hand being lighted up, and the frontage of the theater itself illuminated; the Fuhkien Road (Fourth Avenue) is crowded so densely with Chinamen, that it is difficult to walk along amongst them, and the entrance to the theater is also crowded—*jinricshas* and sedan chairs and their coolies being the chief obstructions. The loud beating of gongs, the singing, or rather screaming of actors, and the laughter of the Celestials inside, are heard as soon as we come to the entrance, and our friends are fully convinced that the fun is already going on "fast and furious." (Clark 1894, 1–2)

For Clark, theatergoing was embodied not only by the density and diversity of material spaces (such as the shops and teahouses along the street) but also by the movements of the crowd, the noises, and the emotions of the audiences. In a more poetic and fantastic way, Chi Zhizheng tried to grasp the experience of walking among the milling crowds of theatergoers under the electric lights. Despite his preferences, typical of male literati, the author vividly described how walking on the street of theaters became a new urban experience:

> I remember the year of 1878, when I started a trip to visit Hankow, Tianjin, and Shanghai. The most prosperous area among these cities was then

the Baoshan Street of Shanghai, though today Fourth Avenue is the most bustling spot. Every evening when the sun went down in the west, beautiful horses would come up from the east. Teahouses and bars were filled with a lively atmosphere, beautiful figures, and the perfume of clothes. When the summer heat was gone and the mild cool breeze touched the willow twigs, young woman wearing heavy cosmetics would all come to windows and doors, waving to the passers-by. I wrote a poem describing the scene: "Paper-made fans (held in the hands of these women) fly like butterflies in the sunset, resting on every railing of the twelve mansions." During the night, the street stretched along like two long shining lines of light, like two winding dragons. Those who walked through the street sensed from both sides successive impressions formed from the melodies of flutes, hardwood clappers, songs, laughter, the noises of horse-drawn carriages, and human voices. These sounds and images flew up and mixed in the air. How fun it was! (Chi Zhizheng [1891] 1989, 142–59)

Vividly conveyed here is a bustling and colorful atmosphere concentrated in one place. The real fun was the very act of walking along the avenue and feeling the party-like atmosphere all around. No traditional urban space could generate this movement of crowds, the vitality of theatergoing, or the lively atmosphere produced by the massive flux of people and troupes in and out of Shanghai. The street became a passageway filled with vitality, embodying a new form of urban experience.

I have tried to describe a new cosmopolitan culture of activity and "everybody-ness" of the so-called foreign miles of Shanghai. But whose invention was that culture? Who were its agents? Tracing these questions will take us to a subaltern history where the forces previously categorized as *yin,* meeting the modernity of the "foreign miles," became the origin and driving force of cosmopolitan culture in Shanghai. The cultural and institutional bases of Baoshan Street and Fourth Avenue would have been completely different without the influx of two distinctly *yin* groups. The first was a collection of semi-illicit theater managers and actors who had escaped the cultural purge of the post-Taiping Restoration. The second group included singsong girls and other female performers who would have been categorically forbidden from the stage in other cities. Unruly theatergoers also contributed to this *yin* chaos by treating the theater not only as a site of entertainment and for passing the time but also as a place for flirting, pickpocketing, and fighting. These marginal and unorthodox elements certainly fell into Governor

Ding Richang's concept of *yin*. Yet they were a driving force of the cosmopolitan culture of the Baoshan Street and Fourth Avenue, unrecognized next to the international traders and foreign goods consumers.

The founders of the early theaters on Baoshan Street and Fourth Avenue belonged to groups the Qing state saw as "illicit" or "semi-illicit." Some had been involved in the Taiping upheavals in one way or another, others had offended local or central authorities, and still others had been outlawed for any of a variety of reasons. Most had neither social nor institutional status, and many lived without documents or under fake identities. The literati of the time would certainly have defined them as scoundrels and troublemakers; without their affiliation with the theater world, they would have remained invisible in the criminal underworld of the city. But because of the unique circumstances, they were able to import an anarchic and anomalous potential from outlying regions throughout the Restoration. A close look at the social and political status of early Shanghai theater managers reveals just how problematic the social and political identities of the founders of Shanghai theater were. As Table 1 shows, most of the fourteen identifiable theater managers among forty theaters either had histories of being arrested or were on the run from the state or from individuals.

The managers of the first two Beijing opera theaters, Mantingfang (founded 1867) and Dan'gui (founded 1867), illustrate two types of outlaw identities among theater managers: scoundrels and political villains. The Mantingfang Theater was founded by an apparently Cantonese man who obtained British citizenship, Luo Yiqing (Chen Wuwo, [1928] 1997, 68). Lo was known at the time not so much as an opera lover but as a famous local scoundrel nicknamed "Tiger" who ran a gambling shop in the International Settlement. After the settlement's municipal police prohibited gambling, Luo began to invest in theaters. He used the profits from his gambling shop to build the first Beijing-style theater in Baoshan Street. To give his new theater the requisite cachet, Luo made trips to the capital to invite famous actors to perform down south. Beijing actors with truly high status did not, of course, accept his offer. He also solicited Beijing opera actors from Tianjin and formed a troupe. He sold theater tickets at a relatively low price, and the first few performances attracted huge audiences. "People in Shanghai went to the theaters as if they had gone mad."[32]

Table 1. Theater Managers in Shanghai, 1860s and 1870s

Name	Character of Manager	Theater and Year
Unknown	"Scoundrels"	Yigui, 1863
Lu Jixiang	Suzhou Kunqu actor	Sanya, 1863
Luo Yiqing	"Local wanton," a Chinese Briton	Mantingfang, 1867
Liu Weizhong	Ex–illegal arms dealer with the Taipings	Dan'gui 1, 1867
Xiong Wentong (known as Xiong Jin'gui)	Former Taiping troupe actor	Jin'gui, 1870
Zhou Dasheng	Actor	Yongni, 1874
Du Dieyun	Actor, rival of a high official	Dan'gui 2, 1874
Wu Chanqing	Comprador, a friend of actors	Daguan, 1875
Wang Bingkun	A magistrate who invited many former Tongchun actors to perform at his theater	Tianxian, 1874
Yang Yuelou	Actor, later arrested	Heming, 1877
Sun Juxian	Actor, offended the Empress Dowager[a]	Shengping, 1878
Tong Si	Ex-outlaw, Tianjin hoodlum[b]	Jin'gui, 1878
Li Chunlai	Former Taiping troupe actor	Tongle, 1878
Tian Jiyun	Actor, offended the Empress Dowager[a]	Jin'gui 2, 1880

Notes:

[a]Sun Juxian and Tian Jiyun, Xu Muyun suggested (*Zhongguo xiju shi* [A history of Chinese theater] [Shanghai: Shijie shuju, 1938], 77), were both performers in Nanfu, the troupe registered at court. Both offended the Empress Dowager but managed to have themselves reported dead to avoid possible punishment. After they were removed from the Nanfu cast list, they went to Shanghai.

[b]Qiefu, "Zhi Jin'gui xuan" [A record of the Jingui troupe], in "Getai xinshi'" [New history of operatic singing], in *Jubu congkan* [Theater series, 1918], comp. Zhou Jianyun (Shanghai: Shanghai shudian, 1990), 39.

Sources: He Ma and Zheng Yimei, *Shanghai jiuhua* [Speaking of old Shanghai] (Shanghai: Shanghai wenhua chubanshe, 1956); Huang Xiexun *Songnan mengying lu* [The shadows of dreams of the south of the Song River], reprinted in *Biji xiaoshuo daguan* [Compiled works of travelogues, 1883], comp. Zhou Guangpei et al. (Yangzhou: Jiangsu guji keyinchu, 1984); Yao Min'nai, "Nanbei liyuan lueshi" [A brief history of opera troupes in the north and the south], in *Jubu congkan* [Theater series, 1918], comp. Zhou Jianyun (Shanghai: Shanghai shudian, 1990), 1–9; ZGXQZBWH [Zhongguo xiquzhi bianweihui, or the Editorial Committee of Record of Chinese Theater], comp., *Zhongguo xiquzhi: Shanghai juan* [Gazetteers of Chinese theater: Shanghai] (Beijing: Zhongguo ISBN zhongxin, 1990); Zhu Jianyun, comp., *Jubu congkan* [Miscellaneous materials about opera and opera circle] (Shanghai: Jiaotong tushuguan, 1918).

Dan'gui Theater was founded three months later, across the street (on Daxin Road) from the Mantingfang (ZGXQZBWH 1990, 634). The founder of Dan'gui Theater, Liu Weizhong, known nowadays as the father of Shanghai Beijing opera theaters, was an even shadier character. Liu was a native of Dinghai County in Ningbo who had gained a *jinshi* degree (the highest degree in the civil service examination) in 1847 and earned his career as a fourth-rank official collecting grains and taxes for the Qing army.[33] However, his official career ended when he was found smuggling arms to the Taiping Rebels. Provincial officials put up wanted notices, but he escaped, hiding in opera troupes and eventually becoming familiar with the Sanqing troupe in Beijing, led by a great actor, Cheng Changgeng. Liu did not himself become an opera singer, but he quickly learned the business. In 1866 he came back to Shanghai to have the charges against him dropped. The next year, Liu transformed the house of a friend into a theater near Mantingfang (ZGXQZBWH 1990, 634).

With his connections among officials and actors, Liu was able to collect 45,000 taels of silver to build Dan'gui Theater and to organize an excellent troupe populated with famous actors from Beijing (Tang Zhenchang et al. 1989, 243), including Xia Kuizhang, Xiong Jingui, Feng Fuqing (1848–1889?), Wang Guifen, Dong Sanxiong, Zhou Changshan, and Zhou Changchun. Among them, Xia and Xiong were ex-members of the Taiping troupe Tongchun. Dan'gui Theater's tickets were cheaper (0.8 yuan per person) than Mantingfang Theater's, and Dan'gui offered free food and tea service. Its generous salaries attracted more and more Beijing opera actors, and Liu had to build branch theaters, Nan Dan'gui Theater and Bei Dan'gui Theater (Xue Liyong 1996, 117–18).[34]

The Hui opera managers and actors who came from the Jiangnan region also had dubious identities. When the Mantingfang Theater sponsored by the Cantonese British failed in a year-long competition with the Dan'gui Theater for audiences, Jin'gui, a Hui opera theater (founded 1870), soon appeared on the same street. The manager and actors of Jin'gui also had dubious backgrounds. Founder Xiong Wentong was himself a well-known Hui actor and had been involved with the Tongchun troupe organized by the Taiping leader Chen Yucheng (Li Hongchun 1982, 43–50). Most of the Hui actors performing in his Jin'gui Theater had also done stints in the Tongchun troupe. These included actors mentioned in the second section of this chapter, including Ren Qi, Meng Fubao (that is, Meng Qi), Li Chunlai, and Wang Hongshou (Yao Min'ai [1918] 1990, 1–9). Li Chunlai and Wang Hongshou were managers respectively of Tongle and Tianbao Theaters. Around 1874, the Tianxian Theater was founded at the junction of Baoshan Street and Shilu Road (ZGXQZBWH 1990, 636). The performers of Tianxian once again included most of the Hui actors who had played in the Taiping troupe Tongchun, such as Wang Hongshou, Meng Qi, and Ren Qi (Yao Min'ai [1918] 1990, 1–9). Wang Hongshou was secretly descended from a salt-merchant family persecuted several decades before. The following section contains a more complete account of Wang Hongshou. It is sufficient here to note that his biography reveals the decadence of the salt-merchant culture and the rebelliousness of Taiping pop culture joining together.

The Beijing opera theater and the Hui theaters were managed by semi-outlaws engaged in a fierce competition for spectators. The Hui opera perform were experienced and subtle; the Beijing opera actors had long-standing reputations.[35] When the Beijing opera manager, Liu Weizhong, opened branch theaters of Dan'gui, Tianxian Theater, with its Hui-based actors, followed suit with a branch called the Yijin Theater (1877) on Baoshan Street. The success of Dan'gui (1867–1877) and Jin'gui (1870–1877) attracted more theaters as well as shops into the surrounding area. In 1877, Baoshan Street saw the appearance of Heming Theater, which was closed shortly afterwards, and Daguan Theater, which later changed hands and was renamed Yongni Theater (Yao Min'ai [1918] 1990).

The second group of entertainers to bring fame to Fourth Avenue were the singsong girls. Hailing from a low-profile and problematic social sector, singsong girls, as Gail Hershatter (1997) shows, were part of that anomic, anonymous, and commercialized city that could make a fool of the modern individual who had just triumphed in mastering the sophistication of the modern life. These women performers formed a cultural front of the defiant and decadent *yin* activities of the time. During the heyday of the New Dan'gui (1884–1889), Fourth Avenue attracted many *tanci* storytellers who inevitably included many women from the Jiangnan region, particularly Suzhou. In his travelogue, Chi Zhizheng mentioned at least twelve *tanci* storytelling "pavilions" *(lou)* on Fourth Avenue, each with an elegant name and its own star singsong girls.[36] Clark noted that within a year the storytelling sites on the Fuzhou Road (Fourth Avenue) had increased suddenly from one or two to more than half a dozen:

> The number is said to have thus increased within such a short period in consequence of the Taotai's recent proclamation, which prohibits females visiting any of the many opium shops in the settlement.... The music is mostly ballad music. These Celestial "nightingales" are, without exception, courtesans, and (those of two of the "sing-song" houses excepted, where Cantonese exclusively flock, and where the performers sing in the Cantonese dialect) all natives of Soochow *fu*. (Clark 1894, 56–57)

The women performers in Shanghai appeared in the writings of the literati in the 1870s, if not earlier, and by the 1890s they had already had a three-decades-long history of performance service in and out of the opium dens owing to the lack of stable performing sites. As Clark noted, instead of dispersing after the Taotai's order, they created their spaces for singing *tanci* and formed an important part for the *re'nao,* or prosperity, of the International Settlement.

The advent of women performers and singsong girls on the public scene added an ambivalent vogue and unfamiliarity to the culture of Baoshan Street and Fourth Avenue. Their appearance skewed the cosmopolitan spirit from simple enjoyment of entertainment pleasures toward a decadent anarchism with threatening undertones. This danger was reflected in the half-alluring, half-menacing image of a singing girl in a *zhuzhici* poem of the 1870s:

> Mandolin sounds echo in the air
> She flushes as she takes her catwalk to the stage
> Softly fondling the music,
> She asks pardon for not having made her greetings
> Alas! As the songs last into the night
> Your desire deepens in the flesh
> Beautiful flowers never last, yet
> It stole your soul to be on the run with
> Gentleman can't you see,
> Her song of *pipa* offers only emptiness.
> (Wang Tao [1875] 1989, 114)

Behind the description of this scene, it is easy to discern the fear and struggle taking place. The female performer and her manipulative power now occupied a distant space—a space in which her body language, her attitude, and her way of fondling a music instrument are the only, anonymously defined, authority of urban culture. Women performers were spaces to most city goers. The singing women thus reinforced the literati's sense that they were losing control over the cultural realm. And as space they could not be easily erased from cosmopolitan urban culture. The tie between the uncontrollable space and women performer is represented in the writing of Huang Xiexun. While theatergoing on Fourth Avenue could be a wonderful and fantastic experience of the urban, it was also something morally bad for him. In the following passage, for example, moral concerns repeatedly interrupt his fantastic description of the modern urban street:

> The bustling core of northern Shanghai used to be on Baoshan Street. The present-day money pit is centered around Fourth Avenue. Every evening in the light of sunset, beautiful horses come from the East. Clouds of young women swagger through the street. Flirtation and coquetry are found along the way. Even an iron-hearted man finds it hard to resist this seduction! Our life, working for others without benefiting ourselves, is hard enough, and we do so for the sake of surviving. But why do we still want to lose our will and mind to (sexual) temptation? The careers and wealth of those rich young boys, once they fall into this trap, will be ruined within a few years. So you young men, be careful! (Huang Xiexun [1883] 1984, 127)

As this passage shows, uncomfortable attitudes toward women performers and women theatergoers disrupted the flights of fantasy and enjoyment of the urban scene. This became evident when contemporary pictorials began to depict Shanghai prostitutes in the public scene (Figure 7). The gathering of prostitutes and singsong girls on Fourth Avenue helped, to borrow Gail Hershatter's term, to introduce a "dangerous pleasure" into the process of relocating the uncontrollable practices in the new urban space.[37] Considering that women were banned from attending the theater in the provincial capital, female theatergoers in Shanghai themselves exemplified an anomalous, if not rebellious, cultural behavior.

From the 1870s to the early 1900s, the semi-illicit theater managers and dangerous woman performers/prostitutes redefined the bustling core of Shanghai's "foreign miles" with the energy of chaos. This bustling new urban space became the point of intersection first between *fanhua* and *yin* and then between *yin* and *luan* (chaos)—revealing the operation of very different forces from those that had appeared in the history

Figure 7. *Goulan zoushui* (Water Leaks in a Brothel). From Dianshizhai huaguan, *Dianshizhai huabao* [Dianshizhai pictorial] (repr., Guangzhou: Guangzhou shi guji shudian, 1883).

of capital. The history of modernity (capital, trade, foreign concession, electricity, horse-drawn wagons, and weekly working schedules) collaborated unwillingly or willingly with other historical subjects (scoundrels, troublemakers, courtesans, and threatening, decadent singsong girls) to create this new urban space. One may even say that these figures reinvented the "foreign miles"—Baoshan Street and Fourth Avenue—into a specific cosmopolitan space on their own terms.

Conclusion: The Beginning of the Chaotic Era

In an interesting way, the festive culture of Fourth Avenue in Shanghai can best be seen as unruly or chaotic, rather than erotic and decadent. Fourth Avenue witnessed the birth of a distinct cultural milieu with the potential for both chaos and creative vitality. The chaotic potential was reflected not only in the semi-illicit managers, the "dangerous," "pleasurable" women, and theatergoing itself, which were central components of the invention of a chaotic cosmopolitan culture in Shanghai. Unlike the staid and civilized ambience of modern theaters, going to the

Figure 8. *Xiayou niangming* (Losing Life in Pleasure Seeking). From Dianshizhai huaguan, *Dianshizhai huabao* [Dianshizhai pictorial] (repr., Guangzhou: Guangzhou shi guji shudian, 1883).

theater in the late Qing era carried with it a certain chaotic potential. *Qingdai xiqu ziliao* (Documents of Theatrical Activities of the Qing Dynasty), compiled by Tanaka Issei (in Tanaka Issei 1989), reveals that theatergoing was a primary occasion for law-breaking activities.

By the late nineteenth and early twentieth centuries, teahouses and theaters were among the most eventful places in the city—the sites of fights, pickpocketing, and flirtation, places where people showed off their finery or hid their identities. A good example of this new urban scene can be found in the depictions in the *Dianshizhai Pictorial* in the 1880s. The artists who worked for *Dianshizhai* certainly grasped the turbulent time by bringing the chaos of theatergoing to the fore, mixing theatergoers and consumers in a startling view of the unruly new cityscape. Figure 8, *Xiayou niangming* (Losing Life in Pleasure Seeking), depicts a scene based on a journalistic report from a town in northern China, where a local gay man named Jin took revenge on Wei Si, the escort of a local official. According to the notes appearing at the top of the picture, Wei Si had publicly told off Jin for flirting with an actor. The

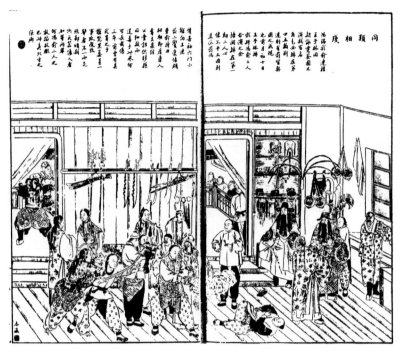

Figure 9. *Tonglei xiangcan* (Harming the Same Kind). From *Dianshizhai huabao daquan* [The complete collection of the *Dianshizhai pictorial*] (Shanghai: Shanghai Dianshizhai huaguan, 1884–1890), vol. 6, no. 52: 59.

next day, Jin brought a sword to the theater and killed Wei. Figure 9, *Tonglei xiangcan* (Harming the Same Kind), shows an actor who was shot dead at the rear of the Yongni Theater in Shanghai by another actor because of a conflict of interest. Figure 10, *Jiezei nanfang* (Smart Theft), depicts a skilled elderly thief from Shanghai who stole a watch from an official in Beijing and then returned it. The theft was so skillful that the Beijing official did not even know when the watch was returned to his wrist. Figure 11, *Diyi lou zai* (The Disaster of Pavilion Number One), depicts the frenzied scene that ensued when a well-known teahouse on Fourth Avenue caught fire.

Though they share no common story, these pictures display how theatergoing operated as a focal point for a panoply of chaotic social events. In Figure 8, for example, the artist reconstructs the event by focusing upon the chaotic scene instead of on Jin and Wei themselves. It was not the personal conflict but the atmosphere, the vigor of unruly passions, and the violence of actions that characterized the urban scene.

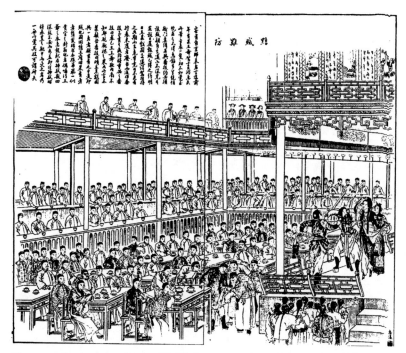

Figure 10. *Jiezei nanfang* (Smart Theft). From *Dianshizhai huabao daquan* [The complete collection of the *Dianshizhai pictorial*] (Shanghai: Shanghai Dianshizhai huaguan, 1884–1890), vol. 7, no. 68: 52.

Figure 9 also shows clearly that theater was not only a performance site but also the stage of actual social dramas and subcultural events. This is also true for Figures 10 and 11, in which the crowds are presented as enormous bodies with distinctive forms of movement and stillness. The massive flow of theatergoers to the many performances, a scene absent from other cities in the post-Taiping era, supported the crowds of consumers who flocked to Fourth Avenue shops and generated the thriving street life of Baoshan Street. The theaters provided a performance space for these unpredictable actors, who formed the human base of the flowing, prosperous, pleasurable, and fantastic landscape of the city's bustling core. Compared to *Prosperous Suzhou* (Figure 4), with its *shengshi* ideals, the illustrations of *Dianshizhai Pictorial* unmistakably convey the disorder of a chaotic time. Here the chaos and uncontrollable energy can be seen replacing the *yin* stage of development. If disordered energy was only potential in the *yin* state, the chaos depicted here shows that unruly energy in full flower.

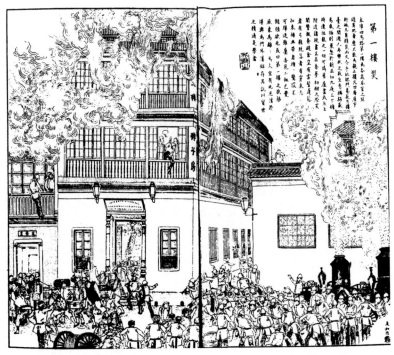

Figure 11. *Diyi lou zai* (The Disaster of Pavilion Number One). From *Dianshizhai huabao daquan* [The complete collection of the *Dianshizhai pictorial*] (Shanghai: Shanghai Dianshizhai huaguan, 1884–1890), vol. 9, no. 80: 58.

It was not long before the Opium War, Gong Zizhen, one of the last creative thinkers of the New Text school of Neo-Confucianism, developed a novel version of the Three Ages through his use of the term "*shuaishi*," the decadent age. *Shuaishi* took its place next to *luanshi* (the chaotic age) and *zhishi* (the age of order) as the opposites of the "prosperous age" (Gong Zizhen 1961). In the decadent age, society and the world were able to maintain order, but they lost their true vitality.[38] A principal reason for this decline in vitality was that political institutions were corrupt and in decline and were therefore unable to promote forms of talent and vision that would be compatible with the rule of the universe. Written during the Daoguang reign (1823–1852), Gong's work was obviously meant as a criticism of the culture and politics of his time. Born into an era of deepening crisis brought about by increasing population and corruption, he predicted the coming of a *haojie* (rebellious knight-errant)—a hero operating outside the authority of the state—who would herald the coming of the chaotic age. His criticism and his prediction of a coming chaotic age attracted little attention during Gong's lifetime, but his vision was fulfilled by events that took place after his death: the Opium War, the Taiping Rebellion, and numerous other rebellions and insurrections marked the era in which the imperial world of the Qing, or imperial history itself, was dissolving. What Gong did not foresee, however, were that the rebellions also represented a type of social and cultural vigor that could perhaps release those creative visions and talents that had lain dormant in the old regime.

FOUR

In Search of a Habitable Globe

The unruly urban festivity discussed in chapter 3 took on a global dimension with the end of Qing imperial authority. En route to Shanghai, this urban festivity developed its own traditions of justice and morality, traditions that signified the dissolution of the Qing imperial world. In Shanghai, it established connections with overseas revolutionary cultural trends to such an extent that those trends formed a revolutionary "cultural nexus" (to borrow Prasenjit Duara's concept [1988]) that contested the old nexus that had kept late-imperial society together. This new cultural nexus gave the urban society of Shanghai an alternative globality, represented by Chinese and Korean assassins, African Americans in the United States, the tragic fate of Poland, and the suffering of the Filipinos and overseas Chinese. This sense of globality was asserted in 1905 in the movement to boycott U.S. manufactured goods. Led by members of the Shanghai Chamber of Commerce, the boycott was mobilized through newspapers, literature, public gatherings, organization and association announcements, public speeches, posters, and the efforts of student activists, who went shop by shop and street by street to persuade the urban masses. Here, the urban festivity that the Qing imperial order had tried so hard to control had grown into a political ideal of a festive world community characterized by an air of "everybody-ness," by the feeling that all were included, regardless of color, race, class, or nationality.

To elaborate on Duara's definition: The interactions between state and society in late-imperial China generated not a class culture or a public sphere in fixed terms but a cultural nexus connecting cultural practices that on the surface seemed far apart (Duara 1988, 21). All cultural practices—elite and popular, national and local—were shifting within the same web of cultures that was the foundation of the stability of the Qing state and of its elite group. The urban festivity presented here was a similar nexus that knitted together different positions and different versions of festive culture. But that festivity was generated from fragile interconnections between the state and the literati, connections that were already fragmented at this point, when the imperialist world was imminent. Instead of working to establish a stable or closed system that reconciled differences, this urban festivity nexus was in constant transformation and expansion. Because of the concentration both of artists and writers and of audiences and readers, a piece of work would quickly take other forms in other fields. As elements of festive culture, such works were transformable to other genres and spaces, highly self-regenerating, fast-spreading, and free-associative in their meanings and contexts. In short, they were more free-floating and random than they could be in the cultural nexus that had maintained the imperial system. Thus, they gave rise to something that can be called "radical festivity."

Postimperial Heroes: From Assassins to Anarchists

The earliest "operas of the time," *Zhang Wenxiang Ci Ma* (Zhang Wenxiang's Assassination of Ma Xinyi; 1870, revised 1893) and *Tie gongji* (Iron Rooster; 1870s), which were based upon contemporary incidents, won the hearts of the Shanghai public in the 1870s. Even at that early moment, the chaotic era that Gong Zizhen had foreseen was already beginning to give way to a political and moral alternative. It was evident that the semi-illicit actors not only provided the external base for the urban milieu of Fourth Avenue but also gave rise to something best described as the spirit of an urban subculture that undercut the legitimacy of the imperial order of the Qing state. For the purposes of this book, I am talking about the plays not as individual literary works or art forms but as elements or motifs of a festive culture. They were organs of urbanism that were free-associative and were constantly transforming. As such, these plays brought to the surface of urban festivity the fear, anger, and trauma experienced by those who had lived through the Taiping Rebellion and the Opium War. They also gave voice to those principles of morality and justice that had been deeply violated by officialdom during this time, thus contesting political authority's intrinsic forms of urban festivity. Long prior to the 1911 Revolution, the urban public of Shanghai had already been prepared for the radical challenge to Qing authority and the collapse of the Qing world.

Assassination of Ma Xinyi reflected popular reaction to a well-known lawsuit of 1870. Ma Xinyi, newly appointed governor of Jiangsu and Zhejiang as well as a state official honored for his achievements fighting the Nian rebels, was publicly assassinated in Nanjing. The assassin, Zhang Wenxiang, surrendered peacefully to the authorities, leaving both the court and high officials in shock. After interrogating him, Qing officials executed Zhang publicly as an ex–"Taiping rebel" and a "sea rover" who had taken revenge on the Qing governor for the treatment of his fellow bandits.[1] This assessment conflicted with stories leaked to the public during the interrogation, but it embodied the political rationale of the Qing state that the assassin was a "rebel" against the state.

The true reasons for Ma's assassination are still debated today. Although both his connection with Muslims and the envy of powerful members of the Xiang army have been suggested as possible reasons,[2] the most widely believed conclusion at the time focused on Ma's personal morality. Before he became governor, Ma had been a "buddy" of Zhang Wenxiang and Cao Erhu during the Nian fight, where they vowed to help each other as "brothers."[3] After becoming a high-ranking official, Ma did not keep his vow. As the story has it, he instead seized Cao's wife, making her his courtesan, and coldheartedly had Cao arrested and killed for a crime he did not commit.[4]

Zhang, in this version of the story, had sought revenge for his friend and himself. Sentencing Zhang as a "rebel" concealed the governor's abuse of power and personal greed. Whether the story was true or not, Zhang's sentence resulted in a torrent of public criticism, and popular opera took the lead in expressing disapproval of the state's verdict. In 1871, even before the case was completely settled, the popular opera actors Meng Qi and Wang Hongshou had created a play that was, at least in Zeng Guofan's conception, "satirical toward governor Ma" (Zeng Guofan 1936).[5] While the original script is no longer available, it was famous at the time for ostensibly providing the only unofficial version of the story (Zhang Xiangwen [1929] 1968, 7:43a–45a).[6] Performance of the play was quickly forbidden, but it effectively turned the tone of public opinion toward sympathy for Zhang.[7] Partially because of the opera, the public tended to see and remember Zhang not as a "*zei*" (rebel), as he was called in the official sentence, but as a *xia* (hero), and he was lionized in popular culture for dying in order to achieve justice for his victimized friend (Zheng Zhicheng 1996, 454–66).[8] Zhang defended those basic human principles that Ma had violated: loyalty, friendship, consistency, brotherhood, and affection. His brave action showed a readiness to make sure justice was served without considering his own loss. Here, the morality and justice of the human heart were separated from the state order and aligned with the rebellious and the weak instead of with the powerful interests of those associated with the state.

Iron Rooster also illustrated the irreconcilability of this split between a popular sense of justice and morality on the one hand and state politics on the other. *Iron Rooster* was a crude remake of *Hong Yang zhuan* (Legend of Hong Xiuquan and Yang Xiuqing), a forty-six-episode opera series performed for the Taiping rebel army celebrating their victories over the Qing state (Li Hongchun 1982, 44–46). The play was revised dramatically to fit the tastes of the Empress Dowager by changing key Taiping figures from heroic protagonists into villains.[9] Yet personal morality remained one of the basic themes of the play. The revised play borrowed from the record of an actual historical figure, Zhang Jiaxiang, a minor rebel leader who surrendered to a Qing general in exchange for official recognition at the outbreak of the Taiping Rebellion.[10] He was then sent to fight the Nien rebels to demonstrate his loyalty to the emperor. His bravery impressed the general so much that he accepted Zhang as his stepson. The version of the opera available today plays with the meaning of "betrayal" and "loyalty," a binary opposition central to both the theatrical tradition and nineteenth-century political ideology.[11]

The opera's plot is quite complicated but can be summarized as follows: The rebel Zhang was a spy sent by the Taiping leader to the camp of Governor Xiang Rong. Knowing that Zhang was an excellent fighter, Governor Xiang sent out his own soldiers, with one of them disguised as Zhang, to attack the Taipings in order to make the Taiping leader distrust Zhang. As expected, the Taiping leader was fooled and killed Zhang's wife and son in anger. Having no knowledge of Governor Xiang's trick, Zhang was deeply hurt and took revenge by killing a fellow spy who had been assigned to assassinate Governor Xiang. To express his gratitude, the governor offered his first daughter to Zhang to replace the wife he had lost. The daughter, however, did not want to marry a former rebel and committed suicide on the night of the wedding. Though sad, the governor nevertheless married his second daughter to Zhang. This won Zhang's heart. From then on, Zhang became not only Xiang's son-in-law but also his bodyguard, even risking his own life to protect Xiang from his political enemies.

The story operates on two levels, with an implicit disparity between them. On the surface level of the political order, Zhang found his way to becoming a "loyal" subject of the Qing state by changing his allegiance from the Taipings to the emperor. The initial impetus for this change was the governor's trickery and Zhang's misunderstanding of the Taiping leader's actions. Although this was enough to turn Zhang into an enemy of the rebels, it does not fully explain his support of the governor or why he became his son-in-law. The father-son bond between the former rebel and the Qing governor requires a special reciprocity. This leads us to the second level of the story: The changing relationship between Xiang and Zhang from enemies to relatives was the result of personal, rather than political, reciprocity—an exchange of faith, gratitude, and recognition. Xiang showed his faith in Zhang by offering his own daughters and putting his prestige on the line. Zhang accepted the recognition Xiang offered and, in return, was willing give Xiang all his loyalty, even his life.

This second level of the story can be traced to the conventions of an ancient, if minor, tradition in the martial arts focusing on *en* and *yi* as ideal human bonds.[12] As one often sees in *yin* martial-arts writings, such as *Outlaws of the Marsh* and *Three Kingdoms* and their subsequent theatrical and storytelling versions, to receive such faith from another man was centrally important. An expression of faith of this kind demanded a return of devotion. The exchange of faith and mutual recognition embodied in the father-son relationship between Zhang and Xiang went beyond family ties to a higher level of moral reciprocity, becoming a form of *yi* (absolute mutual devotion).

At this second level of the story, the personal reciprocity that characterized the martial-arts intersubject relationship transformed the definition of what it meant to be a loyal subject of the Qing Empire: Xiang and Zhang built their intersubjective bond on personal moral reciprocity, and their loyalty to the empire was only an extension of this personal bond. This subaltern form of community is especially evident in martial-arts works such as *Three Kingdoms, Outlaws of the Marsh,* and, more recently, *Lu mudan* (Green Peony), a martial-arts novel situated in Yangzhou in the eighteenth century. The decadent, rebellious *yin* elements in the latter two books are especially obvious, since both novels pit the principle of personal reciprocity against that of political reciprocity. Personal morality is central in these books, functioning as the glue that holds together politically powerless rebel groups and semi-illicit martial-arts communities. Personal reciprocity is represented in martial-arts literature and theaters as a principle of community action and cohesion existing outside state authority, thus mapping out an alternative to being a political subject of the empire.

It may be worth mentioning here that the lives of the operatic artists (that is, the semi-illicit actors) who brought these tales of personal loyalty to life were endowed with a rich source of festive culture that did not look to the Qing state as its immediate central authority. Wang Hongshou, one of the writers of and main actors in *Assassination of Ma Xinyi* and *Iron Rooster,* can be taken as an example of those traveling actors whose performances were banned by officials. The son of a navigation official in Nantong County in Jiangsu, he was the only survivor when his family was executed after his father offended an official of higher rank. Wang escaped by hiding in a big suitcase; then, concealing his true identity, he joined a traveling opera troupe. Already familiar with both the Kunqu and Hui opera arts practiced by the private troupes his father had patronized, he added to his skills as he learned from the different teachers he met on his travels. He joined the Tongchun troupe as a teenager. There he met Meng Qi, his coactor in the two plays, and, later, many others who were drifting around, half in exile, as a result of the ban on *yin* theaters (Li Hongchun 1982, 43–50).[13] When he came to Shanghai, Wang became a student of the famous Beijing opera actor Mi Xizi, whose role as Guan'gong, the godlike hero from the martial-arts novel *Three Kingdoms,* was so vivid that officials had to ban its performance in Beijing (Li Hongchun 1982, 50–53).[14]

Wang was popular in Shanghai theaters after the 1860s, and throughout his wandering life, he learned, performed, and composed Guan'gong operas. Drawing on the martial-arts subcultures from Anhui, northern China, and the Lixia River region (Li Hongchun 1962, 418), he reinvented the theatrical convention of these operas by opening up a new repertoire of Guan'gong plays, new plays in which personal loyalty and friendship often intervened in urgent political matters.[15] He also developed a new role type for Beijing opera's male protagonists known as *hongsheng*, a "red-faced" persona who was younger, more active, and skilled in acrobatics with the sword and horse (Li Hongchun 1962, 405–6; Li Yuanlong 1960, 27–31).[16] A personal reciprocity that had been deeply violated by political authority left obvious traces upon the dramatic structures of both of Wang's contemporary plays, *Assassination of Ma Xinyi* and *Iron Rooster*.

It is obvious that the personal reciprocity of the martial-arts tradition was not strong enough to result in the formation of any intellectually based alternative community, but as a form of festive culture, it disrupted the political justice and imperial authority by frequently reoccurring, transforming, and free-associating with other new meanings. *Iron Rooster* was so popular, even as a dramatic rewrite of the original play, that by the turn of the century it had expanded to twice its original length. *Assassination of Ma Xinyi* returned to Shanghai theaters in the 1890s after having been banned in 1871 and was performed by different opera troupes at different sites during the same period of time. The ban actually made the play even more famous. Upon its return, not only did it revitalize the martial-arts operas in Shanghai theaters, but it also took on the form of civic drama (1907), *tanci* ballad (1910–1920) and, later, spoken drama in the local dialect (1930s).

A Radical World

The beginning of the twentieth century, marked by the looting of Beijing by the army of the Eight-Nation Alliance during the suppression of the Boxers (1900), unmistakably indicated the imminence of a world of absolute power. Modernization or reform was no longer the key to China's survival in such a world, even though the state-led reform, the New Policy, was on the way. During 1902 and 1903, several Qing policies, particularly some of its international policies—such as allowing the Russian army to garrison the northeastern city of Fengtian as well as considering borrowing the French army to pacify internal rebellions— provided fuel to the state's political and cultural enemies. Nationalism, or anti-Manchu sentiment, spread rapidly among Chinese students in Japan and influenced the literati in Shanghai through the print media, various study societies, theater, and literature.[17]

In 1904, on the eve of the Russo-Japanese War, the well-known actor Wang Xiaonong brought to Chunxian Theater *Guazhong lanyin* (The Fall of Poland), his new-style Beijing opera based upon Poland's defeat by Turkey. According to Rebecca Karl's insightful analysis, this performance highlighted the Chinese intellectuals' reading of the relationship among Russia, Korea, and Japan, a relationship that was seen as a regional embodiment of the contemporary global situation (Karl 2002, 27–49). I believe, furthermore, that the performance also marked the ripening of a new urban nexus of something that might be called "radical festivity," a nexus formed by the connections among the members of the subcultural traditions of semi-illicit theater, student groups abroad, and intellectual journalism in Shanghai and Tokyo. The history of these groups came together to make Shanghai the central site of this radical festivity.

Let us first take a look at what had become the semi-illicit theaters in Shanghai at the beginning of the twentieth century. At this point, the eighteenth-century flower operas had become southern-style Beijing opera (that is, operas developed in the south but combining Hui and other northern operatic styles), and in Shanghai the southern-style Beijing opera gave rise, in a theater-reform movement, to a more Westernized "civic drama" (Wenmingxi), or spoken drama (Yu Zhibin 1989; Chen Bohai and Yuan Jin 1993, 425–59). In addition to the "operas of the time," reform-minded artists brought to the Shanghai public operas intended to be politically educational, such as *Pan leishi touhai* (The Martyr Pan) and *Heiji yuanyun* (A Homeless Soul), to create a consciousness of resistance and an anti-opium-smoking sentiment. "Foreign-dress" operas adapted from translated works—such as *Napoleon* (1904) (Ah Ying 1957), New *"La dame aux camelias"* (an adaptation of the younger Alexandre Dumas's *La dame aux camelias;* 1909), *Mrs. Walter's Occupation* (an adaptation of a Bernard Shaw work; 1910) (Tarumoto 2002), *Guazhong lanyin* (The Fall of Poland; 1904), and *Heinu yutian lu* (Black Slaves Appeal to Heaven, based on Harriet Beecher Stowe's *Uncle Tom's Cabin*) (Wang Lixing 1992)—were performed in 1905 and 1907 by various troupes (Figure 12).

It is worth noting that, in the artists' circles, the theater-reform movement was initiated by the sons and students of the first generation of semi-illicit actors. The most important promoters of theatrical reform, Xia Yueshan (1868–1924) and Xia Yuerun (1878–1931), were sons of Xia

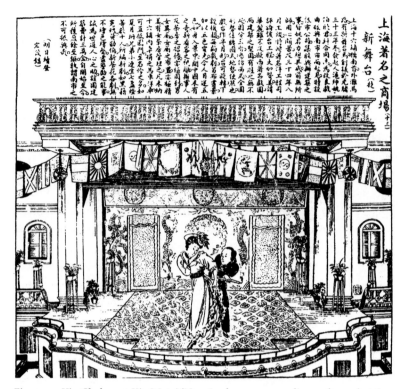

Figure 12. *Xin Chahua at Xin Wutai* (New *La dame aux camelias* performed at the New Stage Theater). From Huan qiu she, *Tuhua ribao* [Pictorial daily news] (Repr., Shanghai: Shanghai guji chubanshe, [1909–1910] 1999), 1:151.

Kuizhang, an ex-member of the Tongchun troupe organized by the Taiping leaders. Before they founded the first modern-style theater, the New Stage in Shanghai in 1908, they had already invited their students and friends, as well as their colleagues Pan Yueqiao, Feng Zihe, Xiong Wentong, and Wang Xiaonong, to perform a new repertoire in inventive styles (Zhang Zegang 1988, 31–36). As the 1911 Revolution drew near, the Xia brothers and Pan Yueqiao became actively involved in the political events of the Revolution. Their passage from sons of semi-illicit actors to theater reformers and then revolutionaries indicated the trajectory of urban festivity itself.

Theater reform was closely related to radical journalism. By 1904, Shanghai had already become the cradle of radical anti-Qing journalism. The state's ban on *Subao* (The Paper of Jiangsu), which had published such well-known anti-Manchu essays as "Geming jun" (Revolutionary Army) by Zou Rong (1885–1905) and "Bo Kang Youwei zhengjian shu" (Rebuttal to the Political Proposal of Kang Youwei) by Zhang Taiyan (1869–1936) in 1903, made radical anti-Qing journalism even more famous. *Zhejiang chao* (The Zhejiang Tide), *Jiangsu,* and *Hubei xueshengjie* (The Student Circle of Hubei), radical journals organized by students in Japan and printed in Shanghai, called upon the urban society, with their powerful words and youthful spirit, to express their urgent concerns regarding the political situation in China in the contemporary world.

Other radical journals circulated in Shanghai, such as *Jingzhong ribao* (Tocsin), *Anhui baihuabao* (Vernacular News of Anhui), and *Zhongguo baihuabao* (The Chinese Vernacular News), enlightened their readers about specific international political conflicts that the imperialist world brought to China after the suppression of the Boxer uprising, such as the Russian army's move toward northeast China, British ambitions concerning Tibet, and French encroachment in the southeast. The journalists of *Jingzhong ribao, Anhui baihuabao,* and *Zhongguo baihuabao* had all been personally involved in the practices of the new theaters during the first surge of anti-Qing, or "revolutionary," spirit in Shanghai culture. To this point I shall return shortly.

Translated works that introduced their readers to the radical changes in the world—the rising and falling of nations as well as the struggles and revolutions of the people—also contributed to the cosmopolitan cultural milieu of Shanghai. These works were serialized in the journals mentioned above or published in book form by student societies, intellectual societies, and presses in Shanghai or Tokyo before being reprinted in Shanghai. Of the 139 translated titles listed in *Xinhai Geming Shuzheng* (Books of the 1911 Revolution), 74 were narratives of radical change in other countries in the world, in the form of nonscholarly histories, biographies, novels, and *tanci*-ballad scripts (Zhang Yuying [1941] 1953, 140–83). The rest focused on philosophy, law, political theory, and historiography. A well-read Chinese adult in Shanghai or Tokyo could, in the short period from 1900 to 1908, find books about the U.S. War of Independence and Civil War; the independence of Switzerland; the struggle for freedom in Vietnam; at least one title about the fight for freedom in Ireland; two or more titles about the struggle for independence in Scotland; more than one story about the Russian Revolution against the tsar; at least two titles about the resistance to U.S. control of the Philippines and the search for independence in that nation; two about the struggles in colonial India; two about the fate of Egypt; three titles about the fight for independence in Greece; four different narratives about the French Revolution, in a variety of forms, including translated history, *tanci* ballads, and biography; five titles about tragedy and struggle in Poland; two titles about anarchism in Europe; and two titles about the important and sweeping changes in nineteenth-century Europe (Ah Ying 1953, 184–203; Feng Ziyou 1954, 276–97; Zhang Yuying [1941] 1953, 140–83).

These journals and books brought to Shanghai's urban society two images of the world. One alerted readers to the imminent reality of the imperialist world, represented not only by the European and American encroachments already mentioned but also by the suffering of Koreans, Filipinos, Vietnamese, Indians, and Poles under the colonial and impe-rialist domination of Japan, the United States, France, Britain, and Russia, respectively. Nothing made it clearer that the Qing's state policies letting such things happen to China were no longer legitimate.

The other image, though, provided by scattered journalistic writings and rough narratives, was that of an alternative world, or a world in revolution. Such a radical world pointed no longer to modernization following European and American models but, rather, to a pursuit of freedom and independence following the examples of those in the non-West: the anti-tsarist movement in Russia; resistance movements in Egypt, Portugal, revolutionary France, independent Italy, Poland, Scot-land, the Philippines, Switzerland, Greece, India, and Vietnam; and so on.[18] At least in imagination, the contest between such a radical world and the imperialist world cut across national borders.

These two images of the world came into frequent juxtaposition to one another. There was the newspaper *Eshi jingwen* (Russia Watch, founded in 1903), and there were also legendary texts about Russian revolutionaries and Russian and eastern European anarchist heroes and heroines, as shown in the historical novels *Eluosi geming dafengchao* (The Great Tide of Revolution in Russia), *Xuwu dang* (Anarchists), and the story of a fictional Sophia in *Dongou nuhaojie* (East European Hero-ines).[19] While the actual French state and army were pursuing colonial interests in Asia, the (re)constructed legendary figure of Madame Roland was upholding a revolutionary France—a France that to Chinese read-ers was a probable comember of an intellectual and international com-munity. By the same token, although the Chinese audience perhaps saw the U.S. achievement of independence from the British Empire as admirable, the Philippine resistance to U.S. power reflected in *Feilubin xiake zhuan* (Legend of Filipino Knights), serialized in *Xin xin xiaoshuo* (The New "New Fiction"; 1904), was even more appreciated.

The tension between the imperialist world and the radical world passed from the print media to the Shanghai theater, particularly to the reformed opera theater, and in this way illustrated the free-associative, fast-spreading nature of urban festivity. The imperialist expansion and its criticism presented by radical journalism, such as *Tocsin* and its predecessor, *Eshi jingwen*, became sources of the repertoire of the reformed Shanghai theaters. For instance, the Wenmingxi drama (a half-spoken, half-sung performance) actor Wang Youyou, who was then a student at the Minli High School of Shanghai, taking as his inspiration a letter published in the paper *Eshi jingwen*, wrote a play called *Zhang Tingbiao beinan* (The Death of Zhang Tingbiao), which was performed by the school's student troupe (Wang Lixing 1992, 283–88). The letter and the play narrated an incident in which Russian soldiers garrisoned in northeast China had forced more than 5,000 Chinese into a river (*Eshi jingwen*, December 2–3, 1903). After the script was published in the journal *Guomin xinwen* (Citizen News), another amateur student troupe at Nanxiang Junior High in Shanghai performed it (Wang Lixing 1992, 283–88).

The overlap between radical journalism and reformed theater was most evident in the founding of the *Great Theater of the Twentieth-Century*, organized by the editor of *Tocsin*, Chen Qibing (1874–1933), and the semi-illicit opera artists Wan Xiaonong and Xiong Wentong (Karl 2002; Zhang Zegang 1987, 78–81). Together with *Tocsin* and the *Vernacular News of Anhui*, where the leading activist Chen Duxiu was the chief editor, the radical journals published theater reviews, written by the intellectuals Chen Duxiu and Jiang Zhiyou, performing schedules (*Tocsin*, August 26, 1904), and play scripts such as Wang Xiaonong's *Guazhong lanyin*, an opera based on Poland's fall to Turkey (*Tocsin*, August 20–31, 1904). Just *Guazhong lanyin* alone embodied the free-associative nature of festive culture, arising from the interaction of news, journalistic circles, translated histories, and theatrical activities. The opera was probably based on books on Polish history, of which at least two translations were available in Shanghai by 1904 (Zhang Yuying [1941] 1953, 176).[20] The playwright was himself a semi-illicit actor as well as a radical cultural activist. The play circulated both in the print media and in the theaters.

The mutual reference among radical journalism, book culture, and the theater readily brought the "radical world" together with the already-existing semi-illicit theatrical tradition represented by *Assassination of Ma Xinyin* and *Iron Rooster,* the disruptive tradition that had long contested the authority of the Qing state. Assassins and assassination, both as actual events of the time and as dramatic actions in the theater, became the key to the affinity between the "radical world" and the "disrupted empire." As word of the political assassinations by anarchists in France and by the nihilists in Russia spread to East Asia through the news media and translated literature, the symbolic goal of assassination in the theater began to be transformed, from enacting personal justice against corrupt authorities to carrying out a radical solution to a political dilemma.

From the 1890s to the 1900s, Shanghai theaters and public culture displayed an array of assassins, originating from different parts the world, acting for different purposes, and targeting political authorities of different sorts. *Assassination of Ma Xinyi* and *Iron Rooster* were joined by journalistic reports, play scripts, and theatrical performances as well as serialized pictorial stories of other assassins and stories of nationalists, of resistance to colonization, of French and Russian anarchists, and of radical anti-Qing organizations. An Chung-gun, the Korean hero who assassinated the Japanese prime minister Ito Bokubi, appeared first in the news, then in the classical verse of script (1901), then in the theater (1904), and finally in pictorial serializations (Huan qiu she [1909–1910] 1999, 1:15) (Figure 13). Around 1904, an unsuccessful attempt was made to assassinate the governor of Guangxi, Wang Zhichun, who was said to have sold local properties to the French. The event appeared first in the news, then as *The Jingu Xiang Teahouse,* a play performed at Chunxian Theater, and then in script form in the *Grand Twentieth-Century Theater* (1904).

Also appearing at the time were stories and play scripts about female Russian anarchists and early French revolutionaries who acted as assassins or heroines and helped the powerless to achieve freedom, represented by the fictional Sophia and historical Madame Roland mentioned above, as well as by the novels *Nü xiake* (Female Knight-Errant, 1907) and *Huang Xiuqiu* (Embroiling the Globe). Contemporary hero and heroine Qiu Qin and Xu Xilin, who attempted to assassinate Qing emperors, appeared not only in their legendary life stories but also in numerous

Figure 13. *An Chonggen cisha Yiteng bowen* (The Assassination of Ido Bokubi on *Tuhua ribao*). From Huan qiu she, *Tuhua ribao* [Pictorial daily news] (Repr., Shanghai: Shanghai guji chubanshe, [1909–1910] 1999), 3:453.

tanci ballads and poems. Through the operas about assassins and assassination, the subculture of semi-illicit theaters was internationalized and became a part of the "radical world." This progression from presenting semi-illicit assassins on stage to presenting anarchist assassins not only projected the end of the Qing world but also indicated a total change in urban festive culture, from what had originally been simply *yin* or "disruptive" or "chaotic" to something radical and political.

At the Loss of the "Fair World"

In 1904–1905, a movement opposing U.S. discrimination against overseas Chinese, originating in San Francisco and Honolulu, joined existing cultural traffic between Shanghai, Tokyo, and diasporan Chinese. This movement drew both the imperialist world and the radical world closer to the cities of China. The result was a boycott of U.S. goods in

Shanghai and Guangzhou in 1905. The significance of this movement from a cultural and historical point of view was that it put into circulation the search, the longing, for a fair world community. The search for such a fair world was initiated by overseas Chinese and by political figures in exile abroad, who felt acutely what it meant to be people "without a state." Shanghai became an important terminal that turned that search for an imagined inhabitable world community into a call for such a world. Because of the city's environment of radical urban festivity, this cultural pursuit of a fair world peaked in Shanghai and passed its spirit on to other places in augmented form.

Actions opposing U.S. discrimination against overseas Chinese originated in San Francisco, a city on the other side of the Pacific Ocean. Although the history of overseas Chinese in the Americas was relatively short compared to the history of Chinese in other regions, it began as early as the gold rush in the late 1840s. When U.S. officials solicited laborers from China in 1852, there were already Chinese living in California; and when the infamous Chinese Exclusion Act was passed in 1882, Chinese overseas laborers had already constructed modern facilities in California and other states. The Exclusion Act was passed to restrict the economic and political rights of Chinese laborers and to expel them from the United States in order to reduce the impact of its ongoing economic crisis.[21] The most important effect of the act was its enforcement both of unequal exchanges of labor and capital, in particular, and of racism against the Chinese, in general. Without revealing the discriminative content of the act, U.S. officials approached the Qing state in 1882 with an agreement stating that the United States would no longer solicit laborers.[22] This agreement was renewed once in 1893, after which the restrictions and discrimination against Chinese in the United States became more violent and were extended to include Chinese students, travelers, and, particularly, Chinese merchants and entrepreneurs (Liang Qichao [1905] 1982, 387–426).[23] The next renewal of this agreement was dated June 1904.

Overseas Chinese in San Francisco reacted to this policy early, but it was not until the turn of the century that their actions became known among the political elites of the diaspora, who became the enemy, passively or actively, of the Qing state only after the Boxer uprising of 1900. Before June 1904, the date set for the renewal of the agreement, the community in San Francisco held several meetings and drafted a long public letter, containing over 100,000 signatures, to seven U.S. governmental bureaus (Liang Qichao [1905] 1982), asking for an end to the discrimination. The community also pleaded with the Qing state to refuse to extend the agreement.

Negotiations between the United States and China on the agreement came to a dead end when Liang Cheng, the representative of the Qing government, refused to sign an agreement that made no substantial change (Liang Zheng 1905). In February 1905, the U.S. government sent William Woodville Rockhill (1854–1914) to China to meet with Qing officials about the stalemate. The Chinese community in the United States telegraphed relevant organizations in Shanghai, Guangdong, and other places to ask for their support in rejecting the renewal (*Zhongwai ribao*, April 13, 1905). Merchant organizations in Shanghai gathered several times to discuss possible strategies for ending the act (*Zhongwai ribao*, April 15, 1905). Although the U.S. cultural politics of endowing "people" with "national" or "racial" character was unfamiliar to early Chinese immigrants, it helped the Chinese abroad come up with a counterstrategy by granting "goods" a national brand.[24] Eventually, in May 1905, under the personal leadership of members of the Shanghai Chamber of Commerce, a boycott of U.S. goods *(dizhi meihuo yundong)* broke out in Shanghai.

The boycott as a social and cultural *movement* (to accept Karl Gerth's use of the term) made opposition to discrimination from afar an urban event in China.[25] Urban festivity was developing in this movement. Boycotting rapidly became a focal point of public urban life, a common theme of urban events. It generated numerous and frequent urban activities, ranging from organizational gatherings of different associations and unions, to public announcements by a variety of professional and other clubs and societies, to public lectures, street posters, shop displays of U.S. goods, and so on. Writers and artists volunteered to give public lectures at all sorts of meetings held in schools, at society gatherings, and in gardens. Student volunteers organized persuasive campaigns in which they spread throughout the city—going door to door, street by street, and neighborhood by neighborhood—persuading small shop owners not to buy or sell U.S. goods. Journalists made the boycott and related events the headlines of the daily news. Demonstrations and crowds marched through the main streets of the city calling for others to join the boycott.

As an urban movement, not only did the boycott give Shanghai an opportunity to express anger at and objection to the discrimination in more aggressive ways than could be expressed from afar, but it also generated echoes of objection to similar discrimination occurring locally. Riots against local discriminative policies took place even after the peak of the boycott.[26] In short, Shanghai became an urban nexus on the move.

Such a radical urban nexus, I shall add, was mobilized not merely because of economic need but because of a deeper urge for an ideally livable world. The intensified imperialist encroachment on China at the turn of the twentieth century had already made surviving in the increasingly unjust world an urgent issue. This nexus had much to do with generating radical groups who objected to the Qing foreign policy and even denied the legitimacy of the Qing state itself. The U.S. discrimination against Chinese laborers was the last straw for the already crisis-ridden Qing government. Since 1903, *Tocsin* and other papers in Shanghai had repeatedly warned their readers of encroachments by Russia and Japan in the Korean Peninsula, by France on the Yunnan borders, and by Britain in Tibet. At that point, newspapers beyond Shanghai, such as *Xin Zhongguo bao* (New China, founded in 1900 in Honolulu) and *Fujian ribao* (Fujian Daily), expressed concern about the new global power, the United States. The United States did not become a superpower until after World War II, but it had established itself as a global player when it launched policies aimed at securing economic control of overseas laborers through military means and when it seized the Philippines and Hawaii as its military bases. A keynote essay entitled "Ni dizhi jinli ce" (A Proposal to Resist U.S. Discrimination against the Chinese), published in *Xin Zhongguo bao* (New China) in 1903, noted:

> In the past, Europeans had been fighting each other to dominate Africa. After possessing Africa, their object of competition pointed to China. The United States sought to join this world competition. That was why it remade its foreign policies, took over Honolulu by force, attacked Cuba, and occupied the Philippines. The rich in the United States desired to use their excessive power globally; therefore, they violated others' rights elsewhere. Honolulu was militarily crucial in the Pacific Ocean; therefore, the United States turned the island into its second naval base to forcefully guard its international trade. The Philippines were the doorway to southeast China; therefore, the United States occupied them to control the trade routes overseas. (Quoted in Ah Ying 1960, 282–83)

Xin Zhongguo bao was the first political Chinese newspaper to be founded overseas. It was established in Honolulu by Liang Qichao and was associated with the diasporan ex-reformist organization Zhongguo weixin hui (The Society to Reform China) (Shi He, Yao Fuzhong, and Ye Cuidi 1991, 341). The essay brought to the fore the global perspective behind the local issue of discrimination and asked the public to see the structural inequality in the world exchange of laborers, capital, and resources. The issue implied in the above passage was not merely the U.S. attempt to turn the Chinese economy into a market for American products, though that was worrisome; nor was it merely discrimination against the overseas Chinese. The implied question, rather, was related to the unjust world to come: Could any people live happily under the shadow of a global power that treated the Filipinos, the Cubans, the Hawaiians, and the overseas Chinese so unfairly?

Perhaps it was this question raised in Honolulu—that of the treatment of overseas Chinese—that so attracted readers, writers, theatrical artists, and journalists in Shanghai. From 1905 to 1907 Shanghai saw the publication of a couple of dozen poems and songs, five novels, several dramas, nine books of documentary and historical writings, and numerous journalistic pieces specifically dealing with the issue (Ah Ying 1960, 2–19). From April 21 to April 23, 1904—just a few months after the essay quoted above appeared in print— *Tocsin* in Shanghai published, among other reports on the theme, a keynote essay entitled "Lun Meiguo lingru huamin" (On U.S. Discrimination against Chinese People). This essay echoed and referred to the article quoted above and stressed the fact that "fairness" in the world had been violated by the anti-Chinese discrimination in the United States. Other Shanghai newspapers—such as *Shibao* (China Times), *Zhongwai ribao* (News of Home and Abroad), and *Nujie bao* (Women's World)—were also actively introducing readers to the issues and facts related to U.S. policy toward the overseas Chinese. According to these papers, a boycott was clearly a way of objecting to the unfairness that was being imposed upon the Chinese at home and abroad. The essay published on April 21 in *Fujian riri xinwen* (Fujian Daily News) voiced this feeling of unfairness simply and directly:

> They (the people of United States) are human beings. So are we. They come to our country without being invited and are well-treated by our treaty. But when we want to go to their country, we are blocked. Their

workers came to our country and made a profit, yet still under our protection. When our workers wanted to go to their country and make a profit, they were prohibited.... I haven't experienced anything in the whole world as unfair as this. (Quoted from Ah Ying 1960, 604–5)

Not surprisingly, in an essay published in *Shibao* just a couple of weeks before the decision to implement a boycott was made, the journalist indicated that a boycott in Shanghai was one way to acquire a fair trade-off in this unequal and unfair cross-ocean exchange:

Since the United States placed restrictions upon Chinese people in order to protect the interests of American workers, we could therefore restrict U.S. goods to protect indigenous products. At least in this way, no one owes the other, and each country could act for its own survival in fair terms. (*Shibao*, April 20–21, 1905)

In a word, the aim of the boycott was to urge a fairer international exchange or to equalize an unequal exchange. Boycotting was a way of objecting to the unfair world that the United States, following the steps of older imperialists, was creating.

Literary works and theatrical performances, along with the journalism in Shanghai, formed an important cultural front for the movement. Literary and theatrical works expressed the shock, the pain, the confusion, and the anger felt at the loss of the "fair world" more effectively than could journalistic and historical texts. Whereas the discrimination against overseas Chinese was an issue of minority rights and taxes in San Francisco and an issue of international politics in the journals of Honolulu, in Shanghai's literature and theater it was a violent violation of the basic principles of individual humanity and human community. As early as 1847, Zhang Weilin, the author of the long poem *Jinshan pian* (The Mountain of Gold), had already found U.S. hostility toward Chinese gold-rushers to be in conflict with the principles of the cosmos of which humans were only a humble part. "Earth offers mankind gold and silver; Shall then humans decide whom not to share with?" (quoted in Ah Ying 1960, 8–9). The author obviously noted the absence in the United States of the belief that all human beings were one.

In 1882 Huang Zunxian (1848–1905), who was then governor of Guangdong Province and who wrote a lengthy poem entitled *Zhu ke pian* (Dismissing the Guests), found the Chinese Exclusion Act to be in direct "conflict with President George Washington's political ideal of liberty" which assumed "everyone to be on an equal footing" ([1882] 1960, 3–4).[27] For Huang, this violation of "George Washington's political ideal of liberty" was at least rhetorically comparable to the loss of "the era of the great harmony" *(datong shi)*, which ancient Chinese saints said had been lost. The disappearance of "the era of the great harmony" meant the loss of the internal quality of the human race represented by the oneness of all to all others, the principle of fairness, the peace and the compassion of the human heart. As a result of this loss, Huang saw the overseas Chinese as suddenly becoming homeless and stateless, drifting about on a strange globe, and thus vulnerable to victimization by all (ibid., 3).

Indeed, this loss of an inhabitable world was a shared feeling and was expressed in different forms. A remote but more positive expression of this loss can be found in Kang Youwei's *Da tong shu* (The Book of Great Harmony), which was written around the same time period. "The great harmonious world"—based upon compassion, a basic human attribute that Kang Youwei assumed everyone held in his or her heart—was little more than a dream of a political utopia, which, ironically, indicated the lack of a habitable world on the real globe.

Perhaps it was the realization of the fatal loss of a fair, livable world that filled the relevant literary writings in Shanghai with anger, grief, and melancholy. The word and the sense of *ku,* "misery" or "suffering," characterized both *Ku Shehui* (A Country of Misery) (1905), an important piece of fiction about the experience of the overseas Chinese, and its sequel, *Ku Xuesheng* (A Suffering Student Abroad) (1906). Melancholy and grief, like mourning, became the only internal traces of the world that had been lost. But as such, they were also an important means to regaining that world.

Jieyu hui (The Burned), a novel by an important late-Qing writer, Wu Jianren (1866–1910), is an allegorical view of this loss. The novel does not describe the life of the overseas Chinese directly but, rather, focuses on the emotional experiences of a wife whose husband was kidnapped and sold to the Americas by a remote "uncle" who profited from the transoceanic labor trade. The wife has lost not only the "world," consisting of her husband and family, but also the hope of a peaceful life when she fell into the hands of the "uncle."

Although she wants to end her own life several times, her soul, through mourning all that has been lost, searches for her missing husband through dreams and prayers. Her grief for the missing family member not only saves her own life but also keeps her husband alive on the other side of the Pacific Ocean. Here, the wife's longing for her husband, an emotional and spiritual action, becomes the agent of reunion and redemption. Grief and melancholy, in this sense, were other forms of longing. It was in the longing for the survival of her husband as well as the other "stateless people" in the world that hope for the self also lay.

Uncle Tom's Cabin in China

Longing for a livable world made the grief of other people and other races one's own individual grief as well. This explains why the Chinese translation of the title of *Uncle Tom's Cabin*, the influential story of slaves in America by Harriet Beecher Stowe (1811–1896), was *Heinu yutian lu*, literally, "Black Slaves Appeal to Heaven." Nothing more accurately conveys the longing for a better world than the word *"yutian*," "appeal to heaven."

This also explains why, from the very beginning, the translation of *Uncle Tom's Cabin* circulated hand in hand with texts about the overseas Chinese. The book, translated by Lin Shu and Wei Yi, was published in woodblock in Hangzhou in 1901. By the end of 1905, its popularity had already warranted a couple of reprints in Shanghai, its inclusion in anthologies of fiction, reference to it in numerous works, and its adaptation by Wang Xiaonong into a Beijing opera performance. It was also transcribed into a spoken drama and was staged in Tokyo in 1907 by Chinese students who were then studying in Japan. In the same year, the spoken drama was performed in China by an amateur troupe that traveled from Shanghai to the northern cities of China.

The translators' prefaces to the 1901 edition established a clear connection between the experiences of African Americans and of Chinese in the United States. Both translators referred to the ongoing U.S. policy of expelling Chinese laborers. Wei Yi, in particular, called for readers to be aware of the possibility of being enslaved. Lin Shu, on the other hand, focused on the possible similarities between the slavery of African Americans and the experiences of overseas Chinese in the United States. Although Uncle Tom and the other characters were fictional, their fate

can mirror the actual situation of Chinese laborers (in the United States). It has been evident that the Chinese in Peru and other places have recently been abused. It is hard to anticipate the suffering of the "yellow race" in the future. I can only hope that the readers do not think that what is recorded here is merely a ridiculous fiction! (Lin Shu [1901] 1960a, 661–62)

By borrowing the narrative of African American slaves to voice the situation of the overseas Chinese, Lin Shu set his view apart from the general view of African Americans and Chinese held by his contemporaries. Lin's contemporaries often made subtle distinctions between the Chinese and the African Americans based on the supposed cultural inferiority of the latter. Huang Zunxian, for example, while expressing the grievance caused by the unequal content of the Chinese Exclusion Act, wondered why the black people, though "less cultured," were allowed to stay where they were, but the Chinese were expelled so harshly ([1882] 1960, 3–4). Liang Qichao followed suit when writing about the issue (Liang Qichao [1905] 1982, 387–426). Lin Shu, on the other hand, urged his readers to focus on the interchangeable experiences of the African Americans and the overseas Chinese. In his preface, he warns the reader of a historical continuum between enslaving Africans on one end and discriminating against Chinese on the other:

After research, we know that the history of enslaving African black people in America's California started in 1619, when a Dutch warship took and sold twenty or so black slaves to Armstrong village. This was the beginning of white people's enslaving of black people. At this time there was not even a United States. Washington founded the United States for and according to the principle of public good. He did not seek after his own personal power. But the system of slavery was so hard to remove that he did not end slavery while he was alive. It was not until Lincoln's time that the system of slavery was formally abolished. But not long after that, the ways that had been used to treat African black people were extended to treat people with yellow skin. ([1901] 1960b, 658)

Within the limit of racial terminology, Lin Shu was able to show a parallel between enslaving Africans and abusing Chinese. Obviously, the way the overseas Chinese were being treated made Lin Shu question the true significance of the abolition of slavery in the United States. Like Huang Zunxian, Lin Shu too sees the discrimination against the Chinese as a betrayal of the political ideals of liberty of both George Washington and Abraham Lincoln.

Lin Shu observed a difference between African slaves and overseas Chinese only in this continuum of slavery and racism. After giving a brief history of the enslavement of Africans in the United States, Lin Shu went on to elaborate the history of Chinese laborers in California.

> At the beginning, they went as laborers. After years, they sent savings from their salary back home. Some Americans thought the Chinese laborers would take away their silver and therefore abused the Chinese, prevented them from settling, and forbade them from coming. For this particular reason, yellow-skinned people might have been treated worse in the U.S. than the black-skinned. ([1901] 1960a, 658)

Whether the Chinese might have been treated worse was impossible to say, as Lin himself quickly admitted. But Lin's account pointed to a specific labor-capital relationship distinct from that of "master and slave." Chinese laborers were free laborers; therefore, they were seen as competitors for silver and were excluded and discriminated against in the United States. Lin laid bare here the crucial political problems that the United States would have to face for decades or centuries after the abolition of slavery: racism, global expansion, minority politics, and betrayal of the spirit of democracy in dealing with international affairs, as well as the politics in immigration, discrimination, and law-making. Not only the overseas Chinese but also other races, though not enslaved in the United States, might very well be mistreated to the same extent. "Some white people can only treat people of other races with discrimination, and the suffering of people of Poland, Egypt, and India might be even worse (than what was described in *Uncle Tom's Cabin*)" (Lin Shu [1901] 1960b, 662).

Not surprisingly, *Uncle Tom's Cabin* gave expression to sorrowful feelings and grieving for other people's suffering and for the loss of a livable world of fairness. As Lin Shu clearly indicated, the other people's loss of the inhabitable world was actually also the loss of the Chinese, since they shared that world. Here, in translating and reading about *Uncle Tom's Cabin*, grief and sorrow became, or acted as, sympathy and compassion, which Kang Youwei had found to be the origin of Datong, the great harmonious world (1935, 2–14). In the preface to a historical work about the Chinese Exclusion Act in the United States, *Tongbao shounue ji* (The Suffering of Fellow Chinese), published in Guangzhou in 1905, the author described how the Chinese experience made even more heartbreaking the experiences of the African American slaves and the Poles he had read about in the translations of *Uncle Tom's Cabin* and *The Fall of Poland*:

Years ago, when I read *Black Slaves Appeal to Heaven,* my heart became
heavy and down-trodden with sorrow. Later, when I read *The Fall of
Poland,* my heart again was downtrodden and full of sorrow. Now, I read
The Suffering of Fellow Chinese, and my heart is once more filled with
grief and sorrow, so heavy that I don't even know how to put them in
words. (Anonymous [1905] 1960, 522)

To a heart capable of compassion, the misery of the overseas Chinese
repeated twice, at least on an emotional level, the trauma of the experiences of the African American slaves and the Poles. A work that could
connect these three experiences had to be, itself, one of compassion. In
the preface to *Uncle Tom's Cabin,* it was suggested that reading the book
could be called a "compassionate association" or "compassionate reading" that expressed cultural and political concern about what the world
had become.

Beside the Poles and the African Americans, compassionate associations were also made between the Chinese and the Cubans who were
subjugated by the United States (Zheng Guanying [1905] 1982, 6–7). The
same kind of compassionate associations were made between the overseas Chinese in the United States and those in Australia. In a similar
way, the anonymous author of a new Yuefu lyric poem, *Tan xiang shan*
(Honolulu), compared the misery of the overseas Chinese in Hawaii
with the sad history of the Jews of the Diaspora who were adrift and
discriminated against for centuries:

Honolulu used to be a thriving city of commerce
Now burned into dry dirt as the ruin of the palace of Ah-fang!
Nothing is left except your tears over the tons of losses
Taxes mount high, Chinese forbidden
(We) walked with tiptoes on earth but
Could not find even a place to stand, and
Abused in the south of Australia and the north of the United States!
. . . .
Can't you see the traces of tears that the Jewish Diaspora
Left on the roads behind their wandering footsteps?
My heart trembles in the chill, at such a thought of Jews!
(Anonymous [1905] 1982, 14)

The compassionate association between the Chinese in Hawaii and the
Jews of the Diaspora represented here could not make a world of Datong,
but it was enough to build an imagined community of which they were
a part in the same way that the Poles and the African Americans were.

This global community came from the sense of simultaneity created by a vernacular print market (Anderson 1984), yet it reiterated the utopia that Kang Youwei had discussed in *Da tong shu*, a community that eliminated national boundaries, which compassionate thinking could not comprehend.

Compassionate associations involved not only sharing and understanding the experiences of others but acting on their behalf as well. A subject who feels for someone else may in turn act for this someone else. This explains why *Uncle Tom's Cabin* was revised in further adaptation. Whereas the boycott movement was short-lived because of conflict between those who were and were not involved in trade with the United States, the adaptation of the African American story continued. The translated *Uncle Tom's Cabin* traveled from Shanghai to Japan, where it was transformed into a spoken drama and performed by an amateur troupe of Chinese students, Chunliu (Spring Willows), in Tokyo in 1907.[28] The performance was well-received by Japanese journalists, writers, and theater critics (Chen Dingsha 1987, 20–57). More importantly, this performance may well have been the way that the story of American blacks first came to be known in Japan. Certainly, it was through this performance that the compassionate association between African Americans and Asians that had been nurtured in Shanghai was disseminated outside of China for the first time.

The synopsis of the performance gives us a hint to how the "compassionate subject" became the "acting for" subject, and how, through the "acting for," grief and longing eventually paved the way to a better world. The performance consisted of five acts.

Synopsis of *Black Slaves Appeal to Heaven*
As Performed in Tokyo, 1907

Act 1. The House of Mr. Shelby

Begins with the introduction of the main characters: Eliza, George, their son, and Tom, and ends with Mr. Shelby agreeing to sell Tom and the son of Eliza and George to Haley, the slave trader to whom Shelby owes money.

Act 2. A Celebration at the Whitney Cotton Factory

Begins with a scene of celebration at the Whitney factory with singing and dancing and the introduction of guests who have been invited to attend the celebration. The factory owner bestows a medal on George but is stopped by Harris, George's previous owner, who is jealous of his success and wants to take him back.

Act 3. Parting

Eliza overhears the slave trader's plan of taking away her son and Tom. She asks help from Shelby's wife but does not get any promise. George returns with the news that he cannot work at the factory anymore. He does not want to return with Harris and plans to escape.

Act 4. At Tom's Cabin

Eliza runs in with her young son and warns Tom of his danger.

Act 5. Fight at the Rock

George and his friends escape and meet Eliza on the way. Harris and his men chase after them. George and his friends fight for their liberty and escape successfully. (Ouyang 1984, 141)

There are two aspects of this adaptation that are worth special attention. First, the drama shifted the work's focus from Tom, a more inward-looking Christian, to George, a more outspoken and rebellious figure. Another interesting detail is the fact that Tom was listed as being in the last act, the big escape. As student actor Ouyang Yuqian recalled, the ending of the novel, in which Tom is beaten to death, was changed. According to the synopsis, Tom's appearance in "Fight at the Rock" suggests that he escaped with George and Eliza (Ouyang 1984, 142). Lin Shu and Wei Yi's translation had already reduced the Christian color of Tom's virtue, and here, in the spoken drama, Tom's passivity was further diminished. George and Eliza's choice determined Tom's future as well. The adaptation and the transformation of the original novel emphasized the agency on the slave side. This change in plot brightened up the story.

The brighter nature of the drama was also manifested in the way the actors dressed in the production. It is interesting to note that skin color was not at all the only way that the black people were represented. Rather, as Ouyang Yuqian recalled, the actors chose clothes and hairstyles that they thought would be "touching." Even though Tom was depicted in the novel as having short hair, the actors who played both George and Tom seem to have chosen to wear their hair long, as is seen on the next page of the playbill. The slave girls, portrayed by Ouyang Yuqian himself and others, danced in long gowns (Ouyang [1959] 1990).

The clothing worn in this performance was a mixture of styles worn by people from different countries and from different historical periods; it is possible that they were chosen not only according to what the actors thought was touching but also on the basis of what was available to rent in Japanese theatrical costume shops (Li Chang 1987, 252–308).[29]

For a variety of complex reasons, though, the bright appearance of the main figures enhanced the effect of the final act of the drama, "Fight at the Rock" (Figure 14). The effect of this act can be seen in the drawing provided in the playbill. In this drawing, the Western "scroll-effect" was made horizontal and, more importantly, it was annotated on the sides with titles and the synopsis done in Chinese calligraphy. Adapting both Western scroll-effect design and European figure drawing, this picture did not depict either the main characters, George and Tom, or the other slaves as being "black." They appeared, instead, with long hair and in traditionally heroic poses. The Caucasian slave hunters, in fact, were drawn in dark and negative ways. This "dark" quality was only given to those who failed to treat others as fellow human beings.

The second aspect of the play I want to discuss is the way that George's technological invention, a relatively unimportant detail occupying a mere two pages in the novel, was turned into an entire act of celebration in this production. This interesting transformation brought to life a "colored moment" of creation in human history (if not a colored temporality) that was easily effaced. From the synopsis printed on the playbill, one can see that many details that did not exist in the novel were added to Act 2: George's winning a medal and giving a speech at a ceremony to which many guests have been invited and who end up enjoying a great dance party. According to Ouyang Yuqian's reminiscences, these guests were played by friends of the Chunliu members, who came from different countries and could play these roles in whatever ways they liked (Ouyang 1984, 134–74). As a result, in the celebration scene, there were Chinese who sang Beijing opera, Indians who played "Indian aristocrats," and Koreans, Japanese, and many others who danced on the stage in their own ethnic clothes (156). Ouyang Yuqian commented that although the celebration scene did not correspond to the novel in any way, he and his coactors had no reference for what it would have realistically looked like anyway. "We just did what we thought of, but the scene was very lively and the audiences loved it" (142). In this way, the act monumentalized

Figure 14. The playbill from the Chinese performance of *Uncle Tom's Cabin.*
From Zhongguo yishu yanjiu yuan Huaju yanjiusuo [Institute of Spoken Drama,
Research Institute of Chinese Academy of Art], comp., *Zhongguo huaju shiliaoji*
[Compiled source materials of the history of spoken drama] (Beijing: Wenhua
yishu chubanshe, 1987), volume 1, n.p.

the slave's technological invention by making it the reason for celebration, the cause for a cosmopolitan gathering, and the reason for the coming theatrical festivity.

The limited records of the Tokyo performance clearly showed the influence of the literary and cultural aspects of the boycott that had been nurtured in Shanghai. In the circulation of *Uncle Tom's Cabin,* the grief and misery of those who were enslaved and those who were discriminated against were transformed into a compassionate act of liberation. The images of the overseas Chinese and the African American slaves, too, were transformed. They were not seen merely as cosufferers of racism and discrimination but as radical fellow human beings capable of fighting for freedom in a compassionate imagination. As the spoken drama and its performers traveled back to China from Tokyo, these transformations, in turn, enriched the meaning of the "radical urban festive culture" of Shanghai. The ideal of this radical festivity was not necessarily revolutionary in a political sense. It was, rather, a radical ideal about mutual humanity, regardless of all differences—differences that had served as reasons for acts of discrimination in the United States, the country of "liberty and equality for all."

Conclusion

In the short period of time from 1900 to 1907, Shanghai was characterized by a festive culture of semi-illicit actors, journalists, political diasporans, writers, members of chambers of commerce, and students traveling between Shanghai and Tokyo. During this time, the city saw a galaxy of books, journals, telegraphs, and translations providing images of Asian and European assassins; Polish, Filipino, and Vietnamese revolutionaries; and Russian and French anarchists. In addition, publications about the plight of the overseas Chinese and translated versions of *Uncle Tom's Cabin* mobilized a boycott movement in the city. This cultural nexus was the basis of Shanghai's urban festivity. And in the process, urban festivity itself became associated with a higher cause: It did not merely reflect a dreamlike state of togetherness in which everyone was having fun; more importantly, it expressed the anxiety, anger, and objection that was being felt about an imminent world in which unequal exchanges of resources and labor, discrimination, and racism were dominant. This anxiety, anger and objection to such a world order demonstrates how the urban festivity that emerged around the boycott movement was a radical festivity.

The 1905 boycott, I would like to note here, was the beginning of a series of similar but even larger movements, most typically the May Fourth movement of 1919 and the demonstrations against the May Thirtieth Massacre in 1925. These two movements involved ten to a hundred times as many demonstrators as the 1905 boycott. The leadership of these movements changed, too. The Shanghai General Workers Union and the Shanghai Student Associations played more active roles in these later movements than did the Shanghai Chamber of Commerce. Yet the rational or cultural logic remained the same: to object to the unjust world order that was about to determine the fate of the people and the land of China. The later movements continued to take the position and to use the methods that had mobilized the 1905 boycott. Journalism, literature, public speeches, posters, shop-by-shop and street-by-street canvasses, picketing, strikes, and exhortations not to buy or sell Japanese and British goods all became familiar aspects of urban life in Shanghai. Like the

1905 boycott, these later movements too had dual political and cultural targets. While the boycott of 1905 targeted both the Qing state and the foreign policy of the United States, the May Fourth movement denied the authority of both the post-Qing government and those powers at the Versailles Conference (April 28, 1919) who awarded the former German leasehold of Jiaozhou to Japan (instead of returning it to China). What I suggest here is that the radical urban festivity discussed in this chapter provided one crucial cultural condition for the birth of the unruly urban public of Shanghai.

PART III
Interiors Projecting the Globe

FIVE

Reenvisioning the Urban Interior:
Gardens and the Paradox of the Public Sphere

The last part of the book deals with the practices of urban space that came along with the inside-out-turn of the Qing Empire and that reflected the disharmonious overlapping between imperial and imperialist histories. This section of the book focuses in particular on those cross-cultural spatial constructions in gardens, entertainment centers, and proto-malls in Chinese cities upon which the changing urban societies of China projected various versions of their reading of the globe as well as their ideal of "the world." The central concern of this and the following chapter is the question of how to conceive the meaning of "modern facade" or "cosmopolitan landscape" in a city of a noncapitalist or a complex society, if they are neither imitative nor derivative of the Modern City of the West.

The intellectual background of such a concern can be traced to the theoretical writings about the Modern City in the West. The emergence of urban interiors of the "world"—such as crystal palaces, arcades, malls, and the structures of world expositions in nineteenth-century European and American cities—represented two related aspects of the Modern City in Western terms. They reified the "production of space" in the industrial capitalist era (Lefebvre 1991), on the one hand, and on the other, the global circulation of commodities, capital, labor, and cultures (Driver and Gilbert 1999). Lefebvre saw the urban space of the industrial era as involving not only technology but also the class relations of production (1991, 259–60), so much so that he saw modern Paris, for example, as a product of "class strategies" (1995, 77, 112–13). Walter Benjamin

(1997, 1999), though he too took urban spaces to be the product of "the age of mechanized reproduction," also saw them in terms of consumption: The ambiguous modern subject, or *flâneur*, not only contemplated the urban modernity while wandering about the city but also sipped coffee behind the glass windows, consuming "the landscape of the round" (1999, 422–23). For still other urban critics, these manufactured urban spaces, as materialized class visions of the "world," were inevitably the sites where the racial and cultural discriminations were most obviously arranged and rearranged (Abu-Lughod 1999; Rydell 1984). These urban spaces represented the globality of the Modern Time projected by the bourgeois class in the West.

Urban interiors of "the world," however, "emerged" beyond the metropolises of the industrial capitalist West and in the cities of the Qing dynasty's heyday, cities that had experienced neither colonization nor even an industrial "modern" moment. The upper-class urban interiors of eighteenth-century China were embodiments of a cultural vision of the world and of multiculturalism, though this vision was arguably less imperialist than that projected by world expositions in London or St. Louis a century later. China's principal heartland cities, too, were characterized by a reversion of the interior (human, Chinese) and the exterior (cosmos, non-Chineseness) in cultural and geographic terms. In Yangzhou, one of the focal cities of late-imperial China and on which this chapter will primarily focus,[1] high-class residents used these urban interiors, built with precious materials from the frontiers of the Qing Empire and with Eurasian styles here and there, to manifest a multiculturalism camouflaged within the glory of the Manchu state. Versions of these transnational urban spaces appeared in Shanghai only a few decades after the decline of Yangzhou in the early nineteenth century. Travelers to Shanghai during the 1880s could observe "authentic" European-style landscapes, without necessarily missing the afterlife of hybrid gardens of the Jiangnan cities, including the imperial Yangzhou. Transcultural urban interiors appeared in Yangzhou *before* being introduced into the more or less industrialized Shanghai. And conversely, Shanghai, a site of modernity in Asia, retained the previous versions of globality.

This "Yangzhou before Shanghai" formula highlights the existence of an earlier, Asia-based cross-cultural urban space that thrived a century or more before the flowering of "world cities" in the heart of modern capitalism. It disputes the notion that the "bourgeois" materiality is original and inevitable, but, more important, it raises questions that are at the center of the concern of this and the following chapter: How are we to conceptualize *the urban*—the social dimension of the city (Lefebvre 1995)—as well as its historical change in the face of modernity in a non-Western and noncolonial context? How do we conceive, for example, the relationship between the two (or more) versions of urban globality, the eighteenth-century version(s) embodied in Yangzhou and the nineteenth-century version(s) of Euro-American cities and Shanghai? Shall we see their relationship as translational (Chakrabarty 2000), conflicting, or collaborative (Liu 1962)? Who would be the earlier, and the later, subject(s) who envisioned the "world," and how do we name these agents—as a Chinese bourgeois class, or quasi-bourgeois classes, or nonclasses? The chapters in this part do not mean to provide ultimate answers to the questions but intend to treat the questions with the seriousness they deserve.

This chapter finds that the Yangzhou-Shanghai transition reflects what I call a "decentering turn" in China's urban society and the "submergence" of the upper class, a process during which Shanghai was turned into a political and cultural frontier positioned against both the Qing Empire and Western imperial systems. I start by exploring the Yangzhou gardens, which reached their apogee in the late eighteenth century, as a spatial manifestation of new cultural conceptions in the rising Qing Empire and among the high-ranking literati and merchant-officials who built them. I then turn to Shanghai, which by the mid-nineteenth century had replaced Yangzhou as the transposition center of the Qing while acquiring new status as a treaty port. I focus on the overlapping codings of the Hardoon Garden and the Zhang Garden, which I interpret as a revival of eighteenth-century cosmopolitan culture within a "frontier" city of the nineteenth-century world. Finally, I examine the way the "submergence" (vis-à-vis emergence) of China's quasi-bourgeois class reinvented Shanghai's overcoded urban interiors into critical public spaces, where discussions and actions of resisting Qing imperial politics and the imperialist pressures of foreign states took place. Shanghai gardens were transformed symbolically and practically into a critical front aimed against both imperial and imperialist powers.

Bringing the Empire to the Interior

Even though the Qing dynasty in the eighteenth century was a transregional military power and controlled a powerful export economy, the urban materiality of its heartland was no less centralized and "multi-cultural" than that of its European counterparts in terms of its collection and concentration of knowledge and resources from afar. The wealth and power of a strong, dominant social class were instrumental in projecting the urban elites' imaginary conception of the world onto the city's urban space; values often seen as unique to European modernity, such as productivity and technology, were also part of the urban landscape of the Qing. This section demonstrates that in many ways, the urban materiality of eighteenth-century China preceded similar developments in the West.

In terms of building urban interiors, it was Yangzhou, not Shanghai, that was the early flagship of the Qing Empire. It was known for rich, ostentatious grand interiors that were reputed to surpass all other gardens in the Jiangnan region. By "interior" I refer not merely to indoor space but also to the aestheticized garden area built within an enclosure. This type of space articulates and expands the psychological interiority and functions to separate what is internal from the external. As Tobei Mayer-Fong's work on Yangzhou history (2003) shows, the city had been transformed from a particularly bloody site of Ming resistance to the Manchu army into a prosperous transportation hub and a center of economic transactions and cultural exchange.[2] As the Qing dynasty established its rule, the memory of the bloody history of the Manchu invasion was systematically repressed, local landmarks were reconstructed, and literary culture was recoded (Mayer-Fong 2003, 75–127, 165–95).[3] As the dynasty prospered, Yangzhou was completely transformed. The new urban spaces of Yangzhou were manifestations of the prosperity and productivity that derived from the vast territorial expanse of the empire and were not simply reflections of local culture. These spaces were designed not only for private pleasure but also for frequent large gatherings of a high society populated by traveling literati, artists, and official-scholars, as well as the Emperor Qianlong (1736–1795) himself. The cultural imaginary embodied in these grand interiors thus represented symbolically the full scope of the empire.

By the eighteenth century, the residents of the city had been joined by powerful elites, especially the salt merchants, who had official titles and who appropriated literati status (Mayer-Fong 2003; Ho Ping-ti 1954). As a multiethnic empire founded through conquest, the Manchu state established various flexible political, military, economic, ethnic, and cultural institutions in order to turn different groups into its subjects. Because salt was a crucial resource for industrial and military use, the Qing state sought to monopolize salt production by controlling a specific social group, the salt merchants. Salt merchants were granted official titles along with absolute power over the salt business. They were privileged in that they gained secure official positions without having to go through the strict civil service examination that was the standard route to officialdom for all Chinese. They were urbanized and lived in luxury.[4] However, in their total dependence on the state, their social and economic positions were insecure.

In many ways, the salt merchants' rise as a powerful upper-class group in the Qing Empire paralleled that of the bourgeoisie in the West, except that the salt merchants did not have the legal and economic right to manipulate the production and distribution of materials. Economically, they were state managers, not owners, of the dynasty's most important monopoly—the production and transportation of salt—and they accumulated vast wealth through their dominance of this sector of the economy (Zeng Yangfeng 1998). But the salt merchants also played an increasingly visible role in helping the Qing state define itself culturally. Over the course of just a few generations, the salt merchants acquired and displayed a variety of cultural resources: taste, talent, musical and theatrical expertise, art and book collections, erudite classical and scientific knowledge, and European scientific and technical devices (Mayer-Fong 2003; Ho Ping-ti 1954).[5] They had the honor of receiving Qing emperors on their grand tours, first the Emperor Kangxi (1662–1722), and then his grandson Qianlong.[6] These tours allowed the salt merchants to turn Yangzhou into a material display of their cultural ideals with the authority conferred by imperial power. Endorsed by the emperor himself, the new urban spaces constructed by the salt merchants ensured the city's position as the great interior of the Qing Empire.

To welcome the emperors, Yangzhou's elite families turned the natural surroundings of the city, even their own properties, into a variety of landscapes, including Islamic and European landscapes. These constructed landscapes exhibited specific themes, which I discuss in what follows, that have been thought unique to Western bourgeois culture: sovereignty, the sublime, exoticism, productivity, and technology.

The Yangzhou elites' embrace of imperial sovereignty was strikingly displayed in the architectural face they presented to the world. The city's entrance was made to symbolize its residents' willingness to be subjects of the Qing dynasty. It was customary for the emperors to arrive in Yangzhou by passing under a bridge built at the northern threshold of the city. This bridge stood as the main entrance to the city. In the context of the geography of the empire as a whole, Yangzhou was symbolically the northern entrance to the region of Jiangnan, China's heartland, and it was the frontier of the Manchu state before the Manchu conquered the south. The bridge at the north end of Yangzhou thus symbolically marked the division between Manchu north and the Han-dominated south. Neither the salt merchants nor the emperors would have been unaware of the symbolic meaning of this geographic division. It was on the bridge, at this symbolic and geographic division, that the salt merchants of the city inscribed the characters *Ying'en qiao* (The Bridge of Welcoming Grace). The characters faced north, the direction from which the emperor would appear along the river (Zhao Zhibi [1775] 1983: 44). The character *en* invoked a cliché often used by imperial subjects to acknowledge the benevolence of an emperor who holds the mandate of heaven. Prepared for the emperor, the bridge thus demonstrated the civilian hosts' self-identification as loyal subjects of the Qing dynasty (Figure 15). The name of the river was also changed, to the River of Welcoming Grace. The bridge was thus a territorial landmark that transformed a natural river of the region into the property of the dynasty and guaranteed its submission to imperial sovereignty.

The architectural style of Yangzhou was a material transcription of its sublime status, a self-conscious exhibition by its elite residents of its cultural superiority. In their shapes and grandeur, imperial architectural styles were, of course, supposed to embody the mandate of heaven and imperial sublimity, but it was taboo to reproduce these styles. Buildings in Yangzhou, however, followed the models of imperial palaces recorded in *Gongduan yingzao lu* (The Imperial Records of Construction and Architecture).[7] With much variation, Yangzhou residential architecture displayed imperial grandeur and spaciousness by emphasizing multiple divisions and the number of thresholds in the halls. Large halls had three front bays and two side bays (known as five-set halls), usually with multiple layers of roofs. Another variation had five facades and two side facades, with multiple layers of roofs (a seven-set hall) (Li Dou [1795] 1984, 373–407).[8] The multiple bays and layers of roofs brought a palatial style to residential buildings. A scholar, calligrapher, and connois-

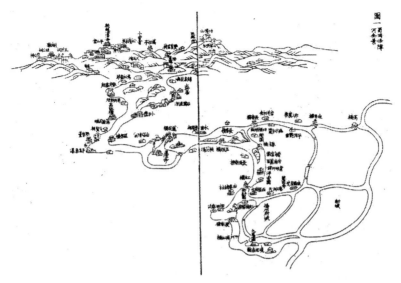

Figure 15. Diagrammatic map of Ying'en River. Ying'en Bridge is the left of the two bridges on the right side. From Zhao Zhibi, comp., *Pingshan tang tuzhi* [The map gazetteer of Pingshan Pavilion] (Taipei: Chengwen chubanshe, [1775] 1983), 1:44a.

seur from Wuxi, Qian Yong (1759–1844), was struck upon his arrival in Yangzhou by the palatial magnificence of its architecture, and he particularly praised the way ordinary buildings—*ting* (halls)—in the gardens were built with the look of "a palace" *(dian)* (Qian Yong 1979, 326–27). These palace-like halls were wider and taller and had more roofs than the buildings one usually found in typical garden residences in Suzhou and Hangzhou. These buildings often transgressed the traditional code, according to which the number of thresholds and roof layers of an official residence were supposed to fit the rank of the official.[9] This transgression, together with the labyrinthine architectural detail and luxurious display of artifacts, further positioned the city's residents as imperial subjects, that is, above ordinary citizens and civil servants.

The exoticism of Yangzhou's material culture was a conscious manifestation of an urban society capable of luxurious consumption, with a high demand for rare goods from afar. As the urban heart of the empire, the city imported luxury goods from the Qing's vast frontiers and boasted fashions no less exotic than those found in the bourgeois interiors of nineteenth-century European cities. Built by the wealthy, the city and its gardens wove together different architectural styles, using rare materials obtained from the far reaches of the empire and from foreign lands as varied as Burma, Arabia, and Europe.[10] Precious woods were imported, including phoebe *nanmu*, redwood, red sandalwood, pear wood, ginkgo, littleleaf boxwood, and the more ordinary cypress. Precious building materials, such as stone from Anhui *(Xuan shi)*, from Lingbi Mountain *(Lingbi shi)*, from the bed of Taihu Lake *(Taihu shi)*, and shipped from Gaozi County *(Gaozi shi)*, were used (Li Dou [1795] 1984).[11] Marble was shipped from Sichuan and Qinghai; jade, from Yunnan and Burma;[12] and clocks, large pieces of glass, and other exotic European goods, from Guangdong and overseas (Li Dou [1795] 1984, 163). The city's residents consumed these materials in huge quantities: *Nanmu* and other precious woods were used not only for the main parts of many buildings but also to build the entire structure of a palace, or *dian*. Crockery made of porcelain was manufactured in four colors, and there were nine types of colored glaze roof decorations (Li Dou [1795] 1984, 384–85). These exotic and artsy materials were the stuff of upper-class spectacle, and flaunting the easy consumption of these precious goods was essential for the city of Yangzhou to gain its status as the flagship of the empire.

European arts and crafts formed a specific kind of exoticism in the eighteenth-century upper-class culture of the Qing. This exoticism was fashionable in painting, crafts, and architecture. European architectural styles and images of actual foreign residences (such as the Thirteen Foreign Factories in Guangzhou) appeared as motifs in Qing travel writing and in oil paintings by Chinese artists in the early nineteenth century (Lee and Philadelphia Museum of Art 1984, 35, 38, 39).[13] Just as European chinoiserie architecture was reproduced from images on teapots, embroidery, and other imported Chinese crafts (Honour 1962; Crossman 1991), the Eurasian gardens in eighteenth-century Yangzhou were very likely also to be replicas of images from Western-style paintings, travel writing, and practical technological books that were circulating in the court and among the elites. Yangzhou architecture deliberately played with *xifa*, namely, European styles and architectural technologies (Zhao Zhibi [1775] 1983, 261–64). A renowned Yangzhou native, Li Dou, noted that at least four major gardens contained structures that were deliberately built in Western style.[14] The salt merchants fashioned their residences in various exotic ways: constructing halls with the depth of European design, attaching verandas to the fronts of buildings, decorating buildings with clocks or clockworks and mirrors, and using glass as a building material (Li Dou [1795] 1984, 367, 140–41, 257–58, 162–63).[15]

Exoticism was important to the formation of the Yangzhou upper-class identity just as it was to the European bourgeoisie. Whereas Chinese exoticism can be traced back to the court culture of the Qing, which was built upon the tribute system, commerce, and missionary connections, European exoticism accompanied colonialism and forceful possession of slave labor and global resources (Spurr 1993; Pratt 1994; McLintock 1995).

Finally, technology and productivity played a crucial role in Yangzhou elites' material transcription of the ideals of empire. Eighteenth-century Yangzhou was known for its scientific cosmopolitanism. The city was home to both formal and informal networks of renowned astronomers and mathematicians, who assembled technological and scientific knowledge from classical and translated sources (Hu Minghui 2002). Manifestations of this technological imaginary were especially evident in the properties of several Yangzhou families who transformed their estates into landscapes displaying the significance of production and agriculture. Two of these landscapes, recorded as "Hanshang nongsang" (Agriculture and Sericulture by the Han River) and "Xinghua cunshe" (Village of Apricot Flowers), were conceived after the drawings from *Yuzhi gengzhi tu* (The Kangxi Edition of Agriculture and Sericulture, Illustrated), a book that was signed and filled with poems by Emperor Kangxi.[16] These landscapes included buildings in imitation of those of the textile industries illustrated in *Yuzhi gengzhi tu*: a raw silk factory, drying rooms, and dye houses (Zhao Zhibi [1775] 1983, 2:23b–24a). There was a section on energy where Western-style windmills *(fengche)* were displayed side by side with Chinese waterwheels to honor "ways of replacing human energy with clever mechanical designs" (Zhao Zhibi [1775] 1983, 2:23a).[17] This particular landscape was an elaboration of a poem that the Emperor Kangxi had contributed to the "Shuiche" (Waterwheels) section in the *Yuzhi gengzhi tu* in which he appraised the progress of agricultural technology from the previous dynasties to the present (Jiao Bingzhen 1879, 1:23–24). These representations of agriculture and sericulture were an integral part of imperial interiors, and they exalted development, technology, and productivity with no less enthusiasm than did European and American world fairs.

Although these architectural visions of productivity, advances in technology, and commodification of the vast resources imported from the empire's frontiers were in principle "premodern" and "noncapitalist," they reflected intensifying conflicts similar to those produced by "development" in other parts of the world. The concentration of capital and resources, on the one hand, and increasing population and social unrest, on the other hand, eventually led to a crisis for the Qing Empire.[18] The centralization of the salt merchants' wealth allowed them to compete with the state for resources and, as some officials found, stymied the state's efforts to enlarge its tax base. In 1792 the state came up with a reformed salt policy aimed at reducing the monopoly of the salt merchants and opening channels for competition in the salt economy (Li Ming-ming and Wu Hui 1977). The new policy did not completely overcome the larger crisis facing the empire, but it did dramatically undercut the political and economic privileges of this group of elites. The bond between the imperial state and imperial subjects was effectively broken from this point on, and the salt merchants lost their role as the most powerful official-merchant group in the empire.

An even larger crisis struck Yangzhou: The Grand Canal, the crucial south-north transportation line that had been the central geographic feature of the city's rise to power, was damaged by repeated floods in the early nineteenth century. The damage to the Grand Canal produced a huge financial burden that the Qing state, already facing financial problems and resource shortages, was reluctant to shoulder. The state gave up regular maintenance of the Grand Canal and began to ship grains and salt via other channels, including through the port of Shanghai (Leonard 1996). This change further undermined the economic base of Yangzhou and with it the cultural preeminence of its once-wealthy residents. With the fall of the salt merchants and with dwindling financial resources, Yangzhou lost its role as the dream city of the empire. Traveling literati noted that the garden sites recorded in Li Dou's 1775 book had disappeared during the short time between 1820 and 1830.[19] Only a few politically and economically powerful figures could afford to build new gardens, and sons of many salt-merchant families survived by selling off the precious building materials in their gardens (Chen Congzhou 1983, 3–19).

My point in drawing attention to the prominence of Yangzhou's architecture before Shanghai emerged on the scene is not to recall the glory of the Qing Empire but to note that the crisis and collapse of a "dream city" could be experienced by the upper classes of any country or region. The collapse of the urban imagination at this moment in China was closely linked to an urgent internal crisis (uneven distribution of wealth, large-scale unemployment, corruption) that was greatly intensified by the shortage of resources within the Qing Empire. The state's policy aimed at fixing the problem led to an undercutting of the power of the salt merchants. The Western bourgeoisie, comparably speaking, "survived" such crises only by exploiting non-European resources in the New World and Africa. As Kenneth Pomeranz's superb analysis (2000) of the "rise" of industrial capitalism illustrates, colonialism, slavery, and migration from the Old World to the New helped ease the constraint of resources shared by the core zones of Europe, China, and other parts of the world. The colonial experience even enhanced the ties between the bourgeois class and their emerging imperialist nation-states.[20] The fall of Yangzhou, in this sense, indicates a split between the state and a powerful upper-class group resulting from the pressures of insufficient resources and other crises.

The fall of Yangzhou during the 1820s was the beginning of a great geographic shift of China's urban centers from the heartland to the coast. The scale of this shift was broadened by the Taiping Rebellion, which further pushed the economic and cultural centers of the Qing toward the coast. Viewed in light of the fall of Yangzhou, the rise of Shanghai was not so much the beginning of a globality brought about by the West as it was a remedy for the unavoidable internal decay of the existing globality, which was comparable to rather than derivative of the sources of the material imagination of the European bourgeoisie.

The Decentered Cosmopolitan Interior

It was only after the Opium War that images of a "closed China" contrasting with a "cosmopolitan West" began to circulate widely in Western media. These images initiated a discursive process that might be called the "indigenizing" of China's urban past. French Lazarist missionary Evariste Régis Huc's book *The Chinese Empire* was one of the earliest to emphasize that the "Chinese mind" clung only to its own ideas and impressions (1855, 45, 666). An American journalist put the idea more precisely: "The civilization of Europe was the product of the interfusion of diverse types of culture from Judea, Greece, Rome, Egypt, and the remote countries of Western Asia. The civilization of China was indigenous" (Mason 1939, 73). This orientalist discourse, characteristic of the nineteenth century, could emerge only from the deliberate erasure of an earlier globality that had allowed cultural exchanges between China and the rest of the world, including Europe. This erasure in turn attributes the birth of Shanghai entirely to a new globality centered around the West. To reverse this erasure, I would like to emphasize the fact that until the 1880s, the landscape of urban interiors in Shanghai very much continued, even revived, the kind of cross-cultural cosmopolitanism in urban landscapes of the Chinese cities before this point. The question one should explore is not how modernity or globality penetrated China but, rather, how the older, ongoing projection of the world we saw in Yangzhou came to meet and fuse with the new imperialist world?

As I have repeatedly indicated, Shanghai represented a reconstructed urban culture at a very unique position: the overlapping edges of both the Qing Empire and Western imperialism, particularly that of the British Empire. Being at the *overlapping* edges of these two empires meant Shanghai was exposed to double powers: Its urban landscapes were doubly imprinted, for example, by groups with allegiance to both the Qing and the British empires. Having just survived a prolonged fight with the Taipings, the Qing Empire began its cultural, military, and economic Tongzhi Restoration in the coastal regions. In Shanghai, enterprises supported by state monopoly brought to the city the Yangwu (Foreign Affairs) institutions and such official concerns as arsenals, shipyards, navigation companies, and textile factories (Liu 1962). The city also became the locus of a powerful network of transregional elites, featuring prominent policy makers such as Minister of Foreign Affairs Li Hongzhang and Governor-Generals Sheng Xuanhuai (1844–1916) and Liu Kunyi (1830–1902).

Meanwhile, Shanghai also derived part of its identity from the war-related trade of the British Empire. Although Britain no longer had the ability to colonize China directly, British subjects and merchants flocked to Shanghai to enjoy the unprecedented political and economic opportunities generated by regional wars and military buildups. British citizens occupied important seats in two of the most important institutions for international trade and governance, the Qing Customs (Da Qing haiguan) and the Shanghai Municipal Council. Figures such as Rutherford Alcock (1835–1911) and Robert Hart became the most respected transnational residents in Shanghai, while gaining respect in England and the international community as well.[21]

In addition to the presence of both imperial and imperialist control, the city witnessed multiple processes of social, political, and cultural

Figure 16. Japanese-style building in Hardoon Garden. From Shi Meiding, comp., *Zhuiyi: Jindai Shanghai tushi* [Looking back: A photographic history of old Shanghai] (Shanghai: Shanghai guji chubanshe, 1996), 65.

hero of the British Empire, "British character" came to highlight this rising self-consciousness within the European bourgeoisie (Hevia 1995, 57–83). In the light of the changes undergone in the heartland of the British Empire, Hardoon's residence was marked by a multiculturalism deemed pitiful, ugly, overdecorated, and thus inferior according to the aesthetic criteria of the new British Empire. The fact that the Hardoon Garden was Hardoon's home made it difficult not to see the fracture between his choice of style and the aesthetic criteria emerging in the British metropolis. The double nature of his residence, which is at once "other" to British bourgeoisie and "home" to himself, marked, once again, the ambiguous identity of its owner. The combination of the "other" and the "home" provides a possibility of a decentered, peripheral version of the imperial aesthetics. This peripheral version preserved the aesthetics lived before the "imperial" became "British."

The European-style Zhang Garden (Figure 17) tells the story of border crossing from a different direction (Xiong Yuezhi 1996, 1998).[27] The garden's cultural coding was tied closely to the newly revived official-merchant sector, the Yangwu sector of the late Qing period. The Zhang Garden was built by a Wuxi merchant named Zhang Honglu (also known as Zhang Shuhe) (Wu Xin and Yao Wennan [1918] 1970, 27:4a).

Figure 17. The Zhang Garden. From Shi Meiding, comp., *Zhuiyi: Jindai Shanghai tushi* [Looking back: A photographic history of old Shanghai] (Shanghai: Shanghai guji chubanshe, 1996), 64.

Zhang was a *taotai* for the Guangdong government and was close to well-known ex-compradors Xu Run (1838–1911), Zheng Guanying (1842–1922), and Tang Tingshu (1832–1892). These merchant elites resembled the wealthy and powerful salt merchants of Yangzhou, and they shared with those merchants certain conceptions of urban interiors.

Zhang purchased the property for the garden from a British company, Blenkin, Rawson and Company in 1882 (Xiong Yuezhi 1996), just after beginning work at a Foreign Affairs firm, the China Merchants Steam Navigation Company (CMSNC), where he was responsible for river transportation (Wu Xin and Yao Wenner [1918] 1970, 27:4a–4b).[28] The tie between the birth of this garden and the rising political and economic network of the Foreign Affairs group was obvious because it was the "merchant capitalists" Xu Run and Tang Tingshu, the core merchants of the Foreign Affairs enterprises, who recommended Zhang for a position in the company (Zhang Houquan 1988, 45–46).[29]

Actually, Zhang had worked for the company and for the group before he was formally hired. In 1879 he visited Luzon and Singapore as a trusted official (connected with Li Hongzhang himself) to investigate the economic situation and to find new stockholders for the company

(Zhang Honglu 1879–1880). Other trips to Nepal, Bangkok, and Vietnam were quite fruitful, contributing to the establishment of a branch of the company in Bangkok (Li Hongzhang 1921, 12:31; Zhaoshang ju 1880). These overseas trips as an official functionary of the empire were probably an important impetus for Zhang Honglu's desire to build a European-style garden. As Craig Clunas has pointed out, building a stylish garden was the most typical way for Chinese elites to gain sociopolitical status and aesthetic authority, while ensuring the connections necessary for continued profits in the economic sphere (1996, 18–19). Zhang Honglu was no exception. Having joined with Xu Run, Tang Tingshu, and Zheng Guanying (who came to the company as an adviser during the same period), Zhang Honglu became a member of the "merchant capitalists," a group Yen-p'ing Hao found so prominent in the late-nineteenth-century Chinese economy and society (Hao 1986).

Although the status of the Hardoon Garden was based on sinicization, that of the Zhang Garden was based on occidentalism. Zhang rebuilt Fanon's original garden, named Weichun yuan (Fragrant Garden), enlarging it from twenty *mu* to more than seventy *mu* and reconstructing it along the lines of a typical European-style estate. According to the *Shanghai Gazetteer*, Zhang constructed the European-style buildings in the garden after he purchased it (Wu Xin and Yao Wenner [1918] 1970, 17:14a). As photos of the Zhang Garden show (Figure 17), the open space at the entrance, the large lawn, and the wide, straight road that led from the entrance to the main building are constructed in a classic European style (Shi Meiding 1996, 64). Although we have no detailed information about the history of the buildings, the pointed roofs, the curved window frames, the columns, and the hallways with arched ceilings revealed, even displayed, the owner's easy access to resources from both within and outside China (Xiong Yuezhi 1996).[30] This is especially evident in the Western-style buildings, including a relatively tall structure named Haitian shengchu (Where the Sky Meets the Sea) and another large structure, capable of seating over 1,000 people, called Ankaidi, named after the Chinese transliteration of the word "arcadia."[31] As one can see from drawings of the time, Ankaidi was a complex five-story edifice attached to a pair of two-story buildings, with elegant and impressive arched ceilings and decorative glass windows (Figure 18).[32] All together, the Zhang Garden introduced a new sense of space into the gardens of Shanghai. Ankaidi was not merely a building in the Western

Figure 18. Drawing of Zhang Garden. From Huan qiu she, *Tuhua ribao* [Pictorial daily news] (Repr., Shanghai: Shanghai guji chubanshe, [1909–1910] 1999).

style but a work of Western architecture; the Zhang Garden was not a garden that contained Western-style landscape; it was physically a Western space.

Zhang's dream space displayed an upper-class sense of cultural territory that was larger than that of the eighteenth-century salt merchants' gardens. In Yangzhou, European style was a flavor, not an essence, and was at the side, not the center, of the space. The Zhang Garden, however, deliberately asserted its authentic European identity through its nonnative materials, the fact that the previous owner of its land was a foreigner, and its spatial designs, which appear to have been the work of foreign architects. Even the name of the main building, "Ankaidi," reflected the process of decentering: Instead of translating the meaning of the name into Chinese, Zhang kept it as a three-syllable transliteration of English. This authentic European estate suggests a disparity between the political and economic status of Zhang Honglu and the cultural identity of his garden. As an ex-*taotai* holding a crucial position in an official enterprise—the CMSNC—during the country's Self-Strengthening movement, Zhang nevertheless desired to become culturally "other" in terms of his residence. Zhang's effort at making his residence a cultural "other" betrayed a profound desire to cross real and symbolic borders between cultures and empires.

Was the upper-class culture represented by the Zhang Garden a (self-) colonializing culture? I tend to see the garden as an expression of a desire similar to the CMSNC's wish to remove geographic, technological, and economic barriers to ocean trade.[33] One important element underlying the cultural coding of the Zhang Garden was the ambitious commercial aspirations developed by the CMSNC, with the help of imperial resources and capital. The aspiration was twofold: Domestically, the CMSNC sought to compete with and underbid foreign shipping firms working in Chinese waterways so as to reclaim domestic profits that had so far been under the monopoly of the foreign firms; internationally, it sought to develop its own cross-ocean trade routes and networks.

On the domestic waterways, it managed to bankrupt the American Shanghai Steam Navigation Company and buy its assets in 1891, thus consolidating a dominant position in the market (Zhang Houquan 1988, 102–10; Liu 1962, 52–68). Meanwhile, the company advanced to establish cross-regional partnerships with Southeast Asia as well as transoceanic trade routes to both the Old and the New Worlds.[34] Between 1872 and 1883, the CMSNC extended its routes until its ships navigated among Shanghai and the Japanese cities of Hiroshima and Yokohama, stopped at the Southeast Asian ports of Manila, Saigon, Singapore, and Colombo, then crossed the Arabian sea to the Mediterranean before arriving in London (Zhaoshang ju 1880). In 1881 the *Meifu*, a 28,225-ton ship the company had recently purchased, carried 966,371 pounds of tea and other goods to London, the heart of the Old World. From 1879 on, the company's *Hezhong* sailed to San Francisco, the edge of the New World, via Honolulu (Zhang Houquan 1988, 61, 62–64). In 1883 Tang Tingshu, the merchant-official in charge of the company, even paid a two-month visit to Brazil, exploring the possibility of cross-Pacific trade between Shanghai and Latin America (Tang Tingshu 1884). These international voyages were intended to make the CMSNC a powerful competitor to foreign companies both within and beyond China's waterways.

The Zhang Garden reflected these aspirations for economic and geographic expansion by embodying a dream of voyages to Europe and the Americas, even if only allegorically. Although Zhang had traveled abroad only once—to Southeast Asia in 1879—he probably shared the aspiration of others in the company of sailing to Europe and America.[35] The architectural style of Ankaidi marked the owner's self-identification as a world citizen, at home both in China and abroad, both host and guest in the authentic landscape of "the West" created within the garden's walls. The garden allowed Zhang to play with foreign landscapes and, more important, to inscribe them, according to the custom of Chinese travelers, with a non-Western, Chinese signature. He juxtaposed Western landscapes and Chinese symbols—for instance, installing a Suzhou-style "flower and lantern boat" in the garden and then inviting literati and courtesans to drink and sing on the boat, or hosting Chinese folk-cultural activities in the exotic environment. These activities were depicted in well-known lithographic pictorials such as *Fengzheng hui* (Kite-Flying Party; Wu Youru [1908] 1983a, 11) and *Zhang Yuan deng fang* (The Lantern Boat of the Zhang Garden; Wu Youru [1908] 1983b, 14) (Figures 19 and 20). Zhang also turned Ankaidi into a space for many forms of entertainment. The garden boasted a stage for opera performance, a ballad theater, a photographer's studio, a billiard room, tennis courts, a dance hall, and a movie theater open to the public (Zheng Yimei 1996, 192–97).[36] These mixed, cross-cultural settings and activities were unmistakable invitations to the public to experience in imaginary form the newly broadened horizons of travel opened by China's wider contact with the world.

Like manifestations of bourgeois modernity in the West, the Zhang Garden embodied an opening of spatial imagination to the larger world. In a sense, it was comparable to the Parisian arcades, which brought commodities from all directions to form "a world in miniature" (Buck-Morss 1989, 3). As concrete products of newly broadened economic horizons, the Parisian arcades, the Zhang Garden, and to some extent Yangzhou's Eurasian gardens all embraced an idea of hybrid cultural identities and of the fusion of different material cultures. In other words, they all embodied a borderless world in which goods and wealth flowed without restrictions or barriers. From the late eighteenth century on, with the spread of colonial acts of conquest, this type of borderless flow of goods and capital became particularly smooth for the European and

Figure 19. *Kite-Flying Party.* From Wu Youru, *Wu Youru huabao: Haiguo congtan* [Treasures of Wu Youru's painting: Series on "ocean countries"] (Shanghai: Shanghai guji chubanshe, [1908] 1983a), 11.

American bourgeois class. It was different, however, when the flow was initiated by the "Orientals," and conducted from the reverse direction. As we shall see, for Zhang and his group, the gesture of reaching out to include a larger world, although supported by the state, was severely curtailed by the intensifying imperialist domination over world trade. The imperialist domination of world trade was one of the primary reasons for the submergence of such Qing imperial institutions as the CMSNC. The emergence of the colonial world order and the consequent submergence of imperial (but not colonial) institutions such as the CMSNC formed the necessary condition of the "modern era" in different parts of the world.

The commercial voyages of the CMSNC to the West were eventually terminated because of economic competition and for military and political reasons. The company's transoceanic trade ran aground because of the unwelcoming, even hostile, political policies and military actions of Great Britain, France, and the United States. These policies and actions

Figure 20. *The Lantern Boat of the Zhang Garden.* From Wu Youru, *Wu Youru huabao: Mingsheng huace* [Treasures of Wu Youru's painting: Series on "well-known sites"] (Shanghai: Shanghai guji chubanshe, [1908] 1983b), 14.

were designed to defend the Western imperialist dominance of the global maritime orders. According to the authors of *Zhaoshangju shi,* the U.S. government's heavy taxation (a fee plus 10 percent of the cargo) and discriminatory policies (such as depriving Chinese who rode the ships the right to [re]enter the United States) helped to bring an end to the CMSNC's Shanghai–Honolulu–San Francisco route (Zhang Houquan 1988, 61–62). French and British warships "accidentally," most often navigating illegal routes, hit and caused quite a few of the company's ships to sink, including the Pacific ocean liner *Hezhong* (Tang Zhenchang et al. 1989, 269–71). The British and French companies active in South Asia formed an alliance to manipulate prices in order to squeeze out their new competitor from China (Zhang Houquan 1988, 59–65).

These actions so severely discouraged the company from making long-distance ocean voyages that after the mid-1880s, the route to Vietnam and Thailand was the only regular international voyage that remained (Zhang Houquan 1988, 62).[37] If we also take into consideration the Chinese Exclusion Act (1882) in the United States and the Sino-French War (1883–1885), it is hard not to see that "indigenizing China" was necessary in constructing a global political order that ensured imperialist control over sea routes and international trade.

The interruption of the CMSNC trade expansion and its possible impact on the imagined cultural space of the Zhang Garden revealed an unfulfilled process of recentering or reterritorialization of the state-supported upper-class culture. This lack of fulfillment led the efforts of trade expansion in a non-West region such as China down a tortuous path. The successful adaptation of European landscapes and the psychological and technical accomplishments of transoceanic navigation remained a "desire" rather than a fulfilled task. Instead of a smooth process of "world trade," as one sees in the history of nineteenth-century European bourgeois culture, such a process in China was blocked by military action and imperialist politics.

Like other economic institutions that benefited from imperial monopoly, the CMSNC's failure to expand abroad, as well as its corruption and financial misreports, attracted much criticism from within China (Ping Biqing 1983, 167–70).[38] After repeated investigations by the Qing court, Zhang Honglu was finally removed from his position and sent back to his hometown, perhaps made into a scapegoat for the losses suffered by the company.[39] He first rented out his garden and then in the 1890s came back to serve as garden manager (Xiong Yuezhi 1996). However, he never returned to the navigation business. The end of Zhang Honglu's career was similar to the fate of the Yangzhou merchants, but this time it was the result of pressure from not one but two imperial orders—the Qing Empire and the "world order" originating on the other side of the Pacific and Atlantic oceans. The fate of the Zhang Garden is emblematic of an upper class whose naive cosmopolitanism was displaced by the emerging military structure of the world.

What is important here is not so much the interruption or the unfulfilled process itself but what resulted from it. Wallerstein (1989) and Michael Hardt and Antonio Negri, among others, would perhaps see this process as one and the same with that of a globalizing capitalist class triumphing over its regional competitors.[40] But what happened in the Zhang Garden thereafter seems to refute that single-minded vision. The unfulfilled process led to a deepened sense of crisis in upper-class culture and the Qing Empire and eventually to a historical course in which former competitors of the European bourgeoisie gave way to political rivals of the bourgeoisie; state managers, to critics; and order keepers, to order breakers. Rather than paving the way for metropolitan capitalism, the submergence of the upper class in China created barriers. The Zhang Garden was one site of such barriers. It changed from a bourgeois-like urban interior into a public space.[41]

Toward a Critical Frontier

From the fall of the Yangzhou salt merchants to the fall of the Yangwu (Foreign Affairs) group, gardens as a form of urban landscape recorded a crucial dialectical turn: a transformation of the political core of the Qing Empire into a boundary culture on the edges of both the Qing state and foreign imperialism. This section is intended to show that the semi-abandoned Zhang Garden, along with its material relics of a broken dream of commercial expansion into a borderless world, subverted what would have otherwise been the Chinese counterpart of a European bourgeoisie. Indeed, after the Sino-Japanese War, the Zhang Garden was recoded and rewritten, not by new designs or construction but by new activities that transformed the garden into a crucial site for the dissemination of political criticism directed against both the Qing Empire and outside imperialist powers. Instead of bringing the outside world inside, the garden became a place where former Qing subjects were transformed into critics, even enemies, of the imperialist powers as well as of the domestic political order. As the center of power moved from Yangzhou to Shanghai, the imagined civilian interior of the Qing Empire became, in effect, a confrontational frontier.

From early on, criticism and suspicions about Foreign Affairs enterprises, particularly critical voices from within official and educated classes, had been directed against both Qing official politics and the policies of "foreign states."[42] Some opposed the Yangwu enterprise, and others pressured the Qing state to further reform Foreign Affairs practices. The state monopoly on modern industry was ended, and the "ten years' potency protection," which Li Hongzhang had initiated to guard official enterprises against foreign and Chinese competitors, was abandoned in the 1890s. From the 1870s to the 1890s, these criticisms and suspicions became more and more pronounced each time a new outside power attempted to impose another version of the world order on China. Critical voices rose to a roar after the Sino-French War, which took place along the Vietnam-China border and which destroyed the regional navy established by a branch of the Foreign Affairs office. Protests reached a new peak after the Sino-Japanese War, and the reformist projects of Kang Youwei and Liang Qichao can be seen as little more than a crystallization of a long-simmering discontent. By the turn of the twentieth century, criticism and suspicion had moved beyond their original targets in the Foreign Affairs group to the cooperation between the Qing state and the imperialist nations in determining the fate of the people and the region.[43]

Disagreement and internal criticism of state politics and problems had long been common among the Chinese elites.[44] What was unprecedented in these new criticisms of Qing authority was that they were not limited to China's domestic affairs but took on international affairs as a primary target. Among these criticisms a new subject emerged: the turncoat, even the betrayer, of Qing imperial power. And it was these turncoats who brought both new activities and new meanings to Shanghai's urban interiors.

These new critical voices could not have materialized without being nurtured by protected urban spaces within the city itself. The Zhang Garden was unmistakably one of the most important of these. The question of who had access to certain urban spaces had been a political and cultural issue throughout the Qing dynasty, and this debate intensified in Shanghai after the 1880s under the increased penetration of foreign capital. Qing rulers had always been on their guard against urban spaces where crowds could gather, and large gatherings were forbidden within the city (Tanaka Issei 1987, 143–60; 1989). Yet in the mid-nineteenth century, Shanghai emerged as an exception to this general rule, because its International Settlements were only minimally cooperative with the Qing state in forbidding social and cultural "vices" of this kind (Wakeman 1995, 97–162).[45] On the other hand, there had been repeated confrontations between Chinese communities and the Shanghai Municipal Council over land and space as the latter sought to expand the International Territories after the 1880s (Goodman 1995, 158–72). In addition to expanding the borders of the foreign settlements, the Municipal Council sought to racialize the public space by restricting Chinese residents to enter the British park at the Bund. Shanghai's urban space was also influenced by an influx of new capital from the United States and Southeast Asia during the 1890s, when foreign interests took over much of

Shanghai's real estate market (Muramatsu 1991). Under these conditions, the Zhang Garden became one of the few large urban spaces to which the public still had easy open access. From the late 1890s on, the garden was made available for both public entertainment and political affairs (Xiong Yuezhi 1996, 1998).[46]

By the turn of the twentieth century, the Zhang Garden had become the incubator of a newly awakening political consciousness that reacted to the intensifying penetration of transnational capital and Qing state policy. Although the Zhang Garden had been primarily a site for public entertainment, it by now began to house a variety of formal public meetings and organizational activities. The topics of these conferences and gatherings ranged from establishing anti-Qing or revolutionary nationalist organizations, to delivering public lectures, conducting meetings of native-place organizations, urging the Qing state to resist French military force, and debating Russian territorial ambitions in northeast China. The size of these conferences ranged from fewer than 100 to more than 1,000 people. Table 2, drawn from *The Chronology of Modern Shanghai* (Jindai Shanghai dashiji), though incomplete, gives us a glimpse of the public use of the Zhang Garden during the first few years of the twentieth century.

The dissenting and critical nature of these activities is the most striking feature of these garden meetings. The organizers and speakers—many of them anti-Qing activists and radical journalists—used this formerly peaceful upper-class interior as a place to gather and to foment rebellion. The garden meetings allowed for a mix all sorts of people, including well-known writers, regional reform-minded educators, students from China and Japan, amateur scientists, and female students. The Zhang Garden was transformed from a site for upper-class dreams—a wealthy merchant's park devoted to public entertainment and festivities—to a political meeting place for an eclectic group of political activists. Indeed, they had turned an interior space associated with Qing central authority into a borderland: The social base of the imperial order became the threatening front lines of a battle with the imperial court. The point was even recognized by the court in Beijing. Zhang Zhidong, for example, identified the Zhang Garden as a hotbed of rebellious activities. In a telegram to Governor-General Liu Kunyi, Zhang Zhidong indicated that the meetings in the Zhang Garden were organized by *xindang* (new party) and that their lectures were full of rebellious terminology such as "*zizhu*" (self-governing or sovereignty), "*ju'e*" (resistance against Russia), and "*ziyou*" (freedom) (Zhang Zhidong 1918). He went on to mention details such as the presence of national flags from many countries, including a Russian flag that was burned by the crowd at the site. In his view, the true aim of these activities was to organize a movement to overthrow the state.

The activities in the Zhang Garden soon spread to other gardens in the city. Urban spaces became more connected than ever before through the public conferences and lectures that took place in them. The criticism of Qing policy toward Russia, for example, turned Yu yuan, a Jiangnan-style private garden, into a site for public meetings critical of the regime. A very active intellectual club, Dui E tongzhihui (The Resisting Russia Club), for instance, was founded in Yu yuan in 1903. More than 100 people joined the club at the site (Tang Zhenchang et al. 1989, 395–96).

Another good example is the 1905 movement to protest U.S. discrimination against Chinese laborers. Started by the Fujian merchant leader Zeng Zhu, the movement gained the support of native-place and professional associations, students, literati, women's organizations, schools, and shopkeepers. Public meetings and lectures associated with an anti-U.S. boycott movement were delivered elsewhere in the city as well, connecting previously isolated urban spaces. The Gongzhong yanshuo hui (Association of Public Lectures) featured such intellectuals and writers as Cai Yuanpei, Wo Woyao, and Wang Kangnian. These and other figures organized a string of lectures at different sites throughout the city (Tang Zhijun et al. 1989, 567). The forty public lectures and conferences organized during 1905 took place at a variety of sites, ranging from the headquarters of native-place and professional associations, to public and private gardens, to schools and learned societies (Tang Zhijun et al. 1989, 599–605). The boycott continued for almost half a year, despite the orders from Qing officials and the protests of foreign authorities. Table 3 shows a breakdown of these lectures.

These unusual political meetings held in what had been upper-class settings reveal a fundamental change in the Qing dynasty's upper class itself. Scholarship dealing with the media and popular culture of this period tends to take the changing Shanghai public culture as the beginning of a new political culture (Nathan and Lee 1985), the birth of a freer public sphere (Xiong Yuezhi 1998). This scholarship insightfully

Table 2. Uses of Zhang Garden, 1900-1905

Date	Events	Initiators	Attendance
1900	Meeting organized by Nationalist activists; themes included rejecting Qing rule and establishing the Nationalist Party of China	Tang Caichang, Zhang Taiyan, Yan Fu, Rong Hong	80
1901	Meeting organized by well-known intellectuals to urge the Qing state to reject signing a treaty with Russia	Wang Dehan, Wang Kangnian, Wen Qinfu	200
March 1901	Meetings attended by writers and intellectuals promoting Nationalist sentiment and urging rejection of the treaty with Russia	Wu Woyao, Wen Xinyao, Huang Zongyang	1,000
April 27, 1901	Public speeches against the Russian invasion	Wang Kangnian and others	1,000
April 30, 1901	Public meeting on organizing Guomin zonghui, a "House of Citizens," designed to represent citizens' views on international affairs related to China	Feng Jingru, Yi Jifu, students	1,200
1902	Chinese Educational Society welcomed the return of Wu Jinghuan and Sun Bojun from Japan	Zhongguo jiaoyu hui (Chinese Educational Society)	
1902	Chinese Educational Society event about assistance to travel and study in Japan	Chinese Educational Society	
1903	Shaoxing native-place gatherings organized by well-known intellectuals and scholars to establish the Shaoxing Educational Society	Du Yaquan, Cai Yuanpei	
1903	Public lectures given by Ma Junwu, Cai Yuanpei, and others on the topic of discrimination against Chinese persons in the Osaka Exposition	Chinese Educational Society (weekly meetings)	

Table 2. Uses of Zhang Garden, 1900-1905 *(continued)*

Date	Events	Initiators	Attendance
1903	Public gatherings of students and others to criticize Wang Zhichun, the Guangxi governor who sold land to France and used the French army to suppress local rebels		
April 1903	Gentry and merchants from various provinces organize a meeting on public resistance to the French army. Cai Yuanpei, Zou Rong, and others give speeches.		300-400
April 1903	Gentry and merchants from eighteen provinces meet to resist Russian occupation of northeast China		1,000+
April 1903	The Siming Native-Place Association meets for public lectures about resisting Russian occupation of northeast China and criticizing Qing foreign policy.	Siming Native-Place Association (Siming gongsuo)	1,000+
May 1903	Monthly meeting of Chinese Educational Society	Chinese Educational Society	
1905	Students of Zhendan public school take photographs to commemorate their resignation from school in protest of the college's curriculum.		1,400

Source: Drawn from Tang zhijun, Wu Qiandui, and Xu Yuanji, comps., *Jindai Shanghai dashiji* [Major events in modern Shanghai history] (Shanghai: Shanghai cishu chubanshe, 1989).

explores the change in China's public culture more or less in relation to, and engaging with, Habermas's theory of the public sphere. Because media and popular culture are not the main concerns here, it is sufficient for me to caution that the linkage in this scholarship between an *emerging* public sphere and a *rising* bourgeois class—a linkage that was self-evident in Habermas's work—is questionable.

Table 3. Sites of Public Lectures and Conferences Supporting the
Boycott Movement in Shanghai, 1905

Gardens and residences (public and private)	11
Native-place and professional associations	14
Schools and study societies	8
Unknown	7
Total	40

Source: Drawn from Tang Zhijun, Wu Qiandui, and Xu Yuanji, comps., *Jindai Shanghai
dashiji* [Major events in modern Shanghai history] (Shanghai: Shanghai cishu chubanshe,
1989); Tang Zhenchang, Shen Hengchun, and Qiao Shuming, comps., *Shanghai shi* [History
of Shanghai] (Shanghai: Shanghai renmin chubanshe, 1989). For a much-extended list of
activities that covers a longer period of time, see Xiong Yuezhi, "Wan Qing Shanghai siyuan
kaifang yu gonggong kongjian kouzhan" [Public space and the open access to private gardens
in late Qing Shanghai], *Xueshu yuekan* [Scholarly monthly] 8 (1998): 73–81.

Many scholars warn us, at times indirectly, of the problematic side
of making such a linkage in the Chinese context (Judge 1996; Mittler
2004, 168–72). Yet I feel the need to further (re)define the change I have
attempted to describe. I hope to have demonstrated in this chapter that,
unlike in the European history that Habermas narrated, it was the submergence, not the emergence, of the upper-class group that gave way to
a modern critical public sphere in China. Democratic and revolutionary in spirit, its participants were not the counterparts of the European
bourgeois class but its critics. Given the unfulfilled reterritorialization
described in the preceding section, the critical public allegedly "originating" from the Zhang Garden can be seen as a result of the decentering of the upper class. Indeed, this decentering had come full circle and
had become dissenting.

In this sense, the urban interior of Shanghai became a cradle for new
political agencies seeking to oppose or at least detach themselves from
the imperialists as well as from the Qing state. In doing so, they also
detached themselves from their "class" status, which was usually defined
by their close relationship to the state. They instead became closer to
the "crowds" in the public space. Actors appearing in these urban spaces
were no longer representatives of a class or a group; rather, they represented a wide, united front that included all sorts of people, ranging
from outspoken political activists such as Cai Yuanpei and Tang Caichang
and talented writers such as Wu Woyao and Li Boyuan, to merchant
leaders such as Zeng Zhu, students, women's movement leaders, public
educators, shopkeepers, and many others.

A similar phenomenon appeared in the 1905 boycott movement that arose in response to U.S. discrimination against overseas Chinese. Merchants, students, writers, educators, shopkeepers, and other anonymous men and women of the "crowd" fundamentally transformed the role of the city through their involvement in the boycott; they turned the city from a semicolonial outpost into the cutting edge of an incursion into imperialist prerogatives. This movement was short-lived, and the political agency it nurtured can thus be seen as situational. Nevertheless, its brief trajectory was significant enough to invert the political interior of the Qing onto its political frontier and to create historical barriers to the proliferation of the racial and political policies of world capitalism in contemporary Shanghai and, by extension, modern China.

Conclusion

This chapter has attempted to bring a new perspective to late-imperial Chinese history—usually seen from the point of view of colonialism—by examining some of the features and the meanings of Shanghai's grand urban interiors and their transformation during the nineteenth and early twentieth centuries. What I have presented is a threefold argument. First of all, as the urban interiors of eighteenth-century Yangzhou make clear, transcultural spatial features that are conventionally thought of as uniquely "modern" and "Western" are found in China and may be related to the formation of an upper-class urban culture that subjected itself to the rule of the Qing Empire. These late-imperial adaptations of "modern" landscapes require us to reconsider Shanghai in terms of Yangzhou, the nineteenth-century metropolis in terms of the nineteenth-century cosmopolis, and the "Western" in terms of the Eurasian.

Second, as my analysis of the Hardoon Garden and the Zhang Garden has shown, the urban space of Shanghai embodied both Western influences and the revival of an eighteenth-century Eurasian multiculturalism. This revival found its political and economic agency in a group of Qing official-merchants who dreamed of building commercial connections with both the Old and the New Worlds via advanced navigation technology and the Qing state's centralizing policies. The continuation of an earlier tradition of multiculturalism and state-protected industries after Shanghai became a treaty port puts into question the way the "modernization" of a Qing upper class was undercut. Urban interiors such as the Zhang Garden were part of such a process. My conclusion is that the interruption of this process by Western warships, maritime world order, and immigration policy led the cultural territory of the Chinese "urban class" toward a path dissimilar from that of the "modern" bourgeoisie. On this path, the urban class in China faced the crisis of industrial capitalism much earlier than the bourgeoisie in the West. And the unfulfilled process of reterritorialization led the "urban class" to form an alternative urban public.

The third part of my argument is also the most important: The crises and problems produced by Foreign Affairs responses to exterior manifestations of the modern generated an ironic dialectical turn among elites within the Qing Empire. The gardens of Shanghai became sites where Chinese elites, who could have formed a bourgeoisie comparable to that of the West, instead became turncoats questioning imperial policies. These actors played the role of critics, even enemies, of the Qing Empire and its powerful other—the imperialist states of the West. This opposition happened when the urban spaces of Shanghai became fragmented by increasingly obvious racial policies and transnational capital at the turn of the twentieth century. Urban interiors such as gardens, which had been the haven of upper-class tastes, now became central sites for the public lectures and political meetings from which these criticisms originated, thus transforming the civilian interior of the Qing Empire into a cultural frontier confronting both the Qing state and Western imperialist policies.

SIX

The Rise of an Entertainment
Cosmopolitanism

The fact that the critical public took gardens as the early sites of their activities revealed Shanghai's specific spatial structure and the pattern of landholding. At the overlapping territories of empires, Shanghai's center for urban activities would hardly be those conventional public spaces such as the city temple or areas around the city gates, even though those were still central to most Chinese cities. Nor would the tall buildings and Nanjing Road of the International Settlement be likely to represent any social or communal centers for the Chinese. Gardens and school lecture halls thus joined the city temple to become the heart of the city's public life. This chapter switches to explore the way the semicolonial city government's landholding and real estate policies transformed the urban spaces of Shanghai. Although the actors of multiple empires continued to fashion their own urban spaces, a unique lessor/lessee system of landownership further narrowed down the potential spaces for unruly practices after the beginning of the twentieth century. The uses of urban space, including entertainment space, and spatial symbolisms were restructured accordingly in Shanghai.

The world capitalist's real estate system came to dominate the urban space of Shanghai rather early, during the last days of the Qing Empire. This was done through what can be called the "propertization" of land, a process in which the semicolonial city government turned the leased land of the International Settlement into real estate property. By comparison, industrial capitalism and international trade, though crucial to the birth of the Modern City in the West, only partially influenced further changes in the urban history of Shanghai. Various parties, ranging from the Shanghai Municipal Council, to the emerging real estate speculators among Shanghailanders, to big and small Chinese and foreign stockholders, were competing over Shanghai real estate. As a result, the distribution of urban space among social groups was greatly changed. So was the cultural meaning of space and the material projections of the ideals of the city and the world.

The process of what I call the propertization of land in Shanghai was set off during the third expansion of the International Settlement in 1899, initiated by the Shanghai Municipal Council. The expansion enhanced a specific type of economy: the economy of finance, insurance, and real estate and the opium economy. This economy defined the urban facade of the Bund as well as its relationship to the urban crowd, of whom 90 percent were anonymous, unprofessional Chinese. This in turn provided the spatial condition within which emerged two other types of urban facades: One was the commercial district, marked by the European new classical style, with skyscrapers and department stores, represented by those built by Southeast Asian merchants who leased the land on Nanjing Road; and the other was what I call "proto-malls" or "amusement estates," which combined entertainment and small businesses in an urban site. The spatial rhetoric of the proto-mall deserves a specific examination since it retranslated the world expositions through the mediation of Japanese reproductions. This "retranslation" of the spatial format of world expos symbolically presented a pastiche of utopia, or a fantasy of the world, generated by the lesser bourgeois of a relatively anarchical state, post-imperial China. This lesser utopia or fantasy was in its own way commenting upon the reality of the world at war.

Establishing a European Vista (1890–1917)

At the turn of the twentieth century, the imperialists' hunt for colonies and concessions at the inner and outer peripheries of China reached a new stage. By the late 1890s, France had already seized Vietnam as well as the Southeast Asian sea routes, Russia occupied the New Territory in the north, and Japan controlled the Korean Peninsula. After the army of the Eight-Nation Alliance suppressed the Boxer uprising and looted the Forbidden City of Beijing in 1900, the United States seized the Philippines and its navigation routes, Germany occupied Qingdao and established its sphere of influence in the Shandong Peninsula, and England was vigorous in its efforts to get Tibet under its control. "Dividing up China" into "spheres of influence" by different "expanding" countries became a shared interest among both early and latecoming imperialists. Compared to earlier processes of colonialism, the imperialist violation of Chinese sovereignty assumed much more complicated forms, involving issues of law and order, the rent and sale of real property, taxation and tariffs, favored-nation treaties, and translation.

It was during this period that the Shanghai Municipal Council, the administrative headquarters of the British and American Settlements established in 1864, launched its third and largest expansion of the landholdings of the International Settlement. Taking the fiftieth anniversary of the International Settlement as the occasion, the council initiated a plan for establishing real estate markets and asked the Qing state for an expansion of the territory.

Up to this point, three expansions had been made to the territory granted by the original Land Regulation (1845), all aiming at enhancing the "independence" and value of property in the settlement. The first expansion of 1848 extended the size of the British Settlement from 830 *mu* to 2,820 *mu* of land before American Settlements amalgamated with the British (Hsia 1929). Since its founding, the Municipal Council had repeatedly asked the Qing state for permission to expand the settlement. The rationale of the council was quite clear: Explicitly, it asked for space in which to house the increasing population of the settlement; and implicitly, it lived upon the widening tax revenue (800,000 taels from foreign residents but 1.25 million taels from the Chinese).[1]

A more nefarious strategy for acquiring land was to construct roads beyond the border of the settlement without the actual agreement of the Chinese side. By 1884 British and American companies, as well as the Municipal Council, had already made several attempts to build roads, railways, and water-pipe systems beyond the legitimate boundaries of the settlement without the consent of the Chinese or local governments. The Municipal Council then requested that these structures be put under its control and within its territory.

In 1893 the land of the International Settlement was extended again, from 2,820 *mu* to 10,676 *mu* (China, Maritime Customs 1906; Zhang Ren-long 1998, 491–93). Within a mere five years, the settlement again asked for an expansion. The 1899 expansion was the third and, thus far, the most dramatic: It enlarged the landholdings of the Shanghai Municipal

Council from the 2.75 square miles it had encompassed in 1893 to 8.75 square miles, that is, from 10,606 *mu* in 1893 to 32,111 *mu* in 1899 (China, Maritime Customs 1906).[2] Correspondingly, the real estate assessment of the settlement increased by 269,050 taels of silver, and the assessed value reached 37,644,752 taels in total (Hsia 1929, 98).

Moreover, since the settlement now included a large number of residences from Jingan Road to Xinzha Road as well as big manufactories built along Yangshufu Road, the Municipal Council obtained 30,508 taels of silver in extra taxes from the Chinese population during the first six months of the expansion. The French Concession was relatively slower to expand. By 1898 the French Concession had expanded its landholdings from the 1,023 *mu* it had encompassed during the 1850s to a new total of 2,135 *mu*. But during the following fifteen years, the French Concession devoted itself to fifteen projects of road construction beyond its borders without the consent of the Chinese government. Its largest expansion occurred around 1914, when Yuan Shikai made a deal with the French in the hope that they would support him in his quest to become the new emperor. Around the turn of the twentieth century, foreign settlements in Shanghai obtained several times more land than they had had during the previous decade (Figure 21).

The expansion of the International Settlement benefited urban planning for the real estate market more than the "public." As Ernest Hauser (1940) noted over sixty years ago, this expansion alone made Shanghai a "city for sale," a profit machine with no cost. The fact was that a mere ten years after the expansion, the land accessible exclusively to foreign merchants had increased three to four times, and this alone would make construction and real property a hot business in densely populated Shanghai. The Municipal Council did have a city construction plan that included a police station *(Xunbufang)*, a municipal hall with a market exclusively for foreigners, a Chinese farmers' market, a cemetery, the Hong Kong market, the Victorian hospital, and a playground (China, Maritime Customs 1906, 2). But the true impact of this expansion was the emergence of real estate business in the city and, actually, in China as a whole. Big existing foreign companies such as Sassoon and Company (1832–); Jardine, Matheson, and Company (1832–);Brandt and Rodgers (1900–1954); and the Landwide Estate Company (1888–1956), founded by the Hong Kong and Shanghai Banking Corporation, as well as figures like Silas Hardoon and Ellis Kadoorie, had all become real estate dealers

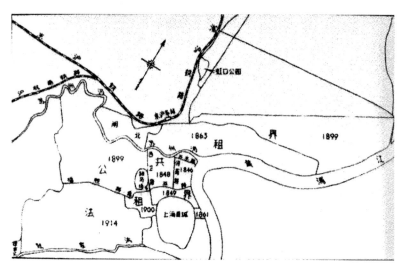

Figure 21. Map of the expansion of international settlement. From Shi Meiding, comp., *Zhuiyi: Jindai Shanghai tushi* [Looking back: A photographic history of old Shanghai] (Shanghai: Shanghai guji chubanshe, 1996), 242.

during the 1890s. Hardoon was so excited by the booming real estate market that he left the Sassoon business to form his own real estate company (Jackson 1969, 201–2). The real estate market was centralized in a few hands in the 1890s. Muramatsu Shin's work (1991, 82–89) shows that the five top clans of British merchants, mostly Jewish families, who had profited the most from the opium trade of the nineteenth century, held more than half of the land of the Middle district of the International Settlement in the 1890s (see Figure 22). Around the turn of the twentieth century, new companies joined the competition. Among the well-known real estate dealers were the China Realty Company (1902–?) founded by American merchant R. H. Parker, the Raven Trust Company (1913, later changed to Asia Realty Company) founded by Frank Jay Raven, and Credit Foncier d'Extreme Orient (1907–1956) founded by merchants from Belgium. In the French Concession, there was the International Savings Society founded by Jean Beudin and Rone Fano in 1909.

The price of land in Shanghai reached sky high after the 1899 expansion, and a new form of economic dominance was rapidly established in the border city. The Sassoon family provided one of the best examples of the rapid growth of property wealth in the overseas "bourgeois" sector of the British Empire due to the booming Shanghai real estate market. In 1877 the Sassoon family, known for accumulating wealth through

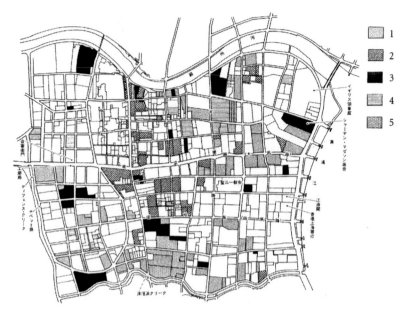

Figure 22. Landholdings of five families in Shanghai: 1 = Sassoons; 2 = Hanburys; 3 = Jardine, Matheson, and Co.; 4 = A. Myburgh, Alexander; 5 = H. J. Craig. Remade by Muramatsu Shin, *Shanhai, toshi to kenchiku: 1842–1949-nen* [Shanghai: The city and the architectures, 1842–1949] (Tokyo: PARCO Shuppankyoku, 1991), 92, after the map in *Shanghai Land Assessment Schedule, English Settlement, 1890* (Shanghai: Kelley and Walsh, 1890) and the map in *Shanghai, toshi to kenchiku: 1842–1949-nen* [Shanghai: The city and the architectures, 1842–1949] (Tokyo: PARCO Shuppankyoku, 1991).

opium deals, owned only one piece of real estate, 8.7 *mu* purchased from the Heard property in the Qiongji yanghang, founded by American merchants. By 1921, however, the Sassoon family had already become the owners of twenty-nine pieces of real estate, altogether 298 *mu*, in Shanghai. The same land the family had purchased in 1877 for 80,000 taels of silver was now valued at 1,702,500 taels of silver (Zhang Zhongli and Chen Zengnian 1985, 41, 42). The price of land in the middle districts in 1890 ranged from 9,500 to 10,000 taels of silver per *mu*. From 1903 to 1907, the price of land in the International Settlement increased from 12,000 to 35,000 taels of silver per *mu*. The real estate market as well as construction projects continued booming in Shanghai when Europe was at war in the second decade of the twentieth century. In 1927 the price of land on Nanjing Road reached 200,000 taels per *mu* (Wu Chengming 1956, 71).

The emergence of a real estate market brought about by the expansion of the settlement marked the departure of Shanghai from its Chinese imperial predecessors, Yangzhou, Suzhou, or Guangzhou. It brought into the city a different world economy that has been vaguely called capitalism. I say "vaguely" because, to many, the word "capitalism" is misidentified with the so-called modernity of industry, technology, science, and wealth that the Western world brought to the Chinese scene. The "modern facade" of Shanghai was characterized as a place where Chinese met, for the first time, the phenomenon of science represented by *sheng, guang, hua,* and *dian*—namely, the knowledge of sound and light, of chemistry and physics.

These characterizations were not wrong except that they missed the crucial point that, ironically, hardly any of the most profitable foreign enterprises in Shanghai involved industrialists, scientists, or technologically advanced factories. It was, rather, another type of capitalist world economy, what might be called the FIRE-O economy—namely, finance, insurance, real estate, and the opium trade—that dominated the wealth and the city facade of Shanghai. Abu-Lughod, in her study of the long history of American global cities, has shown that the FIRE economy (finance, insurance, and real estate) was an early feature in capitalist urban development rather than a recent phenomenon (Abu-Lughod 1999, 2). Some historians of China, too, have long been aware of the same economic feature in the history of Shanghai. Foreign investors in China, as more than one study shows, put a much lower percentage of their investments into industry and manufacturing than into real property, finance, insurance, and the transportation concerns that served the opium trade. Western investment in industries such as manufacturing and mining was 6.9 percent of the total foreign investment in 1914, 11.6 percent in 1931, and 9.6 percent in 1936 (Wei Zichu 1950, 7), but the investment in insurance, banking systems, and transportation was 41 percent in 1914 and 50 percent in 1918 (Wu Chengming 1956, 54–57).[3]

Above all, the foreign finance sector earned a fortune in China through real property "rent" and non-market-based finances such as initiating loans for the war indemnities that the Chinese government was charged first by Great Britain and then by the Eight-Nation Alliance and Japan. The land of the International Settlement was, itself, a big piece of semi-colonial real property that exemplified the success of the FIRE-O expansion in Asia.

Figure 23. Map of land-price distribution in Shanghai around 1890: 1 = 9,500–10,000 taels (of silver) per *mu* of land; 2 = 7,500–9,000 taels per *mu*; 3 = 5,750–7,000 taels per *mu*; 4 = 4,000–5,000 taels per *mu*; 5 = 2,000–3,750 taels per *mu*. From Muramatsu Shin, *Shanhai, toshi to kenchiku: 1842–1949-nen* [Shanghai: The city and the architectures, 1842–1949] (Tokyo: PARCO Shuppankyoku, 1991), 83.

The price of land in the English Settlement was 1.5 taels of silver per *mu* during the 1840s. Fifty years later, the land price for the top area near Fuzhou Road had reached 10,000 taels per *mu*. Land price was high on the east side of the city and gradually became lower toward the west side. Remade by Muramatsu Shin after the map in *Shanghai, toshi to kenchiku: 1842–1949-nen* [Shanghai: The city and the architectures, 1842–1949] (Tokyo: PARCO Shuppankyoku, 1991).

The real property market thrived and dramatically changed the urban facade of the city of Shanghai during the next couple of decades. Four districts were clearly distinguished through this expansion. The East Middle district was the original settlement at the core of Nanjing Road and the Bund, where the foreign banks and shops were centered. Real estate prices went sky high in this district. Other districts, the North and the East, were ranked second in terms of land price. Muramatsu Shin has shown us the cost of land by district by 1890 (Figure 23). Whereas "public Space" for the Chinese did not strike a chord in the urban planning of the Shanghai Municipal Council,[4] wealthy international and domestic city builders concentrated on the golden district of the East Middle region of the city, namely, the Nanjing Road and the Bund. Most of the banks that stood upon the Bund were built between 1900 and

1927. The free-flowing money and the massive construction needs in Shanghai attracted European architects, who flocked to the city. From 1887 to 1914, according to Muramatsu Shin, twenty-six members of the Royal Institute of British Architects came to Shanghai, whereas, prior to 1887, there had been only two members present in the city (Muramatsu Shin 1991, 112).[5] Architects from Germany and other countries, too, were hired to build the German Night Club and other buildings. High-rise buildings appeared on the Bund skyline, competing with each other for height and might on the city's landscape. With wealth and privilege, the buildings on the Bund formed the landscape of Shanghai and made the city a showplace of international wealth and power in Asia. This was best shown in a photograph of the Bund taken in the 1920s (Figure 24).

A careful look at the historical photo shows that among these magnificent buildings were those of the best-known financiers, insurance agencies, real estate speculators, and former opium dealers of the time. Of the six British banks in Shanghai, five were built along the Bund. These included the Hong Kong and Shanghai Banking Corporation, or Huifeng yinhang; the Mercantile Bank of India, a branch of EWO (that is, Jardine, Matheson, and Company); the Chartered Bank of India, Australia, and China; the R. and O. Banking Corporation; and the E. D. Sassoon Banking Corporation (Shanghai tongshe [1936] 1984, 272–74). The new classical mansion of the Hong Kong and Shanghai Banking Corporation was rebuilt in 1921, at a cost of 10 million taels of silver, which at the time equaled two years' bank profits. The building stood on 9,338 *mu* of land, whose price equaled two years' profits. The most prominent building was that of E. D. Sassoon and Company. Built in 1909, the building was the tallest in Shanghai. Its pointed top displayed the wealth and the might of its owner and thus stirred a competition over styles and height on the Bund. The German Club was turned into the Bank of China when China declared war against Germany and took the property in 1917. The building was almost the same height as Sassoon's. Anecdote has it that the original blueprint was for a building taller than the Sassoon building next door but that the neighboring bank strongly objected. As a result, seventeen floors were built underground. In 1920, EWO rebuilt its forty-year-old three-story building into a new, government-style mansion with a dome.

New European classical designs were occasionally given an "oriental" flavor (such as by the decorative bronze lions at the front gate of the

Figure 24. The Bund. From Shi Meiding, comp., *Zhuiyi: Jindai Shanghai tushi* [Looking back: A photographic history of old Shanghai] (Shanghai: Shanghai guji chubanshe, 1996), 19.

Hong Kong and Shanghai Banking Corporation). Expensive building materials, such as large pieces of granite, and new classical marble figures placed around the buildings—all these made the Nanjing Road on the Bund a facade of property, fashion, and power dominance. Other buildings that helped make the worldly facade of Shanghai included the offices of insurance companies, the residences of high-ranking officials, the telegraph company, and so on. Here, on the real property of the Bund, the urban facade was characterized as much by its form and style as it was by its essence and content.

The magnificent architecture along the Bund of Shanghai monumentalized the landscape of a specific FIRE-O frontier of the expanding world of capitalism, the landscape of the might of finance and property. Starting from a translated disagreement, Shanghai's International Settlement developed from a residential area for its foreign community into an expanding real property of the semicolonial FIRE-O class of the world. They may or may not be easily classified as "bourgeois," but they were definitely representatives of one world capitalist frontier: FIRE-O economic agencies using imperialist power. In this "capitalist" frontier landscape of Shanghai, therefore, the manufacturing industry and technology were less prominent than finance, land and road taxes, loans for war indemnity that were safeguarded by military power and unequal treaties, and international politics. The "modern facade" of Shanghai did not originate merely from capitalist "productivity." The surplus values were drawn not only from exploiting the laborers but from selling and reselling the land at prices a hundred thousand times higher than its actual fixed rent. This led to the real-propertization of Shanghai. The twisted owner/tenant, lessor/lessee relationships that existed between foreign states and the Chinese state as well as between foreign owners and Chinese lessees quickly brought forth the problems of sovereignty, imperialism, cultural differences, war, translation, international membership, and representation. This set of questions differentiated Shanghai, a city at the frontier of world capitalism, from the "modern cities" at, in the words of Wallerstein, the "cosmopolitan core." It also distinguished Shanghai from the colonial cities where the problems of sovereignty and the politics of representation took a different turn.

Packaging the Many (1910–1920)

By the same token, Shanghai saw an urban crowd that came from regions unfamiliar to the nineteenth-century Karl Marx and the authors of *The Lonely Crowd*. Such people came to Shanghai for all sorts of reasons. As a trading center, the port had long received native-place associations from the Ningbo, Guangzhou, Shanxi, Zhejiang, Shandong, Anhui, and Fujian provinces together with their restaurants, hotels, and opera troupes (Goodman 1995). And, as mentioned earlier, among the most prominent causes for inbound migration were the wars and other crises. Refugees and sojourners from all over the eastern provinces arrived via either the newly built trains or the traditional river routes. The civil war between the Taipings and the Qing brought the first dramatic increase of population in Shanghai's history. The Sino-Japanese War of 1894 and the Japanese encroachment in the Korean Peninsula continued to bring Koreans and migrant laborers from the north as well as Japanese from across the ocean. The Russo-Japanese War of 1904 brought White Russians, Koreans, and other migrants from the north to Shanghai (Ristaino 2001). The erosion of the Jiangnan region brought a large number of small shopkeepers and their families (Lu Hanchao 1999). Female workers and prostitutes also arrived in the city, and the sons and daughters of both well-to-do and poor families came to the new parochial or church schools in Shanghai (Hershatter 1997; Cong Xiaoping 2001). The Boxer uprising and its suppression, the German dominance in the Shandong Peninsula, and the economic downturn along the northeastern side of the Yangtze River brought into the city numerous unskilled laborers from the northeastern provinces, who worked in Shanghai as rickshaw pullers, dock coolies, movers, cargo workers, road cleaners, bath attendants, garbage collectors, and domestic workers

(Honig 1992). Tobacco companies, fabric factories, printing presses, and arsenals collected workers from all over the eastern provinces.

The urban facades generated by the real-propertization of Shanghai yielded peculiar representations of this urban crowd. These people, when they left the wars and crises at home and came to Shanghai, actually repackaged Shanghai's landscape into different types of facades. Although they were the largest population in the city, they obtained different representations by different agents' specific designs of the spaces and landscapes. The spectacular landscape of the Bund, besides overtly denying the Chinese entrance to the park, either assigned them the position of being mere spectators instead of participants, passersby rather than customers, or regarded them as simply meaningless as they passed through the scene. But the crowd did appear in two other types of facades. They would be packaged as happy consumers in one and as mass players of modernity in the other, before turning into threatening forces capable of strikes and all sorts of political movements in the coming years.

Whereas the Bund along the Huangpu River represented the grandeur of finance and real property, the portion of Nanjing Road located a couple of blocks west of the Bund became the commercial district of the city. This commercial district was formed when Hardoon, the second-largest real estate developer (after the Sassoons), leased out his titled property on Nanjing Road to Ma Yingbiao, who had succeeded in business in Southeast Asia. By 1914, when Ma expanded his business to Shanghai, he was already the owner of the Yonghseng Company in Macao (founded prior to 1894), a Sincere store in Hong Kong (founded in 1899), and another in Guangzhou (founded in 1909). The lease and the building itself on the Nanjing Road cost Ma and his partners 1.2 million yuan. Two years later, Hardoon leased another piece of land to another enterprise developed among the Southeast Asian Chinese, the Wing On Company International created by the Guo brothers. The rent alone was 500,000 taels per year. Starting as a small fruit shop in Sidney, Wing On had established its business network in Fiji and its department store in Hong Kong (1907) before the erection of the Yongan building on the Nanjing Road (1917).

Built by British architects A. Scott Jr. and J. T. W. Brook, the department stores became the first pair of skyscrapers on this part of the Nanjing

Road. Although not the first examples of European-style architecture, they proclaimed their mightiness by being several stories high and by glowing at night with neon lights. The Sincere building stood on twenty-five *mu* of land and extended 250 yards along the road, and its seventh floor reached to about 270 feet tall (*Far Eastern Review* 1916); thus, it undeniably dominated the urban landscape of Nanjing Road. The Wing On department store stood right across the street from Sincere on eight *mu* of land. It was a six-story-tall high-rise built like a European castle. It challenged Sincere with a castle-style rooftop and extremely decorative neon lights.[6]

Besides being sublime commercial space, these department stores housed a crowd now recognized as consumers, or imagined consumers, as well as sightseers from all around. The buildings extended invitations to the crowd. On high, they created a garden-style vista point so that the crowd could enjoy viewing from the rooftops. Teahouses and *snap* shops (food and gift shops, food stands) were situated within the castle-like designs of the rooftops. On the ground, the walkways pleased the crowd with arcades and protected the passersby with shade. Clearly, the buildings were now consumable spaces for the crowd. Not only the goods in the department stores but also the exotic architecture, the light, the interior, the glass display windows, the food in a fresh atmosphere, and the feeling of power that went with looking out from the seventh floor above Nanjing Road were the objects of consumption. Thus, the word "sightseer" became synonymous with "consumer." In a way, the department store on Nanjing Road provided Chinese consumers/sightseers with a spatial qualification for world membership. Its architectural style, its fixed prices, its well-decorated and well-lighted counters, and its invitation to the crowd all sent the message that this store was not a local space but a worldly one, or at least a space that was capable of being nonlocal and worldly.

The third type of urban facade consisted of a specific spatial institution, the playground, or amusement resort, which usually took the form of a renovated structure redesigned for recreation. Chinese real estate dealers with smaller amounts of capital usually devoted themselves to minor architectural renovations on Nanjing Road. With these pieces of architecture, they created places where ordinary Chinese could "play" with the toys of modernity. A playground, or, indeed, an architectural structure of any sort with a playground as its interior, represented this type of "facade." It usually contained roof gardens, elevators, metal-and-glass roofs, mini-galleries of industrial toys, mirror mazes, moving pictures—together with teahouses and restaurants, these structures became the most popular stopping places for the milling crowd of Nanjing Road.

A real estate dealer, Jing Runshan (d. 1915?), first initiated the renovation of this type of space at Daxin jie (present-day Hubei lu) between Fourth Avenue and Nanjing Road.[7] At the suggestion of Huang Chujiu (1872–1931), a slippery merchant from Hangzhou, Jing added a metal-and-glass rooftop to the three-story theater building of Xin xin wutai (The New New Stage) in 1912. It was named Louwailou (Mega-pavilion, or Pavilion beyond Pavilions) (Qian Huafo [1947] 1984, 66; Yang Yaoshen 1994, 118–20). Louwailou made maximum use of its space by adopting the British and Japanese fashion of roof gardens. Originally, the rooftop area was added for sightseers, but it soon turned into a glass terrace for entertainment. Although the building was hardly a skyscraper, an elevator, which was still a novelty to the Shanghai public, helped impress the travelers with the vertical experience of the city (Chen Cunren 1973, 235–39). Different layers of entertainment appeared as the elevator rose. The first floor was a theater that was already well known. The second floor excited visitors with a hall of mirrors and with billiards and many other games. On the rooftop were gathered musical bands, tea tables, and flower displays. For no extra cost, visitors could enjoy performances of such things as the *tanci* ballad, the flower drum, Shanghai and Suzhou comic operas, and foreign circuses (Qian Huafo [1947] 1984, 66–68) (Figure 25).

Louwailou became many spaces at once: It was, at the same time, the theater, the circus, the billiards room, the tea house, the museum of bizarre things and modern innovations, the site for exotic experiences, and the a place to see vistas from on high.[8] It was also reproducible because of its low cost. Within a couple of years, Shanghai saw a dozen imitations of the Louwailou, such as the Tianwai tian (Another Heaven, or Heaven beyond Heaven, its name clearly modeled after Louwailou's) and Xiuyun tian (Heaven of Embroidered Clouds). The popularity of this spatial format marked the development of a low-rise landscape where "modernity" was played.[9]

The last type of urban facade soon popularized itself as amusement estates or even featured proto-malls. Generally called *Youle chang,* these

民國四年八月十五日上海新聞報刊載的"樓外樓"廣告

Figure 25. Advertisement for Louwailou. From Chen Cunren, *Yin yuan shidai shenghuo shi* [Life in the era of silver dollars] (Hong Kong: Chou Chih-weng; Tsung ching hsiao Wu hsing chi shu pao she, 1973), 263.

were huge, centralized structures that served as the first "shopping centers," full of theaters, showrooms, restaurants, shops, and all sorts of places for playful and consumptive activities. Inside, these playgrounds served as precursors of present-day malls, with multiple floors, welled interiors, a central hall, corridors, and numerous inner spaces, including teahouses, mini-museums, opera theaters, storytelling places, galleries, circuses, cinemas, playhouses, and restaurants featuring different regional cuisines. Outside, these amusement estates took up the style of world expos and were built as replicas, either on the whole or in part, of other well-known monuments and architectural structures. The most representative among these larger estates was Xin shijie (The New World, Figure 26), built in 1914, and the Great World, built in 1917 (Chen Congzhou and Zhang Ming 1988, 211).

The original New World was a new classical style building, but the second branch was designed and built by Arthur Dallas (of Atkinson

Figure 26. The New World. From Shi Meiding, comp., *Zhuiyi: Jindai Shanghai tushi* [Looking back: A photographic history of old Shanghai] (Shanghai: Shanghai guji chubanshe, 1996), 82.

and Dallas Architects and Civil Engineers, founded in 1897) in imitation of the then fashionable Shanghai-Suzhou Train Station. Constructed in 1907, the train station was finished with an Arabian touch (Chen Congzhou and Zhang Ming 1988, 211). The Great World was built in the French Concession at an initial cost of 800,000 yuan (Yang Yaoshen 1994, 119).[10] It took up 14,700 square meters (that is, more than 43,500 square feet) after being expanded onto a piece of wasteland in the French Concession. By the 1930s, it held 4,000 seats, and it welcomed approximately 7,000 to 20,000 visitors each day.[11] The architectural style of the Great World, if any, combined the ancient Roman–style circular theater with Chinese kiosks. The founder of the Great World asked architect Zhou Huicun to rebuild the structure (Chen Congzhou and Zhang Ming 1988, 211), adding a three-story Western-style tower to the front, which was meant to symbolize, ironically, the power of a Buddhist pagoda. A. C. Madison Scott, who had spent his youth in China and become a fan of Chinese operas, provided descriptions of the estate that confirmed its own advertisement: "It was a large, reinforced concrete complex laid out with courtyards, roof gardens, a cinema, shops, galleries, stalls—in truth, all the fun of the fair," and it was the "new temple of pleasure that outdoes all the rest" (1982, 76). With their huge capacity for visitors, the amusement estates obviously defined the crowd as players of the modern.

The emergence of such spatial institutions reflected the impact of the process of propertization of land in Shanghai, however indirectly related it may seem to be. The rise of tourism is only a partial explanation for the appearance of these spaces. It contributes more to our understanding if we also consider the fact that the founders of these proto-malls were themselves speculators brought forth by the newly developed real estate economy in Shanghai. Known as the "king of Shanghai land" (*dipi dawang*), the founder of Louwailou and the New World, Jing Runshan, was a shrewd comprador who worked for the first American real estate company in China, the China Realty Company (Shanghai wenshi ziliao 1987, 293). Louwailou and the New World were, very probably, his personal investments in the land market under the title of the China Realty Company (Chen Dingshan 1956). Although most Chinese merchants had little opportunity to participate in the real estate market in terms of both title and capital, Jing Runshan was one of the very few who actually got access to the real property of the settlement. As a comprador, he should have been informed enough to seize the right deals, and he was rich enough to afford a couple of small pieces of real property, but his property and architectural structures were in secondary locations, were much smaller in size, and were less magnificent than those of foreign real estate dealers.

Huang Chujiu, who later established the Great World, did not have the good fortune to be a comprador in a real estate company, but he managed to stay close enough to the new form of economy. Coming from a humble origin, Huang's first success was in medicine (Wang Renze and Xiong Shanghou 1984, 267–74; Ping Jinya 1982, 146–57). Huang's "brain nourishing tonic" (*ailo bu'naozhi*), a so-called Western-style potion invented by a supposed medical man, "Doctor" T. C. Yale, brought him both profit and luck in his early years. Known for being one of the "sneakiest" in the Shanghai merchant circle, Huang and his friend, the popular writer Sun Yusheng (1863–1939), split from the New World and became its competitor. The Great World was underwritten by people from a variety of socioeconomic backgrounds, ranging from a nexus of forgotten celebrities to past revolutionary heroes who had been turning into small stock buyers since the second decade of the twentieth century.

In 1919 Huang established a Day and Night Bank (Riye yinyang) next door to the Great World (Shanghai tongshe [1936] 1984, 2, 232). There were rumors that the personal savings of the wife of the northern warlord Zhang Xun, Wang Keqin,[12] whom Huang Chujiu had managed to befriend as a result of his association with opera star Zhou Fenglin, provided an indispensable portion of the capital needed for the opening of the bank (Chen Cunren 1973, 66–68).[13] With its low minimums, long hours, and flexible schedules for stock exchange, the Day and Night Bank attracted low-income customers, including laborers, gamblers, prostitutes, and small shopkeepers (Shanghai tongshe [1939] 1984, 2, 268–74).

Soon the Jiangnan Stock Market (Jiangnan jiaoyi suo, 1920–?), in which Huang was indirectly but necessarily involved, was also founded next to the Great World. The stock exchange was initiated within a personal network during the craze for the Shanghai stock market in 1920. In this year, an in-group member of the Great World, Yang Liaosheng, invited his celebrity friend from Beijing, Lian Huiqing, to prepare the founding of the Jiangnan Stock Market (Jiang Shangqing 1970, 150–63).[14] An unlikely variety of people were involved in the Jiangnan jiaoyi suo, ranging from a doctor who had graduated in Germany, to actresses, the Republican revolutionary hero Niu Yongjian, and even the Tianjin warlord Wang Tingzhen (Ping Jinya 1982, 146–57). Because Huang could not sit on the board of the Jiangnan Stock Market, he opened a Shanghai Night Stock Market (Shanghai yeshi wujuan jiaoyi suo, founded 1920) instead.

The Day and Night Bank was not very well respected among Shanghai bankers because of its small capacity and its low-income customers,[15] and the Jiangnan Stock Market did not last long because of the fall in the value of silver and the worldwide economic depression. But Huang, the son of a local medical man, grabbed the opportunity to become an investor and to establish social and political resources based upon a FIRE-O economy. He became one of those who knew both the monetary value and the symbolic value of land and space but could not dominate the market in Shanghai. It was this type of player who founded the spatial institution of the proto-malls.

As the rising land and stock market so easily swept the elites of the newborn Republic off their feet (as mentioned above), it is not difficult to imagine the impact that the propertization of the International Settlement had on the ordinary people in Shanghai and its outlying environs. The most immediate result was that as real estate prices escalated, space in Shanghai became simply unaffordable for many small businesses and traveling troupes. Opportunities for opening small shops and service businesses, as so many had done prior to the 1899 settlement expansion, became increasingly sparse in the International Settlement and French Concession Shanghai. It is likely that many service businesses did not have stores and that their proprietors had to carry their businesses on their shoulders.

As real estate speculators, the founders of the New World and the Great World managed their proto-malls in similar ways, as Hardoon would have done. Namely, they leased out the space in their estates, but at times these leases were built not in terms of capital but, rather, in terms of fame and centrality. Huang Chujiu, for example, contracted out the property he rented from the French Concession to all sorts of small service stands. And to make the contract rent cheap enough, his contracts with performers were defined by the hour so that the same showroom could be used nonstop for different kinds of performances and shows. According to the advertisements for the Great World, during an average day beginning at two o'clock in the afternoon and ending at midnight, a single theater offered a dozen different performances and shows. The Great World, as a whole, mounted several hundred shows each day. Because the rent was said to be inexpensive, restaurants, teahouses, and small service businesses were also collected into the Great World. The origin of the proto-mall in Shanghai, in this sense, partially reflected the fact that the real estate market had squeezed the small shops and theaters into a single place like the Great World.

Compared with the mall of today, the Great World and Louwailou were by no means "bourgeois" because of the existence of the numerous "petty service businesses" that had clustered there. Although by the 1920s the Great World had come to serve as a precious space for passing time in the increasingly crowded downtown region, it was, from the beginning, a space for all sorts of tiny little "petty service businesses" that could not possibly have found places of their own. When visiting Shanghai in 1931, Austrian film director Josef von Sternberg (1894–1969) noted his distinct urban experience in the Great World. His description of the Great World's offerings is everything except flattering, but it is also so vivid that it deserves to be quoted at length here:

The establishment had six floors to provide distraction for the milling crowd, six floors that seethed with life and all the commotion and noise that go with it, studded with every variety of entertainment. When I had entered the hot stream of humanity, there was no turning back even had I wanted to. On the first floor were gambling tables, singsong girls, magicians, pick-pockets, slot machines, fireworks, bird cages, fans, stick incense, acrobats, and ginger. One flight up were the restaurants, a dozen different groups of actors, crickets in cages, pimps, midwives, barbers, and earwax extractors. The third floor had jugglers, herb medicines, ice cream parlors, photographers, a new bevy of girls, their high-collared gowns slit to reveal their hips, in case one had passed up the more modest ones below who merely flashed their thighs; and under the heading of novelty, several rows of exposed toilets, their impresarios instructing the amused patrons not to squat but to assume a position more in keeping with the imported plumbing. The fourth floor was crowded with shooting galleries, fan-tan tables, revolving wheels, massage benches, acupuncture and moxa cabinets, hot-towel counters, dried fish and intestines, and dance platforms serviced by a horde of music makers competing with each other to see who could drown out the others. The fifth floor featured girls whose dresses were slit to the armpits, a stuffed whale, storytellers, balloons, peep shows, masks, a mirror maze, two love-letter booths, wish scribes who guaranteed results, rubber goods, and a temple filled with ferocious gods and joss sticks. On the top floor and roof of that house of multiple joys a jumble of tightrope walkers slithered back and forth, and there were seesaws, Chinese checkers, mahjongg, strings of firecrackers going off, lottery tickets, and marriage brokers. (von Sternberg 1965, 81–83)

The ideological implication, the gaze, and the tone embedded in von Sternberg's comment deserve a separate lengthy analysis. It is sufficient to mention here that von Sternberg had obviously fantasized the Great World into a metaphorical space of the "other" and the "unknown"—a dark space mixed with lure and sin, frivolity and secrecy, odd exotica, and "oriental" peculiarity, potentials for adventure and mystery. Such a space has often been seen in European literature and films, such as Joseph Conrad's *Heart of Darkness,* the movie *Indiana Jones,* and von Sternberg's own film *Lady from Shanghai.* Yet his belittling account still shows the fact that the space held many small service stands that had once been found on the street corners of the city. This was, at least in part, the result of the real-propertization of the International Settlement. The fact that the interior of the amusement estate was packed so fully with all sorts of people and small businesses indicates how the land hegemony of the FIRE-O class had squeezed small services into cheaper rental spaces. They were made "petty," pettier and even pettier still than the changing consumers in the sublime heaven of the department stores, not to mention the members of the clubs on the Bund. A double trivialization can be identified here: The Austrian film director visually trivialized and mystified what the land market had already spatially trivialized.

The "World": Pastiche to Paraphrase (1910–1917)

Triviality, of course, was not the idea that the founders of the New World and the Great World had in mind when they built the proto-malls. In fact, despite the expansion of the real property and the land market that tended to clear small businesses from the city's streets, the founders of the New World and the Great World had their own vision of what it could mean to own space in Shanghai. Their vision of such an urban institution was represented by the way they named their estates, spaces that, in certain ways, resembled an entire "world." Tracing the historical origin of this approach to naming would lead us a long way toward the spatial format of world expos by way of Japanese mediation. Curiously, the cultural self-representation of both the New World and the Great World showed not only a close connection with the spatial imagery of world expos but also a ridiculous distortion of it. I suggest that to a large extent, the proto-mall and the dubious petty identity (petty bourgeois, or *xiaoyezhu*, and petty urbanites, or *xiaoshimin*) of its crowd may, as well, contain an implicit retranslation of the way the "world" had been displayed in the West—and later in Japan—since the late nineteenth century.

It was no accident that the New World and the Great World both used the word "world" to capture the spirit of their spatial institutions. In fact, the cultural enterprises of the Great World and the New World came about first as cross-cultural adaptations of the playground Shin Sekai (The New World), an early expo-style urban device built expressly for Asia's early world fair in the city of Osaka in Meiji Japan (Yoshimi Shunya 1992, 146–52). The story has it that Huang Chujiu and Sun Yusheng had visited Osaka in person and were so inspired by the grand theatrical complex in the city that they imitated not only the idea but also the name of the architectural complex. The original building of Shin Sekai, though it does not exist today, was itself an imitation of the entertainment sections of the world expositions, which originated in Europe and America (Hotta-Lister 1999).

Whether the Shanghai New World was a physical replica of the Shin Sekai or not, the two Shanghai entertainment estates did, in principle, carry some features that were unmistakably expo-style. The architectural styles of the New World and the Great World, for example, were full of "citations" of different styles and codified parts of other constructions. They contained a mimicry of European new classical architecture, copies of literati gardens, pastiches of the train station as mentioned earlier, ersatz "natural" vistas, replicas of battlefields, displays of industrial inventions, and exotic landscapes. Like most of the world expos, they included performances by different local theaters and foreign circus and dance troupes as well as folk and exotic performances representative of other "cultures." As imitations of a Japanese adaptation of a world expo, the spatial formats and names of the New World and the Great World became more symbolic and complicated in a cross-cultural context.

The world exposition was both the product and one of the producers of the new world order in the form of technology, industry, trade, and culture since the late nineteenth century, and Meiji Japan was actively participating in this process. In the West, the important work of the world fairs accompanied the development of an industrial capitalist world in which the concept of the "membership" of each nation became reified. As expositions, these fairs, organized in different countries, aimed at offering a cross-section for the international exchange of commodities, technologies, machines, arts, information, and inventions. They may have served these purposes quite well, as technological innovations did spread quickly this way. Yet at the same time, this institution could not help but enhance and reinforce the formation of a global community of industrial capitalism.

Different world fairs took similar routes to presenting the "world community" of nations and ethnicities appearing at once, in one space, here and now, by evaluating their products, arts, cultures, and the "forwardness/backwardness" of their peoples. The Columbian Exposition in Chicago (the Chicago World's Fair of 1893), for example, divided the space of each exhibit hall by nationality, race, and ethnicity rather than by goods. Never would any world expo blur the boundaries between nations, races, and ethnicities. The anthropological or entertainment sectors of these world expos often provided performances by groups from the "civilized world" as well as displays of costumes and cultures of the "primitives," and hence an institutionalization of the hierarchy of nations, races, cultures, ethnicities, and "primitive civilizations" was created "for all to see" (Gainor 1995). The Midway Plaisance, the first entertainment section of this sort, appeared in the Chicago World's Fair in 1893. That event marked the moment when the U.S. elite began to flood popular culture with their imperialistic, racist *principles* and served to deepen the class and racial conflicts that continue to plague the nation and the world (Rydell 1984).

During the Meiji period, Japan was more prepared to participate actively in world expos as a nation and was eager to be recognized as a member of the world trade and industrial community that such institutions represented. The Chinese were also active participants, contrary to many existing notions, but as individual merchants rather than as a nation. World expos were interpreted as purely commercial or trading opportunities rather than as a means to earning "membership" in the international community built to enforce the world order. From 1863, delegations from China participated in most of the world expos, but it was not until 1910 that the Qing state was formally involved in organizing one. Yet this Chinese interpretation, emphasizing the apolitical aspects of trade and exchange, seemed to make China less acceptable to the community of world expos. Not only were goods from China perceived as being less refined than those from Japan—which was probably true, since most of the Chinese delegations were organized by individual merchants such as Hu Xueyan or Robert Hart, the British man in charge of the Qing Customs who used exposition trips as excuses for grand vacations—but the Chinese "nation" was also devalued.

In his critical study of the American world fairs, Robert W. Rydell, in *All the World's a Fair* (1984), has demonstrated how these events helped to both establish and promote racial discrimination toward Asian Americans. According to Rydell, human exhibitions were deliberately designed to serve as "living proof" that the Asian nations were primitive civilizations. As a result, the world fairs actually legitimized the U.S. imperialistic foreign policy toward China and other parts of Asia (Rydell 1984,

235–36). In the Philadelphia Centennial Exhibition (1876), although the goods from China were high-quality silks, jade, and ivory carvings, "China" was identified as a "closed empire," and its people were cast as "coolies" with long pigtails who preferred to treat themselves to opium pipes rather than cups of green tea (ibid., 30–31). In the 1893 Chicago World's Fair, even though China did not participate as a nation or a culture, "Chinamen" and Chinese culture were still put on exhibition as a source of amusement—not respect—in the Midway Plaisance (ibid., 48–49). The planners of the New Orleans and Atlanta exhibitions made so many efforts to design and propagate displays of "strange nationalities and wild animals" that Chinese Americans who attended the fair were surrounded by thousands of onlookers making all manner of insulting comments (ibid., 94–96).[16]

The Japanese did not necessarily receive any better treatment in the world exhibitions of the nineteenth century, but the Meiji state definitely accepted the principles and the requirements for membership in the industrial world community that were embodied by the world expos. In Japan, the world exposition was adopted as a way to promote technological invention and to spread information as early as 1878 (Yoshimi Shunya 1992, 21–43). Meanwhile, the world order reinforced by the world expos was also accepted in Japan as a welcome rationale for the nation building of the Meiji state well before it launched the Sino-Japanese War in 1894 (ibid., 22–24). The intellectual appeal of Japan's "separation from Asia," for example, can be seen as one important piece of evidence supporting the idea that one influential group in Japan was willing to actually subjugate itself to the world order of industrial capitalism by self-constructing itself into a non-Asian culture (Tanaka 1993). Japan's victory in the Sino-Japanese and Russo-Japanese wars eventually won the nation recognition from, and hence membership in, the West.

By the time the Shin Sekai playground was established in Osaka in 1911, the Japanese state had long since claimed its cultural and military superiority in Asia and had already begun to consciously make urban planning a tool to be used for regulating leisure and popular sentiment in the service of an orderly industrial society with both military and imperialistic purposes (Hotta-Lister 1999; Yoshimi Shunya 1992). Shin Sekai was built right at that moment. It was a materialization of the rationalized leisure and entertainment area of Japan's new industrial city, Osaka. Using the ideal of the European industrial and exposition cities, Osaka was planned as a city made up of different zones that divided work and leisure areas, consumption and production areas, residential and office areas, and private and public areas (Yoshimi Shunya 1992, 35). Shin Sekai, in this sense, was the spatial symbol of rational modernity.

The New World and the Great World's adaptations of Shin Sekai, or world exposition, were obvious not only in their choice of names but also in their use of significant modern cultural motifs typical of the world expos, such as images found in science and technology. Shin Sekai sought to exhibit the glory of scientific and industrial innovations, and so did the Great World and the New World. Shin Sekai, for example, followed the convention of world expos in the West and offered the crowd a Ferris wheel. The Great World did the same by installing a lesser model, the *sheng gao ti* (Ferris wheel), to catch the public's fancy. To capitalize on such scientific innovations, the Great World also installed a mechanical model of a "flying boat" *(feichuan),* which circled in the sky above the Great World.[17] The New World, on the other hand, went underground to exploit the technological advances of the day and opened an aquarium that was connected by a subterranean tunnel to the architectural replica of the newly built railway station (Chen Dingshan 1956, 4–5). Shin Sekai displayed a detailed electronic, panoramic, ice-sculpture model of the battlefields of the 1905 Russo-Japanese War in northeast China, obviously for the purpose of boosting public sentiment for the national glory of its military victory (Yoshimi Shunya 1992, 12). The panorama was so precise that one could point out the location of the cannons in Lushun Harbor (Yoshimi Shunya 1992, 21). The Great World, too, exhibited a neon model of a large-scale war, not to promote patriotism but to display the ongoing battles of World War I.[18] Moreover, both the Great World and the New World exhibited rare animals from various places, which was a clear—though playful—replica of a popular device of the early world fairs that was related to the emergence of the fields of biology and zoology. Similarly, a display of dwarfs was also widely advertised (*Da shijie bao*, February 17, 1918).[19] Finally, the Great World and the New World gathered numerous folk and ethnic entertainers from all directions, thus making the proto-malls counterparts to the Midway Plaisance, the entertainment section conventionalized through the world's exposition where the theaters of all nations gathered.

But Shanghai differed from Osaka in being located at the overlapping frontier of different empires, where access to resources, rather than developing industries, was the center of economic concern for the Mixed Council (the administrators of the International Settlement). And (unlike the Meiji emperor) Yuan Shikai, who seized the presidency of the Republic of China, also seemed uninterested in capitalizing on the cultural politics of world expositions. The New World and the Great World, as copies of Shin Sekai, provided unintended retranslations of the institution of world expos in a different context. Whereas Osaka's Shin Sekai, forced by the modernizing Tokyo, characterized itself by its "newness" or its universal modern style, the architecture of the Great World looked somewhat unplanned and "postmodern" and had a "kitschy," pastiche style.

For example, although it followed Shin Sekai in the pursuit of scientific and technological innovations, the Great World was also significantly influenced by the Chinese garden, embodied in its tall, curved external walls and pavilion-style roofs (Figure 27). The main hall, or the Hall of the Republic, was decorated with "literati-style" paintings and calligraphy and was where people sat with friends drinking tea and enjoying "literati-style" fun.[20] An announcement of the Great World's grand opening told potential visitors that inside there was "a garden and a roof garden," a goldfish and Mandarin duck pond, and a special palace, as well as several pavilions and kiosks that were waiting for poetic inscriptions (*Shenbao*, July 11, 1917). These pavilions and kiosks displayed ten vistas *(jing)*, each with a descriptive caption such as "an old rockery in front of a mountain house" *(shoushi shanfang)*, "a pavilion of great spectacle" *(daguan lou*, which imitated the Great Spectacle Pavilion in the *Dream of the Red Mansion*, at least in name), "a lesser Penglai island" *(xiao Penglai*, named after the famous fantasy island), "a lesser Lu Mountain" *(xiao Lushan)*, "a flower field" *(huaqi)*, "a kiosk for ascending the clouds" *(deng yun ting)*, "a vista of flying kiosk and floating boat" *(feige liuzhou)*, and so on (Tu Shipin et al. [1948] 1968, 315). I tend to characterize these features of the Great World as "garden kitsch," because all these vistas were made in the architecture itself; hence they kept only the spirit of what could actually be found in the homes of the upper classes. The heights and panoramas as well as the ideas of rockeries, ponds, woods, or flowers provided by the literati who wrote poetic lines for each vista were clearly, though only partially, "kitschy" continuations of the garden tradition.

Figure 27. The Great World in 1917. From Shi Meiding, comp., *Zhuiyi: Jindai Shanghai tushi* [Looking back: A photographic history of old Shanghai] (Shanghai: Shanghai guji chubanshe, 1996), 82–83.

The Great World's reconstruction in 1925 displayed a further change in the pastiche facade. The reconstruction manifested the owner's attempt to readapt his proto-mall to the rapidly Westernizing landscape of Nanjing Road. Besides building more stories to increase the height, the most important change was to add a tower in the front. The tower was meant to be a pagoda, since that had been suggested by a local feng shui expert. But it was built as a Western-style tower with the pillars and arches so often seen in the late-Victorian expositions in England and the United States (Figure 28).[21] By adding this tower, the front of the Great World changed from "garden kitsch" to "exposition kitsch." Following the advice of the feng shui expert even further, Huang Chujiu changed the location of its main entrance. Its old entrance had faced away from the downtown region of Shanghai, but the new entrance now faced toward it. With this new entrance, the Great World relocated itself at the junction of Edward VII Avenue (present-day Yan'an donglu) and Xizang lu (present-day Xizang zhonglu) (Chen Dingshan 1956, 237).

By rebuilding itself, the Great World joined, or at least identified itself with, the modern urban scene of Western spectacle, or the spectacle of the "world," in Shanghai. Ironically, the very kitsch or pastiche effect that the building carried with it had little in common with the rationalized industrial spectacle one saw in Shin Sekai; nor was the unintended pastiche imbued with the spirit of the supremacy of industrial capitalism, as the world expos usually were. A von Sternberg or a Japanese minister would have said that the Great World ridiculed the world expo, if it had not been such a bad mimicry of it.

The retranslation of the institution of the world expos went beyond the level of unplanned, irrational, ridiculous pastiche. Borrowing the

Figure 28. The Great World after 1925. From Shi Meiding, comp., *Zhuiyi: Jindai Shanghai tushi* [Looking back: A photographic history of old Shanghai] (Shanghai: Shanghai guji chubanshe, 1996), 83.

world expo format and applying it in a superficial or kitschy manner, the New World and the Great World became the first cultural enterprises that projected spatial manifestations of the imagery of the "world" and its membership. This "world" and its membership were characterized not so much by distinctions between civilized and primitive nations as by the incorporation of an aggregation of all sorts of different "local cultures." Huang seemed to have wanted his "world" to contain all sorts of differences, and, according to the reminiscences of a Sutan opera actor, he sought out local opera performers by offering them a unique sort of exchange: They would come to perform in the Great World without paying rent, and in return they would earn not money but celebrity and fame.

Appearance in the Great World was, itself, a kind of membership. These "members" were represented by multiple and incoherent units. Sometimes they represented nations, sometimes regions, sometimes even smaller localities. Distinctions were drawn in a variety of ways: by nation, region, community, and, most often, dialect and genre. Depending on the day, theaters were clearly listed by their localities, such as Beijing opera theaters, Suzhou theaters, Changzhou and Wuxi theaters, and so on.[22] Local and traveling troupes occupied different theaters at different moments. These included *huagu* or drum ballads that were performed widely in the Anhui, Jiangsu, and Zhejiang provinces in different dialects; *la xuan ge*, "songs of dragging strings," a type of country entertainment developed in the poor areas of northern Jiangsu; Suzhou light local operas that were known for their erotic themes; *duizi xi*, "dialogue songs," which had developed among the Huai laborers; female story-tellers from Jiangnan; *xuanjuan*, "singing of the scripts," a form derived from folk religious chanting; Shanghai local light operas; folk circuses from the streets of different cities; juggling shows and traveling circuses as well as gambling games such as *denghu*, "lantern tiger," and "*shimi*," "poetry riddles." Quite a number of foreign troupes and circuses performed in this proto-mall, alongside a wide variety of other genres and representatives of many different local cultures. These performances included Japanese circuses, Japanese film series, the early American comic moving pictures Kaisidong (the "Keystone Series," perhaps the movies of Keystone Studios), Russian dance and circus troupes, Greek circuses, and European dance companies. All together, the Great World had shaped a membership that included the following:

Beijing (Little Beijing opera troupes)
Tianjin (Tianjin drum ballads)
Suzhou (Suzhou light opera, *tanci* ballads, male and female
    performers)
Yangzhou (Yangzhou storytelling)
Shaoxing (popular songs, literate storytelling)
Ningbo (popular songs)

Subei (La Xuanzi, or "country" music; *taiping geci*, or
  folk-religious chanting)
Wuxi (civic opera, martial arts)
Changzhou (popular songs, storytelling)
Yangzhou (Women's theater, "Mao'er" theater)
Japan (circus, troupes of magician, movies)
Greece (Greek Magic Show, circus)
Russia (dance performances)
Europe (dance company)
United States (Keystone movies)

Rather than being a representation of "all nations," what appeared in this symbolic "world" were those who distinguished themselves from others not so much by national subjectivity or character as by everything that the process of nation building opposed: their geographic positions, their languages or dialects, their generic features, and their cultural costumes. Moreover, the Great World made no effort to draw a line between "advanced" and "backward" civilizations. The dwarf exhibition was cruel but had little to do with providing "living proof" of primitive and thus inferior cultures. If one takes the arrangement in the Great World as an unintended retranslation of the entertainment sector of a world expo, then it is clear that to the owner Huang Chujiu and his staff of literati, the imagery of the "world" was that of a borderless, rank-free community with casual entrance requirements that, therefore, sidestepped the criteria used in world expos (race, nation, modern versus primitive civilization).

One may even say that the Great World, in a way, displayed a significant lack of knowledge about world expos, and that as a result, the Great World blurred the national borders that were so clearly institutionalized in the world expos and ignored world expos' basic racial membership requirements for entering the world community. Therefore, it gave the public a vague—even false—impression that the "world" really was a borderless place, free of discrimination and political hegemony. Huang's image of the great urban interior continued what Zhang Honglu, the Foreign Affairs figure of the China Merchants Steam Navigation Company (discussed in chapter 5), tried to impress the public with in the Zhang Garden. Compared to the Zhang Garden, of course, Huang's Great World embodied, in symbolic ways, an enlarged membership that was opened to the locals as well as to the petty urbanites.

The absence of an industrial capitalist government behind the scene of the Great World reminds us that the specific historical moment Huang faced was different from that of Zhang Honglu. Zhang's outbound world ambition was curbed by the imperialist naval powers and their dominance of the commercial sea route, and the Foreign Affairs group as a state-supported industrial enterprise had run aground after the Sino-Japanese War. But Huang was excited about the personal opportunities brought forth by the 1911 Revolution. Only in such a political vacuum could a semi-illicit commoner like himself lease a piece of land and try his luck on the stock market. The new historical moment ended his pitiful history as a fake foreign drug dealer and helped him obtain a decent identity. Taking advantage of the new opportunities offered in the Republic, Huang got himself honored as an executive member of the Council of the Chamber of Commerce in 1914, and he even bought himself an official title from the warlord government despite the fact that he had no political ambitions of his own.

Founded right after the Chinese World Exposition in 1910 at the dawn of the new Republic, the Great World, in a way, carried out Huang Chujiu's fantasy of his "world" in an era called "Republic." The Great World clearly marked the time in a manner that the Zhang Garden had not by building a Gonghe ting (Republic Hall), at the center of the "world." The Republic Hall did not so much represent a sign of new polity as it served as a celebratory kind of spatial rhetoric. The word "Republic" was used to refer to the open flows of people, theaters, and shops and as a metaphor for public space, "everybody-ness," and even "democracy." In a sense, Republic Hall became an indicator of the stateless nature of the time as well as the imagery of the Great World. Contrary to what was true of the world expos, people, rather than states, were deemed to be of greatest importance when Huang collected theaters in which performers spoke in every dialect in the proto-mall of the Great World. Dialects, in this sense, identified people who came from distant places. The term "gonghe" was translated into something irrelevant to the "republic" of the Western world. In the Great World, "gonghe" meant the "coexistence" and "mixture" of different groups, people, and cultures. And that indicated the actual spirit of the imagery of the "world" and the stateless community of the Great World.

What exactly was the new meaning of space that the Great World might have created? If one considers that Huang Chujiu lived on the border between histories, then two juxtaposed pictures may come to mind. On the one hand, he was induced, however willingly or unwillingly, into the FIRE-O economy brought forth by the capitalist expansion; and he himself did become involved in it, even if only in trivial ways. On the other hand, he brought with him the desire and the ambition to get his share in a world of *gonghe,* in a "world" open to everyone without border and hierarchy. The Great World, in a sense, resulted from the way that Huang's fictitious vision of *gonghe* came to redefine the phrase "to get one's share" and perhaps even served to reorient the gravity of the FIRE-O economy brought forth by the expansion of the International Settlement. To further surmise in this vein, the center of this world of *gonghe* could, of course, be located in the New York Stock Exchange or in the heart of Europe, but it could appear, as well, in this very specific space located in Shanghai, particularly since Huang himself had already acquired a piece of its property.

The implication of this reorientation or sharing of the economic world of *gonghe* is clearly evident in the one difference between the Zhang Garden and the Great World, that is, the representation of the locals. Like Zhang Honglu's, Huang's symbolic estate erased all "world" borders. But unlike the Zhang Garden, where visitors were invited to embark upon an imaginary voyage to the exotic "other world" represented by its European landscapes, the Great World's "world" appeared in the here and now. This "world" was the terminal for the inbound movement of all the incoming people, goods, and capital (in however small or large amounts) from all over the globe. All the marks of identity were unmistakably indicated by their "distances" and their "origins" from far beyond. Yet at the same time, these incomers were equally distinctively locals and translocals, and their way of mixing in the spatial arrangement of the Great World symbolically exemplified the popular connotation of *gonghe* (that is, coexistence and medley). Indeed, as the capitalist world system expanded by way of the FIRE-O economy, the stock form of capital seems to have flowed much more smoothly when moving inbound to Shanghai than it did when the Chinese ships moved outbound toward the Old and New Worlds. But by putting together an assembly of local theaters, the Great World unexpectedly rewrote the "world" centering around *capital* in terms of the trafficking of *peoples,* including laborers, and *their cultures.*

The Great World, in this sense, spatialized the residue of the noncapitalist world in the midst of FIRE-O market. Only by remembering that *gonghe*, or coexistence and medley, was once the meaning of the proto-mall can one understand the complexity of the relationship between Shanghai and its surrounding areas prior to the founding of the Nanjing GMD government. Local opera troupes looked upon performing at the Great World not as victimization as primitives in front of the civilized city but as an acknowledgment of their membership in the contemporary world and thus as ensuring their status in their hometown communities. Visitors to the Great World were not all members of the upper class. This did not prevent an unknown artist of the early 1920s from presenting the Great World in the spectacular, fantastic, cosmopolitan manner seen in Figure 29. Most noteworthy in this drawing is the style of the tower and the format of the central hall surrounded by rows of theaters, certainly capturing the magnificence of the structure of this cosmopolitan site. The clouds behind the tower romantically emphasized and exaggerated the height—or the imagined height—of the space. Women's hairstyles and fashionable dresses and the movement of humanity presented a utopian vision of the modern world that allowed the peaceful coexistence and cohabitation of every people. This visualized utopia of *gonghe*, of course, served as a self-beautifying celebration of becoming "modern" in Shanghai, if one remembers von Sternberg's depiction of the Great World, but it also captured an inevitably ironic retranslation of the "world fair." It was just what the world fair was missing.

An important result of the Great World's retranslation of the world expo was the plural type of subjectivity it brought forth. Whereas the park on the Bund categorically rejected the Chinese, the Great World presented an open world to the incoming crowd. The cheap entrance fee attracted legions of sojourners from the eastern provinces, who came not only to discover how local and provincial they were but also to recognize their own dialects and their own theaters as well as the different dialects and performances of others.[23] They came to experience the city, which itself had become a world. They were invited to play with modern toys and were asked to assume different postures and identities in ways even more extreme than had been once presented in the Zhang Garden. The sightseers were anticipated and imposed by publications such as *Da shijie bao* (Great World Paper), which was specially dedicated to the happenings of the Great World as having been designed for those

Figure 29. Drawing of the Great World. From Chen Cunren, *Yin yuan shidai shenghuo shi* [Life in the era of silver dollars] (Hong Kong: Chou Chih-weng; Tsung ching hsiao Wu hsing chi shu pao she, 1973), 267.

who could enjoy all differences at once. These "differences" ranged from folk acrobats to the Ferris wheel, a flying boat dragged by an engine, roller skating, a World War I battlefield, Keystone movies, Western foods, galleries, rockeries, and performances in both familiar and strange languages.

Let there be no confusion: The Great World's synchronic representation of coexistence and equally exchangeable differences only concealed the historical process of deepening imbalance and polarization between Shanghai and its neighboring "localities"—Suzhou, Shaoxing, Ningbo, and Subei. The new ethnic distinctions were being drawn along the lines of who was rich and poor in the city (Honig 1992). These discriminative categories of race, class, and ethnicity did prevail in Shanghai's social scene. But these identities and categories did not constitute the subjectivity I am talking about here. Still, in the space of the Great World, one can see the work of a specific subjectivity or character—the sense of who we are in relation to others. This subjectivity was quite different from that of the other citizens, national subjects, and colonial subjects we have seen. It might be called a retranslative subjectivity, a subjectivity formed from a cluster of subjective positions, each of which was a translation of the other.

A Shanghai subjectivity that was born in the playground was a plural subjectivity—plural not only in the sense of the coexistence of different subjective positions but also in the sense that different positions served as translators of each other. This was best illustrated by a light comedy opera, *Zhaicaixin* (Picking Cabbage Hearts) that played in the Great World between 1914 and 1917 (Shanghai xiqu yanjiu hui 1927, vol. 3).[24] The structure of the play is man finds woman, but it is set against the background of the outbreak of World War I and shows the increasing tension between the city and the country. In flirting with a young woman, the male protagonist assumes many postures—a comprador in a Western-style jacket and hat, an orphan of a literati family, a *tanhuang* singer who picks up others' opinions and puts them into the lyrics of his songs, and, of course, a boy who wants to find a relatively trustworthy girl. The protagonist speaks from several different positions. In the voice of the comprador, he talks about the panic brought on by the war, but that panic is limited to a specific social group once he reassumes his naive identity as a boy pursuing a country girl. When imitating the *tanhuang* singer, he gives voice to those who lament such things as hit-and-run car accidents, the lack of education for all children, and the exploitation of women. Thus, the urban life of Shanghai is criticized as he attempts to escape by following the girl to her village home. Yet while masquerading as a comprador in the village, he is seen as a "promising" match and is accepted as the girl's fiancé. Over the course of the piece, the protagonist assumes a variety of disguises, and he encounters multiple interpretations of them. In the end, as a result of his struggles with many different roles, he comes to realize a kind of caution or self-awareness about the limits of different subjective positions.[25] What was seen here was not a national or a bourgeois character, nor was it a local or primitive subject like those one would have seen in most of the world expos. Rather, what was seen here was an interactive character involving subjects from all levels of culture. The interaction could be interpreted as affirming, critical, or both; and it brought to the urban crowd a strategy for understanding its complicated and deceptive cosmopolitan world.

Dream On, Dream Off

The success of Huang Chujiu's vision of a "world" centered in the here and now with free entrance and open membership inspired him to invest more heavily in the real estate and stock markets. Unlike the aspirations of Zhang Honglu, who dreamed of sailing abroad, Huang Chujiu's dream was Shanghai-centered, but it took on multiple faces. The Day and Night Bank and the Jiangnan Stock Market provided the financial base that enabled Huang Chujiu to invest in more business and construction enterprises. Originally noted as a "medicine king," Huang continued to initiate the manufacture of medicinal and nutritional products after the founding of the Great World. He rebuilt his two medicine factories, the Zhong Fa dayuaofang (Chinese-French Dispensary, founded in 1903) and the Zhonghua zhiyao gongsi (Drug Manufacture of China, founded in 1913), into multi-storied buildings decorated, respectively, with blue and yellow porcelain exteriors. After extending their sales to Southeast Asia, he also attempted to compete with the British tobacco companies by founding his Dachang tobacco company (1923). His investment in manufacturing was the glass manufactory Gongyi (1923); his contribution to public welfare was the Shanghai Contagious Diseases Hospital (Shanghai shiyi jijiu yiyuan, 1927), a philanthropic medical institution. By this time, both capital and goods seem to have flowed smoothly in and out of Huang Chujiu's hands. The success of the Great World facade as an entertainment, consumption, and financial corner in the French Concession was so well established that the price of land in its neighborhood went up several times. Huang Chujiu, a merchant who had grown big witnessing the growth of the real estate market of Shanghai, wanted to try the real estate business, even to build a portion of the city himself. This, however, would later prove to be the end of his dream of the world.

Huang's ambitious move into the real estate market seemed to go smoothly at the beginning, but it soon turned sour at the end of the 1920s. He was able to purchase and lease a huge piece of land at the center of the International Settlement from a Chinese real estate dealer, Qian Yangyuan, and some of his neighbors. When the paperwork was complete, the piece of land now in his name covered three whole blocks of Nanjing Road's most central point, starting from the present-day Shanxi Road and running all the way west to Zhejiang Road (Qin Luzhi 1999, 189). On this property, he constructed twenty to thirty new buildings that reflected his vision of a prosperous street. The first floors of these buildings housed shops and teahouses, and the upper floors provided offices and suites. The fashionable architectural style took time and money to build, and Huang had to use quite a lot of the savings from his Day and Night Bank. When the pretty new buildings appeared on Nanjing Road, they were empty and lacked lessees. Huang Chujiu managed to fill the spaces with his own businesses, but he did not have enough capital to survive the depression without going bankrupt. Soon he found that the Day and Night Bank, the institute that had been bringing in capital, was losing customers. The network of the Shanghai Green Gang, which was then the pet of Chiang Kai-shek, not only penetrated the Great World but also heavily squeezed the Day and Night Bank (Wang Renze and Xiong Shanghou 1984, 268–74). Under all these pressures, Huang's "world" began to fall apart.

The unpopularity of the new properties was closely related to the social unrest and new economic and political conflict within the country and to the worldwide depression that had come to Shanghai at last. In 1927 a workers' movement had threatened the Municipal Council and the Chiang Kai-shek government. Having recently seized power in the GMD government, Chiang Kai-shek had used both the police force and the army to subdue the Shanghai workers' movement as well as a variety of student demonstrations. Meanwhile, he also mobilized the underground world, such as the Green Gang, to control the urban neighborhood and the Shanghai economy. The Green Gang leader Huang Jirong, who became the owner of the Great World after Huang Chujiu died, "helped" Huang Chujiu's rapid fall and centralized the financial agencies around Chiang's core banks (Martin 1996, 193–95). The worldwide depression had hit Shanghai in 1931, and many real estate dealers became increasingly conservative, letting only the really powerful companies participate in more speculative pursuits like the businesses in Huang's new buildings. It was unlikely that these powerful companies would share Huang's vision. The flow of capital stagnated during the depression. Nanjing Road, at this economic downturn, did not prosper any more than it ever had.

By the end of the 1920s, the Great World had met an ironic end. In the second decade of the twentieth century, Huang had created the urban facade to celebrate a world of "liberty" and economic opportunity that a commoner like himself could, with some luck, seize. His proto-mall featured the coexistence of different peoples and cultures, local and foreign, under one sky, and he called it his "world." The end of his story shows exactly the opposite: that he could lay his hands on real estate in the International Settlement only because the bigger real estate dealers did not want to risk investing at a time of revolution and depression. This proved to be exactly the reason for his bankruptcy. What was falling apart was really the "great world" that Huang had envisioned and that the public had once been convinced could be. The bankruptcy of the Day and Night Bank hit its lower-class customers, who were the majority of its clientele, most severely—namely, the small shopkeepers, un-skilled laborers, rickshaw pullers, service workers, prostitutes, and com-moners who Huang thought had benefited, like himself, from the Republic. Huang himself died of a heart attack and other diseases in 1931, in the midst of the crisis of the Day and Night Bank. The Huang family was said to have offered their own property to compensate the bank's customers for their losses, but the compensation simply went into the pockets of those who ended up with Huang's leftover property.

The Great World, during this ordeal, fell into the hands of Huang Jinrong, the head of the Green Gang and the buddy of the newly emerged military and economic power, Chiang Kai-shek (Martin 1996). Huang Jinrong's gang had become increasingly powerful and obtained a domi-nant position in the Shanghai public life during the late 1920s due to his close relationship with Chiang.

As the Great World was renamed Rong's Great World (Rongji dashijie, named after Huang Jinrong), the stateless Republic Huang Chujiu had once envisioned gave way to a new state organ of the GMD. As we know, at this period, from the end of the 1920s into the beginning of the 1930s, Chiang Kai-shek had just usurped the presidency of the GMD, cracked down on the Communists in Shanghai, and moved the capital from Beijing to Nanjing (in 1927). The Nanjing government at once con-trolled the army and police force (Wakeman 1995) and the top Chinese families of the finance-based international economy. The Nanjing period (1927–1937) of the Republic, therefore, was marked by the marriage of army and police, of bankers and financiers domestic and abroad, and of the state and former underground society. The Shanghai urban space of the 1930s was surely transformed by the ever-improving collaboration between the Chiang Kai-shek power and the Shanghai Municipal Council. It is ironic, but not surprising, that the Shanghai of the Nanjing period is probably the most widespread image of the city today.

CONCLUSION

Chinese Cosmopolitanism Repositioned

The city and urban cultural life described in this volume have a lot to do with what can be called at large a Chinese cosmopolitanism, or cosmopolitanism in a Chinese context.[1] I use the word "Chinese" to refer to a collection of cultural-historical as well as textual resources rather than to a political and social entity, and the word "cosmopolitanism" to refer to a set of political, material, intellectual, and emotional practices. Though not merely ideas and discourses, these practices do connect with a connotation of "cosmos" or "universe" *(tian xia)* in Chinese thought. As Mizoguchi has concisely put it, in Chinese political and moral thinking it is the *tian xia*, the cosmos or the universe, rather than the state or the emperor, that stands for the highest call for the public *(gong)* or public good (1989, 74–95).[2] Unlike in the European post-Enlightenment tradition, in which heaven was the opposite of the secular human world, here the ultimate public is conceived as the greatest justice and hospitality that the universe provides for all life forms. Seen from the perspective of the cosmos or the universe, the "ultimate public" is by no means the opposite of any "private" or individual existence. Rather, it speaks through the healthy, friendly coexistence of every form of being—natural phenomena, a variety of life world(s), spatial orientations, harmonious social relationships, and a prosperous (not necessarily profitable) economy, as well as in everyone's sense of worth and unanimous happiness. The city, as the center that circulates people, goods, and culture, is the chosen site of this cosmopolitanism. It should only be natural for urban life to bear the ideal of the ultimate public good at sociopolitical, material, moral, and emotional levels.

This book approaches this subject in light of the insights of Jacques Derrida and tells the story of how the city became the home of cosmopolitanism by being a *refuge* for it, rather than its ought-to-be *origin.* Derrida suggested that it is the "city of refuge" and the great hospitality it offers that carries on the meaning of cosmopolitanism (2001, 4–5). In the context this book provides, I would like to note, it was cosmopolitanism as well as its various practices that were in exile and were in constant search for a new haven. It is obvious to everyone that the harmonious coexistence of all life forms that Chinese cosmopolitanism assumed is not as much a lost past as it is a lack (or at least a sporadic lack) in human history. Yet the connection between city life and the practices of this cosmopolitanism is too historical to be considered unreal. Instead of seeking for the absolute reality in this cosmopolitanism, it is more productive to recognize the way this cosmopolitanism existed: It existed not as a completed structure but, rather, as a remnant, residue, anomaly, and, to some extent, disruptive and uncontrollable element. A city of *refuge* receives what is already incomplete, what is dissident and unruly. The sociopolitical and cultural practices described in this book became closely involved with the city Shanghai because they were themselves refugees at firsthand.

To be more specific, I have tried to show that during what I call the inside-out-turn of the Qing Empire, the cosmopolitanism I am talking about was repositioned in both semantic and physical terms by being such a refugee. It was released, transformed, and transferred to a new site. It was released from the imperial regime that consisted of heaven, earth, and the human race and was transformed into a postimperial cultural and political pursuit for the new. It escaped the confinement of imperial and imperialist systems and survived in nonexclusive and retranslative practices of cultural differences. It left behind the rigid cosmic-human relationship and opened itself to an unruly practice of modern globality, a globality that created room for an alternative to the imperialist world order. The unruly cultural practices, as I have argued throughout these pages, emerged with the unraveling of Neo-Confucianism, and in turn helped to unfreeze the Chinese cosmopolitanism from their crystallization within the Qing regime. They also helped turn the spirit into a cultural alternative to the multiculturalism produced by what Wallerstein would call the "cosmopolitan core" of the capitalist world system.

To conclude, I would like to elaborate further on the repositioning of Chinese cosmopolitanism by revisiting some key concepts discussed above, such as "unruly cultural practices," the "history of noncapital," and "retranslation." These concepts enable us to understand this Chinese cosmopolitanism as both a rare historical value and a cultural and political practice, rather than as a philosophy or a national ideological system. I would also like to examine the ways the cultural practices that brought about Shanghai began to decrease. This decrease had to do with two important events that significantly redefined Shanghai: The first was the irreconcilable internal split between "retranslational" and "revolutionary" intellectuals around 1917; the second was the ascension to power of the Jiang Jieshi faction of the GMD government through the 1927 anti-Communist coup, which largely limited the choices of being politically and culturally nonconformist while at the same time being cosmopolitan.

Unruly Practice and Cosmopolitanism

Unruly cultural practice and "retranslation," due to their decentering power, were vital to the transformation of the Chinese cosmopolitanism I am talking about. Generally speaking, I see in the unruly and insubordinate cultural practices the fortitude of the creativity and multiplicity that had been crystallized in the imperial structure and that were released during the crisis-driven shift of the urban centers. Somewhat like what Wallerstein calls "anti-systemic movements" (1991), the unruly practices were the forces that pushed Shanghai's urban culture off the track of cultural rigidity, hierarchy, rationalized power structures, and hegemonic master codes. Retranslation, which I borrowed from Chakrabarty and elaborated on in the introduction and throughout the chapters, can be described as a collection of ways of cultural decolonization. It served to create room for cultural and historical multiplicity and to deconstruct the domination of imperialist and colonialist cultural hegemony. If the unruly practices were the creative social and cultural practices that repositioned cosmopolitanism in Shanghai, retranslation, then, was a special and necessary way of being unruly.

Questions naturally arise. What exactly is the relationship between the unruly practices and the concept of cosmopolitanism? Is it possible to discuss this relationship conceptually, without having to repeat the entire historical narrative?

To explore these questions, let me turn to Mikhail Bakhtin's *Dialogical Imagination* (1981) where the "unconquerable," desystematic nature of the unruly practices finds a home.[3] As someone whose intellectual resources differed from those that gave rise to structuralist thinking in Western Europe, Bakhtin remains one of those rare thinkers who actually endows us with tools to go beyond the usual systematic imagination of modernities, empires, world systems, and multiculturalism that are said to be cosmopolitan. As a cultural theorist, he drew our attention to the distinction between the *social-ideological* use of language and the system of language (Bakhtin 1981, 275), between the dialogue (dialogic language) and the monologue (monologic language) (ibid., 270). In his terminology, a monologue or monologic utterance conveys meaning through a single source, characteristically a closed system or a speaker or author, and is therefore "isolated, finished . . . divorced from its verbal and actual context" (Morris 1994, 34–35). Driven by a centripetal momentum that draws things toward a center, monologia is a unitary system that can be easily used by various mechanisms, including the state apparatus. Dialogic language, on the contrary, is the product of social contexts that require a speaker, a listener, and, most importantly, a social-ideological relationship between the two (Bakhtin 1981, 331–53). It is driven by a centrifugal momentum that tends to push things in all directions (Morris 1994, 74–77). Therefore, dialogic utterance adds multiplicity and fluidity to language by including a wide variety of ways of speaking and different rhetorical strategies and vocabularies generated by various contexts (Bakhtin 1981, 272). The unruly practices that set off the radical changes in the Qing cultural system can be best translated to the category of dialogic utterance.

Bakhtin's inspiration is more than that. His greatest contribution lies in the fact that, while giving full endorsement to differences, he refreshed the very concept of the whole. A centripetal system of the monologue is by no means a representation of the whole or the universal; rather, it is a cancellation of it. Because this is so, "alongside verbal-ideological centralization and unification, the uninterrupted process of decentralization and disunification go forward" (Bakhtin 1981, 272). Yet for Bakhtin, this decentralization or disunification does not mean fragmentation, just as unruly practices did not. Rather, it opens to a different concept of the whole, a whole of different, heterogeneous utterances. This is what Bakhtin calls *heteroglossia,* which refers to a stock of different ways of speaking and writing, different rhetorical modes, and different vocabularies established in social-ideological relationships among all sorts of speakers and listeners (ibid., 301–31). Heteroglossia is not a system but the imagined, edgeless whole of the variety of ways of speaking.[4] Heteroglossia remains such a whole exactly because it does not reify differences; nor does it make differences into a discriminative, singular system. To extend Bakhtin's concepts into sociocultural and political arenas: I see cosmopolitanism as the best translation of heteroglossia.

To an extent, both the unruly and the retranslational practices I am talking about were ways of being cosmopolitan in the sense that they liberated heterogeneity, or heteroglossia, without leading to separation and discrimination.[5] Historically speaking, they pushed culture toward multiplicity, fluidity, and even anarchy, for the very redemption of the heterogeneous whole. As I have attempted to show, the unruly practices that ushered in the decentering process of the Qing Empire originated from an eighteenth-century (and earlier) task of reconstructing a nondiscriminatory political prototype from proliferated and fragmented textual traces, some of them forgeries. This contradiction between the perfect continuum of polity and culture and its fragmented materializations designated *difference* itself as the primary condition within which that very nondiscriminative ideal world is desired. The argument between the New Text and the Old Text schools of Confucianism was as much about the authenticity of classical texts as it was about the multiplicity and diversity of the origins of political models (Elman 1984; Wang Hui 2004). The key issue now lay in how to reach the ideal world of nondiscrimination from the world of difference and multiplicity. The gap between the nondiscriminative ideal world and its fragmented, contradictory materializations set off perpetual pursuits of a world of *datong* (the ideal of Chinese cosmopolitanism) through desystematization. These pursuits of *datong* were unruly and, to use Bakhtin's word, dialogic in their very logic: It was exactly for the sake of the great harmonious world that they would drive history centrifugally away from any regime that reified difference into sets of systemized discrimination.

The centrifugal pursuits of the political and cultural ideal in China since the eighteenth century, which could be the effect of the unraveling of Neo-Confucianism, formed an unprecedented body of heteroglossia that redefined Chinese cosmopolitanism in various ways. The shattering of the orthodox moral philosophy based on a lineage of sage-kings, as we have seen, gave way to other "dialogic utterances," such as the teachings of the "uncrowned king" and the "people" (Elman 1984). During the nineteenth century, dialogic utterance about the ultimate ideal polity was no longer limited to the realm of Neo-Confucianism. It appeared, for example, in the Taipings' "Heavenly Kingdom," in which there was no hierarchy or discrimination, as well as in the movement boycotting U.S. goods, which was a refusal of the discriminative world order. It also took shape in anarchism, and later on in the ideals of the Republic, socialism, or any imagined "world" that sounded nondiscriminatory to its advocates at the time. Each context, whether it was the New Text Confucian scholars, the Chinese Christians, the Russian and eastern European influences, the Japanese connection, or the Chinese overseas, had its own social-ideological speakers and listeners, as well as their distinct relationships. As a result, by the beginning of the twentieth century, the ultimate ideal of the human world was no longer fixed by any singular "system"; rather, it had become a heteroglossia itself.[6] Chinese cosmopolitanism was set free from the imperial system as these utterances came to desystemize the cosmic-political connection in which imperial legitimacy was rooted.

The shifts of urban cultural centers attested that intellectual and textual history was not the only home of the unruly practices of the changing cosmopolitanism. During the shift of urban cultural centers from the heartland cities to Shanghai, the unruly practices redefined Chinese cosmopolitanism in the realms of technological transmission, book culture, theater culture, entertainment, consumption, and space building. Compared to intellectual and textual history, in the field of urban cultural history, the transition of Chinese cosmopolitanism was made, in a sense, not only more tangible and accessible but also more profound.

This volume shows the specific ways in which the cosmopolitanism I am talking about was repositioned from the heartland cities to Shanghai. The cosmopolitanism was embodied, for example, in the practice of infinite translatability among knowledge systems. Unlike earlier missionary translations, which tended to eliminate knowledge itself in the name of Creation, the practices of science and technology in the Jiangnan Arsenal became negotiations between the fixed categories of Chinese learning and Western learning. The negotiated translations even de-systematized "science" in the sense that they led to an uncontrollable proliferation of knowledge so vast it threatened the very *disciplinary* function of scientific knowledge itself. Here, the cosmopolitanism de-territorialized itself by investigating connections between the cosmic order and the human world, then reterritorialized itself in the dialogic utterance of "science" guided by the spirit of unlimited translatability. In the realm of book culture, we can see how cosmopolitanism changed its configuration when philology changed its focus. Philological practice became, instead of a methodology and a scholarship that ushered in the reconstruction of cosmopolitan antiquity, the means to negotiate with the universal scientific modernity threatening to colonize Asia. Although the very difference of minor histories tended to disappear in the face of an exclusive system of modernity, the unruly philological method helped preserve the histories and the multiplicity of sciences. The de-elimination of distinct histories from a pseudo-universal system of modernity was itself the practice of cosmopolitanism.

Similar transitions took place in aspects of theater culture and in the configuration of urban space. Beneath the recurring urban festivities that had been repeatedly categorized as *yin* during the Qing dynasty, there was a hidden fortitude of redefining *shengshi*, the "prosperous era" or a "heaven-blessed society." Instead of making the "heaven-blessed society" a celebration of imperial order and royal legitimacy, the prac-tice in the name of *yin* turned *shengshi* into an unruly urban festivity where a bandit's morality interacted with the imperial morality, where a folk sense of injustice interacted with the imperial meaning of justice. This negotiation between folk justice and imperial rule foreshadowed the way "world" became emotionally and morally meaningful. Finally, Shanghai theaters were able to stage a representation of justice for the colored people that confronted the injustice of the world order. Cosmo-politanism thus survived in the festive culture of Shanghai.

The configuration of urban space was also turned into "utterances" of the changing cosmopolitanism I am talking about. Cross-cultural landscapes in the upper-class gardens transformed from the symbols of imperial interior to symbols of a cultural and economic imperial fron-tier. A transnational status of architecture was replacing the imperial status, before this architectural taste was itself downplayed by the anti-

Qing and anti-imperialist sentiment. The "world" space for "commoner" entertainment, on the other hand, shared little part of the world system even though it was built after the style of the world expositions. Rather, it revived a heteroglossic collection of spatial visions of the world.

These and other aspects of urban culture convinced me that Chinese cosmopolitanism was repositioned from a cosmo-centric, imperial-based multiplicity to a set of practices of difference in the modern global-ity. The unruly cultural practices that empowered this change were con-stantly fragmentary, sporadic, situational, and dialogically oriented. And yet, with a centrifugal momentum they were able to transform public actors and reshape the focal point of that cosmopolitanism. Of course, the repositioned cosmopolitanism was hardly more "Chinese" than any other cosmopolitanism seemed to be. But the mechanism that had settled the Chinese cosmopolitanism with the modern globality was still his-torically specific. The historical specificity of Chinese cosmopolitanism determined the unique way the historical and cultural China—already multicentric as it was—defined as well as connected itself to modern globality. In other words, the historical specificity was crucial to the polit-ical significance of Chinese cosmopolitanism. To elaborate on this signifi-cance, let me turn to the issue of retranslation and history of noncapital.

Retranslation and History of Noncapital

As a specific type of unruly practice, cross-cultural retranslation was crucial to the repositioning of Chinese cosmopolitanism. In the most general sense, retranslation had long been a cross-cultural practice and had served to maintain the consistency of textual knowledge for the cultural hospitableness of the late-imperial order.[7] Not until the very textual genealogy of Neo-Confucianism was unraveled from within did that retranslation change from a fixed format to a cultural strategy. Retranslation became a way to decolonize, to deal with cultural differ-ences in the modern world without losing the sense of the whole, and to provide a cultural and political alternative to the global modernity.

"Retranslation" in this later sense can be easily understood in Bakhtin's terms. In the context of colonialism, retranslation itself is one way of transforming the colonialist monologic language into dialogic languages, thereby leading toward heteroglossia. The imperialist or colonial dis-course is monologic since it requires a passive listener or a listener who accepts the position defined for him or her by the speaker or colonizer. Retranslation, however, refashions the colonial or imperialist monologue on the listener's side. Retranslation creates more than one listener position, or more than one speaker-listener relationship. It takes place among at least three parties: the monologic/colonial speaker, the colonized/listener, who is now the retranslator, and other colonized/listeners. Sometimes, the retranslator puts the monologic/colonial speaker in the position of respondent. It replies to the colonial speaker as well as to other listeners in their own rhetorical modes and vocabularies. Here, the listener-to-listener relationship is like that between self and alternative selves. When the self of the listener is erased by the monologic language of the colonizers, other selves remain to uncover it.

Having said this, I do need to stress that retranslation does not provide a true alternative without a framework of human history, particularly that of the history of noncapital; as I have indicated, the history of noncapital refers to a history where capital and commodity work but do not dominate. In other words, to connect to the "history of noncapital" necessarily means any retranslation will be political and critical. To elaborate on this connection I shall recapitulate the issue of historical difference discussed at the beginning of the book.

As I indicated in the introduction, the theoretical conceptualization of this volume is greatly inspired by Chakrabarty's account of History 2, or subaltern history, namely, the history of what was "not yet conquered" by and was actually "unconquerable" by the capitalist system. Chakrabarty situated the distinction between the two types of histories close to Marx's notion of the internal crisis of capitalism. In Chakrabarty's elaboration of Marx's concept, the repetitive and mechanical abstract labor at the core of capitalism (that is, History 1) inevitably finds its enemy in the life-world where the heterogeneity of human beings is the ruling principle (that is, History 2 or History 2s). For critics and historians, retranslation is the critical tool to emancipate History 2s from the hegemony of History 1. Although these ideas are all well put, Chakrabarty has yet to theorize clearly how the "not yet conquered" or the "unconquerable" histories reside not only within the inner human experience but also in records, movements, organizations and institutions. In this sense, the unfolding of History 2s does not necessarily confirm the thesis "the subaltern does not speak."[8] On the contrary, the records, movements, and organizations of the History 2s make retranslation an obvious critical task.

To further clarify the political significance of retranslation and its role in transforming Chinese cosmopolitanism, I see a theoretical necessity to expand "subaltern history," or History 2, into "the history (or histories) of noncapital." To an extent, this is to move the concept of History 2 out of the experience of India and to situate it within the global experiences of other regions and countries of the world. Prasenjit Duara makes the effort to take decolonization as a global phenomenon in which each different context and location generated its own form. One sees in Duara's book that different priorities have been established in China, Africa, and India to carry out the dual task of decolonization, the task of defeating imperialism in the political arena and the task of defeating colonialism in the cultural field (Duara 2003, 1–2). But viewed together, the anti-imperialist and anticolonial movements in these different places form, beside a visible history of decolonization, episodes of a history of noncapitalism at large. In a sense, History 2s, or the history of noncapital in my terminology, should be considered a larger history, longer in time and wider in scale, than the history of capitalism. Such history travels in time and space, internally and externally, in silence and in voices, and it leaves traces and records in movements, organizations, even in governments all over the globe. Subaltern history and types of decolonization were different "utterances" within a "heteroglossia" of the history of noncapital.

Retranslation is something politically and culturally meaningful only when such a history of noncapital exists. And vice versa, retranslation is politically and culturally important only because it brings a history of noncapital into existence, no matter how momentarily. As a larger history, the history of noncaptial does not have a system or fixed units. But it does have concepts, languages, traces, records, material forms, and social fabrics. If the traces of the history of noncapital were used as source languages for capitalism to translate from, then they can also serve as target languages to retranslate into. Mastering the traces of the history of noncapital—traces in the form of words, cultural principles, social groups, and practices of materiality—means to obtain the basic literacy of retranslation. When based on such a wide vision as well as on the literacy of human history, a retranslation could actually serve as a tool to be used in creating a cosmopolitanism of noncapitalism. A retranslation could provide the subject of the history of noncapital with the tools for making distinctions as well as connections, for launching cultural exchanges, for engaging in political negotiation with the subject of the history of capital. These implications of retranslation, I maintain, formed the core of the Chinese representation of the world during the period I am talking about. To put it in a simple way: These implications made the Chinese cosmopolitanism I am talking about a cosmopolitanism of the Third World (and was by no means the only one).

To a large extent, this repositioning of Chinese cosmopolitanism benefited from the fact that in China the history of noncapital overlapped with, instead of being subsumed in, the history of capitalism. By "overlap" I mean that the history of noncapital was outside the history of capitalism, even though it was gradually incorporated into the latter. Unlike the critique of capitalism in Western Europe and North America, in China, as it was perhaps in Africa and India, the critique of capitalism and its cultural values actually had two fronts, as Duara observed (2004, 1–3). To rephrase Duara's words in the context of this volume: The critique of capitalism had, on the one hand, a front of pursuing constant revolution in political, social, and cultural fields. The pursuit found its affinity in modernity (or modernities) itself, which served, in the history of capital, as a critique as well as a threat to organized, reified, institutionalized capitalism. On the other hand, the critique of capitalism in China also had a front of anticolonialism, which was also a critique and a threat to capitalism but which was derived from the angle of what capitalism is not. The major ways to subvert capitalist culture on this front include, for example, retranslation, preservation of traces of minority history, and criticism of a West-centric value system from a non-Western perspective. This second front provided the necessary condition for Chinese cosmopolitanism to reposition itself near the Third World.

Although it was fortunate that the history of noncapital generated the cosmopolitanism I have tried to present, it was unfortunate that this cosmopolitanism did not advance to a fuller cultural and political formation. This is in part due to the fact that the dual critical fronts, or the dual missions of resisting capitalism, while broadening the edge of critique, also caused a problem for Chinese history. The two fronts of critique did not always progress together, and they actually developed in different forms at different speeds. The first of these two fronts developed more fully since the decentralizing unruly practices that had disabled the Qing regime were relatively easy to transform into a novel pursuit of the new. The unruly was combined with the reformist and the revolutionary in the social, cultural, and political realms. The second critical front, the front of anticolonialism, however, did not develop into an intellectual project or continuous cultural practice as it did in India and Africa (Duara 2004, 2). Because of lack of urgency, the task that required a much wider range of literacy in more than one type of histories was repeatedly delayed. This unfinished mission of anticolonialism limited the way Chinese cosmopolitanism grew into fuller theoretical, intellectual, and political formations.

As China marched further into the twentieth century, the unbalanced distribution of Chinese cosmopolitanism in different cultural fields became more obvious. The unruly practices—the fortitude that had brought the Qing dynasty to an end and had turned Shanghai into a new location of Chinese cosmopolitanism—split. The reformist and revolutionary type of unruly practices gradually parted from retranslation or decolonization. In many cases, the mission of revolution and constant renewal seemed to have sidestepped the mission of decolonization and retranslation. An immediate disadvantage was that the literacy of noncapitalist history was thwarted in the repeated circulation of new state apparatuses, new cultures, new sciences, new languages. This split, in my view, eventually weakened the cultural creativity of the unruly practices as well as the continuous development of Chinese cosmopolitanism. Its effect has lasted to the present day.

1917: Between Antitradition and Anti-Imperialism

In this and the following sections, I will elaborate the split in unruly practices and its effect upon Shanghai's urban culture from a more detailed, historical perspective. The split between the different types of unruly practices, particularly between the radical and retranslational, can be historically dated to two crucial years, 1917 and 1927.

In this book I have attempted to show the unruly and insubordinate cultural practices that brought Shanghai under siege from both Qing and imperialist cultural regimes. These pursuits, for example, accelerated alternative scientific and technological learning and pressured the Qing state into abolishing civil service examinations and announcing the reform project known as the New Policy in 1902. This was followed by activist philological practices that engaged the imperial and imperialist orders of words and terminologies. In the same context, the vernacular festive culture of *yin* proved to be insubordinate to Qing state control and provided the necessary environment for the emergence of a radical cosmopolitanism prior to the 1911 Revolution. Finally, the submergence of the top economic groups, rather than the emergence of a "bourgeois class," turned the significant part of the elite into critics of the Qing and the imperialist world order. Demonstrations targeting the unequal global exchange of labor and capital marked the creation of an urban public insubordinate to the world cultural regime and to the modern urban order of the bourgeoisie. Shanghai became a rebellious city at the double edges of empires and presented an urban culture that actively engaged in international politics and culture. Thus it was the new site of the transformed Chinese cosmopolitanism.

During the first decade of the twentieth century, however, the pursuit of renewing the cultural and political ideal was already beginning to show internal divisions that later turned into conflict. This division and conflict significantly redefined Shanghai as a cultural center. The earliest sign of the disagreement was seen in the debate between Liang Qichao and the more radical anti-Manchu revolutionaries between 1905 and 1908 (Bernal 1976, 129–97).[9] Focusing on the newspapers *Xinmin bao* (New Citizen) and *Minbao* (People), the debate unfolded along the lines of whether it was imperialism or the Manchu state that was the primary target of revolution (ibid.). The disagreement did not generate a huge conflict but it did create a division in Tokyo, Hawaii, Shanghai, and other cities between reformist intellectual leaders who preferred a constitutional regime and the more radical groups who sought to overthrow Manchu rule through a national revolution. The division cut across existing organizations, such as the influential Chinese Educational Society. It also appeared between older and newly established organizations as well, known by such different categories as "constitutional" and "revolutionary" (Zhang Yufa 1971, 1975).[10] This division reflected the irony of being at the overlapping edges of dual empires: While the duality of the dominant power created alliances between the critics of the Qing and critics of imperialism, it also determined the split between the critics themselves.

The division between the reformists and the revolutionaries dissolved at the sociopolitical level when the Republic was established in 1912, but it left an irreconcilable gap in the cultural arena. The fall of the Qing dynasty did not remove the cultural task of fighting imperialism, or indeed of fighting colonialism from a non-Western perspective. At the outbreak of World War I, those who took anticolonization as the most important cultural goal attempted to show the shortcomings of Western modernity from a non-Western viewpoint. Du Yaquan, then chief editor of the Commercial Press's intellectual journal, *Eastern Miscellany*, wrote a series of articles about World War I, questioning what Western modernity had brought to the human world (Huters 2005). These intellectuals also sought to preserve the subhistory of non-Western culture under the imperialist cultural regime. Examples presented in this volume are the efforts of Du Yaquan and his colleagues at retranslating botanical terminology and Zhang Yuanji's attempt to control the circulation of classical resources (see chapter 2).

Nationalists and radical intellectuals, on the other hand, preferred a total "New Culture" that would remove existing cultural practices to the point of promoting complete Westernization. Cai Yuanpei, head of the Educational Bureau of the new Republic, launched European-style education in the universities. Chen Duxiu, captain of the New Culture movement in 1917, sought to sweep away any traces of tradition. It is quite clear that for Chen, the imagined ideal West was reduced to "Mr. Science" and "Mr. Democracy," figurative images of the mainstream West. The "minor West"—Poland, Russia, Ireland, Greece, and others—that the late-Qing writings had once brought to life no longer registered on his map of the New Culture.

Not surprisingly, a debate over "culture" erupted between 1917 and 1919 between the *New Youth* circle, who, together with radical advocates of the New Culture, were centered at Beijing University, and the circle of *Eastern Miscellany*, which was an organic intellectual journal of the Commercial Press in Shanghai (Huters 1999, 2005). The core of the debate, in today's vision, centered around what the task of the New Culture should be—combating tradition or combating colonialism. The New Culturalists took "tradition" as the enemy. They campaigned for a vernacular that was devoid not only of any references to classical texts but also of any rhetorical devices. Their most extreme proposals included campaigning for the replacement of the Chinese written language with a romanized writing system and calling on Chinese youth to read only Western books. The anticolonial synergy that had just come of age among the former cultural reformers was now labeled a "conservative" endeavor. By the mid-1920s, when the students who had studied in Europe and the United States secured their central positions in leading institutions of higher education (Shu Xincheng [1933] 1973), the task of combating tradition had replaced the task of combating colonialism. Even the Commercial Press, an enterprise known for its philologists and alternative sciences, was now willing to call upon groups and curriculums that were more characteristically "modern" in the "Western" sense.

After 1917, campaigning against the imperialist cultural regime ceased to be a *cultural* task or a culture-specific task among the cultural practices of China. By this I mean that in China after 1917, the imperialist cultural regime that had provoked West-centralism, racism, and a world hierarchy of civilizations was no longer the target of cultural criticism from a non-Western perspective. Combating imperialism was no longer a philological task or a task of evidential historiography; nor was it an alternative scientific task any longer, a culture-specific task of performing culture or a task of material culture. Anti-imperialism no longer meant the preservation of subhistories or the plurality of knowledge against the imminent hegemony of European modernity. It no longer meant decolonization through the retranslation of universal models of knowledge back into heterogeneous models.

This is not to say that anti-imperialism ceased to be a non-Western practice in China. Rather, I am trying to show that the non-Western perspectives and non-Western cultures ceased to be considered valuable and useful resources in the critique of imperialism, even though they were, in fact. As a result, whereas prior to the New Culture movement, reform-minded intellectuals—ranging from activist philologists, historians, and alternative scientists to classical writers—were still allies of the more radical anarchists and revolutionaries on the front line of cultural advances, after 1917 the cultural attempts of the former group were sidestepped. The radicals began, instead, to collaborate with students who had returned from abroad, as represented by the loose alliance between Chen Duxiu and Hu Shi in the New Culture movement, which originated at Beijing University. Correspondingly, the indigenous practices of using classical texts were compartmentalized as "Chinese" and "traditional" and remained as residues of the past or of an old regime.

This result of the debate between *New Youth* and *Eastern Miscellany*, as Theodore Huters has pointed out, redefined Shanghai's role as a cultural center (1999). In Shanghai, as elsewhere, the cultural frontier moved toward Westernization at the price of sacrificing the minor West and the non-West that had once been comembers of an imagined community of an anti-imperialist world. The radical practice of New Culture in Shanghai, therefore, became distanced from the ongoing performances of the social and political tasks of anti-imperialism in the city. These anti-imperialist actions took the form of constant urban movements that had become a tradition and a spectacle in Shanghai ever since the 1905 movement to boycott U.S. goods (Remer 1933; Bergère 1989). The city witnessed another movement to boycott foreign goods in 1908, the May Fourth movement of 1919, the workers' strike protesting the May Thirtieth Massacre in 1925, and general strikes and demonstrations in 1927, to mention just a few. There were no less than 151 organized strikes in 1927, with the number of participants ranging from a little over 1,000 to 39,308 per strike (Ren Jianshu 1996, 348). While demonstrations were becoming semipermanent in Shanghai, however, the high culture or the New Culture began to drift apart. The urban movements after 1905 had almost no association with the practice of the New Culture. As Duara has pointed out, although there were vigorous anti-imperialist movements in China, "the need to critique the West culturally—to ideologically decolonize in the manner of a Frantz Fanon or Mahatma Gandhi," was not felt (2004, 2). There was an obvious gap between the local movements of anti-imperialism and the Westernized New Culture during the 1910s and 1920s. Not until after 1927 was this gap noticed among Chinese intellectuals.

1927: "The Paris of the East" in Another Light

The year 1927 was far more important than 1917, since it marked the conclusion of the urban history of the already-split cultural pursuit of the new. It marked the most crucial turning point in China's urban history since 1862, when Suzhou and Hangzhou fell.

During 1926 and 1927 Lu Xun, a well-known Chinese writer, experienced two violent incidents that marked the turning point of Chinese polity in two continuous years. On March 18, 1926, the militarist government in Beijing opened fire on demonstrating students. Among the victims was Liu Hezhen, a young woman studying at Beijing Women's

Normal Collage where Lu Xun was teaching. He resigned from the Educational Bureau in protest against the massacre and wrote a touching memorial to Liu Hezhen. Just over a year later, on April 12, three days after Lu Xun had given a lecture, "Revolution and Literature," at Guangzhou's Huangpu Academy of Politics, the Jiang Jieshi government ordered attacks on demonstrators at Guangzhou and Shanghai. Hundreds of strikers, as well as innocent women and children at both sites, were shot dead. Zheng Zhenduo and other intellectuals who witnessed the GMD's massacre in 1927 said it had "surpassed the brutality of Duan Qirui's militarist massacre of students" in 1926 and had "outdone the cruelty of the British authorities during the May Thirtieth Massacre (1925)" (Zheng Zhenduo et al. [1927] 1980). The Nanjing decade between 1927 and 1937, known as a decade of peak prosperity for the Shanghai economy, signaled a new era in which the Chiang Kai-shek clique established its military dominance through "white terror."

The 1927 anti-Communist coup generated several effects beyond the Communist-related issues, effects that significantly changed the nature of Shanghai as a city. Politically speaking, Shanghai during the Nanjing decade was similar to Paris during the regime of Georges Haussmann, when the city was rebuilt after the bloody crackdown on the Paris Commune. Following the crackdown, Paris went straight to high capitalism under strict political control: Haussmann's urban planners widened the streets of Paris, cleared away small shops, (re)built, along extremely symmetrical lines, boulevards where no confrontation could last long, and established public parks consciously designed and embellished for bourgeois tourists. Paris became the product of a bourgeois "class strategy" that aimed at preventing Parisian workers from dominating the city space and promoting the further commodification of everyday urban life (Lefebvre 1995, 74–78; Harvey 2003, 93–116). More than half a century later, the Jiang Jieshi government had a similar "class strategy" for rebuilding Shanghai after the anti-Communist coup. The nationalist government, for example, rebuilt Zhongshan Road, making it Shanghai's widest north-south arterial route. The government also registered and restructured the street numbers of the entire city's residences (Ren Jianshu 1996, 352). The sports fields, large memorial squares, and public parks constructed in the years following the coup were all designed, in one way or another, to remove the spatial facilitation of continued strikes and resultant chaos.

But the "class strategy" of rebuilding Shanghai was performed in more direct administrative and political terms. It was written, for example, in the way Shanghai changed from a county administration to a city government. The city government was originally intended to take over control of the city from the militarist regime after the North March. It became an instrument through which the GMD government enforced military control over radical practices in the city. Chiang Kai-shek nominated people to fill key positions in the Shanghai city government, including the commander of the Shanghai Guardian Troop, the head of the Bureau of Politics, the head of the police force, and the head of the Security Bureau (Ren Jianshu 1996, 326–27). The GMD army and police force applied military and political coercion to public life by prohibiting demonstrations against foreigners; the GMD government established a special committee to monitor the workers' unions, and it created the Industrial Bureau and Agricultural Department to organize workers and peasants in official terms (ibid., 329, 330, 352).

Economically speaking, Shanghai became the national center of capital circulation and, to an extent, the largest personal bank for Chiang Kai-shek's circle after 1927. The GMD's triumph over the northern militarists had a national impact in terms of the distribution of capital. The Nationalist government confiscated the capital reserve of the north (Beijing and Tianjin), which had previously been in the hands of militarists, as part of the spoils of victory and moved it to Shanghai. Prior to confiscation, the north's capital was considerable, representing 69.1 percent of national capital in 1921. After the confiscation, in 1928, Shanghai contained 75.3 percent of national capital (Sheehan 2000, 55). The Japanese invasion of northeastern China further moved the capital from Tianjin to Shanghai in 1931 (97.9 percent in 1935) (ibid.). Even though the French scholar Marie-Claire Bergère described the time between 1911 and 1927 as the "golden era of Chinese bourgeois" (1989, ch. 5), an urban class or an urban culture of Chinese bourgeois did not begin until the 1930s, after the Nanjing period. However, small business proprietors, who had always populated Shanghai, did not necessarily benefit from this centralization of capital. Rather, some became the victims of competition with larger banks that were controlled by the Chiang family and their relatives and associates. Huang Chujiu's Day and Night Bank was a classic example of victimization by the gangster society close to Chiang Kai-shek.

At the sociocultural level, the Chiang Kai-shek regime was known for banning books, shutting down newspapers and journals, and arresting and even murdering critics and left-wing writers. Even though left-wing writers and critics remained active in the city after 1927, many of them had to hide their political identities from the public sphere and go underground constantly. Meanwhile, new social and cultural models were promoted after 1927. For instance, although Green Gang boss Du Yuesheng was involved in the anti-Communist coup of April 1927 (Martin 1996, 145; Ren Jianshu 1996, 315), he was portrayed as the representative of the knight-errant (xia and haojie) spirit and as a Confucian gentleman (junzi) and a person of humanity (renren) (Martin 1996, 147–49). The cultural politics of making this Green Gang boss a heroic figure in popular culture erased and distorted the entire past of the unruly practice. What was considered "heroic" in popular late-Qing culture meant "revolutionary" and "insubordinate" to the current powers. But what won Du Yuesheng the reputation of being a knight-errant was his secret alliance with Bai Chongxi and the Chiang Kai-shek government in the crackdown on insubordinates, the kidnapping of union leaders, and the secret killing of anyone who was politically offensive. As a social hero and a Shanghai "notable," Du Yuesheng in turn collected cultural capital by staging free performances by leading Beijing opera stars (ibid., 149) and by patronizing local opera troupes in Shanghai.

What did Shanghai become after 1927? In the late 1920s and early 1930s Shanghai became, on the one hand, a more internationalized avant-garde culture that seemed to have naturally carried on the unruly pursuits for the new and the innovative. This avant-gardism mixed modernistic and left-wing literary and artistic imaginations and created its own cultural space in journals, galleries, book stores, coffee shops, cinemas, and clubs, as well as in architectural styles (Lee 1999; Gandelsonas 2002). On the other hand, there seemed to be, as Bergère observed, a "declining" moment of "Chinese bourgeois" at the return of state-run capitalism after 1927 (1989, conclusion).[11] By "declining" she was referring to the fact that the urban class, while struggling between the foreign capitalists and workers' movements, lost the chance to advance a "revolutionary nationalism" that history seemed to have once offered and became instead dependent on the rather reactionary Chiang Kai-shek regime (1989, ch. 6).[12] In cultural comparison to what she saw as "decline" is the crystallization of cosmopolitanism in the upper-class life. Education, book culture, urban space, and theatrical culture were rationalized by planning, management, and censorship. This crystallization was felt even in the rhythms of the fox-trot or tango in bars and nightclubs under the insubstantial glow of neon lights. A feeling of being yoked and of being deprived of the vitality of change expressed itself in a widespread metaphor of death before the dawn of tomorrow, of which Cao Yu's *Sunrise* and Mu Shiying's short story "Five People in the Night Club" provide vivid examples. This cultural crystallization perhaps explains why 1930s Shanghai was the peak of modernity—peak in the sense that the very original and creative energy that had been integral to the unruly cultural practices stopped generating new forms of culture and new stages of history.

It is in this sense that I claimed a weathering of unruly history and Chinese cosmopolitanism from Shanghai. This, of course, does not mean the end of the history of unruly practices itself (Lean 2004).[13] Rather, it refers to the fact that after 1927 Shanghai had gradually changed from what Derrida would call a "city of refuge" (2001, 4) to a city enacting the military and political control of the state. A city belonging to the state, Shanghai no longer offered a "new" culture that was endowed with infinite choices and forms of being unruly and being cosmopolitan. The 1917 New Culture movement had already separated "retranslational" from "the new," that is, it had taken the task of decolonization from the enterprise of modernization. The emotional trauma and antipathy to the GMD caused by the political events of 1927 further dissociated retranslation or decolonization from revolution in the cultural sense. The disgust felt toward political reality led intellectuals to swing between two poles: They either submerged themselves in "pure" arts or pure scholarship or they lowered their literary and artistic standards in seeking symbolic radical solutions to the political problem. Although these were certainly legitimate choices, Chinese cosmopolitanism seemed to be torn apart between crystallization and Westernization on the one hand, and a Communist ideal of internationalism that tended to overpoliticize cross-cultural issues. After 1927, only a relatively small amount of intellectual energy was devoted to cultivating the critical and retranslational literacy that was urgently needed in the new cultural fields such as media, film, architecture, arts, and popular entertainment, as well as in the bar culture and club life. Comparatively, intellectuals spent more energy attacking each other for being too political or too apolitical. This seems to have shown that after 1917 and 1927, in the realm of "new culture," few choices were left for intellectuals and cultural figures to be cultured and cosmopolitan, and to be unruly, nonconformist, and left-wing all at once.

At the Overlapping Moment of Histories

At the turn of the twenty-first century, Shanghai has once again ventured into an overlapping moment of different histories, that of post-socialism and that of globalization. Ironically but not surprisingly, it was the rosy conventional side of 1930s Shanghai that was monumentalized as the "space of the past," standing side by side with the "spaces of the present" rendered by national and international capital. In this monumentalization, the taste of art deco and vanguardism was compressed into a false memory of the international capital system of the 1930s. The renovated architectures along the Bund and Nanjing Road no longer seem to be in the modernistic spirit of art deco but seem to have in affinity with postmodern Las Vegas. Pubs, cafés, and clubs are rebuilt, and the image of modern Shanghai girls on old calendars is reprinted, in the forms of nostalgia rather than vanguardism. The "space of the past" in contemporary Shanghai is itself the outcome of a "politics of disappearance," to borrow Ackbar Abbas's description of Hong Kong (Abbas 1997). That is to say, although traces of Shanghai's noncapitalist past may remain, they become "subtly unrecognizable" (63). This constructed memory of the city effectively brings a capital-oriented "Paris of the East" "back to the future," where the history of postsocialism and the history of global capitalism seem to intersect and conjoin smoothly.

But the fact that European and Asian urbanisms intersected at different historical moments leaves room, hopefully, for alternative interpretations and contested memories. Writing this volume has convinced me that beyond the 1930s there were "other pasts" of Shanghai in which the city was neither a site of the apparatus of the state(s) nor a forefront of international capitalism but served instead as an asylum for cosmopolitanism. Just like Paris in its pre-Haussmann moment, Shanghai in its "other past" reconstructed in this book was a culturally uncontrollable city, living proof of the catastrophe that had turned the Qing heartland inside-out, a center of the unruly but original cultural practices, a site of a noncapitalist history. Through retranslational activities, Shanghai in this pre-1930 period revitalized, as Derrida saw in the "cities of refuge," the law of cosmopolitanism or the ethics of universal hospitality (2001, 17, 19). For along the way, this cosmopolitanism gave way to the 1930s Shanghai urban culture and has become unrecognizable. But I personally believe this "other past" of Shanghai, like pre-Haussmann Paris—a Paris where Charles Baudelaire or even the Paris Commune were alive— deserves to be considered as a crucial part of the literacy of contemporary cultural criticism. This other past of Shanghai hopefully will help us bring cosmopolitanism, the ultimate public, "back to" the more livable "future" that extends beyond the system of global capitalism.

Notes

Introduction

1. Immanuel Wallerstein (1989) has dealt with issues related to the expansion of capitalism into China through, for example, opium smuggling from India, the replacement of the Dutch East India Company, the Opium War, and the unequal treaties.

2. Frank was vague in defining the relationship between an Asian global economy and the capitalist world system. At one point he maintained that the world system was set first by the Asian world economy and that therefore, capitalism, as an advanced economic form, was not the privilege of the West. At another point he argued that the West's eventual control of economic power occurred not as a result of market forces but as a result of noneconomic forces such as military threats and war, and these he does not attribute to capitalism. This vagueness induced many debates (see note 7 below).

3. Hamashita and his coauthor Kawakatsu to some extent adopted the Japanese scholarship produced in the Japanese colonialist period (1940s–1950s) on the Asian economy without a thorough criticism of its possible ideological implications. For discussion of this aspect, see Sun Ge 2003, 56–67.

4. It is an already-established fact that Southeast Asia experienced a period of development and even expansion in world trade during the seventeenth century (Reid 1993; Subrahmanyam 1990). It is important to note, however, that Frank's argument set the moment of "Western hegemony" in Asia at least a century later.

5. According to Liang Jiabin's classic work *Yapian zhanzheng qian Guangdong guoji maoyi jiaotong shi kao* (An Evidential Study of the International Trade in Guangdong before the Opium War; 1960), the number of trading ports varied in different dynasties under different emperors for specific political and economic reasons. In the Sung dynasty, for example, state policy encouraged foreign trade over the ocean but discouraged it across land routes. In the Yuan dynasty, the emperor opened all possible ports to ocean trade before he restricted the number of ports. Such situational policy changes were also typical in late imperial times.

6. Shanghai's significance was real even though direct shipping from Europe to Shanghai, as Linda Johnson revealed, was sporadic at the time (1995, 161).

7. Wallerstein responded by pointing out that Frank, while trying to deconstruct the myth of the "rise of the West," canceled the critique of capitalism (1999). Giovanni Arrighi too thought it important to further explore the connection between the emergence of capitalism and the "rise of the West" (1999).

8. Although the Qing Empire and imperialist powers were all involved in various kinds of domination over smaller countries and groups, that domination took on quite different historical forms. The British Empire, for example, entailed imperialism that was inseparable from the development of global capitalism: waging war and using force to obtain political and economic control of labor, resources, and legal rights as well as production and trade. It is not the task of this introduction to define the difference between the Qing Empire and modern imperialism; rather, it is sufficient here to note that I use the word "imperial" to describe matters related to the Qing and the word "imperialist" to describe those related to political, economic, and military powers that have come hand in hand with capitalism.

9. Xu Baoqiang 2001. While I fully appreciate Xu's ideas of alternative and liberating capitalism, I prefer to keep the distinction between capitalism and noncapitalism for the sake of historical analysis. I will return to this soon, with a more detailed discussion.

10. John Fairbank's main argument was that a closed, stagnant, self-centered China was awakened under the impact of the advanced West and that in this modernizing moment, Shanghai became the cradle of Chinese modernity because of its closeness to the West (Teng and Fairbank 1954). Marxist studies describe Shanghai as having a semicolonial system that impoverished the rest of the country. According to this narrative, while the rest of China remained in a feudal stage, Shanghai alone embraced capitalism, but the imperialists appropriated the profits. This line of thought reversed the liberal narrative of Shanghai but at the same time strangely overlapped with it by designating the West as the true actor and ultimate center in the history of China.

11. I should also add that a huge number of scholarly works are published in Chinese, partly as the result of research projects developed by the Social Science Academy of Shanghai. It is a pity that I cannot list these works here because of their large number.

12. For the salt administration and industry as well as grain transportation, I draw mostly on the following works: Chiang Tao-chang 1976; Adshead 1970; Saeki Tomi 1987, 1956; Wang Zhenzhong 1996; Hsü An-k'un 1998; and Ding Changjing, Liu Foding, et al. 1990.

13. Shih (2001) distinguished two Wests: the "cosmopolitan West" (Western culture in the West) and the "colonial West" (the culture of colonialists in China) as objects of critique (30–40). I suggest this distinction is more applicable to post-1917 Beijing and 1930s Shanghai. In the period I am talking about, namely, from the Taiping Rebellion to the eve of the Nanjing period, another West, that is, a "radical West," was certainly presented in literature and culture.

1. The Shifting Locations of the Translation of Science

1. Philip Kuhn (1980) has discussed the nineteenth-century bureaucratic and military problems as well as relations between the court and the bureaucratic sys-

tem. Benjamin Elman (1990) has given a detailed picture of the problems of curriculum and polity as well as the rivalry between Han Learning and Song Learning. Discussions on civil service examinations and the struggle for knowledge and institutional change from the seventeenth to the eighteenth centuries can be seen in others of his works (Elman 1984, 2000a).

2. In fact, Shanghai was not given even such a priority naturally, as I have mentioned elsewhere (Meng Yue 2000). At first, Zeng Guofan was considering sending the Huai army to Zhenjiang, the city at the meeting of the Yangtze River and the Grand Canal (Zeng Guofan 1985a, 1985b). It was the persuasion of Qian Dingming and other Jiangnan gentry as well as the need for the *liji* tax—of which Shanghai was able to offer more than were other cities after the fall of Suzhou and Hangzhou—to feed the army that eventually brought the Huai army to Shanghai (Xue Fucheng 1966).

3. William J. Haas has provided some valuable accounts of the link between American missionary institutions, bourgeois agents such as the Rockefeller Foundation, and American diplomatic policy in the context of the economic relationship between the United States and China (1996, 17–90).

4. As Elman has shown, the missionaries' Christian beliefs also dominated what they chose to call science and what they excluded. Therefore, their modern moment was a specific by-product of modern Western history.

5. Tan Tai, a compatriot of Ruan Yuan at Yangzhou, in his preface entitled "Chouren jie" (The Meaning of *Chouren*) defined *chouren* as having two meanings: first, people who inherit a family history of being a man of math or a man of a related craft (*jiashi ye ye xiang chuan zhe*), and second, people with special skills in mathematics, astronomy, rites, philology, or musicology (Tan Tai 1962, 1–4).

6. These are *Chouren zhuan xubian* (Biographies of Mathematicians and Astronomers, vol. 2, 1840) (Luo Shilin 1962) and *Chouren zhuan sanbian* (Biographies of Mathematicians and Astronomers, vol. 3, 1886) (Zhu Kebao [1844] (1962), compiled respectively by Luo Shilin (1789–1853) and Zhu Kebao (1845–1903), as well as *Chouren zhuan sibian* (Biographies of Mathematicians and Astronomers, vol. 4) (Huang Zhongjun [1899] 1955). People who compiled and edited the *Biographies* included contemporary mathematicians such as Li Rui, Tan Tai, and Jiao Xun. Ruan Yuan, in "Chouren zhuan fanli" (in Ruan Yuan [1799] 1962), also indicated that excellence in learning, especially in mathematics, could only be achieved through specialization (*fei zhuanjia buneng ban*). For Ruan Yuan and his contributions, see Elman 1998. See also Hu Minghui's dissertation (2004) on eighteenth- and nineteenth-century Jiangnan mathematical culture, particularly that of the Yangzhou circle.

7. About quotas and civil service examination, see Lee 1985.

8. Taking specialty of knowledge as the only criterion, the compilers of *Chouren zhuan* and its sequels included fifty-three foreigners under the term "*chouren*." Thirty-seven were included in the first volume of *Chouren zhuan*; sixteen appeared in the third volume. Many of the prominent *chouren* were experts in both Chinese and Western systems. All these make *chouren* a hybrid, even international, category.

9. Circles of mathematicians and astronomers were a mixture of commoners and official-scholars. Mathematicians such as Xu Youren (1800–1860) and Luo Shilin, for example, served in high offices. Xiang Mingda (1789–1850) and Dai Xu (1810–1860) were not interested in studying for a degree (see "Xiang Mingda" and "Dai Xu" in Zhu Kebao [1844] 1962, 767–71, 789–97). "Failures" in the civil service examinations

were not few among *chouren*. Gu Guanguang (1789–1864), for example, became a doctor while studying science on his own after he failed (Zhu Kebao [1844] 1962, 799–802).

10. Horng Wann-sheng's dissertation (1991) on nineteenth-century translations of Western mathematics as well as his study of friendship groups among mathematicians and astronomers (1993) both addressed the issues of curriculum, society, teacher-student networks, private academies, and friendship clubs.

11. See Benjamin Hobson's *Bowu xinbian* (Collection of New Scientific Knowledge) ([1855] 1864). The book was first published in Guangzhou, then reprinted by London Missionary Press in Shanghai. For missionary publications at the time, see Xiong Yuezhi 1994, 152–60.

12. To preserve the *chouren* tradition, Hua Hengfang was himself turning into a writer of biographies of mathematicians. His work *Jindai zhouren zhushu lu* (On Works by Recent Mathematicians and Astronomers; [1899] 1962) covers the period beginning with the last few decades of the nineteenth century. This work is always compiled as an appendix of the fourth volume of *Biographies of Mathematicians and Astronomers*.

13. I have measured the technological "success" of the Jiangnan Arsenal in terms of shipbuilding and gunnery in more detail elsewhere (Meng Yue 1999).

14. It was believed that the arsenal was "certainly capable of constructing warlike material on a more extended scale than can be done by Japan" (Anonymous 1895, 126–43). For contemporary discussions, see Meng Yue 1999 and Takehiko Hashimo 1999.

15. Translation between different knowledge systems, as we all know, is likely to be influenced by cultural and historical elements that are not necessarily scientific and are therefore highly problematic in the scientific perspective. But since my purpose is not to give a scientific evaluation of the translations but to examine what made Shanghai the center of knowledge, the cultural and historical practice of translatability is what I would like to emphasize.

16. "*Suanxue*" was a conventional term often used in late-Qing documents to refer to science. In 1887, for example, after quite a few denials, the Zongli yamen (the Administration of Foreign Relations) approved the establishment of a *suanxue* category *(suanxue qushi)* in the civil service examination to recruit persons capable of conducting matters of sciences and technology (Elman 2005). The term "*bowu,*" on the other hand, was widely used to refer to science in missionary publications. Benjamin Hobson's book on science and technology was entitled *Bowu xinbian,* even though "*bowu*" rather carried the meaning of erudition. For a similar discussion about "*bowu*" and "*gezhi,*" see Wang Hui 1996, 21–82.

17. Here I follow Joseph Needham's translation of the term (1954, 48). The scope of the term was broader than *suanxue* but narrower than *bowu*.

18. Joseph Edkins, Martin William, and Wang Tao were planning to prepare "an outline of new learning" ("Taoyuan zhushu zongmu" [Complete List of Works by Taoyuan], in Wang Tao 1889).

19. The term "*gezhi jia*" was often seen in *Scientific and Industrial Magazine* as well as in *Global Magazine*.

20. Thanks to Benjamin Elman's study on the topic, we know that the imagined opposition between *gezhi* studies and *kexue* marked the problematic caused by

ideological binaries between premodern and modern, science and nonscience (2000b, 1–43).

21. "*Gezhi*" is an abbreviation of "*gewu zhizhi*," or "attainment of knowledge through the investigation of things."

22. Indeed, when the authors of *Biographies* focused on the genealogy of *chouren* in their prefaces, they were symbolically objecting to the Neo-Confucian genealogy of knowledge.

23. About the origin of *gezhi zhixue*, see Elman 2000b, 2005.

24. When the concept of *gezhi* was used, for example, to translate Aristotle's *Four Elements of Physics* (in Chinese, *Kongji gezhi*), it began to refer to a philosophical system about the world less rigid than that of Neo-Confucianism. See Ji Wende 1991, 119.

25. *Gezhi congshu* was compiled by the famous Ming bookseller Hu Wenhuan (fl. 1596).

26. Wang Hui (1996) has offered a careful discussion of the complex meaning of "*gezhi*" in his essay. I would like to add that for the Jiangnan Arsenal circle, the term "*gezhi*" did not have the same connotation as in its earlier usage, as Wang Hui sometimes suggests, but bore a new connotation of industrial knowledge.

27. Dai Xu's works, such as *Duishu jianfa* (Logarithm Subtraction), *Si yuan yujian xicao* (A Detailed Study of *Si yuan yujian*), and *Xiangshu yuanshi* (The Origins of Astronomical Mathematics), were written in specific philological terms.

28. An excellent discussion on commensurability and incommensurability in the Chinese context is found in Hart 1999, 88–114. In a broader sense, scientific translation, like other translation, can be seen as transaction (Lydia Liu 1999, 1–13).

29. In organizing these contests, Wang Tao and Fryer invited high-ranking, reform-minded officials to offer topics for the participants and to read and rank the essays. The best three or four essays won awards from the institute. The contests were held four and sometimes six times a year every year from 1886 to 1896. For details of these contests, see Wang Erh-min 1980; Biggerstaff 1956, 1961.

30. The four prize winners were Jiang Tongyin from Taican County, Wang Zuocai of Jiangsu Province, Zhu Chengshu from Shanghai, and Zhong Tianwei from Guangdong.

31. Xue Fucheng actually used both the classifications of modern sciences and the associative methods of the evidential studies. On the one hand, Xue adopted the European classifications for technology, such as the study of light (*guanxue*), the study of manufacturing (*zhongxue*), or the study of the steam engine (*qixue*), to systematize useful knowledge scattered throughout both the classical and contemporary books. Although by the late nineteenth century these classifications had been replaced by more modern terms, such as "physics," "chemistry," and "biology," Xue's system was "revolutionary" as a way of categorizing different learnings compared to the philological way of storing knowledge, that is, storing knowledge in terms of books' titles, authors' names, methods, and characters. On the other hand, however, Xue followed the rules of evidential studies, namely, elaborating certain knowledge by tracing its origin as well as its ramifications for later applications. The phenomenon of amber picking up a seed was first described in *Bowu zhi* (Broad Learning of Things) by Zhang Hua (1983, 232–300) and was discussed by Li Shizhen (1518–1593) in his *Bencao gangmu* (Chinese Materia Medica), "Mubu, mulie" section. The optic

art of lenses and mirrors *(yangsui tongjian)* was recorded in *Mengxi bitan* (Notes by Mr. Dream of Stream) by Shen Guo (1031–1095).

32. *Shou shan ge congshu* (Collectanea of the Holding Mountain Studio), *Zhi hai* (Sea of Signs), compiled by Qian Xizuo (d. 1844), *Xi yin xuan congshu* (Collectanea of the Studio of Cherished Time) compiled by Li Xiling, *Lian yun yi congshu* (Collectanea of the Bamboo Hut) compiled by Yang Shangwen, *Hai shan xian guan congshu* (Collectanea of the Studio of the Fairies of the Seas and Mountains) compiled by Pan Shicheng (who won the degree of *juren* in 1832), and *Huang Qing jingjie xubian* (Qing Exegesis on Classics, Supplementary Editions) by Wang Xianqian (1842–1918) became particularly famous because they preserved rare scientific texts. My thanks to Benjamin Elman for bringing the publication of *Huang Qing jingjie xubian* to my attention.

33. Matheson's *Aid Book to Engineering Enterprises Abroad* was translated by Fryer and Zhong Tianwei and published in 1894. Part one of the original book was translated under the title of *Gongcheng zhifu* by Fryer and Zhong.

34. Zhu Kebao has explained the meaning of *yangsui* and its relationship to *geshu* (methods of optics): "The name of *geshu* was from *Mengxi bitan. Yangsui* was to manufacture metal, probably gold, and make it into a mirror" ([1844] 1962, 814).

35. This book was similar to *Wuli xiaoshi* except it lacked the latter's cosmological statement.

36. The Emperor Guangxu began to take charge of political matters in person in the early 1890s after the Empress Dowager formally retired from imperial business.

37. For example, Zhang Zhidong differentiated mathematical texts and mathematicians in terms of three categories: "Western way *(xifa)*," "Chinese way *(zhongfa)*," and "both *(Jianyong zhongxi fa)*" (Zhang Zhidong [1874] 1963, 3831–67).

38. My thanks to Xiong Yuezhi at the Shanghai Academy of Social Sciences for commenting on this point.

2. Semiotic Modernity

1. Many studies have been done on the vocabularies of this period. For the Japanese travelers, travel writing, and their impact on Chinese culture, see Fogel 1995, 1996. For a discussion of the components of Meiji vocabularies, see Lydia Liu 1995; Masini 1993.

2. For the best works among many, see Mittler 2004; Judge 1996; Karl 2002.

3. This principle shows itself in the way "*kexue*," a word from Meiji Japan referring to science and technology, replaced "*gezhi*," the earlier word for science and technology that had been in use in China for decades.

4. There has been interesting scholarship on the Commercial Press in many languages. The pioneer studies that consider the history of the Commercial Press as a whole include the following: (1) historical statistics and studies by such scholars as Zhuang Yu (1931), He Shengnai (1931), Wang Yunwu (1973), and Jean Pierre Drège (1978); (2) historical studies of the crucial figures of the Commercial Press by, for example, Manying Ip (1985) and Wang Shaozeng (1984); and (3) book catalogs, such as those of the Commercial Press (Shangwu yinshuguan 1981, 1987, 1992). Aspects of recent scholarship are represented by Reed (2004), Tarumoto Teruo (1979, 1988, 1983), Nakamura Tadayuki (1989, 1990, 1993), and Sawamoto Ikuma (1993).

5. The calculation is my own.

6. Another source suggests that the Baos' father actually did not die until his sons had grown up. See Chang Zhou 1992, 642–55.

7. For the establishment of the Lowrie Institute, see Farnham 1910. The information provided here about Xia Ruifang and other founders of the Commercial Press is taken from Zhang Xichen 1987, 102–24; Cai Yuanpei 1987, 1–2; Jiang Weiqiao 1987, 3–5; Zhuang Yu 1987b, 6–8; Chang Zhou 1992, 642–55; Meng Sen 1992, 17–20; Gao Hanqing 1992, 1–13.

8. The initial 3,750 yuan was gathered from eight people and divided into seven-and-a-half shares, making each share worth 500 yuan (Gao Hanqing 1992, 1–13). For more about disagreements and agreements among scholars on the establishment of the Commercial Press, see Sawamoto Ikuma 1993, 1–50.

9. According to Gao Hanqing (1992, 5), one of the founders of the press, Xia Ruifang, managed to obtain low-cost paper, which allowed them to produce *Tongjian jilian* for much less than the woodblock copies of their competitors. Whereas the woodblock copy of the encyclopedia cost ten to twenty yuan, the Commercial Press's reprint cost less than three yuan. The press sold about 10,000 copies.

10. *Waijiao bao* was founded by Cai Yuanpei, Du Yaquan, Zhang Yuanji, and Wen Zongyao in 1902. The journal was first published by Putong xue shushi (The Studio of General Sciences) and was organized by Du Yaquan. In March 1903 it was printed by the Commercial Press. See Zhang Shunian 1991, 39–43.

11. According to the reminiscences of Gao Hanqing (1992, 1–13), the important positions in management were filled by Chinese, with a Japanese inspector. The Commercial Press accepted the supervision and training given by Japanese technicians on certain skills until the collaboration ended in 1914.

12. The exact phrase used in an advertisement was "English and Chinese School Books, Specially Reprinted, with Full Translations in Chinese, from the Series of School Books Published by the Christian Literature Society for India" (quoted from plate 8 in *Shinmatsu shosetsu* 16 [Spring 1993], 13).

13. It is not surprising that the bilingual layout became the visual symbol of intellectual journals that were printed by the Commercial Press. Reform journals such as *Changyan bao* (Journal of Free Speech, 1898) and *Waijiao bao,* and the missionary journal *Gezhi xinbao* (Scientific Review, 1898), as well as new journals such as *Kexue* (Sciences, 1915, a journal established by Hu Shi [1891–1962] and other students abroad) and *New Youth* (1915), all had Chinese and English titles (as well as French in some cases) displayed on the cover page (Shangwu yinshuguan 1997, 8).

14. Shenbao Press and missionary presses used to invite one or two ex-Hanlin bachelors (Cai Erkang for Shenbao, Wang Tao and Li Shanlan for London Mission Press) to take care of proofreading and the compilation of their classics. Translation departments in the official publishing houses usually consisted of several scholars, as was the case in both the Jiangnan Arsenal and the Nanyang Public Academy. Concerning the possibility that the owner of Shenbao himself participated in editorial projects, see Wagner 1995, 423–43.

15. Elman (1984) has long pointed out that philologists in the seventeenth and eighteenth centuries, including in the New Text school of evidential studies, were not merely a scholarly society but also a political one. The combination of these two tendencies—that is, having specific skills in textual studies and political engagements—became much more obvious around the turn of the twentieth century.

16. One of his ancestors was Zhang Junchang (*jinshi* degree of 1655), who was famous for having directly criticized the Ming emperor. He was forced to retire early, and left to enjoy his large collection of books, which had attracted many literati.

17. Zhang learned English through a private teacher. At the press, he and Kuang Fucho, a member of the Guangdong literati who also worked at the press, exchanged ideas in English, since neither one understood the other's dialect (Mao Dun 1987, 140–97).

18. My thanks to Benjamin Elman for bringing this point to my attention and for sharing the document on the Zhuang lineage, *Biling Zhuang shi zupu* (The Lineage Record of the Zhuangs in Wujin).

19. The title *Yaquan* came from the combination of two terms in chemistry, "*ya*" and "*quan*." Later he took this as his own name.

20. These six books are *Mingzhi zhengdang xiaoshi* (A Brief History of the Political Parties in the Meiji Period), by the Tokyo Daily News Press, translated by Chinese students in Tokyo; *Aiji jinshi shih* (Modern History of Egypt), translated by Chinese students in Tokyo; *Diguo zhuyi* (Imperialism); *Jinshi lujun* (Modern Infantry), translated by Tao Senjia; *Geguo guomin gong si quan kao* (A Study on the Public and Private Rights of Citizens in Different Countries), translated by Chinese students in Tokyo; and *Geguo xianfa lun* (On Laws in Different Countries), translated by Chinese students in Tokyo.

21. Qian Mu studied in this school and, according to him, the textbook edited by Yu Fu and Ding Baonan was actually very practical and easy to understand (Qian Mu 1986, 18–25).

22. The textbooks break down into (1) elementary Chinese, ten volumes; (2) sciences, three volumes; (3) arithmetic, four volumes; (4) self-cultivation, ten volumes; (5) mathematics, six volumes; and (6) calculation using the abacus, two volumes.

23. The complete set of books for this level were (1) Chinese, edited by Zhang Yuanji et al., eight volumes; (2) history, edited by Zhuang Yu, four volumes; (3) geography, edited by Yao Zujin, four volumes; (4) sciences, four volumes; (5) mathematics, three volumes; (6) calculation using the abacus, four volumes; (7) self-cultivation, four volumes; (8) agriculture, four volumes; and (9) commerce, four volumes.

24. Wenming Press contributed twenty types or so, and the other thirty-some types were split among more than five other presses.

25. The Shenbao Press's *Juzhenban congshu* (Collection of Precious Classics) naturally took the lead in this trend (Wagner 1995, 1999).

26. At the time, Xia Ruifang offered 80,000 taels of silver, which was more than two-thirds of the press's entire budget, to purchase the collection.

27. The Chinese scholars are listed according to the number of strokes in their surnames: Kong Qinglai, Wu Deliang, Li Xianglin, Du Jiutian (a nephew of Du Yaquan), Zhou Yueran, Zhou Fan, Chen Xueying, Mo Shulue, Xu Jiaqing, Huang Yiren (who held a Ph.D. in botany), Ling Chanhuan, and Yan Baocheng.

28. Some would argue that the idea of studying and categorizing all plants rather than individual plants served a Darwinian worldview much more directly than it did a colonial one. But from the point of view of the colonized countries and cultures, the Darwinian worldview and colonialism worked hand in hand to oppress the local cultures or the cultures of the colonized.

29. The following is an example taken from *Zhiwu mingshi tukao*: "Jingtian. Jingtian is ranked high in the *Classics of the God of the Plants* and was painted well

in the *Pictorial Classics of the God of the Plants* of the Song dynasty. Its contemporary name is 'flaming grass.' In the capital it is called 'eight treasures,' and also 'nail of the Buddha.' It is planted in pots and put on top of the roof. In the south, it flowers in late autumn. Li Shizhen believed that the 'nail of the Buddha' recorded in *Jiuhuang bencao* was the same as jingtian. But the flower known today as jingtian is light red in color and random in shape, without the white milk (that Li described); therefore, it must be a different kind. The Peasant of Lingxi says: 'Jingtian also called Shenli. In both north and south, it is kept in pots on the roofs and is used as a symbol of fire prevention. . . . The popularity of this usage, however, indicates the lack of efficient government management of disasters. . . . If no one thinks of preventing a fire before it happens, then even potted Jingtian won't be very helpful'" (Wu Qixun [1848]1960, 286–87). ("The Peasant of Lingxi" is the persona Wu Qixun chose for himself.)

30. Here, "the Kaibao edition of *Materia Medica*" refers to *Shen nong ben cao jing* (The Sacred Classics of *Materia Medica*).

31. Kou Zongli is the name of a scholar who appeared often in Li Shizhen's *Bencao gangmu*.

32. Here I am borrowing Robert Darnton's well-known analysis of the *Encyclopédie* in the French cultural history *The Great Cat Massacre and Other Episodes in French Cultural History* (1984) to illustrate the effect of preferring alphabetical as well as stroke orders to modern botanical categorization.

3. Urban Festivity as a Disruptive History

1. According to Gu, early theaters in Jiangnan were built on large boats, and during the Yongzheng reign (1723–1735), after a certain Guo built a theater in Suzhou, theater-building became popular. Up to the Qianlong period (1736–1795), the city saw "large numbers of merchants living around the Jinlu (Suzhou). Banquets were held constantly and operas were performed every day at several dozen theaters, and these provided a living for at least tens of thousands of common people" (Gu Gongxie [1785] 1917, 40–41).

2. The restoration of Jiangnan's theaters was slow; in Suzhou it took four decades to restore several dozen. Suzhou Kunqu actors joined troupes in Ningbo before the Taipings took Suzhou. Among them were *dan* actors nicknamed Xiao Laixi, Xiao Dongzhi, and Xiaomian Aning. They joined the Lao xuyuan troupe in Ningbo, where they remained. This partially explains the popularity of opera in Ningbo during the post-Taiping era (ZGXQZBWH 1990, 48). According to Wang Changchou, a Kunqu opera actor, his father Xiao Laixi and other actors went with the Taipings to Ningbo in 1848 (Zheng Xuepu and Guo 1986, 70–93).

3. These meanings, of course, are put together by scholars to divert readers from seeing things in a larger historical context. It is not surprising to learn that some early meanings were dropped in later periods. But in the case of *"fanhua,"* there was no radical rupture in the history of the word. Even the earliest uses of the word remain as one of the meanings of the contemporary term.

4. From "Nigu 3," a poem by the Tang dynasty poet Wei Yingwu (732–792?). The full stanza reads like this: "Jingcheng fanhua di, xuangai lingchen chu" [The capital city is the busy and fashionable site, extravagant wagon-tops loom with the dawn].

5. Quotation from a poem by the Tang dynasty poet Song Zhiwen (656–713).

6. Perhaps for these reasons, Emperor Qianlong made the street life of Suzhou into an "imperial" possession when he transplanted a Jiangnan street into his royal garden, Yuanmingyuan.

7. According to Dong Zhongshu, the Three Ages have two levels. At the political level, each age has a separate set of political institutions and rites. At the cosmos level, the transformation and movement of the universe followed cosmological principles, such as the five phases and theory of the alternation between yin and yang. For a discussion of Dong Zhongshu's political concepts and philosophy of cosmology, please see Queen 1996.

8. *Shengshi zisheng* was also the name of a tax base in which the Bureau of Population Registration registered newly emerged families, as described in the *Da Qing huidian shilie* (Annotated Legal and Governmental Documents of the Qing Dynasty).

9. Both the cosmopolitan materiality and cosmopolitan spirit I am talking about here are different from "international" or "transnational" subjectivity. Cosmopolitan materiality and cosmopolitan spirit existed beyond the framework in which "nation," national community, and national states became the measurement of differences and distances.

10. The chief editors were Huang Wenyang (b. 1736) and Li Ching; the editorial board was made up of Ling Tingkan (1757–1809), Cheng Mei, Chen Zhi, and Jing Ruwei. All of these men came from the Jiangsu and Zhejiang areas (Li Dou [1795] 1984, 104–16). According to Huang Wenyang, the dramas they worked on included both the available old and new scripts and those contributed by *Suzhou zhizao* (The Suzhou Bureau of Tribute) (Huang Wenyang 1989, 163).

11. The publication of the libretto of *Zhui bai qiu* (1770–1780) was a crucial event at the time. With respect to scholarly works, Jiao Xun (1763–1820) alone, for example, wrote several works on the theater, such as *Qukao* (Study of Music), *Jushuo* (On Opera, 1805), and *Hua pu nongtan* (The Peasant's Discourse on the Flower Dramas, 1819 [Jiao Xun 1959–1960]). The people who wrote about plays and scores ranged from officials and scholars, such as Jiao Xun, to much less well known literati, such as Ye Tang (1724?–1799?), who wrote *Nashuying qupu* (Music Scores Printed by Nashuying, 1792–1794) and *Simeng qupu* (Complete Music Scores for Operas of "The Four Dreams," 1792–1794).

12. The generic and hierarchical aspects of the "elegant" *(ya)* and the "flower" *(hua)* genres are well known. Generically, Kunqu opera was characterized by its poetic lyrics, which, once uttered in the Wu dialect, fit aesthetically into classical, written music scores that can be traced back to the Song dynasty. Hence, Kunqu opera was called the "elegant genre." The "flower" dramas, on the other hand, refer to (other) regional or local dramas, which usually did not have scripts and were heavily dependent upon individual performances. Hence, the flower dramas were also called *luantan* (performed without script). See Hsü 1985, 64–65. Kunqu opera has twelve roles, whereas *luantan* usually has two main roles and several assistant roles. Kunqu emphasizes music, soliloquy, and choreography, whereas the flower genres focus on dialogues, body languages, and the like. See Li Dou [1795] 1984, 126–28; Niu Chuanhai 1977, 48–54.

13. To quote Jiao Xun: "The lyrics from the Wu area (i.e., Kunqu opera from Suzhou area) are complicated. Even though Wu melodies accord with the principles of music, listeners would still not be able to understand a thing without reading the

texts of the lyrics. The content of the Kunqu plays ... was mostly love stories and flirtations, and therefore, does not touch the depth of humanity. The flower dramas (i.e., local and northern-style operas), on the other hand, inherited the artistic tradition of the Yuan dramas. Their plots focus mostly on morals (conflicts) and are therefore gripping. Their lyrics are simple and frank; thus woman and children understand them" (Jiao Xun 1959–1960, 8:1–8).

14. This distinction habitually bore hierarchical meaning, with the ya, or "elegant," at the top and the hua, or "flower," at the bottom.

15. Not only did local opera troupes travel, but so did Kunqu opera troupes. Suzhou Kunqu troupes, for example, were divided into city-based troupes (suocheng ban) and traveling troupes (jianghu ban, such as the Literary Troupe of Rivers and Lakes). The city-based troupes also traveled often (Gu Duhuang 1987, 87–88).

16. Tanaka Issei (1987, 1989) pointed out long ago that the Qing state treated moral corruption as a political enemy because it led to gatherings of large crowds that threatened the social and political order.

17. Gu Duhuang noted that the Shaoxing martial-drama troupe that had been registered in Suzhou and allowed to perform outside the provincial capital was known as Kunyi xiao ruichin zhi and was had been founded in Shaoxing in 1884 (1987, 118–32).

18. Wuban was a type of troupe performing martial drama. It originated in Shaoxing and was characterized by martial-arts performances and by the content of its dramas. The martial drama was contrasted to civil drama (wenxi), which emphasized the singing aspects of the performance and included fewer military events in the play.

19. As Gu Duhuang (1987) has noted, the Kunqu troupe Quanfu ban spent five-sixths of each year traveling outside Suzhou from 1890 to 1919.

20. Wang Tao ([1875] 1989) commented, "While Jiangsu and Zhejiang provinces were sacked by bandits (the Taipings) and the entire southeast half of China had hardly any peaceful land left, Shanghai on the contrary became far more prosperous than it ever was" (115).

21. They were called Wenle yuan (Wenle Theater) and Fengle yuan (Fengle Theater). Wang Tao ([1875] 1989) mentioned the performances of traveling troupes in Shanghai during the Taipings (9).

22. The author went to Shanghai from his hometown Nanchang in Jiangxi Province in 1866 and stayed a year. He then wrote down what he had experienced. In 1874, when he went to Shanghai again, the manuscript was stolen. He rewrote the book from memory. The record contained not only his experiences from 1866 but a mixture of images of Shanghai life from 1865 to 1874 (Shanghai tongshe [1936] 1984, 191–93).

23. The author of the book does not give the source for this statistic. The number, however, was close to that in ZGXQZBWH, 1990, 623–28.

24. Renao is difficult to render precisely in English. It means a mixture of scenes and activities that are noisy, busy, chaotic, full of life.

25. Here the word "guiyuan" should refer to Dan'gui and Jin'gui Theaters. This poem was written in 1871.

26. There are no accurate statistics on the number of spectators for opera in Shanghai that I am aware of. The number of spectators, however, must have been large considering the frequency of the performances and the large number of theaters.

27. Playbills advertised in *Shenbao* usually contained the names of the principal actors. The total number of actors at a theater was actually much larger. This is attested in Clark's description; as he noted: "Some of the theaters employed about 125 actors, all males, and the principal professionals, who have earned some fame in their own sphere, are thought a good deal of by the people. But the large proportion of the young men and boys brought on the stage are only of the lowest order" (1894, 1).

28. John Clark complained about the music, which he called "Chinese noise," as well as about the fact that while he was in the International Settlement during the warm season, "these almond-eyed Romeos" kept up "their serenading till the dawn of day" (1894, 100–101).

29. *Shenbao* did not advertise Sunday theater performances at this time. Theaters in the British Settlement probably did not have performances on Sundays because of the Church of England's rules. But no source that I have looked into confirms that Chinese theaters closed on Sundays. The statistics in the text are based on the six days from April 3 to April 8, Monday to Saturday, 1876. *Shenbao*, April 3 to April 8, 1876.

30. The Guangdong guild sued Dan'gui actor Yang Yuelou (1849–1891) for seducing a woman from a good family. This was a sensational case, and Dan'gui went bankrupt supporting Yang. For details about the native-place associations and the case, see Goodman 1995, 111–17.

31. The numbers of opium dens and teahouses listed by Ge Yuanxu ([1876] 1989) are much lower in other areas within the British Settlement. The three major avenues closest to the Bund had a total of fourteen teahouses at this time. The author recorded twenty-three opium dens in the rest of the British Settlement.

32. The price of Beijing opera theater about this particular moment in Shanghai is unknown. Lo's price was one yuan, about half the regular price (Chen Wuwo [1928] 1997, 68).

33. He was also the grandfather of the Shanghai industrialist Liu Hongsheng (1888–1956). For biographies, see Xue Liyong 1996, 116–17; Shanghai shehui kexueyuan 1981, 1:3; ZGXQZBWH 1990, 830.

34. Both Dan'guis, however, were short-lived. Nan Dan'gui was ordered to close by the Shanghai country magistrate due to the lawsuit against Yang Yuelou, the famous actor of the Nan Dan'gui, for his "seduction of a woman from a good family." And when the municipal government's plans to put the underground water supply system through the basement of the theater were realized, Northern Dan'gui was quickly sold to others because of considerations of feng shui.

35. The competition is reflected in one of the two *zhuzhi* poems collected by artist Yuan Zuzhi (1887), which indicates that although the performance in Jin'gui was more subtle, audiences, particularly women, liked to go to Dan'gui because Yang Yuelou, the handsome young performer from the private troupe of a high-ranking official, was acting there at the time (Zhou Zhifu 1951, 48–49; Chen Yimin 1993–1994, 48: 187–220).

36. All of these pavilions were multistory mansions with elegant names, such as *Tienlewo*, "Heavenly Pleasurable Hut"; *Xiaoguanghan*, "Little Moon Palace"; *Taohua guan*, "The Pavilion of Peach Blossoms"; *Wanhua lou*, "Pavilion of Ten Thousand Flowers"; *Xiang e xingyung lou*, "Clouds Pause to Enjoy the Songs"; *Xianyue juntian lou*, "Celestial Melodies Echoing the Sound of Heaven"; and so on (Chi Zhizheng [1891] 1989, 157).

37. Gail Hershatter's work on Shanghai prostitutes covers exactly the topics Huang and other literati did not talk about and hence provides a thorough study of the topic of women's history and the urban culture of Shanghai.

38. A crucial part of this vitality, for Gong Zizhen, was talent and vision.

4. In Search of a Habitable Globe

1. Zeng Guofan was assigned to reexamine the case. He kept the original judgment.

2. In *Chunbingshi yecheng* (Unofficial Records by the Master of the Chunbing Studio], Li Yuerui suggested that Ma Xinyi was secretly connected with Muslim rebels in Xinqiang and that Zhang happened to learn the secret from Ma's personal assistant. Zhang's assassination was aimed at ending the life of a dangerous rebel (Li Yuerui [1912] 1995). Gao Baishi's memoirs (1965, 376–79) and Zhao Yashu's recent study (1973, 15–40) suggest that powers within the Xiang army were probably responsible for his murder. These powerful figures from the army envied Ma's position as governor of Jiangsu and Zhejiang.

3. The information about Zhang Wenxiang is taken from Jin Tianyu's *Tianfang lou wenyan* ([1927] 1969) and Zhang Xiangwen's biography of Ma Xinyi (in Zhang Xiangwen [1929] 1968, 7:43a–45a). There were many other records about the case and many other suggestions as to the true motivation for the assassination. Most of these were compiled in Li Ciming, Zhang Daogui, and Ding Fenglin 1986.

4. Most of the records, including those by high-ranking officials who were friends of Ma, such as Mo Youzhi and Wang Kaiyun, tended to imply that Ma had stolen the other's wife—that is to say, Ma was assassinated for his amoral behavior.

5. The case ended during the second month of 1871, and within twenty days Zeng had already penned a description of the satirical play.

6. See Qiao Qin'go's often-quoted stanza: "Qun gong zhang zou fen ming zai, bu ji ge chang du xie zhen" [Even though all the documents are clearly written by different officials, they cannot compare the truthful story voiced at the sing-song site] (quoted from Zhang Xiangwen [1929] 1968, 7:43a–45a).

7. There were other comments and disapproval expressed at the time in the writings of the literati. Wang Kaiyun, for example, wrote in his diary that he did not think that hiding "dark private matters" (*yinshi*) for an honored official was a good way to handle the case. The "*yinsh*" here refers to Ma's seizing another's wife.

8. Zheng Zhicheng has noted that people at the time were so touched by Zhang's devotion to revenge that they thought of him as a heroic assassin instead of as a bandit (1996, 454–66).

9. According to Li Hongchun, the play was shortened by more than two-thirds and the dramatic line was altered tremendously. The Empress Dowager called the play to the Beijing court, and the actor Qian Jiyun rewrote the entire play to avoid political danger. During the revision, it was turned from a depiction of the victories of the Taipings into a description of their disintegration (1982, 44–46).

10. In historical accounts, Zhang came not from the era of the Taiping Rebellion but from the era of the Nien Rebellion. He was a minor bandit who was sent to fight the Nien rebels after having surrendered to the Qing. Unfortunately, I have not been able to verify the actual facts of Zhang's life. My account here is drawn from

secondary sources by Wang Dungen and others. See "Study of *Iron Rooster*" in Wang Dungen [1926] 1989, 3:537–38.

11. An earlier version of the same play had been performed in Dan'gui Theater under a different title in 1880; it was also performed in the Tianxian Theater in 1893. The version I am working with here is from Wang Dungen [1926] 1989, 3:537–56.

12. In one situation, a higher-ranking male offers grace, faith, and recognition to a soldier or a former rebel in order to receive the latter's absolute loyalty and subjection; the soldier in turn devotes his life to the higher-ranking man in return for what he has received. In more publications after the eighteenth century, friendship between males was built upon an ideal exchange in which each entrusts the other with his life.

13. As with many Hui actors who had been teachers or students in the Taiping troupe, Wang's problematic political identity prevented him from performing in the provincial capital, where his personal history would have had to be reported.

14. Mi Xizi was one of the two best Guan'gong performers during the Qing dynasty. The other was Cheng Zhanggeng, a well-known male Beijing opera performer.

15. *Huarong Dao* (On the Pass of Huarong) is an exemplary case of such a play; in it, Guan Yu, the general of Shu, releases Cao Cao, minister of Wei and the country's enemy, in order to return Cao's personal favor (Li Hongchun 1962).

16. Li Yuanlong, himself an actor in the "Guan'gong style," commented that "actors who performed Guan'gong dramas, whether in the southern or the northern opera systems, all followed Wang Hongshou's style of performing the hero" (Li Yuanlong 1960, 27–31).

17. According to Feng Ziyou, extreme nationalist journals founded by Chinese students in Japan, such as *Guominbao* (Citizen News, founded 1901), sent 2,000 copies each month to Shanghai (1965–1968, 2:77).

18. Arif Dirlik's classic 1994 work on anarchism in the Chinese Revolution clearly indicated the radical and international interests of the Chinese revolutionary movement. Here I am dealing with a different manifestation, with a similar inclination in the realm of urban culture.

19. Hu Ying (2000) has offered a sophisticated analysis of the gender and cultural politics embedded in Chinese intellectuals' presentation of eastern European heroines as well as of figures such as Madame Roland. My discussion takes her analysis as its beginning point.

20. Two such books had the same title, *Bolan shuaiwang shi* (The Fall of Poland). One was a book that was published in 1901 in a periodical that presented works in translation, *Yishu huibian* (Journal of Collected Translations), by Chinese students in Japan. The other was a book published in 1904 that was a translation by Xue Zhelong of a Japanese author's work (Zhang Yuying [1941] 1953, 176).

21. According to the Chinese Exclusion Act, it was illegal to hire Chinese laborers; Chinese laborers did not have political rights; and those who hired Chinese laborers would be fined. In 1880 a treaty was signed between the United States and China strictly restricting the numbers and the rights of Chinese workers. In the following years the directive for "restriction" became more discriminatory since it sanctioned a variety of unfair and racist practices directed against the Chinese, including poisoning Chinese laborers, burning Chinese shops for the sake of a clean environment, and unfair taxation. For a record of these treaties, see Rockhill 1904.

22. Huang Zunxian, then governor of Guangdong, complained about the ignorance of the Qing state and criticized the U.S. policy in his long poem *Zhu ke pian* (Dismissing the Guests) ([1882] 1960).

23. The strict definition of "merchant" was embodied, for example, in the regulations stating that a business could only have one legal "merchant" or that workers in factories and businesses related to the manufacture of cigarettes, hats, shoes, and the like did not belong to the category of merchant.

24. This ideological connection between "things" and nation in China can be traced back to the work of earlier writers, such as Zheng Guanying (1842–1922) and his concept of "commercial wars" expressed in his *Shengshi weiyan* (Disaster Warning in the Prosperous Era) ([1894] 1922).

25. As Gerth's (2004) work shows, it was the National Product movement and similar social and political events rather than consumer behavior and habits that provided the impetus for most boycotts in Republican China. These movements provided the "organizational and discursive foundations" for the many boycotts against foreign goods (2004, 168). What I would like to stress in this chapter is that the 1905 boycott of U.S. goods, as a social and cultural movement, was much less characteristically "nationalist" than were other movements Gerth discussed. Indeed, as I attempt to show, the discursive and cultural constitution of this first boycott was endowed with "transregional" and "international" characteristics.

26. As Bryna Goodman has observed, the protest against U.S. discrimination had local echoes: "The Mixed Court Riot, the most violent protest in the International Settlement since its establishment, occurred several months after the peak of boycott activity and involved many of the same activities" (1995, 187). For details of the Mixed Court Riot and its significance, see Goodman 1995, 187–95).

27. One of my editors, Sue, made a very insightful comment that is worth quoting here: "Of course, Washington himself was, for most of his life, a slave owner. He did, eventually, come to decide that slavery was wrong and should end. But it certainly is interesting to note that, basically, his ideal of liberty was somewhat 'skewed' from the outset."

28. This performance was one of the first two experimental spoken dramas offered by the Chunliu troupe in Tokyo. The first performance given by the Chunliu troupe was *Chahua nu,* which was based upon Li Shu's translation of *La dame aux camelias* by Dumas.

29. Sometimes the gender aesthetics of operatic convention also seemed to brighten up the skin color, for the "female" characters (performed by male students) wore heavy white powder in order to create a feminine appearance (Li Chang 1987, 252–308; Ouyang Yuqian [1959] 1990).

5. Reenvisioning the Urban Interior

1. By suggesting Yangzhou's importance in the late imperial period, I do not mean to ignore the disruptive side of the city's social and cultural history. As Tobie Mayer-Fong's study (2003) clearly shows, it was the cultural, social, and political interactions among the literati, the salt merchants, and the court that characterized Yangzhou's development from the devastated city of the Manchu conquest to a

commercial and cultural center of the Qing Empire in the eighteenth century. I shall return to this later. Jonathan Hay's work (2001a) on Shitao is a valuable contribution to studies of the cultural history of Yangzhou.

2. The killing and looting are recorded in *Yangzhou shiri ji* (Ten Days in Yangzhou) by Wang Xiuchu (fl. 1645), who experienced the massacre and reported that at least 800,000 dead bodies were burned in the local temples (1971: 241–42). The publication of this book was banned by Qing authorities.

3. In fact, the "tragic feelings" about political upheavals and the fall of dynasties, which Jiao Xun, a well-known scholar and mathematician from Yangzhou, noted were prevalent in the village performances, continued to be part of the local memory about the city, only circulated in folk genres (Jiao Xun 1956–1960).

4. The urbanization of the salt merchants in the beginning years of the dynasty doubled the size of Yangzhou.

5. Ho Ping-ti's classic 1954 study "The Salt Merchants of Yang-Chou" argued that the salt merchants guaranteed their own continuing influence by transforming their economic resources into cultural prestige and political power. This argument is still valid in many respects, though the relationship between the salt merchants and the Qing state needs to be further explored to capture the power and fate of the social group.

6. Details of the preparations of these trips can be found in official records (Gao Jin et al. [1771] 1983).

7. According to Li Dou ([1795] 1984), architectural and technical information provided by *The Imperial Records of Construction and Architecture*, Jiao Xun's *Qunjing gongshi kao* (Palaces Recorded in the Classics), and Wu Danhuan's *Chengyuan shile* (Studies of Cities and Buildings) was accessible to Yangzhou literati and artisans at the time.

8. The layers of roofs ranged from two to five, and the buildings were called, respectively, *liang juan ting* (two-roof hall), *san juan ting* (three-roof hall), *si juan ting* (four-roof hall), and *wu juan ting* (five-roof hall).

9. See the structure of buildings for certain official ranks recorded in *Gongduan yingzao lu*, for example. These were much less magnificent than are recorded for Yangzhou architecture of this time period.

10. Even the most ordinary stones had to be shipped along the river and cut into cubes before being used for construction. As Li Dou noted, both shipping and carving involved a tremendous number of laborers. The shipping of stones sometimes required 300 strong laborers for one job ([1795] 1984, 385).

11. Craig Clunas (1996, 73–75) has carefully discussed the role of Taihu stone. Li Dou also mentioned that authentic Taihu stone was very hard to ship and handle. He quoted the stone carver Zhang Nanshan and suggested that Jiufeng yuan (Garden of Nine Mountains) was one of only two gardens with authentic Taihu stones. (The other was the Lion Forest in Suzhou, built during the Yuan dynasty.) Li Dou's *Yangzhou huafang lu* also mentions that even the fake Taihu stones needed to be shipped from Zhenjiang ([1795] 1984, 162–63).

12. See Li Dou [1795] 1984, 401. According to Li, the jade was wrapped in leather and carried inland across the mountains on horseback.

13. Literati sometimes had the chance to see both the paintings and the actual foreign buildings of the Thirteen Factories in Guangzhou. Figures such as Shen Fu

and Yuan Mei noted their impressions about the Western-style buildings of the Thirteen Factories they saw in Guangzhou. Shen Fu even commented that the architecture in Guangzhou "looked the same as seen in foreign paintings" ([1808] 1962, 57).

14. I have discussed this and the following points in more detail and for wider social and cultural backgrounds in my dissertation (Meng Yue 2000, 336–32).

15. Glass was not a favorite building material only in Europe; there was also a craze for it in eighteenth-century Yangzhou. The South Garden (Nan yuan; also known as Yanchi ranhan, or "Ink Stone Pond") owned by Wang Yushu from She County of Anhui established two "glass pavilions": One was built with windows made of five kinds of colored glass and was called a "glass house" *(boli fang)*, and the other was a pavilion decorated with three-foot-wide transparent glass windows and was called a "glass hall" *(boli ting)*. Emperor Qianlong visited the glass hall and obviously liked it. He called it a "crystal universe" *(chengkong yu)*.

16. This *Yuzhi gengzhi tu*, drawn by the well-known artist Jiao Bingzhen under the instruction of the Emperor Kangxi, was a reproduction of the twelfth-century work *Gengzhi tu* (Agriculture and Sericulture, Illustrated). The new version contained a preface by the emperor himself and twenty-three pictures on farming *(geng)* and twenty-three on silk production *(zhi)*.

17. Zhao Zhibi described the windmill as follows: "West of the Dream of Clouds is the Garage ('storage,' or *cang*). From the Garage toward the west stood a few windmills made in Western styles. These windmills are there to show that farming and agriculture can be done without human labor" ([1775] 1983, 2:23a–24b). The windmills were probably assembled in the Dutch style, offering a reading of Sino-Dutch relations in terms of crafts, arts, and politics. Holland at the time was one of the most often seen symbols of "the foreign" because the country had exceptionally close political and commercial ties to the Qing royal house before the mid-nineteenth century (Boxer 1988; Zhao Erxun 1976b, 6:169; 1976c, 46:2263).

18. Kenneth Pomeranz (2000) has noted that the conflict between increasing population and limited resources was shared by different core economic zones around the world. It had caused Chinese society to abandon the development of labor-saving technology in order to solve the problem of population.

19. This is expressed in clear terms in the numerous prefaces written by renowned scholars and literati, including Ruan Yuan, to the reprint editions of *Yangzhou huafang lu* of the second and third decades of the nineteenth century.

20. As James Hevia's discussion (1995) on the McCartney delegation to China indicates, the colonialism in Latin America and Africa, where a leading "aristocratic bourgeois" figure such as Lord McCartney gained his political experience, actually helped shape nationalism in the British public sphere.

21. Alcock, for example, was praised by the British prime minister Lord Palmerston for actively solving problems in the region, and his career was highlighted by contemporary biographers (see, for example, Michie 1900).

22. More examples can be listed here. The city celebrated the birthdays of both the queen of England and Empress Dowager in the same halfhearted yet ritual manner. Bryna Goodman's study (2000) of Queen Victoria's diamond jubilee in Shanghai in 1897, though it does not deal directly with the issue of double calendars, shows the split agendas different social groups brought forth in one action of celebration.

The city welcomed different intellectual authorities and became a meeting ground where "Western learning," "Eastern learning," and "Chinese learning" competed for dominance. The city was also open to competing economic forces. Southeast Asian Chinese, for example, competed vigorously with the British for dominance of the tobacco business (Cochran 1980).

23. It took six years to build the Hardoon Garden, which eventually occupied about 170 *mu* of land. A photograph of a corner of the Hardoon Garden in the album compiled by Shi Meiding (1996, 65) shows an excellent example of this style.

24. There few physical traces of the Zhang Garden left today. In its time, it was renowned; it appeared more frequently than any other garden in contemporary literary writings. Several photographs of the Zhang Garden scenes can be found in Shi Meiding 1996, 64–65.

25. For information on Hardoon, the Hardoon Garden, and the cross-cultural reproduction of statues and themes, see Betta 1999. My thanks to James Benn for bringing this study to my attention.

26. Take the mid-eighteenth-century writings of Montesquieu and David Hume as examples: Both posited the natural environment as the determinant factor of the morals of a people, and both denounced the political regime and social and ethical principles of China. Their denunciation soon developed into a "wholesale criticism of China" (Hevia 1995, 70). As Hevia has pointed out, the opposition to things Chinese was actually an assertion of English "national character," of "national culture," and of "Greek and Roman purity" (1995, 66–74).

27. Xiong Yuezhi's essays are pioneer studies of the late-Qing Shanghai gardens in general and of the Zhang Garden in particular. What I seek to explore is a similar spatial manifestation of culture and society from a longer historical cycle and in a cross-cultural context.

28. Another source indicates that Zhang might have actually purchased the land from a French man named Fanon (Wu Xin and Yao Wennan [1918] 1970, 4a–4b).

29. Most scholarship identifies the owner of the Zhang Garden as Zhang Shuhe, a merchant from Wuxi, without noticing his connection with the CMSNC. I would like to emphasize the ties Zhang had with these better-known core figures of the Foreign Affairs enterprises. The term "merchant capitalists" is taken from Yen-p'ing Hao (1986), whose study focuses on the role of Xu Run, Tang Tingshu, and other important compradors during this period.

30. Xiong Yuezhi's study of the architects of Ankaidi shows that the building materials might have been imported from abroad. Also, it was common in the late nineteenth century for foreign residents as well as for Chinese high officials to hire architects from abroad (Johnston and Erh 1993).

31. According to Wu Xing and Yao Min'ai ([1918] 1970, 17:4a–4b), the two main European-style buildings, the Deep in the Clouds and the Ankaidi, were constructed after the Zhang Garden opened to the public in 1885.

32. I apologize for not dealing with the artistic aspect of the image here. For an overall analysis of the Shanghai paintings and pictorial images of this time, see Jonathan Hay (2001b).

33. This is a situation different from the voyages of Zheng He during the Ming dynasty. Zheng He opened up trade possibilities without doing any trading himself, whereas in the case of CMSNC, it was the semi-official company that made the commercial attempt.

34. It is widely accepted among scholars that this policy in its later stages heavily restrained the development of Chinese navigation companies by not allowing other domestic agencies to participate in the economic competition.

35. Actually, the attempt to open long-distance routes to Europe and the Americas was viewed as an important endeavor by many both inside and outside the company. Zhang Peiren, a contemporary literatus, commented that this indicated the restoration of the country's strength (Zhang Houquan 1988, 60–65).

36. Zheng Yimei, a writer and scholar of Shanghai popular culture, has noted that the Zhang Garden provided the earliest model for the "playground" because it offered the Shanghai public a variety of performances and entertainment as well as other forms of public fun. I have elaborated elsewhere on this connection with the playground (Meng Yue 2000, 436–95).

37. Yet the Qing state did not give up the imperial forms of international competition until the New Policy of 1902, which sanctioned the importation of machinery for private parties and individual use.

38. These criticisms, however, were quite diverse. Some focused on the strategic aspects of the company practice, some on its monopolizing policies, and others on its corruption. I return to this point shortly.

39. In 1885 Li Hongzhang reported to the court the bankruptcy of the CMSNC and fired both Xu Run and Zhang Honglu.

40. Michael Hardt and Anthony Negri see deterritorialization of capital and people as smooth processes within a global empire (2000, xii). The concept that the world has developed into an empire without an "outside" excludes the possibility of conceiving different histories that are connected with but not internal to the development of capitalism. In thinking of the globe as an empire that "has no outside," China and other parts of the Third World as well as the former socialist world could only become unimaginable.

41. The idea that the Zhang Garden turned into a public sphere is not new. Xiong Yuezhi (1996) has suggested that the administrative "gap" between the Shanghai Municipal Council and the Qing government over the International Settlement created the opportunity for the emergence of a political public in sites such as the Zhang Garden. I agree with Xiong's argument that the Zhang Garden became the site of a public space after the mid-1890s. Yet I am reluctant to accept his implication that the administrative "gap" of the International Settlement would automatically give rise to such a critical public. Nor would I assume that the entertainment activities that took place in the garden before the late 1890s had direct social and cultural links to political public activities after the late 1890s. I return to this point in the following section.

42. Xue Fucheng, himself involved in Foreign Affairs practices, provided an interesting example. In his analysis of the situation of the CMSNC, he pointed out weaknesses in policy making and operations and criticized the intentions of foreign companies ([1879] 1983, 1:1254).

43. This was best embodied by the movement to resist Russia, during which many criticized both the Qing state's cooperation with Britain in signing the 1904 treaty on Tibet and the Qing-Russian cooperation on border issues.

44. See Elman 1990. Elman's work has shown that during the early years of the nineteenth century, criticism toward "private" abuse of the "public" interest via status and power was common.

45. Wakeman (1995) has suggested that what he calls "vice, narcotics, and reds" accumulated in Shanghai's International Settlement because of its chaotic order and political vacuum.

46. In his discussion of Shanghai's public space, Xiong Yuezhi suggested that the opening of Shanghai gardens to the public led to the birth of a public sphere in the city. My views are close to Xiong's, with one crucial exception: For Xiong, the opening of a public sphere seems to indicate the emergence of a middle-class political and cultural space that was independent from the state, whereas I believe that the history of the Zhang Garden manifested the process of decentering—or the unfulfilled reterritorialization—of upper-class culture.

6. The Rise of an Entertainment Cosmopolitanism

1. The obvious fact is that by the beginning of the twentieth century, "the foreigners paid only eight hundred thousand taels in municipal taxes every year, and the Chinese community in the Settlement paid a million and a quarter" even though they had no political representation (Hauser 1940, 132).

2. Another source indicates that the total land area of the International Settlement in 1899 reached 33,503 *mu* (Zhang Renlong 1998, 491–93).

3. As is well known, transportation was built mainly for the purpose of getting foreign goods into the inner areas of China.

4. Many scholars have assumed that the independent or semi-independent status of the International Settlement was responsible for creating the space for anti-Qing revolutionary and nationalistic movements, including the boycott of American goods. In light of the expansion of the International Settlement, this belief does not seem to hold much water. Anti-Qing and anti-imperialist conferences and lectures, as mentioned in chapter 5, took the Zhang Garden and other gardens and native-places as their sites.

5. The architects included J. M. Cory (who visited Shanghai from 1887 to 1893), W. M. M. Dowdall (from 1887 to 1915), F. M. Gratton (from 1882 to 1900), W. H. Clark (from 1888 to 1889), W. Scott (from 1889 to 1912), S. J. Halse (from 1904 to 1929), B. L. Newman (from 1905 to 1915), R. E. Witch (from 1905 to 1910), F. G. Drewett (from 1905 to 1911), F. G. Johnson (from 1906 to 1907), G. A. Johnson (from 1906 to 1923), L. W. C. Lorden (from 1906 to 1926), A. G. Bray (from 1907 to 1911), J. T. W. Brooke (from 1907 to 1929), A. Scott Jr. (from 1908 to 1911), R. E. E. Stewardson (from 1908 to 1920 and again in 1929), G. L. Wilson (from 1911 to 1926 in Hong Kong and from 1926 to 1929 in Shanghai), and so forth (Muramatsu Shin 1991, 110–15).

6. Photographs of Sincere stores can be found everywhere. Shi Meiding (1996) has provided quite a few.

7. In quite a number of reminiscences, the name "Jing Runshan" is written as "Jing Runsan."

8. In more than one reminiscence, the writers recall that during the so-called Second Revolution in 1913, they gathered on top of the Mega-pavilion, a vantage point from which they could view the attack on the Jiangnan Arsenal.

9. The advertisements these playgrounds placed in *Shenbao* show that they all had a similar format. Traveling troupes often went from one site to another, offering

the same types of shows in each place. Advertisements for Xiuyun tian and Tianwai tian, with detailed information about their shows, can be found, for example, in *Shenbao* for any month in 1917.

10. The information about the architecture of Da shijie, its size, seats, and visitors presented here and in the following paragraph are based on the work of Yang Yaoshen (1994) and on following sources: *Shenbao*, July 14, 1917; von Sternberg 1965, 82–83; Shanghai shehuiju 1934b, 1934c; and Chen Cunren 1973, 237.

11. The number of visitors here are presented in two sources: Yang Yaoshen's estimate is 7,000 per day (1994, 163), which is closer to the number of seats; Wang Renze and Xiong Shanghou's estimation is 20,000 (1984, 268–74), a bit higher than my own yet worth noting here. Although no exact statistics about the audiences at this time are available, we know that in later decades Great World sold about 7,000 tickets per day. See Shanghai shehuiju 1934c.

12. Rumors had spread that Zhang was the real investor in the bank.

13. The bank opened on August 1, 1921, with Huang Chujiu himself as president, Ye Shantao as vice president, and Sun Shenqin as manager. The bank's initial capital was 500,000 yuan when it was founded, which was a small amount at the time. It attracted lower-income people because of its low minimum. The bank was closed after the death of Huang Chujiu on January 19, 1931 (Shanghai tongshe [1939] 1984, 231).

14. The people involved in preparing the stock market also included Bao Shijie, secretary to the warlord Feng Yuxiang; Ping Jinya, a novelist; Ye Hancheng, a medical doctor who had graduated in Germany; Min Caizhang, owner of a hosiery manufacturing business; Zhu Zizhao, the son of an eminent comprador; and Sun Zhengqiu, an actress (Jiang Shangqing 1970, 150–63).

15. It had the reputation of being a *yeji yinhang* (a bank for prostitutes or a layperson's bank), for example.

16. This sort of exhibition in Atlanta involved real killing, just to show the blood of a mother and her dead infant in an Indian village (Rydell 1984, 72–105).

17. "Flying boat," a nickname for airplanes, had appeared frequently in late-Qing popular pictorials (e.g. the *Dianshizhai Pictorial*) and fictions (e.g. *Xin Shitou ji*) (Ming Feng-ying 1999).

18. According to an announcement of the *Da shijie bao*, the exhibition was installed in 1917.

19. Displays of animals, dwarfs, giants, or ethnic people from around the world had been general motifs in all the world expositions since the nineteenth century. The interests in biology, zoology, and anthropology had gradually turned into racism by the turn of the century.

20. As described in a poem: "How fun it was to sit with friends and drink tea in the Hall of Republic, pleasing our eyes with the beautiful paintings and calligraphy on the wall" (*Da shijie bao*, February 18, 1918).

21. This "style" (if it can be called so) was most characteristic of the World's Columbian Exposition in 1893. See, for example, the pictures from *Advanced Guide to the World's Columbian Exposition*, 12, 72, 110. See Bertuca, Hartman, and Neumeister 1996 for a bibliographic guide to the World's Columbian Exposition.

22. A. C. Madison Scott (1982, 76) remembered that the Great World was where he saw a Shaoxing drama, or Yueju, for the first time.

23. For the deterioration of economic and political invention of the "inner land," including the Subei area, see Pomeranz 1993; Honig 1992.

24. The title of the opera frequently appeared in Great World advertisements in *Shenbao* and other newspapers during this period.

25. About the split and multiple late-Qing subject positions in narrative, see Ming Feng-ying 1999.

Conclusion

1. Here I have borrowed the phrase "Chinese cosmopolitanism" from the conference held for Professor Leo Lee's retirement from Harvard University in May 2004 in Cambridge, Massachusetts. I am indebted to the conference briefing written by Eileen Chow, which was a great inspiration on the topic, and to those scholarly works that have developed the issue in different terms. In my view, the concept has an affinity with the internationalism that, according to Rebecca Karl (2002), has characterized the way Chinese nationalism took shape. It is voiced in Wang Hui's work on Chinese thought, particularly his exploration of the changing meaning of "public" in the modern global order (Wang Hui 2004).

2. As Mizoguchi continues to suggest (1989, 2004), in the face of this ultimate public, a state or an emperor was only legitimate when properly performing the heaven-assigned tasks. Indeed, people often overthrow imperial rulers in the name of acting for the heavenly public.

3. I thank Ackbar Abbas for bringing Mikhail Bakhtin to my consideration.

4. At this point Bakhtin makes an interesting departure from structuralist theory, which emphasizes the divide between the signifier (or structure of signifiers) and the signified (or the meanings randomly attached to the signifiers by the structure). To make a rough comparison, Ferdinand de Saussure also emphasized the difference between speech practice and the system of language. According to Saussure, the structure of language exists among all speaking positions but is not in full presence. Each speech act activates the structure as a whole. For Bakhtin, however, utterance is not a speech act that brings forth the otherwise absent structure. Rather, dialogical utterances desystemize the language structure.

5. In this sense, the unruly cultural practices I have focused on were not identical to "chaos"—a disorderly social and mental situation caused by constant irregular performance of the system. Rather, the unruly practices, like Bakhtin's heteroglossia, were born socially and ideologically multiple, heterogeneous, and centrifugal. By the same token, the unruly practices were not "residues" of old systems that refused to be transformed by the system of capital, either.

6. This might explain why China is among those countries having had the most revolutions over the past couple of centuries. Of course, this claim itself deserves to be written about in another book.

7. In the tradition of missionary science in China, for example, every translation was already a retranslation or at least a double translation, since it took place in the collaboration and negotiation between two subjects. In many cases, the missionary translation did not always form new concepts; rather, the source concept was often retranslated into a terminology that was already there.

8. And as I have mentioned, Gail Hershatter dealt with the silence issue long ago (1993, 103–30).

9. The anti-Qing journal *Subao* appeared in Shanghai as early as 1903, but it was not until this debate that the difference between reformers and revolutionaries began to show.

10. According to Zhang Yufa, the number of "revolutionary organizations" was at least 126 (1975, 663, 680). And there were at least 668 "constitutional organizations" (Zhang Yufa 1971, 144). Sang Bing believes the actual number of nonrevolutionary organizations could be much larger, around 2,000 or more (1995, 274).

11. This analysis obviously echoes what Jürgen Habermas described as the disappearance of the "public sphere," namely, a historical downturn in European capitalism caused by the mutual penetration of the bourgeois class and the state at the price of the very independence of civil society (1989).

12. Although Bergère's use of social unit analysis to offer a political narrative is questionable (Cochran 1990, 895–96), she has presented the contrast between a relatively open and active phase of urban history prior to 1927 and the loss of that atmosphere after that point.

13. Eugenia Lean's study (2004) on the way Shi Jianqiao's assassination of Sun Chuanfang affected the urban public in political, cultural, and legal dimensions proves that even in the Nanjing period, what can be identified as unruly practice could mobilize the public and influence legal procedures.

Bibliography

Abbas, Ackbar. 1997. *Hong Kong: Culture and the Politics of Disappearance.* Minneapolis: University of Minnesota Press.

———. 2000. "Cosmopolitan De-scriptions: Shanghai and Hong Kong." *Cosmopolitanism, Public Culture* 12, no. 3: 769–86.

Abu-Lughod, Janet L. 1989. *Before European Hegemony: The World System A.D. 1250–1350.* New York: Oxford University Press.

———. 1999. *New York, Chicago, Los Angeles: America's Global Cities.* Minneapolis: University of Minnesota Press.

Adshead, Samuel Adrian M. 1970. *The Modernization of the Chinese Salt Administration, 1900–1920.* Cambridge, Mass.: Harvard University Press.

Advanced Guide to the World's Columbian Exposition. 1893. Chicago and New York: Rand McNally.

Ah Ying. 1953. "Wan Qing xiaoshuo de fanrong" [The flourishing of fiction in the late Qing]. In *Zhongguo jindai chuban shiliao* [The first compilation of documents on modern Chinese printing and publishing], comp. Zhang Jinglu, 184–203. Shanghai: Shangza chubanshe.

———. 1957. *Wan Qing xiqu xiaoshuo mu* [A bibliography of late Qing fictions and dramas]. Shanghai: Gudien wenxue cubanshe.

———, comp. 1960. *Fan Mei huagong jinyue wenxueji* [Literary anthology of opposition to Chinese exclusion in the United States]. Beijing: Zhonghua shuju.

All about Shanghai: A Standard Guidebook. [1935] 1986. With an introduction by H. J. Lethbridge. Repr., Hong Kong and New York: Oxford University Press.

Anderson, Benedict. 1983. *Imagined Communities: Reflections on the Origin and Spread of Nationalism.* London: Verso.

Anonymous. 1895. "Lessons from the War in the East." *Brassey's Annual,* 126–43.

Anonymous. [1905] 1960. "*Tongbao shounue ji* Fakanci" [Foreword to *The suffering of fellow Chinese*]. Reprinted in *Fan Mei huagong jinyue wenxueji* [Literary anthology of opposition to Chinese exclusion in the United States], comp. Ah Ying, 522. Beijing: Zhonghua shuju.

Anonymous. [1905] 1982. "Tan xiang shan" [The Tanxiang mountain]. Reprinted in *Dizhi huagong jinyue wenxueji* [Literary anthology of resistance to Chinese exclusion in the United States], 14. Taipei: Guangya chubanshe.

Appadurai, Arjun, ed. 1986. *The Social Life of Things: Commodities in Cultural Perspective.* Cambridge: Cambridge University Press.

———. 1996. *Modernity at Large: Cultural Dimensions of Globalization.* Public Worlds 1. Minneapolis: University of Minnesota Press.

———, ed. 2002. *Globalization.* Durham, N.C.: Duke University Press.

Appleton, William Worthen. 1951. *A Cycle of Cathay: The Chinese Vogue in England during the Seventeenth and Eighteenth Centuries.* New York: Columbia University Press.

Arrighi, Giovanni. 1999. "The World According to Andre Gunder Frank." *Review* 22, no. 3: 327–54.

Bakhtin, Mikhail. 1981. *The Dialogic Imagination: Four Essays.* Trans. Caryl Emerson and Michael Holquist. Austin: University of Texas Press.

Bao Tianxiao. 1990. *Chuanyinglou huiyilu* [Reminiscence of the Master of the Chuanying Pavilion]. 3 vols. Taipei: Longwen chubanshe.

Benjamin, Walter. 1997. *Charles Baudelaire: A Lyric Poet in the Era of High Capitalism.* London: Verso.

———. 1999. *The Arcade Project.* Trans. Howard Eiland and Kevin McLaughlin. Cambridge, Mass.: Belknap Press of Harvard University Press.

Bennett, Adrian Arthur. 1967. *John Fryer: The Introduction of Western Science and Technology into Nineteenth-Century China.* Harvard East Asian Monographs 24. Cambridge, Mass.: East Asian Research Center, Harvard University.

Bergère, Marie-Claire. 1989. *The Golden Age of the Chinese Bourgeoisie, 1911–1937.* New York: Cambridge University Press.

Bernal, Martin. 1976. *Chinese Socialism to 1907.* Ithaca, N.Y.: Cornell University Press.

Bertuca, David, Donald K. Hartman, and Susan M. Neumeister, comps. 1996. *The World's Columbian Exposition: A Centennial Bibliographic Guide.* Westport, Conn.: Greenwood.

Betta, Chiara. 1997. "Silas A. Hardoon: A Cultural Intermediary in Shanghai, 1880–1931." Ph.D. diss., School of Oriental and African Studies, University of London.

———. 1999. "Silas Aaron Hardoon and Cross-Cultural Adaptation in Shanghai." In *The Jews of China,* vol. 1, *Historical and Comparative Perspectives,* ed. Jonathan Goldstein. Armonk: N.Y.: A. E. Sharpe.

Biggerstaff, Kight. 1956. "Shanghai Polytechnic Institution and Reading Room: An Attempt to Introduce Western Science and Technology to the Chinese." *Pacific Historical Review* 25, no. 2 (May): 127–49.

———. 1961. *The Earliest Modern Government Schools in China.* Ithaca, N.Y.: Cornell University Press.

Boxer, C. R. 1988. *Dutch Merchants and Mariners in Asia: 1602–1795.* Repr., London: Variorum Reprints.

Breckenridge, Carol A., ed. 2002. *Cosmopolitanism.* Durham, N.C.: Duke University Press.

Bretschneider E. [1898] 1962. *History of European Botanical Discoveries in China.* 2 vols. Leipzig: Zentral-Antiquariat der Deutschen Demokratischen Republik.

Briquet, John Isaac. 1935. *International Rules of Botanical Nomenclature Adopted by the International Botanical Congresses of Vienna, 1905, and Brussels, 1910, Revised by the International Botanical Congress of Cambridge, 1930.* N.p: Jena, G. Fischer.

Brockway, Lucile. 1979. *Science and Colonial Expansion: The Role of the British Royal Botanic Gardens.* New York: Academic Press.

Brokaw, Cynthia. 1994. "Tai Chen and Learning in the Confucian Tradition." In *Education and Society in Late Imperial China, 1600–1900*, ed. Benjamin Elmand and Alexander Woodside, 257–91. Berkeley and Los Angeles: University of California Press.

Buck-Morss, Susan. 1989. *The Dialectics of Seeing: Walter Benjamin and the Arcades Project.* Studies in Contemporary German Social Thought. Cambridge, Mass.: MIT Press.

Cai Jingfeng. 1985. "*Bencao gangmu* zhong de yixue jiaoliu" [The exchange of medical knowledge attested in *Materia Medica*]. In *Li Shizhen yanjiu lunwen ji* [An anthology of Li Shizhen studies], comp. Zhongguo yaoxue shi xuehui [Chinese Association of Studies of Medical History], 200–24. Wuhan: Hubei chubanshe.

Cai Yuanpei. 1918. Preface to *Botanical Nomenclature*. In *Zhiwuxue dacidian* [Botanical nomenclature], 1–2 (prefaces paginated separately). Shanghai: Commercial Press.

———. 1987. "Shangwu yinshuguan zong jingli Xia jun zhuan" [A biography of the president of the Commercial Press, Mr. Xia]. In *Shangwu yinshuguan jiushi nian* [Ninety years of the Commercial Press], 1–2. Beijing: Shangwu yinshuguan.

Cao Juren. [1962] 1996. *Shanghai chunqiu* [Spring and autumn in Shanghai]. Repr., Shanghai: Shanghai renmin chubanshe.

Cao Rong. 1967. *Xuehai leibian* [The categorical compilation of the sea of learning]. Baibu congshu jicheng [Series of a hundred collectanea] 24. Repr. ed., Taipei: Yiwen.

Chakrabarty, Dipesh. 2000. *Provincializing Europe: Postcolonial Thought and Historical Difference.* Princeton: Princeton University Press.

Chang Zhou. 1992. "Shangwu yinshuguan de zaoqi gudong" [The early stockholders of the Commercial Press]. In *Shangwu yinshuguan jiushiwu nian* [Ninety-five years of the Commercial Press], 642–55. Beijing: Shangwu yinshuguan.

Chen Bohai and Yuan Jin. 1993. *Shanghai jindai wenxue shi* [A literary history of modern Shanghai]. Shanghai: Shanghai renmin chubanshe.

Chen Congzhou. 1983. *Yangzhou yuanlin* [The gardens of Yangzhou]. Hong Kong: Sanlian shudian, Shanghai kexue jishu chubanshe.

———. 1994. *Zhongguo tingtang: Jiang nan pian* [Entrance halls and living rooms in China: the Jiangnan chapter]. Shanghai: Shanghai huabao chubanshe.

Chen Congzhou and Zhang Ming. 1988. *Shanghai jindai jianzhu shigao* [A history of architecture in modern Shanghai]. Shanghai: Shenghuo dushu xinzhi sanlian shudian.

Chen Cunren. 1973. *Yin yuan shidai shenghuo shi* [Life in the era of silver dollars]. Hong Kong: Chou Chih-weng; Tsung ching hsiao Wu hsing chi shu pao she.

Chen Dingsha. 1987. "Chunliu she shiji" [The history of the Chunliu troupe]. In *Zhongguo huaju shiliaoji* [Compiled source materials of the history of spoken drama], comp. Huaju yanjiusuo, zhongguo yishu yanjiuyuan [Institute of Drama Studies, Chinese Academy of Arts], 20–57. Beijing: Wenhua yishu chubanshe.

Chen Dingshan. 1956. *Chun Shen jiuwen; Chun Shen jiuwen xuji* [Old memories of spring in the city of Shen River]. Taipei: Shijie wenwu chubanshe.

Chen Duxiu. 1915. "Jinggao qingnian" [A few words for the youth]. *Xin Qingnian* [New Youth] 1, no. 1 (September 15): 5–6. (In this issue of the journal, each essay is paginated separately.)

Chen Shutung. 1987. "Huiyi Shangwu yinshuguan" [Recollection about the Commercial Press]. In *Shangwu yinshuguan jiushi nien* [Ninety years of the Commercial Press], 131–39. Beijing: Shangwu yinshuguan.

Chen Wuwo. [1928] 1997. *Lao Shanghai sanshi nian jianwen lu* [What I saw and heard in the past thirty years about old Shanghai]. Repr., Shanghai: Shanghai shudian.

Chen Xinqian and Zhang Tianlu, eds. 1992. *Zhongguo jindai yaoxue shi* [A history of medicine in modern China]. Beijing: Renmin weisheng chubanshe.

Chen Yimin. 1993–1994. "Jingju shi xinian jiyao" [Essentials of the Peking Opera chronology]. *Xiqu yanjiu* [Theater studies] 46 (June 1993): 187–203; 47 (December 1993): 166–93; 48 (March 1994): 187–220.

Chen Zhongyi. [1899] 1902. "Liyan" [Foreword]. Reprinted in *Huangchao jingshiwen sanbian* [The *Third Sequel to Essay of Statecraft of the Dynasty*]. 80 *juan*: 1–2. Shanghai: Shanghai shuju.

Chi Zhizheng. [1891] 1989. *Hu you mengying* [The shadow of dreams of traveling in Shanghai]. Repr., Shanghai: Shanghai guji chubanshe.

Chiang Tao-chang. 1976. *The Significance of the Salt Industry in Ch'ing China.* Singapore: Institute of Humanities and Social Sciences, College of Graduate Studies, Nanyang University.

China, Maritime Customs. 1898–1933. *Decennial Reports on the Ports Open to Foreign Commerce in China and Corea and on the Condition and Development of the Treaty Port Provinces.* Shanghai: Kelly and Walsh.

———. 1906. *Decennial Reports on the Ports Open to Foreign Commerce in China and Corea and on the Condition and Development of the Treaty Port Provinces, 1892–1901.* Shanghai: Kelly and Walsh.

Clark, J. D. 1894. *Sketches in and around Shanghai etc.* Shanghai: "Shanghai Mercury" and "Celestial Empire" Offices.

Clunas, Craig. 1996. *Fruitful Sites: Garden Culture in Ming Dynasty China.* Durham, N.C.: Duke University Press.

Cochran, Sherman. 1980. *Big Business in China: Sino-Foreign Rivalry in the Cigarette Industry, 1890–1930.* Cambridge, Mass.: Harvard University Press.

———. 1990. Review of *The Golden Age of the Chinese Bourgeoisie, 1911–1937,* by Marie-Claire Bergère. *Journal of Asian Studies* 49, no. 4: 895–96.

———. 1999. *Inventing Nanjing Road: Commercial Culture in Shanghai; 1900–1945.* Ithaca, N.Y.: Cornell University Press.

Cohen, Paul A. 1973. *Between Tradition and Modernity: Wang T'ao and Reform in Late Ch'ing China.* Cambridge, Mass.: Council on East Asian Studies, Harvard University; distributed by Harvard University Press.

———. 1984. *Discovering History in China: American Historical Writings on the Recent Chinese Past.* New York: Columbia University Press.

Commercial Press. 1997. *Shangwu yinshuguan 100 zhounian* [A hundred years of the Commercial Press]. Taipei: Shangwu yinshuguan.

Cong Xiaoping. 2001. "Localizing the Global, Nationalizing the Local: The Role of Teachers' Schools in Making China Modern, 1897–1937." Ph.D. diss., University of California at Los Angeles.

Coolidge, Mary Elizabeth. 1969. *Chinese Immigration.* New York: Arno.

Crossman, Carl. 1991. *The Decorative Arts of the China Trade: Paintings, Furnishings, and Exotic Curiosities.* Woodbridge, Suffolk, U.K.: Antique Collectors' Club.

Da shijie bao [Great World paper]. Shanghai. August 19, 1917–June 7, 1931.

Daniels, Christian, and Nicholas K. Menzies. 1996. *Agro-Industries: Sugar Cane*

Technology; and Forestry. Part 3 of vol. 6, *Biology and Biological Technology*, of *Science and Civilisation in China*, ed. Joseph Needham. Cambridge: Cambridge University Press.

Darnton, Robert. 1984. *The Great Cat Massacre and Other Episodes in French Cultural History.* New York: Basic Books.

Debord, Guy. 1970. *The Society of the Spectacle.* Detroit: Black and Red.

Deleuze, Gilles, and Felix Guattari. 1987. *A Thousand Plateaus: Capitalism and Schizophrenia.* Trans. and with a foreword by Brian Massumi. Minneapolis: University of Minnesota Press.

Deng Xiaoqiu. 1996. "Huaiju de yuanyuan yu xingcheng" [The origin and the formation of the Huai Opera]. In *Xiqu yanjiu* [Theater studies] 51 (June): 181–93.

Derrida, Jacques. 2001. *On Cosmopolitanism and Forgiveness.* London and New York: Routledge.

Dianshizhai huaguan. 1883. *Dianshizhai huabao* [Dianshizhai pictorial]. Series 2. Repr., Guangzhou: Guangzhou shi guji shudian.

Ding Changjing, Liu Foding, et al., 1990. *Minguo yanwu shigao* [A history of the salt industry in the Republican era]. Beijing: Renmin chubanshe.

Ding Richang. 1877. *Fu Wu gondu* [Public documents for pacifying the Wu]. Jiangsu: N.p.

Ding Richu, Shen Zuwei, et al. 1994. *Shanghai jindai jingji shi, 1843–1894* [The economic history of modern Shanghai, 1843–1894]. Shanghai: Shanghai renmin chubanshe.

Ding Shen. 1957. *Wulin cangshu lu* [Records of book collecting in Wulin]. Shanghai: Dudian wenxue chubanshe.

Ding Yusheng. 1868a. "Chajin yinci xiaoshuo" [The search for and prohibition of unlawful erotic ballads and fictions] on May 7, 1868, and May 13, 1868 (Tongzhi 7, Fourth Month, fifteenth day and twenty-first day). In *Jiangsu shengli* [Official regulations of Jiangsu Province], 14a–19b. China: Jiangsu shuju, 1870.

———. 1868b. "Jinzhi kaishe xiguan" [Prohibition against opening theaters] in May 1868 (Tongzhi 7, Fourth Month). In *Jiangsu shengli* [Official regulations of Jiangsu Province], 25a–25b. China: Jiangsu shuju, 1870.

———. 1868c. "Yanjin funu ruguan yincha" [Women strictly forbidden from entering theaters and teahouses] on July 17, 1868 (Tongzhi 7, Fifth Month, twenty-eighth day). In *Jiangsu shengli* [Official regulations of Jiangsu Province], 13a–13b. China: Jiangsu shuju, 1870.

Dirlik, Arif. 1994. *Anarchism in the Chinese Revolution.* Reissue, Berkeley and Los Angeles: University of California Press. Originally published 1991.

———. 2001. "Markets, Culture, Power: The Making of a 'Second Cultural Revolution' in China." *Asian Studies Review* 25, no. 1 (March): 3–33.

Dongfang tushuguan [Oriental Library]. 1933. *Dong fang tushuguan zhilue* [A brief history of the Oriental Library in Shanghai]. Shanghai: N.p.

Downs, Jacques M. 1997. *The Golden Ghetto: The American Commercial Community at Canton and the Shaping of American China Policy, 1784–1844.* Bethlehem, Pa.: Lehigh University Press.

Drège, Jean Pierre. 1978. *La Commercial Press de Shanghai, 1897–1949.* Paris: Collège de France.

Driver, Felix, and David Gilbert, eds. 1999. *Imperial Cities: Landscape, Display, and Identity.* Manchester and New York: Manchester University Press.

Du Shiran, Lin Qingyuan, and Guo Jinbin. 1991. *Yangwu yundong yu Zhongguo jindai keji* [The foreign affairs movement and China's modern science and technology]. Shenyang: Liaoning jiaoyu chubanshe.

Du Yaquan. 1918. "Zhiwu xue da cidian xu si" [Fourth preface to *Botanical nomenclature*]. In *Zhiwuxue dacidian* [Botanical nomenclature], 1–2 (prefaces paginated separately). Shanghai: Commercial Press.

Duara, Prasenjit. 1988. *Culture, Power, and the State: Rural North China, 1900–1942*. Stanford: Stanford University Press.

———. 1995. *Rescuing History from the Nation: Questioning Narratives of Modern China*. Chicago: University of Chicago Press.

———. 2003. *Sovereignty and Authenticity: Manchukuo and the East Asian Modern*. Lanham, Md.: Rowman and Littlefield.

———, ed. 2004. *Decolonization: Perspectives from Now and Then*. London: Routledge.

Durand, Antoine, and Regine Thiriez. 1993. "Engraving the Emperor of China's European Palace." *Biblion* 1, no. 2 (Spring): 81–108.

Elman, Benjamin A. 1984. *From Philosophy to Philology: Intellectual and Social Aspects of Change in Late Imperial China*. Cambridge, Mass.: Council on East Asian Studies, Harvard University.

———. 1990. *Classicism, Politics, and Kinship: the Ch'ang-chou School of New Text Confucianism in Late Imperial China*. Berkeley and Los Angeles: University of California Press.

———. 1998. "Reconsidering the Transition from the Pre-modern 'Chinese Sciences' to 'Modern Science' in China." Paper presented at the Workshop on Interesting Areas and Disciplines: Cultural Studies of Chinese Science, Technology, and Medicine, sponsored by the University of California, Berkeley, Center for Chinese Studies, February 27–28, 1998.

———. 2000a. *A Cultural History of Civil Examinations in Late Imperial China*. Berkeley and Los Angeles: University of California Press.

———. 2000b. "Cong qian xiandai de gezhi xue dao xiandai de kexue" [From premodern gezhi studies to modern sciences]. *China Scholarship* 1, no. 2: 1–43.

———. 2005. *On Their Own Terms: Science in China, 1550–1900*. Cambridge, Mass.: Harvard University Press.

Eriksson, Gunnar. 1983. "Linnaeus the Botanist." In *Linnaeus, the Man and His Work*. Berkeley and Los Angeles: University of California Press, 63–109.

Esherick, Joseph, ed. 2000. *Remaking the Chinese City: Modernity and National Identity, 1900–1950*. Honolulu: University of Hawaii Press.

Fairbank, John King. 1969. *Trade and Diplomacy on the China Coast; the Opening of the Treaty Ports, 1842–1854*. Stanford: Stanford University Press.

———, ed. 1978. *The Cambridge History of China*, vol. 10, *Late Ch'ing, 1800–1911, Part I*. Cambridge: Cambridge University Press.

Fan Jinmin and Chin Wen. 1993. *Jiangnan sichou shi yanjiu* [A study of the history of silk manufacturing in Jiangnan]. Beijing: Nongye chubanshe.

Fang Hao. 1953–1954. *Zhongxi Jiaotong shi* [The history of Chinese-Western exchanges]. 5 vols. Taipei: Zhonghua wenhua chuban shiyeshe.

Fang Yizhi. 1983. *Wuli xiaoshi* [The small knowledge of the principle of things]. Taipei: Shangwu yinshuguan.

Far Eastern Review. 1916. "Building Progress of Shanghai." *Far Eastern Review* 8, no. 4: 144–52.

Farnham, John Marshall Willoughby. 1910. "Shanghai Qingxin zhongxue lanshang ji" [The development of the Lowrie Institute in Shanghai]. In *Qingxin liangji zhongxuexiao qishi zhounian jinian ce* [Volume in celebration of the seventieth anniversary of the Qing Xin School]. Shanghai: N.p.

Feng Fangji. 1982. "Feng Shenzhi xiansheng riji" [Selected diary entries of Mr. Feng Shenzhi]. In *Qing dai riji huichao* [Selected diaries from the Qing dynasty], ed. P. E. A. Liu. Shanghai: Shanghai renmin chubanshe.

Feng Guifen. 1897. *Jiaobin lu kangyi* [Remarks made in the Jiaobin studio]. Repr., Taipei: Wenhai chubanshe, n.d.

Feng Ziyou. 1954. "Xinhai geming shubao yilanbiao" [A general list of books and newspapers published prior to and during the 1911 Revolution]. In *Zhongguo jindai chuban shiliao erbian* [The second compilation of documents on modern Chinese printing and publishing], comp. Zhang Jinglu, 276–97. Shanghai: Qunlian chubanshe.

———. 1965–1968. *Geming yishi* [An unofficial record of the 1911 Revolution]. 5 vols. Taipei: Shangwu yinshuguan.

Feurerwerker, Albert. 1958. *Chinese Early Industrialization: Sheng Hsuan-huai (1844–1916) and Mandarin Enterprise.* Cambridge, Mass.: Harvard University Press.

Flynn, Dennis Owen, Arturo Giraldez, and Richard von Glahn, eds. 2003. *Global Connections and Monetary History, 1470–1800.* Aldershot, U.K.: Ashgate.

Fogel, Joshua A. 1995. *The Cultural Dimension of Sino-Japanese Relations: Essays on the Nineteenth and Twentieth Centuries.* Armonk, N.Y.: M. E. Sharpe.

———. 1996. *The Literature of Travel in the Japanese Rediscovery of China, 1862–1945.* Stanford: Stanford University Press.

Foucault, Michel. 1970. *The Order of Things: An Archaeology of the Human Sciences.* New York: Vintage.

Fox, Robert, and Anthony Turner, eds. 1998. *Luxury Trades and Consumerism in Ancien Régime Paris: Studies in the History of the Skilled Workforce.* Aldershot, U.K., and Brookfield, Vt., U.S.: Ashgate.

Frängsmyr, Tore, ed. 1983. *Linnaeus, the Man and His Work.* With contributions by Sten Lindroth, Gunnar Eriksson, and Gunnar Broberg. Berkeley and Los Angeles: University of California Press.

Frank, Andre Gunder. 1998. *ReOrient: Global Economy in the Asian Age.* Berkeley and Los Angeles: University of California Press.

Frow, John. 1997. *Time and Commodity Culture: Essays in Cultural Theory and Postmodernity.* New York: Oxford University Press.

Fryer, John [Fu Lanya]. [1880] 1953. "Jiangnan Zhizaoju fanyi xishu shilue" [Translation of Western books in the Jiangnan Arsenal]. Reprinted in *Zhongguo jindai chunban shiliao chubian* [The first compilation of documents on modern Chinese printing and publishing, 1840–1918], comp. Zhang Jinglu, 9–28. Shanghai: Shang za chubanshe.

Gainor, J. Ellen. 1995. *Imperialism and Theatre: Essays on World Theatre, Drama, and Performance.* London and New York: Routledge.

Gan Zuolin. 1915. "Jiangnan zhizao ju jianshi" [A brief history of the Jiangnan Arsenal]. *Dongfang zazhi* [Eastern miscellany] 11, no. 5 (May): 46–48; 11, no. 6 (June): 21–25.

Gandelsonas, Mario, ed. 2002. *Shanghai Reflections: Architecture, Urbanism, and the Search for an Alternative Modernity; Essays.* New York: Princeton Architectural Press.

Gao Hanqing. 1992. "Benguan chuangye shi" [The early history of the Commercial Press]. In *Shangwu yinshuguan jiushiwu nian* [Ninety-five years of the Commercial Press], 1–13. Beijing: Shangwu yinshuguan.

Gao Jin, comp. [1771] 1983. *Qinding nan xun sheng dian* [The imperial records of emperors' southern tours]. Repr., Taipei: Taiwan Shangwu yinshuguan.

Ge Yuanxu. [1876] 1989. *Huyou zaji* [Miscellaneous records about Shanghai]. Repr., Shanghai: Shanghai guji.

Gee, Gist. 1918. Preface to *Botanical Nomenclature*. In *Zhiwuxue dacidian* [Botanical nomenclature], 1–2 (prefaces paginated separately). Shanghai: Commercial Press.

Gerth, Karl. 2004. *China Made: Consumer Culture and the Creation of a Nation*. Cambridge, Mass.: Harvard University Press.

Gezhi huibian [Journal of sciences and industry]. 1876–1892. Shanghai: Gezhi shushi.

Gledhill, D. 1989. *The Names of Plants*. Cambridge: Cambridge University Press.

Godley, Michael R. 1978. "China's World Fair of 1910: Lessons from a Forgotten Event." *Modern China Studies* 12: 503–22.

Gong Zizhen. 1920. "Shu Jinling" [On the Actor Jin]. In *Ding'an chuanji* [Complete works of Ding'an], 179–81. Shanghai: Saoye shanfang.

———. 1961. *Gong Zizhen quanji* [Complete works of Gong Zizhen]. Ed. Wang Peizheng. Beijing: Zhonghua shuju.

Goodman, Bryna. 1995. *Native Place, City, and Nation: Regional Networks and Identities in Shanghai, 1853–1937*. Berkeley and Los Angeles: University of California Press.

———. 2000. "Improvisations on a Semi-Colonial Theme, or How to Read a Celebration of Transnational Urban Community." *Journal of Asian Studies* 59, no. 4: 889–926.

Gu Changsheng. 1981. *Chuan jiao shi yu jindai chongguo* [Missionaries and modern China]. Shanghai: Shanghai renmin chubanshe.

———. 1985. *Cong Ma li xun dao Citu leideng* [From Morrison to Steward]. Shanghai: Shanghai renmin chubanshe.

Gu Duhuang. 1987. *Kun qu shi bulun* [Supplementary notes on the history of the Kunqu opera]. Nanjing: Jiangsu guji chubanshe.

Gu Gongxie. [1785] 1917. *Xiaoxia xianji* [Leisure writing in the summer]. Repr., Shanghai: Shangwu yinshuguan.

Gu Lu. [1830] 1984. *Qing jialu* [Ways of life in the Qing era]. Reprinted in vol. 9 of *Biji xiaoshuo daguan* [Comprehensive collection of travelogues and fictions]. Yangzhou: Jiangsu Guangling guji keyinche.

Guomin zhengfu jiaoyubu [The Education Bureau of the Republic]. [1935] 1953. "Jiaokeshu zhi fakan gaikuang, 1868–1918" [The general survey of the publication and distribution of textbooks, 1868–1918]. In *Zhongguo jindai chunban shiliao chubian* [The first compilation of documents on modern Chinese printing and publishing, 1840–1918], comp. Zhang Jinglu, 219–53. Shanghai: Shangza chubanshe.

Guy, R. Kent. 1987. *The Emperor's Four Treasuries: Scholars and the State in the Late Ch'ien-lung Era*. Cambridge, Mass.: Council on East Asian Studies, Harvard University; Distributed by Harvard University Press.

Haas, William J. 1996. *China Voyager: Gist Gee's Life in Science*. Armonk, N.Y., and London: M. E. Sharpe.

Habermas, Jürgen. 1989. *The Structural Transformation of the Public Sphere: An Inquiry into a Category of Bourgeois Society.* Cambridge: Polity Press.

Haller, Mark H. 1963. *Eugenics: Hereditarian Attitudes in American Thought.* New Brunswick, N.J.: Rutgers University Press.

Hamashita Takeshi and Kawakatsu Heita. 1991. *Ajia koekiken to Nihon kogyoka, 1500–1900* [Asian trade circle and the industrialization of Japan, 1500–1900]. Tokyo: Riburo Poto.

Hanan, Patrick. 1998. "*Fengyue Meng* and the Courtesan Novel." *Harvard Journal of Asiatic Studies.* 58, no. 2: 345–72.

Hao, Yen-p'ing. 1986. *The Commercial Revolution in Nineteenth-Century China: The Rise of Sino-Western Mercantile Capitalism.* Berkeley, Los Angeles, and London: University of California Press.

Hardt, Michael, and Antonio Negri. 2000. *Empire.* Cambridge, Mass.: Harvard University Press.

Hart, Roger. 1999. "Beyond Science and Civilization: A Post-Needham Critique." *East Asian Science, Technology, and Medicine* 16 (December): 88–114.

Harumi Goto-Shibata. 1995. *Japan and Britian in Shanghai, 1925–31.* New York: St. Martin's.

Harvey, David. 2003. *Paris, Capital of Modernity.* New York and London: Routledge.

Hauser, Ernest O. 1940. *Shanghai: City for Sale.* New York: Harcourt, Brace.

Hay, Jonathan. 2001a. *Shitao: Painting and Modernity in Early Qing China.* Cambridge and New York: Cambridge University Press.

———. 2001b. "Painting and the Built Environment in Late-Nineteenth-Century Shanghai." In *Chinese Art: Modern Expressions,* ed. Maxwell K. Kearn and Judith Smith, 78–116. New York: Metropolitan Museum of Art.

He Ma and Zheng Yimei. 1956. *Shanghai jiuhua* [Speaking of old Shanghai]. Shanghai: Shanghai wenhua chubanshe.

He Shengnai. 1931. "San shi wu nian lai Zhongguo zhi yin shua shu" [A retrospective account of the print technology in the past thirty-five years]. In *Zuijin sanshiwu nian zhi Zhongguo jiaoyu* [Education in China in the past thirty-five years], comp. Zhuang Yu and He Shengnai. Shanghai: Commercial Press.

Henriot, Christian. 1993. *Shanghai, 1927–1937: Municipal Power, Locality, and Modernization.* Trans. Noel Castelino. Berkeley and Los Angeles: University of California Press.

Herbert, Hilary A. 1895. "Military Lessons of the Chino-Japanese War." *North American Review* 160, no. 6 (June): 685–98.

Hershatter, Gail. 1993. "The Subaltern Talks Back: Reflections on Subaltern Theory and Chinese History." *positions* 1: 103–30.

———. 1997. *Dangerous Pleasures: Prostitution and Modernity in Twentieth-Century Shanghai.* Berkeley and Los Angeles: University of California Press.

Hevia, James. 1995. *Cherishing Men from Afar: Qing Guest Ritual and the Macartney Embassy of 1793.* Durham, N.C.: Duke University Press.

———. 1999. "Looting Beijing, 1860, 1900." In *Token of Exchange: The Problem of Translation in Global Circulations,* ed. Lydia Liu, 192–213. Durham, N.C.: Duke University Press.

———. 2004. *English Lessons: The Pedagogy of Imperialism in Nineteenth-Century China.* Durham, N.C.: Duke University Press.

Higham, John. 1955. *Strangers in the Land: Patterns of American Nativism, 1860–1925.* New Brunswick, N.J.: Rutgers University Press.

Ho Ping-ti. 1954. "The Salt Merchants of Yang-Chou: A Study of Commercial Capitalism in Eighteenth-Century China." *Harvard Journal of Asiatic Studies* 17: 130–68.

Hobson, Benjamin. [1851] 1967. *Quanti xinlun* [The treaties of anatomy]. In *Haishan xianguang congshu* [Collectanea of the Fairy Pavilion on the Ocean Mountain], vol. 60 of *Baibu congshu jicheng* [Series of a hundred collectanea]. Taipei: Yiwen.

———. [1855] 1864. *Bowu xinbian* [Collection of new scientific knowledge]. Repr., Tokyo: Yorozuya Heishirō, Genji kōshi.

Honig, Emily. 1992. *Creating Chinese Enthnicity: Subei People in Shanghai, 1850–1940.* New Haven: Yale University Press.

Honour, Hugh. 1962. *Chinoiserie: The Vision of Cathay.* New York: Dutton.

Horng Wann-sheng. 1991. "Li Shanlan: The Impact of Western Mathematics in China during the Late Nineteenth Century." Ph.D. diss., City University of New York.

———. 1993. *Tan tian sanyou* [Three friends of astronomical studies]. Taipei: Mingwen shuju.

Hoshi Ayao. 1969. *The Ming Tribute Grain System.* Trans. Mark Elvin. Ann Arbor: Center for Chinese Studies, University of Michigan.

Hotta-Lister, Ayako. 1999. *The Japan-British Exhibition of 1910: Gateway to the Island Empire of the East.* Richmond, Surrey, U.K.: Japan Library.

Hsia, Ching-lin. 1929. *The Status of Shanghai: A Historical Review of the International Settlement.* Shanghai: Kelly and Walsh.

Hsü An-k'un. 1998. *Qingdai dayunhe yanxiao yanjiu* [The salt administration and the Grand Canal in the Qing]. Taipei: Wenshizhe chubanshe.

Hu Chunhui. 1984. "Niu Yongjian." In *Zhonghua minguo mingren zhuan* [Famous figures in Republican China], 2:522–35. Taipei: Jindai zhongguo chubanshe.

Hu Guochen, comp. 1992. *Bencao gangmu tongshi* [General explanation of compendium of *Materia Medica*]. Beijing: Xueyuan chubanshe.

Hu Minghui. 2004. "Cosmopolitan Confucianism: China's Road to Modern Science." Ph.D. diss., University of California, Los Angeles.

Hu Xianghan. [1930] 1989. *Shanghai xiaozhi* [A minor history of Shanghai]. Repr., Shanghai: Shanghai guji chubanshe.

Hu Ying. 2000. *Tales of Translation: Composing the New Woman in China, 1898–1918.* Stanford: Stanford University Press.

Hua Hengfang. [1873] 1896. "*Dai shu shu xu*" [Preface to *Dai shu shu*]. In *Dai shu shu* [*Algebra*, by John Wallis]. Trans. John Fryer and Hua Hengfang. Repr., Shanghai: Shanghai shiyin shuju.

———. 1885. *Xing su xuan suanxue bazhong* [Eight works of mathematical studies by the master of Xingsu studio]. N.p.: Shenji shuzhuang.

———. [1899] 1962. "Jindai chouren zhushu lu" [On works by recent mathematicians and astronomers]. Reprinted in *Chouren zhuan huibian* [Compiled biographies of mathematicians and astronomers], comp. Yang Jialuo. Taipei: Shijie shuju.

Huan qiu she. [1909–1910] 1999. *Tuhua ribao* [Pictorial daily news]. Repr., Shanghai: Shanghai guji chubanshe.

Huang Dezhao. 1980. "Zhang Ji." In *Min'guo renwu zhuan* [Biographies of Republican Figures], 2:114–18. Comp. Li Xin and Sun Sibai. Beijing: Zhonghua shuju.

Huang Liang-chi. 1969. *Dongfang zazhi zhi kanxing jiqi yingxiang zhi yanjiu* [A study on the publication and influence of *Eastern miscellany*]. Taipei: Taiwan Shangwu yinshuguan.

Huang Maocai. [1898] 1984. *You Hu cuoji*. Reprinted in *Shanghai yanjiu ziliao* [Collected documents for Shanghai studies], comp. Shanghai tongshe [Society of General Knowledge of Shanghai]. Taipei: Zhongguo chubanshe.

Huang Wenyang. 1989. "*Chongding Quhai zongmu zixu*" [Preface to the revised *Ocean of operas*]. In *Zhongguo gudian xiqu xubai huibian* [Compiled prefaces and afterwords of classical opera scripts], comp. Cai Yi, 2:163. Jinan: Qi Lu shushe.

Huang Xiexun. [1883] 1984. *Songnan mengying lu* [The shadows of dreams of the south of the Song River]. Reprinted in *Biji xiaoshuo daguan* [Comprehensive collection of travelogues], vol. 11, 23 (ce): 374–93. Yangzhou: Jiangsu Guangling guji keyinche.

Huang Zhongjun. [1899] 1955. *Chouren zhuan sibian* [Biographies of mathematicians and astronomers, vol. 4]. Repr., Shanghai: Shangwu yinshuguan.

Huang Zunxian. [1882] 1960. "Zhu ke pian" [Dismissing the guests]. In *Fan Mei huagong jinyue wenxueji* [Literary anthology of opposition to Chinese exclusion in the United States], comp. Ah Ying, 3–4. Beijing: Zhonghua shuju.

Huc, Evariste Regis. 1855. *The Chinese Empire: Being a Sequel to the Work Entitled "Recollections of a Journey through Tartary and Thibet."* London: Longman, Brown, Green, and Longmans.

Hummel, Arthur W. [1944] 1991. *Eminent Chinese of the Qing Period.* Repr., Taipei: SMC.

Huters, Theodore. 1996. "Appropriations: Another Look at Yan Fu and Western Ideas." *Scholars* 9 (April): 296–355.

———. 1999. "Yubo: 1910 nian Zhongguo wenhua lunzhang" [The cultural debate during the 1910s]. *Jintian* 2 (Summer): 261–78.

———. 2005. *Bringing the World Home: Appropriating the West in Late Qing and Early Republican China.* Honolulu: University of Hawaii Press.

Ip, Manying. 1985. *The Life and Times of Zhang Yuanji, 1867–1959.* Beijing: Commercial Press.

Jackson, Stanley. 1969. *The Sassoons: Portrait of a Dynasty.* London: Heinemann.

Jameson, Fredric. 1987. *Zheng zhi, wenhua, lish: Beida jiangyan ji* [Politics, Culture, and History: Lectures at Beijing University]. Trans. Tang Xiaobing. Beijing: Beijing daxue chubanshe.

Jentschura, Hansgeorg, Dieter Jung, and Peter Michel, comps. 1977. *Warships of the Imperial Japanese Navy, 1869–1945.* Trans. Antony Preston and J. D. Brown. Annapolis, Md.: U.S. Naval Institute.

Ji Wende. 1991. *Cong Siku quanshu tanjiu Mingqing jian shu ru zhi Xixue* [Western learning imported during the Ming and Qing as reflected in the Four Treasuries]. Taipei, New York, and Los Angeles: Hanmei tushu youxian gongsi.

Jiang Duo. 1988. "Cong Wuxi Xuejia tandao jiu Zhongguo minzu ziben" [The national capital in old China: The case of the Xues in Wuxi]. In *Zhongguo jindai jingji shi luncong* [Collected works on modern economic history of China], ed. Huang Yifeng and Jiang Duo, 258–66. Shanghai: Shanghai shehui kexueyuan chubanshe.

Jiang Guanyun. 1960. "Jinri zhi yanju jie" [Today's performing circle in China]. In *Wan Qing wenxue congchao: Xiaoshuo xiqu yanjiu juan* [Late Qing literature: Fiction and theater studies], comp. Ah Ying, 50–51. Beijing: Zhonghua shuju.

Jiang Shangqing. 1970. *Wangshi jintan* [Talking about the past at the present]. Hong Kong: Zhicheng chubanshe.

Jiang Weiqiao. [1935] 1957. "Bianji xiaoxue jiaokeshu zhi huiyi" [A recollection of compilation of elementary textbooks]. Reprinted in *Zhongguo jindai chuban shiliao bubian* [Supplementary compilation of the documents of publication in modern China], comp. Zhang Jinglu, 138–45. Beijing: Zhonghua shuju.

———. 1987. "Xia jun Ruifang shilue" [A brief biography of Xia Ruifang]. In *Shangwu yinshuguan jiushi nian* [Ninety years of the Commercial Press], 3–5. Beijing: Shangwu yinshuguan.

Jiangsu sheng bowuguan [The Jiangsu Provincial Museum], comp. 1959. *Jiangsu sheng Ming Qing yilai beike ziliao xuanji* [Selected inscriptions in Jiangsu from the Ming and Qing dynasties]. Beijing: Sanlian.

Jiao Bingzhen and Kangxi. 1879. *Yü zhi Geng zhi tu* [The Kangxi version of *Illustrations of agriculture and sericulture*]. Shanghai: Dianshizhai shuju.

Jiao Xun. 1959–1960. *Huapu nongtan* [The peasant's discourse on the flower dramas]. In *Zhongguo gudian xiqu lunzhu jicheng* [Collected works on classical Chinese operas], 8:1–8. Beijing: Zhongguo xiju chubanshe.

Jin Tianyu. [1927] 1969. *Tianfang lou wenyan* [The literary writings at the Tianfang Pavilion]. Repr., Taipei: Wenhai chubanshe.

Jing Yu. 1954. "Qing dai yinshua shi xiaoji" [The little history of printing in the Qing]. In *Zhongguo jindai chunban shiliao erbian* [The second compilation of documents on modern Chinese printing and publishing], comp. Zhang Jinglu, 339–61. Shanghai: Qunlian chubanshe.

Johnson, Linda C. 1995. *Shanghai: From Market Town to Treaty Port, 1074–1858.* Stanford: Stanford University Press.

Johnston, Tess, and Deke Erh, eds. 1993. *A Last Look: Western Architecture in Old Shanghai.* Hong Kong: Old China Hand Press.

Jones, Andrew. 1999. "The Gramophone in China." In *Tokens of Exchange: The Problem of Translation in Global Circulation,* ed. Lydia Liu, 214–38. Durham, N.C.: Duke University Press.

Judge, Joan. 1996. *Print and Politics: "Shibao" and the Culture of Reform in Late Qing China.* Stanford: Stanford University Press.

———. 2001. "Talent, Virtue, and the Nation: Chinese Nationalisms and Female Subjectivities in the Early Twentieth Century." *American Historical Review* 106, no. 3: 765–803.

Kang Youwei. 1935. *Da tong shu* [The book of great harmony]. Ed. Qian Dingan. Shanghai: Zhonghua shuju.

Karl, Rebecca. 2002. *Staging the World: Chinese Nationalism at the Turn of the Twentieth Century.* Durham, N.C.: Duke University Press.

Kotenev, A. M. 1925. *Shanghai: Its Mixed Court and Council; Material Relating to the History of the Shanghai Municipal Council and the History, Practice, and Statistics of the International Mixed Court.* Shanghai: North-China Daily News and Herald.

Kuhn, Philip. 1980. *Rebellion and Its Enemies in Late Imperial China: Militarization and Social Structure, 1796–1864.* Cambridge, Mass.: Harvard University Press.

Kuo Ting-yee and Kwang-Ching Liu. 1963. *Jindai Zhongguo shi nizhi* [Daily events of modern Chinese history]. Taipei: Zhengzhong shuju.

———. 1978. "Self-Strengthening: The Pursuit of Western Technology." In *The*

Cambridge History of China, vol. 10, Late Ch'ing, 1800–1911, ed. John Fairbank, 491–542. Cambridge, New York, and Melbourne: Cambridge University Press.

Kuwabara Jitsuo 1967. Zhongguo A-la-bo haishang jiaotong shi [The ocean trade between China and Arabia during the Tang, Song, and Yuan dynasties]. Trans. Feng Yu. Repr., Taipei: Taiwan Shangwu yinshuguan.

Lackner, Michael, and Nalascha Vittinghoff, eds. 2004. Mapping Meanings: The Field of New Learning in Late Qing China. Leiden: Brill.

Latour, Bruno. 1993. We Have Never Been Modern. Trans. Catherine Porter. New York: Harvester Wheatsheaf.

Latourette, Kenneth Scott. 1929. A History of Christian Missions in China. New York: Macmillan.

Lean, Eugenia. 2004. "The Making of a Public: Emotions and Media Sensation in 1930s China." Twentieth Century China 29, no. 2: 39–61.

Lee, Jean Gordon, and Philadelphia Museum of Art. 1984. Philadelphians and the China Trade, 1784–1844. Philadelphia: Philadelphia Museum of Art.

Lee, Leo Ou-fan. 1999. Shanghai Modern: The Flowering of a New Urban Culture in China, 1930–1945. Cambridge, Mass.: Harvard University Press.

Lee, Thomas. 1985. Government Education and Examination in Sung China. New York: St. Martin's.

Lefebvre, Henri. 1991. The Production of Space. Trans. Donald Nicholson-Smith. Cambridge, Mass.: Blackwell.

———. 1995. Writings on Cities. Selected, translated, and introduced by Eleonore Kofman and Elizabeth Lebas. Cambridge, Mass.: Blackwell.

Leonard, Jane Kate. 1996. Controlling from Afar: The Daoguang Emperor's Management of the Grand Canal Crisis, 1824–1826. Ann Arbor: Center for Chinese Studies, University of Michigan.

Li Chang. 1987. "Zhongguo jindai wutai meishu piantan" [Scattered discussions on the designs of settings in modern theatrical art in China]. In Zhongguo huaju shiliaoji [Compiled source materials of the history of spoken drama], comp. Huaju Yanjuso, zhongguo yishu yanjuyuan [Institute of Drama Studies, Chinese Academy of Arts], 252–308. Beijing: Wenhua yishu chubanshe.

Li Ciming, Zhang Daogui, and Ding Fenglin, eds. 1986. Zhang Wenxiang ci Ma [Zhang Wenxiang's assassination of Ma Xinyi]. Changsha: Yuelu shushe.

Li Dou. [1795] 1984. Yangzhou huafang lu [Records of the painted boats in Yangzhou]. Repr., Yangzhou: Jiangsu Guangling guji keyinshe.

Li Hongchun. 1962. Guan Yu xiji [Anthology of Guanyu's theme operas]. Shanghai: Shanghai wenyi chubanshe.

———. 1982. Jingju changtan [Reminiscences of my career as a Beijing Opera actor]. Ed. Liu Songyan. Beijing: Zhongguo xiju.

Li Hongzhang. [1905] 1980. Li Wenzhong gong quanji [Complete works of Li Hongzhang]. Comp. Wu Rulun. Repr., Taipei: Wenhai chubanshe.

———. 1921. Li Wenzhong gong quanji: Peng liao han gao [The complete works of Li Hongzhang: Letters to colleagues and friends]. Shanghai: Shangwu yinshuguan.

Li Jiaji, Li Maosu, and Xue Xiangsheng, comps. 1994. Lin Shu fanyi xiaoshuo weikan jiuzhong [Nine unpublished translations by Lin Shu]. Fuzhou: Fujian renmin chubanshe.

Li Ming-ming and Wu Hui. 1997. Zhongguo yanfa shi [A history of the regulations of salt]. Taipei: Wenjin chubanshe.

Li Shanlan and Wylie Alexander. 1857. *Shokubutsugaku* [Study of botany]. N.p.: Bokkai Shokan, Kanpo teishi.

Li Xingyuan. 1982. *Li Xingyuan riji* [The diary of Li Xingyuan]. In *Qing dai riji huichao* [Selected diaries from the Qing dynasty], ed. P. E. A. Liu. Shanghai: Shanghai renmin chubanshe.

Li Yuanlong. 1960. *Jingju suotan* [Scattered reminiscences about Peking opera]. Hong Kong: Hongye shuju.

Li Yuerui. [1912] 1995. *Chunbingshi yecheng* [Unofficial records by the master of the Chunbing studio]. Taiyuan: Shanxi guji chubanshe.

Li Zezhang. 1931. "San shi wu nian lai de Zhongguo chuban ye" [Publication in the past thirty-five years]. In *Zuijin sanshiwu nian zhi Zhongguo jiaoyu* [Education in China in the past thirty-five years], 259–78. Shanghai: Shangwu yinshuguan.

Li Zhiting 1997. *Zhongguo caoyun shi* [A history of tax and transportation in imperial China]. Taipei: Wenjin chubanshe.

Liang Jiabin. 1937. *Guangdong shisan hang kao* [An evidential study of the thirteen foreign factories in Guangdong]. Nanjing: Guoli bianyi guan.

———. 1960. *Yapian zhanzheng qian Guangdong guoji maoyi jiaotong shi kao* [An evidential study of the international trade in Guangdong before the Opium War]. Taichung: Sili Donghai daxue.

Liang Qichao. 1896. *Xixue shumu biao* [Bibliography of Western learning]. Shanghai: Shihwu baoguan.

———, comp. 1897. *Xizheng congshu* [Collectanea of Western government]. Shanghai: Shenji shuzhuang.

———. [1905] 1982. *Ji Huagong jinyue* [U.S. government's Chinese Exclusion Act]. Reprinted in *Dizhi huagong jinyue wenxueji* [Literary anthology of resistance to Chinese exclusion in the United States], 387–426. Taipei: Guangya chubanshe.

———. 1936. "Gezhi xue zhi yange" [The development of the investigation of things]. In *Yin bing shi he ji* [Collected works from the Ice-sipper's studio], 4:3–14. Shanghai: Zhonghua shuju.

Liang Shu-an. 1996. *Zhongguo jindai chuanqi zaju jingyan lu*. Beijing: Shumu wenxian chupanshe.

Liang Tingnan, comp. 1975. *Yüe hai guan zhi* [Record of the Qing customs at Guangdong]. Repr., Taipei: Wenhai chubanshe.

Liang Zheng. 1905. *Note from the Chinese Minister to the Secretary of State on Chinese Exclusion and the anti-American Boycott*. Washington: N.p.

Lin Shu. [1901] 1960a. "Heinu yutian lu yiben liyan" [Foreword to the translation of *Uncle Tom's Cabin*]. In *Fan Mei huagong jinyue wenxueji* [Literary anthology of opposition to Chinese exclusion in the United States], comp. Ah Ying, 661–62. Beijing: Zhonghua shuju.

———. [1901] 1960b. "Heinu yutian lu Xu" [Preface to the Chinese translation of *Uncle Tom's Cabin*]. In *Fan Mei huagong jinyue wenxueji* [Literary anthology of opposition to Chinese exclusion in the United States], comp. Ah Ying, 658. Beijing: Zhonghua shuju.

———. 1981. "Yi yu sheng yu" [Surplus words after the translation]. In *Li hen tian*, 1–5. Beijing: Shangwu yinshuguan.

Lin Zhengqi. 1981. "Lin Xie." In *Zhonghua min'guo mingren zhuan* [Biographies of well-known figures of the Republic of China], 6:34–52. Taipei: Jindai zhongguo chubanshe.

Lindroth, Sten. 1983. "The Two Faces of Linnaeus." In *Linnaeus, the Man and His Work,* ed. Tore Frängsmyr, 1–62. Berkeley and Los Angeles: University of California Press.

Liu, Kwang-ching. 1962. *Anglo-American Steamship Rivalry in China, 1862–1874.* Cambridge, Mass.: Harvard University Press.

———. 1978. "The Ch'ing Restoration." In *The Cambridge History of China,* vol. 10, *Late Ch'ing 1800–1911, Part 1,* ed. John K. Fairbank, 409–90. Cambridge, New York, and Melbourne: Cambridge University Press.

Liu, Lydia. 1995. *Translingual Practice: Literature, National Culture, and Translated Modernity—China, 1900–1937.* Stanford: Stanford University Press.

———, ed. 1999. *Tokens of Exchange: The Problem of Translation in Global Circulations.* Durham, N.C.: Duke University Press.

———. 2004. *The Clash of Empires: The Invention of China in Modern World Making.* Cambridge, Mass.: Harvard University Press.

Liu Shangheng. 1989. *Guji congshu gaishuo* [On the classical collectanea]. Shanghai: Shanghai guji chubanshe.

Lo Yudong. 1977. *Zhongguo lijin shi* [A history of Lijin tax in China]. Taipei: Wenhai chubanshe.

———. 1980. "Lijin zhidu zhi qiyuan jiqi lilun" [The origin and theory of the Lijin tax]. *Zhongguo jindai jingjishi yanjiu jikan* [A series of modern Chinese studies in economic history], 1, no. 1 (1932). Reprinted in *Zhongguo jingji fazhanshi lunwen xuanji,* part 1 [An anthology of essays on the development of Chinese economic history studies], ed. Yu Zongxian, 531–68. Taipei: Lianjin chuban sheye gongsi.

Lu Eting. 1995. *Qingdai xiqujia congkao* [An evidential study of a series of operatic artists of the Qing dynasty]. Shanghai: Xuelin chubanshe.

Lu Hanchao. 1999. *Beyond the Neon Lights: Everyday Shanghai in the Early Twentieth Century.* Berkeley and Los Angeles: University of California Press.

Lufei, Erkui. [1918] 1953. "Lun Zhongguo jiaokeshu shi shu" [On the history of Chinese textbooks]. In *Zhongguo jindai chuban shiliao chubian* [The first compilation of documents on modern Chinese printing and publishing, 1840–1918], comp. Zhang Jinglu, 212–14. Shanghai: Shang za chubanshe.

———. 1920. *Ciyuan* [The encyclopedic Chinese dictionary]. Shanghai: Shangwu yinshuguan.

———. 1992. "*Ciyuan* shuo lue" [A brief introduction to *Ciyuan*]. In *Shangwu yinshuguan jiushiwu nian* [Ninety-five years of the Commercial Press], 158–62. Beijing: Shangwu yinshuguan.

Luo Ergang. 1991. *Taiping Tianguo shi* [History of the Taiping Kingdom]. Bejing: Zhonghua shuju.

Luo Shilin. 1962. *Chouren zhuan xubian* [Biographies of mathematicians and astronomers, vol. 2]. Shanghai: Shijie shuju.

Ma Sen. 1994. *Xi chao xia de Zhongguo xiandai xiju* [Modern Chinese drama in the waves from the West]. Taipei: Shu lin chuban youxian gongsi.

Ma Tailai. 1981. "Lin Shu fanyi zuopin quanmu" [The complete list of translations by Lin Shu]. In *Lin Shu de fanyi* [Translations by Lin Shu], comp. Qian Zhongshu, 60–98. Beijing: Xinhua shudian.

Mackerras, Colin. 1971. "The Growth of the Chinese Regional Drama in the Ming and Ch'ing." *Journal of Oriental Studies* 1, no. 9 (January): 67–78.

———. 1972. *The Rise of the Peking Opera, 1770–1870: Social Aspects of the Theater in Manchu China*. Oxford: Clarendon.

Makino Tomitarō. [1925] 1926. *Nihon shokubutsu zukan* [A dictionary, with pictures, of Japanese plants]. Repr., Tokyo: Hokuryukan.

Mao Dun. [1981] 1987. "Gexin xiaoshuo yuebao de qianhou" [Around the time that Fiction Monthly was reformed]. Reprinted in *Shangwu yinshuguan jiushi nian* [Ninety years of the Commercial Press], 140–97. Beijing: Shangwu yinshuguan.

Martin, Brian G. 1996. *The Shanghai Green Gang: Politics and Organized Crime, 1919–1927*. Berkeley, Los Angeles, and London: University of California Press.

Masini, Federico. 1993. *The Formation of Modern Chinese Lexicon and Its Evolution toward a National Language: The Period from 1840 to 1898*. Berkeley and Los Angeles: University of California Press.

Mason, Mary Gertrude. 1939. "Western Concept of China and the Chinese, 1840–1876." Ph.D. diss., Columbia University.

Mayer-Fong, Tobie. 2003. *Building Culture in Early Qing Yangzhou*. Stanford: Stanford University Press.

McLintock, Anne. 1995. *Imperial Leather: Race, Gender, and Sexuality in the Colonial Conquest*. New York: Routledge.

Mei-hua-an-zhu [Pictures and textual explanations of the spectacles at the Shen River]. [1912] 1972. In *Shenjiang shengjing tushuo*. Repr., Taipei: Dongfan wenhua shuju.

Meng Sen. 1992. "Xua jun Cuifang xiaozhuan" [A biography of Mr. Xia Ruifang]. In *Shangwu yinshuguan jiushiwu nian* [Ninety-five years of the Commercial Press], 17–20. Beijing: Shangwu yinshuguan.

Meng Yue. 1999. "Hybrid Science versus Modernity: The Practice of the Jiangnan Arsenal, 1867–1904." *East Asian Science, Technology, and Medicine* 16 (December): 13–52.

———. 2000. "The Invention of Shanghai: Cultural Practices and Their Transformation, 1860–1930." Ph.D. diss., University of California, Los Angeles.

Merrill, Elmer Drew, and Egbert H. Walker. 1938. *A Bibliography of Eastern Asiatic Botany*. Jamaica Plain, Mass.: Arnold Arboretum of Harvard University.

Meskill, John Thomas. 1994. *Gentlemanly Interests and Wealth of the Yangtze Delta*. Monograph and Occasional Paper Series, no. 49. Ann Arbor, Mich.: Association for Asian Studies.

Metropolitan Museum of Art. 1941. *China Trade and Its Influences*. New York: Metropolitan Museum of Art.

Michie, Alexander. 1900. *The Englishman in China during the Victorian Era, as Illustrated in the Career of Sir Rutherford Alcock*. Edinburgh: Blackwood and Sons.

Ming Feng-ying. 1999. "In Search of a Position: The Paradox of Genre Typology in Late Qing Polygeneric Novel; Romance, Political-Detective, and Science Fiction Novel, 1898–1911." Ph.D. diss., University of California, Los Angeles.

Mittler, Barbara. 1998. "Cong Shanghai baozhi kan Shanghairen xingxiang he shengyin" [Voice and image of the Chinese Shanghailander as seen from the city's newspapers]. In *Zhongguo jindai qiye shehui kongjian*, ed. Zhang Zhongli, 266–71. Shanghai: CASS.

———. 2004. *A Newspaper for China? Power, Identity, and Change in Shanghai's News Media (1872–1912)*. Cambridge, Mass.: Harvard University Press.

Mizoguchi, Yūzō. 1989. *Hōhō to shite no Chūgoku* [China as the method, the world as the goal]. Tokyo: Tokyo Daigaku Shuppankai.

———. 2004. *Chūgoku no shōgeki* [The China impact]. Tokyo: Tokyo Daigaku Shuppankai.

Morris, Pam. 1994. *The Bakhtin Reader: Selected Writings of Bakhtin, Medvedev, Voloshinov.* New York: Arnold.

Mote, Frederick. 1973. "A Millennium of Chinese Urban History: Form, Time, and Space Concepts in Soochow." *Rice University Studies* 59, no. 4 (Fall): 33–65.

Muramatsu Shin. 1991. *Shanhai, toshi to kenchiku: 1842–1949-nen* [Shanghai: The city and the architectures, 1842–1949]. Tokyo: PARCO Shuppankyoku.

Nakamura Tadayuki. 1989. "Kenshō: Shosan inshokan, Kinkodo no goben" [Prove: The cooperation between the Commercial Press and Kinkodo Press]. *Shinmatsu shosetsu* [Late Qing fiction studies] 12 (December): 51–64.

Nathan, Andrew, and Leo Ou-fan Lee. 1985. "The Beginnings of Mass Culture: Journalism and Fiction in the Late Qing and Beyond." In *Popular Culture in Late Imperial China*, ed. David Johnson, Andrew Nathan, and Evelyn Rawski, 360–95. Berkeley and Los Angeles: University of California Press.

Needham, Joseph. 1954. *Science and Civilisation in China*, vol. 1, *Introductory Orientations.* Cambridge: Cambridge University Press.

Niu Chuanhai. 1977. *Qianlong shiqi juchang huodong zhi yanjiu* [Studies on the theatrical activities during the Qianlong time]. Taipei: Hua gang chuban gongsi.

Ouyang Yuqian. [1959] 1990. *Zi wo yanxi yilai* [Since I began to perform]. Repr., Taipei: Lung wen chubanshe.

———. 1984. *Ouyang Yuqian xiju lunwen ji* [An anthology of theatrical essays by Ou-yang Yuqian]. Shanghai: Shanghai wenyi chubanshe.

Perdue, Peter. 2005. *China Marches West: The Qing Conquest of Central Eurasia.* Cambridge, Mass.: Belknap Press of Harvard University Press.

Perry, Elizabeth. 1993. *Shanghai on Strike: The Politics of Chinese Labor.* Stanford: Stanford University Press.

Ping Buqing. 1983. *Xiawai junxie* [Collecting the fragments of history from beyond the clouds]. Shanghai: Shanghai guji chubanshe.

Ping Jinya. 1982. "Mantan Huang Chujiu jiqi shiye" [Random reminiscences about Huang Chujiu and his enterprises]. *Wenshi ziliao xuanji* [Selected materials on the culture and history of Shanghai] 38: 146–57.

Pomeranz, Kenneth. 1993. *The Making of a Hinterland: State, Society, and Economy in Inland North China, 1853–1937.* Berkeley and Los Angeles: University of California Press.

———. 2000. *Great Divergence: Europe, China, and the Making of the Modern World Economy.* Princeton: Princeton University Press.

———. 2002. "Beyond the East-West Binary: Resituate the Development Path in the Eighteenth-Century World." *Journal of Asian Studies* 61, no. 2 (May): 539–90.

Pratt, Mary Louise. 1994. *Imperial Eyes: Travel Writing and Transculturation.* New York: Routledge.

Qian Huafo. [1947] 1984. *Shanshi nian lai zhi shanghai* [Shanghai in the past thirty years], ed. Zheng Yimie. Repr., Shanghai: Shanghai shudian.

Qian Mu. 1986. *Bashi yi shuangqin* [Memoir of my parents at the age of eighty]. Changsha: Yuelu shushe.

Qian Yong. 1979. *Luyuan cong hua* [A series of notes by Luyuan]. Beijing: Zhonghua shuju.

Qiefu. 1918 [1990]. "Zhi Jin'gui xuan" [A record of the Jingui troupe]. In "Getai xinshi'" [New history of operatic singing]. In *Jubu congkan* [Theater series], comp. Zhou Jianyun, 39–40. Shanghai: Shanghai shudian.

Qin Luzhi. 1999. *Haipai shangren Huang Chujiu* [A merchant of Shanghai style: Huang Chujiu]. Shanghai: Shanghai shudian.

Qu Fengqi. 1987. "Tieqin tongjian lou yu Shangwu yinshuguan" [The Commercial Press and "The Pavilion of Iron Harp and Bronze Sword"]. In *Shangwu yinshuguan jiushinian* [Ninety years of the Commercial Press], 324–27. Beijing: Shangwu yinshuguan.

Queen, Sarah A. 1996. *From Chronicle to Canon: The Hermeneutics of the Spring and Autumn Annals According to Tung Chung-shu*. Cambridge: Cambridge University Press.

Reardon-Anderson, James. 1991. *The Study of Change: Chemistry in China, 1840–1949*. Cambridge and New York: Cambridge University Press.

Reed, Christopher A. 2004. *Gutenberg in Shanghai: Chinese Print Capitalism*. Honolulu: University of Hawaii Press.

Reid, Anthony. 1993. *Southeast Asia in the Age of Commerce, 1450–1680*. Vol. 2, *Expansion and Crisis*. New Haven: Yale University Press.

Remer, C. F. 1933. *A Study of Chinese Boycotts, with Special Reference to Their Economic Effectiveness*. With the assistance of William Braman Palmer. Baltimore: Walter Hines Page School of International Relations, The Johns Hopkins Press.

Ren Jianshu, comp. 1996. *Xiandai Shanghai dashiji* [Chronology of modern Shanghai after 1917]. Shanghai: Shanghai cishu chubanshe.

Riesman, David, Reuel Denney, and Nathan Glazer. 1950. *The Lonely Crowd: A Study of the Changing American Character*. New Haven: Yale University Press.

Ristaino, Marcia Reynders. 2001. *Port of Last Resort: The Diaspora Communities of Shanghai*. Stanford: Stanford University Press.

Rockhill, William Woodville. 1904. *Treaties and Conventions with or Concerning China and Korea, 1894–1904, Together with Various State Papers and Documents Affecting Foreign Interests*. Washington, D.C.: Government Printing Office.

Rong Hong. [1909] 1961. *Xixue dongjian ji* [My life in China and America]. Repr. Taipei: Guangwen.

Rowe, T. William. 1984. *Hankow: Commerce and Society in a Chinese City, 1796–1889*. Stanford: Stanford University Press.

———. 1989. *Hankow: Conflict and Community in a Chinese City, 1796–1895*. Stanford: Stanford University Press.

Ruan Yuan. [1799] 1962. *Chouren zhuan* [Biographies of mathematicians and astronomers]. In *Chouren zhuan huibian* [Compiled biographies of mathematicians and astronomers, vols. 1, 2, and 3], ed. Yang Jialuo. Taipei: Shijie shuju.

Rydell, Robert W. 1984. *All the World's a Fair: Visions of Empire at American International Expositions, 1876–1916*. Chicago: University of Chicago Press.

Saeki Tomi. 1956. *Shindai ensei no kenkyū* [The salt policy of the Qing]. Kyoto: Tōyōshi Kenkyukai.

———. 1987. *Chugoku enseishi no kenkyū* [A study of Chinese salt administration]. Kyoto: Horitsu Bunkasha.

Said, Edward. 1994. *Culture and Imperialism*. New York: Vintage.

San Ai. [1904] 1992. "Lun Xiqu" [On theater]. Quoted in Wang Lixing, *Zhongguo jindai wenxue kaolun* [An evidential study of modern Chinese literature], 187–94. Nanjing: Nanjing daxue chubanshe.

Sang Bing. 1995. *Qing mo zhishijie de shetuan yu huodong* [Intellectual societies and their activities in the late Qing]. Beijing: Sanlian chubanshe.

Sang Xianzhi. 1996. "Lun jingju yu wan Qing wenhua" [Beijing opera and the late Qing culture]. *Zhonghua xiqu* 19: 164–176.

Sargentson, Carolyn. 1996. *Merchants and Luxury Markets: The Marchands Merciers of Eighteenth-Century Paris.* Malibu, Calif.: Victoria and Albert Museum, in association with the J. Paul Getty Museum.

Sawamoto Ikuma. 1993. "Shoki shomu inshokan no nazo" [The mysteries about the early Commercial Press]. In *Shinmatsu shose tsu* 16 (Spring): 1–50.

Scott, A. C. Madison. 1982. *Actors Are Madmen: Notebook of a Theatregoer in China.* Madison: University of Wisconsin Press.

Scranton, Philip. 1997. *Endless Novelty: Specialty Production and American Industrialization, 1865–1925.* Princeton, N.J.: Princeton University Press.

Sennett, Richard. 1969. *Classic Essays on the Culture of Cities.* New York: Appleton-Century-Crofts.

Sergeant, Harriet. 1990. *Shanghai: Collision Point of Cultures, 1918–1939.* New York: Crown.

Shanghai shehui kexueyuan [The Institute of Economy, the Shanghai Social Science Academy], comp. 1958. *Shanghai Xiaodao hui qiyi shiliao* [Documents on the small swords in Shanghai]. Shanghai: Shanghai renmin chubanshe.

———, comp. 1981. *Liu Hongsheng qiye shiliao* [Historical documents about Liu Hongsheng's enterprises]. Shanghai: Shanghai renmin chubanshe.

Shanghai shehuiju [Institute of Social Affairs]. 1934a. *Shanghai shi shehuiju jutuan tongji ziliao* [Bureau of Social Affairs' statistical survey of performing troupes]. Shanghai dang'an guan [Shanghai Municipal Archive], Q6–13-(1–747).

———. 1934b. "Shanghai shi shehuiju gonggong yule chang xiyuan dengji yilan biao" [A list of registered public entertainment spaces and theaters. Survey by the Institute of Social Affairs]. Shanghai dang'an guan [Shanghai Municipal Archive], Q6–13–745.

———. 1934c. "Rongji da shijie juan" [Rong's Great World]. Shanghai dang'an guan [Shanghai Municipal Archive], Q6–13–519.

Shanghai shi xiju yuan shangye tongye gonghui [Shanghai Guild of Theaters]. 1954. "Shanghai xiju ye gaikuang: Benhui de lishi yange qingkuang baogao; Wusi nian nianbao; ji xiang rendai dahui de tian" [An overview of Shanghai's theater businesses: Report on the history of our association, 1954 Yearbook, and a proposal to the Conference of People's Representatives]. Shanghai dang'an guan [Shanghai Municipal Archive], 320-4-1.

Shanghai tongshe [Society of General Knowledge of Shanghai], comp. [1936] 1984. *Shanghai yanjiu ziliao* [Collected documents for Shanghai studies]. Taipei: Zhongguo chubanshe.

———, comp. [1939] 1984. *Shanghai yanjiu ziliao xuji* [Sequel to the *Collected documents for Shanghai studies*]. Shanghai: Shanghai shudian.

Shanghai tushuguan [Shanghai Library], comp. 1982–1983. *Zhongguo cong shu zonglu* [Synthetic records of Chinese collectanea]. Shanghai: Shanghai guji chubanshe.

Shanghai wenshi ziliao gongzuo wei yuanhui [The editorial committee of historical materials of Shanghai]. 1987. *Jiu Shanghai de waishang yu maiban* [Foreign businessmen and compradors in old Shanghai]. Shanghai: Renmin chubanshe.

Shanghai xiqu yanjiu hui [Opera study society of Shanghai], comp. 1927. *Xihai: Gailiang tanhuang* [Ocean of operas: Shanghai folk drama]. Shanghai: N.p.

Shangwu yinshuguan [The Commercial Press]. 1979. *Ciyuan* [The encylcopedic Chinese dictionary]. Beijing: Shangwu yinshuguan.

———. 1981. *Shangwu yinshuguan tushu mulu* [The book catalog of the Commercial Press]. Beijing: Shangwu yinshuguan.

———. 1987. *Shangwu yinshuguan jiushinian* [Ninety years of the Commercial Press]. Beijing: Shangwu yinshuguan.

———. 1992. *Shangwu yinshuguan jiushiwu nian* [Ninety-five years of the Commercial Press]. Beijing: Shangwu yinshuguan.

———. 1997. *Shangwu yinshuguan 100 zhounian* [A hundred years of the Commercial Press]. Taipei: Shangwu yinshuguan.

Sheehan, Brett. 2000. "Urban Identity and Urban Networks in Cosmopolitan Cities: Banks and Bankers in Tianjin, 1900–1937." In *Remaking the Chinese City: Modernity and National Identity, 1900–1950,* ed. Joseph Esherick. Honolulu: University of Hawaii Press.

Shen Fu. [1808] 1962. *Fu sheng liu ji* [Six records of my drifting life]. Repr., Taipei: Shijie shuju.

Shi He, Yao Fuzhong, and Ye Cuidi, eds. 1991. *Zhongguo jindai baokan minglu* [Annotated titles of newspapers and magazines in modern China]. Fuzhou: Fujian renmin chubanshe.

Shi Meiding, comp. 1996. *Zhuiyi: Jindai Shanghai tushi* [Looking back: A photographic history of old Shanghai]. Shanghai: Shanghai guji chubanshe.

Shibao [Shanghai times]. [1905] 1962. "Lun Dizhi meiguo huagong jinyue" [On resisting the U.S. policy of Chinese exclusion], April 20, 21. Reprinted in *Fan Mei huagong jinyue wenxueji* [Literary anthology of opposition to Chinese exclusion in the United States], comp. Ah Ying, 601. Beijing: Zhonghua shuju.

Shih, Shu-mei. 2001. *The Lure of the Modern: Writing Modernism in Semicolonial China.* Berkeley and Los Angeles: University of California Press.

Shu Xincheng. [1933] 1973. *Jindai Zhongguo liuxue shi* [History of studying abroad in modern China]. Repr., Taipei: Zhongguo chubanshe.

Skinner, William, ed. 1977. *The City in Late Imperial China.* Stanford: Stanford University Press.

Spengler, Oswald. 1969. "The Soul of the City." In *Classic Essays on the Culture of Cities,* ed. Richard Sennett. New York: Appleton-Century-Crofts.

Spurr, David. 1993. *The Rhetoric of Empire: Colonial Discourse in Journalism, Travel Writing, and Imperial Administration.* Durham, N.C.: Duke University Press.

Stock, Jonathan P. J. 1997. "Huju and Musical Change: The Rise of a Local Operatic Form in East China, to 1920." *ACMR Reports,* Spring: 14–38.

Subrahmanyam, Sanjay, ed. 1990. *Merchants, Markets, and the State in Early Modern India.* Delhi and New York: Oxford University Press.

———, ed. 1996. *Merchant Networks in the Early Modern World.* Aldershot, U.K.: Variorum.

Sun Choucheng. 1936. "Xinyao jie xianjin Huang Chujiu xiansheng shilue" [A biography of Mr. Huang Chujiu, a pioneer of new medicine]. *Xinyao yuebao* [New medicine monthly], May.

Sun Congtian. 1966. *Cangshu jiyao* [Essentials of book collecting]. Vol. 45 of *Baibu congshu jicheng* [Complete collection of a hundred collectanea], comp. Yang Chengyin. Taipei: Yiwen.

Sun Ge. 2003. "Yazhou yiwei zhe shenme" [The meanings of "Asia"]. In *Qiu cuo ji* [Error-checking], 56–67. Beijing: Sanlian shudian.

Sun Yütang, comp. 1957. *Zhungguo jindai gongye shi ziliao* [Source materials on the history of modern Chinese industry]. Beijing: Kexue chubanshe.

Takehiko Hashimo. 1999. "Introducing a French Technological System: The Origin and Early History of the Yokosuka Dockyard." *East Asian Science, Technology, and Medicine* 16 (December): 53–72.

Tan Tai. 1962. "Chouren jie" [The meaning of *chouren*, preface to *Chouren zhuan* compiled by Ruan Yuan]. In *Chouren zhuan huibian*, comp. Yang Jialuo, 1–4. Shanghai: Shijie shuju.

Tan Zhengbi. 1981. *Tanci xulu* [A descriptive catalog of *tanci* ballads]. Shanghai: Shanghai guji.

Tanaka, Stefan. 1993. *Japan's Orient: Rendering Pasts into History.* Berkeley and Los Angeles: University of California Press.

Tanaka Issei. 1987. "The Social and Historical Context of Ming-Ch'ing Local Drama." In *Popular Culture in Late Imperial China,* ed. David Johnson, Andrew Nathan, Evelyn Rawski, 143–60. Berkeley and Los Angeles: University of California Press.

———. 1989. *Chugoku kyoson saishi kenkyu: Chihogeki no kankyo* [Study of Chinese ritual theaters: The environment of local theater]. Tokyo: Tokyo Daigaku Toyo Bunka Kenkyujo.

Tang Tingshu. 1884. "Tang Tingshu bing Li Hongzhang wen" [Tang Tingshu reports to Li Hongzhang]. In *Zhaoshang ju dang'an* [The Archive of the China Merchants Steam Navigation Company]. Beijing Number Two Archive, *zong* 468, *juan* 73.

Tang Zhenchang, Shen Hengchun, and Qiao Shuming, comps. 1989. *Shanghai shi* [History of Shanghai]. Shanghai: Shanghai renmin chubanshe.

Tang Zhijun, Wu Qiandui, and Xu Yuanji, comps. 1989. *Jindai Shanghai dashiji* [Major events in modern Shanghai history]. Shanghai: Shanghai cishu chubanshe.

Tarumoto, Teruo. 1979. "Kinkodo, shomu Inshukan, shozo shōsetsu" [Kinkodo Press, the Commercial Press, and the *Illustrated fictions*]. In *Shinmatsu shōsetsu kenkyu* [Late Qing fiction studies] 3 (December): 300–39

———. 1983. *Shinmatsu shōsetsu kandan* [Scattered writings on late Qing fiction]. Kyōtō: Hōritsu Bunkasha.

———. 1988. "Shoki shomu inshokan wo moto mete" [In search of the early Commercial Press]. *Shinmatsu shosetsu kara* 9 (April): 1–52.

———. 1992. *Shinmatsu shosetsu ronshu* [On late-Qing fiction]. Kyoto: Horitsu Bunkasha.

———. 2002. *Xin bian zeng bu Qing mo Min chu xiao shuo mu lu* [Indexed catalog of fictions during the late Qing and early Republican periods, revised edition]. Jinan: Qilu shushe.

Teng, Ssu-yü, and John K. Fairbank. 1954. *China's Response to the West: A Documentary Survey, 1839–1923.* Cambridge, Mass.: Harvard University Press.

Tian Zhujian and Song Yuanchang, eds. 1987. *Zhongguo ziben zhuyi mengya* [The stems of capitalism in China]. Chengdu: Bashu shushe.

Ting Yusheng. 1877. *Fu Wu gong tu* [Official documents of restoration in the Wu region]. China: N.p.

Townsend, W. J. 1928. *Robert Morrison: Pioneer of Missions to China.* London: Pickering and Inglis.

Tsien, Tsuen-hsuin. 1987. *Paper and Printing.* Part 1 of vol. 5, *Chemistry and Chemical Technology,* of *Science and Civilisation in China,* ed. Joseph Needham, rev. ed. Cambridge: Cambridge University Press.

Tu Shipin, comp. [1948] 1968. *Shanghai chunqiu* [Spring and autumn in Shanghai]. Repr., Hong Kong: Zhongguo tushu bianyiguan.

Tu Weiming. 1999. *Wen hua Zhongguo de ren zhi yu guan huai* [The recognition and the concern for a cultural China]. Banqiao, Taipei: Dao xiang chubanshe.

Vittinghoff, Natascha. 1999. "Why Did Wang Tao go to Hongkong? Some Preliminary Observations and Questions Raised by Unpublished Documents from the Public Record Office [London]." *History and Culture* 1, no. 3: 60–68.

———. 2002. "Useful Knowledge and Appropriate Communication: Strategies of Publishing Houses in the Formative Stage of the Chinese Press (1872–1882)." In *Joining the Global Public: World, Image, and City in the Early Chinese Newspaper (1870–1910),* ed. Rudolf G. Wagner, 210–93. Albany: State University of New York Press.

von Glahn, Richard. 1996. *Fountain of Fortune: Money and Monetary Policy in China, 1000–1700.* Berkeley and Los Angeles: University of California Press.

von Sternberg, Josef. 1965. *Fun in a Chinese Laundry.* New York: Macmillan.

Wagner, Rudolf G. 1995. "The Role of the Foreign Community in the Chinese Public Sphere." *China Quarterly* 142 (June): 423–43.

———. 1999. "The *Shenbao* in Crisis: The International Environment and the Conflict between Guo Songtao and *Shenbao.*" *Late Imperial China* 20, no. 1: 107–38.

Wakeman, Frederic E. 1995. *Policing Shanghai, 1927–1937.* Berkeley and Los Angeles: University of California Press.

Wallerstein, Immanuel. 1989. *The Second Era of Great Expansion of the Capitalist World-Economy, 1730–1840s.* Vol. 3 of *The Modern World-System.* San Diego and New York: Academic Press.

———. 1991. *Unthinking Social Science: The Limit of Nineteenth-Century Paradigms.* Cambridge: Polity Press.

———. 1999. "Frank Proves European Miracle." *Review* (Fernand Braudel Center for the Study of Economics, Historical Systems, and Civilization) 22, no. 3: 355–72.

Wang, David Der-wei. 1997. *Fin-de-siècle Splendor: Repressed Modernities of Late Qing Fiction, 1849–1911.* Stanford: Stanford University Press.

Wang Dungen, comp. [1926] 1989. *Xikao daquan* [Complete anthology of operas, with scholarly notes]. Repr., Shanghai: Shanghai shudian.

Wang Erh-min. 1972. *Qingji bing gongye de xingqi* [The rise of the armaments industry in the late Ch'ing period]. Taipei: Institute of Modern History Academia Sinica.

———. 1980. *Shanghai gezhi shuyuan zhilue* [A brief history of the Shanghai Polytechnic Institute]. Hong Kong: Chinese University Press.

Wang Hui. 1996. "The Fate of Mr. Science in China: The Concept of Science and Its Application in Modern Chinese Thought." In *Formations of Colonial Modernity in East Asia,* ed. Tany Barlow, 21–82. Durham, N.C.: Duke University Press.

———. 2004. *Zhongguo xiandai sixiang de xingqi* [The rise of modern thoughts in China]. Beijing: Sanlian chubanshe.

Wang Jiajian. 1973. *Ma Xinyi shilue xuanji* [Collected documents on the death of Ma Xinyi]. Taipei: Hwakang.

Wang Junnian. 1988. *Zhongguo jindai wenxue lunwen ji, 1919–1949* [An anthology of essays on late Qing and modern Chinese literature]. Beijing: Zhongguo shehui kexue chubanshe.

Wang Liping. 1997. "Paradise for Sale: Urban Space and Tourism in the Social Transformation of Hangzhou, 1589–1937." Ph.D. diss., University of California, San Diego.

———. 2000. "Tourism and Spatial Changes in Hangzhou, 1900–1927." In *Remaking the Chinese City: Modernity and National Identity, 1900–1950*, ed. Joseph Esherick, 10–120, 236–237. Honolulu: University of Hawaii Press.

Wang Lixing. 1992. *Zhongguo jindai wenxue kaolun* [An evidential study of modern Chinese literature]. Nanjing: Nanjing daxue chubanshe.

Wang Renze and Xiong Shanghou. 1984. "Huang Chujiu." In *Minguo renwu zhuan* [Biographies of prominent figures in the Republican era], ed. Li Xin and Sun Sibai, 4:268–74. Beijing: Zhonghua shuju.

Wang Shaozeng. 1984. *Jindai chuban jia Zhang Yuanji* [A modern publisher—Zhang Yuanji]. Beijing: Shangwu yinshuguan.

Wang Tao. [1875] 1989. *Yingruan suozhi* [Fragmented records of Shanghai]. Repr., Shanghai: Shanghai guji.

———. [1876] 1983. *Taoyuan chidu* [Letters from Tao's garden]. Taipei: Wenhai chubanshe.

———. 1886. "Gezhi shuyuan bingxu nian keyi xu" [Preface to the essay contest of the *bingwu* year of the Polytechnic Institute]. In *Gezhi shuyuan keyi* [Course readers and documents of the Shanghai Polytechnic Institute], comp. Wang Tao, 1:1. Shanghai: Shanghai shiyin shuju.

———, comp. 1886–1893. *Gezhi shuyuan keyi* [Course readers and documents in Shanghai Polytechnic Institute]. 8 vols. Shanghai: Shanghai shiyin shuju.

———. 1889. *Chunqiu shuo run zhi ri kao* [An evidential study of the first days of the lunar month, intercalary days, and solar terms of spring and autumn]. Shanghai: N.p.

Wang Tieya. 1957. *Zhongwai jiu yuezhang huibian* [Compiled documents about the treaties and regulations of trade between China and foreign countries]. Beijing: Shenghuo dushu xinzhi sanlian shudian.

Wang Xiaonong. 1957. *Wang Xiaonong xiju ji* [Anthology of plays by Wang Xiaonong]. Beijing: Renmin wenxue chubanshe.

Wang Xiqi, comp. 1964. *Xiao fang hu zhai yidi congchao* [Little Square Pot's collection of travelogues]. Taipei: Guangwen shuju.

Wang Xiuchu. 1971. *Yangzhou shiri ji* [Ten days in Yangzhou]. Taipei: Guang wen chubanshe.

Wang Yunwu. 1973. *Shangwu yinshuguan yu xin jiaoyu nianpu* [The Commercial Press and the chronicle of new education]. Taipei: Shangwu yinshuguan.

Wang Zhaochun. 1991. *Zhongguo huoqi shi* [A history of armaments in China]. Beijing: Junshi kexue chubanshe.

Wang Zhenzhong. 1996. *Ming Qing Hui shang yu Huai Yang she hui bianqian* [The Hui merchants and social changes in the Huai Yang region during the Ming and the Qing periods]. Beijing: Sanlian shudian.

Wanguo gongbao. [1876] 1992. "Ji Shanghai Gezhi shuyuan zaocheng" [The founding of Shanghai Polytechnic Institute]. In *Yangwu yundong shiqi jiaoyu* [Chinese education in the era of foreign affairs: Collected documents], comp. Gao Shiliang, 739. Shanghai: Shanghai jiaoyu chubanshe.

Ward, Barbara E. 1985. "Regional Operas and Their Audiences: Evidence from Hong Kong." In *Popular Culture in Late Imperial China,* ed. David Johnson, Andrew Nathan, Evelyn Rawski, 166–87. Berkeley and Los Angeles: University of California Press.

Wasserstrom, Jeffrey N. 1991. *Student Protests in Twentieth-Century China: The View from Shanghai.* Stanford: Stanford University Press.

Wei Yungong. [1904] 1969. *Jiangnan zhizaoju ji* [Records of the Jiangnan Arsenal]. Repr., Taipei: Wenhai chubanshe.

Wei Zichu. 1950. *Diguo zhuyi dui hua touzi* [Imperialist investments in China]. Beijing: Renmin chubanshe.

Wittrock, Björn. 2000. "Modernity: One, None, or Many? European Origins and Modernity as a Global Condition." *Daedalus,* Winter: 31–60.

Wong, Bin R. 1997. *China Transformed: Historical Change and the Limits of European Experience.* Ithaca, N.Y.: Cornell University Press.

Woodside, Alexander. 1989. "State Scholars and Orthodoxy: The Qing Academies, 1736–1839." In *Orthodox in Late Imperial China,* ed. Liu Kwan-ching, 158–84. Berkeley and Los Angeles: University of California Press.

———. 1994. "The Divorce between Political Center and Educational Creativity in Late Imperial China." In *Education and Society in Late Imperial China, 1600–1900,* ed. Benjamin Elman and Alexander Woodside, 458–92. Berkeley and Los Angeles: University of California Press.

Wright, Arnold, and H. A. Cartwright. 1908. *Twentieth Century Impressions of Hong Kong, Shanghai, and Other Treaty Ports of China: Their History, People, Commerce, Industries, and Resources.* London: Lloyds Greater Britain.

Wright, David A. 1995. "Careers in Western Science in Nineteenth-Century China, Xu Shou, and Xu Jianyin." *Journal of the Royal Asiatic Society,* 3rd ser., 5, no. 1: 49–90.

———. 1996. "John Fryer and Shanghai Polytechnic Institute: Making Space for Science in Nineteenth-Century China." *Historical Journal of Asiatic Studies* 29: 1–16.

———. 1997. "The Great Desideratum: Chinese Chemical Nomenclature and the Transmission of Western Chemical Concepts." *Chinese Science* 14: 35–70.

Wright, Mary C., ed. 1968. *China in Revolution: The First Phase, 1900–1913.* New Haven: Yale University Press.

Wu Chengming. 1956. *Diguo zhuyi zai jiu Zhongguo de touzi* [The imperialists' investment in China]. Beijing: Renmin chubanshe.

Wu Chenyi. 1978. *Qingmo Shanghai zujie shehui* [The communities in the International Settlement in the late Qing]. Taipei: Wenshizhe chubanshe.

Wu Dazheng. 1982. "Ke zhai riji" [The diary of the Ke Studio]. In *Qing dai riji huichao* [Selected diaries from the Qing dynasty], ed. P. E. A. Liu. Shanghai: Shanghai renmin chubanshe.

Wu Jianren. [1906] 1984. *Jue yu hui* [The burned]. Repr., Taipei: Guangya chuban youxian gongsi.

Wu Qixun. [1848] 1960. *Zhiwu mingshi tukao* [An evidential study on plant names, with pictures]. Repr., Taipei: Chien shu chu.

Wu Woyao. [1905] 1984. *Ku Shehui* [The bitter society]. Wan Qing xiaoshuo daxi [Late Qing fiction]. Repr., Taipei: Guangya chuban youxian gongsi.

Wu Xiangxiang. 1965. *Zhongguo xiandai renwu* [Prominent figures in modern China]. Taipei: Ziyou taiping yang wenhua shiye gongsi.

Wu Xin and Yao Wennan. [1918] 1970. *Shanghai xian xuzhi* [Sequel to the Gazetteer of Shanghai county]. Repr., Taipei: Chengwen chubanshe.

Wu Youru. [1908] 1983a. *Wu Youru huabao: Haiguo congtan* [Treasures of Wu Youru's painting: Series on "ocean countries"]. Repr., Shanghai: Shanghai guji chubanshe.

———. [1908] 1983b. *Wu Youru huabao: Mingsheng huace* [Treasures of Wu Youru's painting: Series on "well-known sites"]. Repr., Shanghai: Shanghai guji chubanshe.

Wu Yun. [1869] 1969. *De yi lu* [One with everything: A journal]. Repr., Taipei: Huan wen shuju.

Wu Zhichang. 1988. *Ke chuang xianhua; Xu Ke chuang xianhua* [Random talks on the roads, and its sequel]. Beijing: Wenhua yishu chubanshe.

Wylie, Alexander. 1867. *Memorials of Protestant Missionaries to the Chinese: Giving a List of Their Publications, and Obituary Notices of the Deceased*. Shanghai: American Presbyterian Mission Press.

Wylie, Alexander, James Thomas, and Henri Cordier. 1897. *The Chinese Researches*. Shanghai: N.p.

Xia Dongyuan. 1992. *Yangwu yundong shi* [A history of the Foreign Affairs movement]. Shanghai: Huadong shida chubanshe.

Xiao Luzong juyue hui [The Filipino Society for the Resistance of the Chinese Exclusion Act]. [1905] 1960. "Guomin juyue ge" [Sing to resist]. In *Fan Mei huagong jinyue wenxueji* [Literary anthology of opposition to Chinese exclusion in the United States], comp. Ah Ying, 20–21. Beijing: Zhonghua shuju.

Xiong Yuezhi. 1994. *Xixue dongjian yu wan Qing shehui* [The eastward flow of Western learning and the late Qing society]. Shanghai: Shanghai renmin chubanshe.

———. 1996. "Zhang Yuan: Wan Qing yige gonggong kongjian yanjiu" [Zhang Garden: A study of a public space in late Qing Shanghai]. *Dang'an yu shixue* [Archive and historiography] 12: 31–43.

———. 1998. "Wan Qing Shanghai siyuan kaifang yu gonggong kongjian kouzhan" [Public space and the open access to private gardens in late Qing Shanghai]. *Xueshu yuekan* [Scholarly monthly] 8: 73–81.

Xu Banmei. 1957. *Hua ju chuang shi qi huiyi lu* [Reminiscences of the early stage of Chinese spoken drama]. Beijing: Zhongguo xiju chubanshe.

Xu Baoqiang. 2001. "Ziben zhuyi bushi shenme" [What capitalism is not]. *Shijie* [Horizon], 2: 46–81.

Xu Chaojun. 1936. "Ziming zhongbiao tushuo" [Illustrated explanations of how clocks work]. Reprinted in *Gaohou meng qiu* [Primary search for height and depth]. *Qingchao xu wenxian tonggao* [Annotated classics of the Qing dynasty, a sequel], no. 265, series comp. Liu Jinzao. Shanghai: Shangwu yinshuguan.

Xu Chaojun and Huang Hanmin. 1994. "Zaoqi Shanghai de zibenjia he gongren jieji." In *Shanghai jindai jingji shi di yi juan* [Volume 1 of economic history of modern Shanghai], comp. Ding Richu, 648–83. Shanghai: Shanghai renmin.

Xu Ke. 1917. *Qing bai leichao* [Compiled popular records of the Qing dynasty]. Shanghai: Shangwu yinshuguan.

Xu Muyun. 1938. *Zhongguo xiju shi* [A history of Chinese theater]. Shanghai: Shijie shuju.

Xu Qianfang. 1989. *Yangzhou feng tu jilue* [The cultural custom of Yangzhou]. Yangzhou: Jiangsu Guangling guji keyinshe.

Xu Run. 1927. *Xu Yuzhai zizu nianpu* [The chronic of Xu Run, by himself]. N.p: Xiangshan Xu shi.

Xü Weize. 1902. *Zeng ban dong xi xue shulu* [An enlarged version of the book records of Eastern and Western learnings]. Shanghai: N.p.

Xu Yang and Liaoning sheng bowuguan. [1757] 1988. *Qing Xu Yang Gusu fanhua tu* [Xu Yang's painting of Prosperous Suzhou]. Repr., Hong Kong: Shangwu yinshuguan.

Xu Yinong. 2000. *The Chinese City in Space and Time: The Development of Urban Form in Suzhou*. Honolulu: University of Hawaii Press.

Xue Fucheng. [1879] 1983. *Chouyang chuyi* [Preliminary thoughts on foreign policies]. In *Zhongguo jindai hangyun shi ziliao* [Compiled documents on modern Chinese transportation], ed. Nie Baozhang, 1:12–54. Repr., Shanghai: Shanghai renmin.

———. 1890. "*Gezhi huibian* xu" [Preface to the *Journal of Sciences and Industry*]. *Gezhi huibian* 5, no. 1 (Spring): 2–3.

———. [1891] 1985. *Chushi Ying Fa Yi Bi siguo riji* [The European diary of Xue Fucheng, envoy extraordinaire of imperial China]. Repr., Changsha: Yuelu shushe.

———. 1966. "Shu Hefei xiangbo Li gong yong Hu ping Wu" [Li Hongzhang from Hefei used Shanghai to pacify Jiangsu]. In *Zhongguo jin bai nian shi ziliao chubian* [Compiled documents on the past hundred years of Chinese history], comp. Zuo Shunsheng, 163–72. Taipei: Taiwan Zhonghua shuju.

Xue Liyong. 1996. *Xianhua Shanghai* [Anecdotes of Shanghai]. Shanghai: Shanghai shudian chubanshe.

Xue Suizhi and Chang Juncai, eds. 1983. *Lin Shu yanjiu ziliao* [Documents for Lin Shu studies]. Fuzhou: Fujian renmin chubanshe.

Xuebu [The Bureau of Education]. 1906. *Xuebu diyici shending chudeng xiaoxue zanyong shumu* [The first catalog of the standardized elementary schoolbooks selected by the Bureau of Education]. Beijing: N.p.

———. N.d. *Gaodeng xiaoxuetang zhongxuetang zanyong keben zhi shumu* [Catalog of junior high school textbooks]. Beijing: N.p.

Yamada Keiji. 1995. *Higashi Ajia no honzo to hakubutsugaku no sekai* [The world of botany and the concept of cosmology]. Kyoto: Kokusai Nihon Bunka Kenkyu Senta.

Yang Mo, comp. 1910. *Xijin sizhe shishi huicun* [Compiled facts about the four talents from Xijin]. Wuxi: N.p.

Yang Yaoshen. 1994. *Lao hua Shanghai Fa zujie* [Reminiscences of the French concession of Shanghai]. Shanghai: Shanghai renmin chubanshe.

Yang Zhangsheng. 1886. *Jingchen zalu* [Miscellaneous notes on the flower of dreams]. Shanghai: Tongwen shuju.

Yangwu shi xuehui [Foreign Affairs Historical Society], comp. 1961. *Yangwu yundong* [Source materials about foreign affairs movement]. Shanghai: Shanghai renmin chubanshe.

Yao Gonghe. [1917] 1989. *Shanghai xianhua* [Informal talks about Shanghai]. Shanghai: Shanghai guji.

Yao Min'ai. [1918] 1990. "Nanbei liyuan lueshi" [A brief history of opera troupes in the north and the south]. In *Jubu congkan* [Compiled records of the opera], comp. Zhou Jianyun, 1–9. Minguo congshu, series 2, no. 69. Shanghai: Jiaotung tushuguan.

Ye Changchi. 1989. *Cangshu jishi shi* [Anecdotal poems on book collection]. Shanghai: Shanghai guji chubanshe.

Yeh, Catherine Vance. 1997. "The Life-Style of Four Wenren in Late Qing Shanghai." *Harvard Journal of Asiatic Studies* 57, no. 2: 419–70.

Yeh, Wen-Hsin. 1990. *The Alienated Academy: Culture and Politics in Republican China, 1919–1937.* Cambridge, Mass.: Council on East Asian Studies, Harvard University. Distributed by Harvard University Press.

Yen Huiqing [W. W. Yen]. 1974. *East-West Kaleidoscope, 1877–1946: An Autobiography.* New York: St. John's University Press.

Yiming. 1962. "Tan xiangshan" [Honolulu]. In *Fan Mei huagong jinyue wenxueji* [Literary anthology of opposition to Chinese exclusion in the United States], comp. Ah Ying, 6. Beijing: Zhonghua shuju.

Ying Baoshi and Yu Yue. [1872] 1975. *Shanghai xianzhi* [The Gazetteer of Shanghai]. Repr., Taipei: Chengwen chubanshe.

Yishu gonghui [The Association of Translators]. [1897] 1954. "Yishu gonghui zhangcheng" [The regulation of the Association of Translators]. In *Zhongguo jindai chuban shiliao erbian* [The second compilation of documents on modern Chinese printing and publishing], comp. Zhang Jinglu, 90–91. Shanghai: Qunlian chubanshe.

"Yisu shenci beiji" [The stone inscription of the temple at Yisu, on the third year of Jiaqing, Third Month, fourth day]. 1959. In *Jiangsu Ming Qing yilai beike ziliao xuanji* [Selected inscriptions in Jiangsu province since the Ming and the Qing], comp. Jiangsu sheng bowuguan, 295–96. Beijing: Sanlian.

Yoshida, Mitsukuni. 1989. *Nihon to Chugoku: Gijutsu to kindaika* [Japan and China: Technological exchanges]. Tokyo: Sanseido.

Yoshimi Shunya. 1992. *Hakurankai no seijigaku: Manazashi no kindai* [The politics of the world expositions]. Tokyo: Chuo Koronsha.

Yu Xingmin. 1991. *Shanghai, 1862 nian* [Shanghai in the year 1862]. Shanghai: Shanghai renmin chubanshe.

Yu Yue. 1895. "*Huangchao jingshi wen xubian xu*" [Preface to *The sequel to essays of statecraft of the dynasty*]. In *Huanghcao jingshi wen xubian* [The sequel to essays of statecraft of the dynasty], comp. Ge Shijun, 1. Shanghai: Shanghai shuju.

Yu Zhibin. 1989. "Jiangsu nanfang jingju shishu" [A historical account of the southern-style Peking Opera in Nanjing, Jiangsu Province]. *Yishu baijia*, no. 1: 19–26.

Yuan Hanqing. 1987. "Zixue youcheng de kexue bianyizhe Du Yaquan xiansheng" [The self-taught compiler and editor of science, Du Yaquan]. In *Shangwu yinshuguan jiushi nian* [Ninety years of the Commercial Press], 83–87. Beijing: Shangwu yinshuguan.

Yüan Mei. 1972. *Suiyüan shihua* [Suiyüan's remarks on poetry]. Beijing: Renmin wenxue chubanshe.

Yuan Zuzhi. 1887. *Chongxiu Huyou zaji* [Miscellaneous records of Shanghai, revised]. Shanghai: N.p.

Zeng Guofan. 1936. *Zeng Guofan riji* [Diaries of Zeng Guofan]. Shanghai: Qizhi shuju.

———. 1985a. "Li Hongzhang gaiyou lunchuan fu hu zhe" [Li Hongzhang changed to take the ship to Shanghai]. In *Zeng Guofan Quanji* [The complete works of Zeng Guofan], 4:2123–24. Changshai: Yuelu shushe.

———. 1985b. "Da kenci jiechi zhejiang sheng geguan bing zuncha ge cankuan ji baoju Li Hongzhang caikan zhongji ge zhepian" [A reply to excuse myself from the position of authority over Zhejiang provincial officials and to investigate the matters according to the court's instruction, as well as to recommend Li Hongzhang, who is well able to perform an important role in the country]. In *Zeng Guofan quanji* [Complete works of Zeng Guofan], 3:1804–6. Changsha: Yuelu shushe.

Zeng Yangfeng. 1998. *Zhongguo yanzheng shi* [A history of salt administration in China]. Beijing: Shangwu yinshuguan.

ZGXQZBWH [Zhongguo xiquzhi bianweihui, or the Editorial Committee of Record of Chinese Theater], comp. 1990. *Zhongguo xiquzhi: Shanghai juan* [Gazetteers of Chinese theater: Shanghai]. Beijing: Zhongguo ISBN zhongxin.

———, comp. 1992. *Zhongguo xiquzhi: Jiangsu juan* [Gazetteers of Chinese theater: The Jiangsu volume]. Beijing: Zhongguo ISBN zhongxin.

Zhang Geng. 2003. *Zhongguo huaju yundong shi chugao* [History of the spoken drama movement in China]. In *Zhang Geng wen lu* [Works of Zhang Geng], vol. 6. Changsha: Hunan wenyi chubanshe.

Zhang Guyu. 1987. "Liyuan jiushi erti" [Two pieces of information about the old Shanghai theaters]. In *Shanghai xiqu shiliao huicui* [Compiled documents of Shanghai theaters], comp. Zhou Gongping, 3:11–16. Shanghai: Shanghai yishu yanjiusuo.

Zhang Honglu. 1879–1880. "Bingbao youli nanyang qingxing" [Report on the inspections of Southeast Asia]. In Zhaoshangju dang'an [The archive of the China Merchants Steam Navigation Co.], Beijing Number Two Archive, *zong* 468(2), *juan* 24.

Zhang Houquan. 1988. *Zhao shang ju shi: Jindai bufen* [The history of Zhao shang ju: Modern era]. Beijing: Renmin jiaotong chubanshe.

Zhang Hua. 1983. *Bo wu zhi* [Broad learning of things]. Taipei: Shangwu yinshuguan.

Zhang Renlong. 1998. *Shanghai shizheng gongcheng zhi* [Gazetteer of Shanghai municipal engineering]. Shanghai: Shanghai shehui kexue chubanshe.

Zhang Shunian. 1991. *Zhang Yuanji nianpu* [The chronicle of Zhang Yuanji]. Shanghai: Shangwu yinshuguan.

Zhang Xiangwen [1929] 1968. *Nanyuan conggao* [Collected writings of South Garden]. Taipei: Wenhai chubanshe.

Zhang Xichen. 1987. "Mantan Shangwu yinshuguan" [Casual recollections about the Commercial Press]. In *Shangwu yinshuguan jiushi nien* [Ninety years of the Commercial Press], 102–24. Beijing: Shangwu yinshuguan.

Zhang Xiumin. 1989. *Zhongguo yinshua shi* [A history of print technology in China]. Shanghai: Shanghai renmin chubanshe.

Zhang Yinhuan, comp. 1897. *Xixue fuqiang congshu* [Collectanea of Western learning, wealth and power]. N.p.: Xiao cang shanfang.

Zhang Yuanji. [1911] 1981. "Zhi Miao Quansun" [Letters to Miao Quansun]. In *Zhang Yuanji shuzha* [Correspondences of Zhang Yuanji], comp. Zhang Shunian and Zhang Renfeng, 1–7. Shanghai: Shangwu yinshuguan.

———. 1951. *Hanfen lou jinyu shulu* [Catalog of the unburned books of the Hanfen lou library]. Beijing: Shangwu yinshuguan.

———. 1992. "Dongfang tushuguan gaikuang, yuanqi" [A general introduction to the Oriental Library and its origin]. In *Shangwu yinshuguan jiushiwu nian* [Ninety-five years of the Commercial Press], 21–22. Beijing: Shangwu yinshuguan.

Zhang Yufa. 1971. *Qingji de lixian tuanti* [The constitutional groups in the late Qing]. Taipei: Zhongyanyuan zhongguo jindaishi yanjiusuo.

———. 1975. *Qingji de geming tuanti* [The revolutionary groups in the late Qing]. Taipei: Zhongyanyuan zhongguo jindaishi yanjiusuo.

Zhang Yuying. [1941] 1953. "Xihai geming shuzheng [The books that were prevalent during the 1911 Revolution]. In *Zhongguo jindai chuban shiliao* [The first compilation of documents on modern Chinese printing and publishing], comp. Zhang Jinglu, 140–83. Shanghai: Shangza chubanshe.

Zhang Zegang. 1987. "*Ershi shiji dawutai* chuankan shimo" [The creation of the journal *Grand theater of the twentieth century*]. In *Shanghai xiqu shiliao huicui* [Compiled documents of Shanghai theaters], comp. Zhou Gongpin, 2:78–81. Shanghai: Shanghai yishu yanjiusuo.

———. 1988. "Xiqu gailiang yundong the wutai shijianzhe: Feng Zihe de yishu zhuiqiu" [The practitioner of the theatrical reform movement: The artistic pursuit of Feng Zihe]. In *Shanghai xiqu shiliao huicui* [Compiled documents of Shanghai theaters], comp. Zhou Gongpin, 5:31–36. Shanghai: Shanghai yishu yanjiusuo.

Zhang Zhidong. [1874] 1963. *Shumu dawen* [Annotated bibliography of books]. In *Zhang Wenxiang gong quanji* [The complete works of Zhang Wenxiang], comp. Wang Shu'nan, 6:3831–67. Taipei: Wenhai chubanshe.

———. [1898] 1963. *Quanxue pian* [Persuasion of learning]. In *Zhang Wenxiang gong quanji* [The complete works of Zhang Wenxiang], comp. Wang Shu'nan, 6: 3699–3750. Taipei: Wenhai chubanshe.

———. 1918. "Zhi Jiangning Liu Zhitai, Shanghai Sheng Dachen" [To Governor Liu at Jiangnin and Minister Sheng at Shanghai]. In *Zhang Wenxiang gong diangao* [An anthology of telegrams by Zhang Zhidong]. Shanghai: N.p.

Zhang Zhongli and Chen Zengnian. 1985. *Shaxun jituan zai jiu Zhongguo* [The Sassoons in old China]. Beijing: Renmin chubanshe.

Zhao Erxun. 1976a. *Qing shi gao* [The history of the Qing]. Beijing: Zhonghua shuju.

———. 1976b. "Sheng zu benji" [Biography of the Shengzu emperor]. In *Qing shi gao* [The history of the Qing], 6:169. Beijing: Zhonghua shuju.

———. 1976c. "*Taiwan yudi* xu" [Preface to *Geography of Taiwan*). In *Qing shi gao* [The history of the Qing), 71, 46:2263. Beijing: Zhonghua shuju.

Zhao Yashu. 1973. "Ma Xinyi beici de lailong qumai" [The context of the assassination of Ma Xinyi]. In *Ma Xinyi shilue xuanji* [Compiled records of the Ma Xinyi incident], comp. Wang Jiajian, 15–40. Taipei: Hwakang.

Zhao Zhibi, comp. [1775] 1983. *Pingshan tang tuzhi* [The map gazetteer of Pingshan Pavilion]. Repr., Taipei: Chengwen chubanshe.

Zhaoshang ju. 1880. "Zhaoshang ju yi Xiao lusong, Xianluo fenju lingshi shendong wengao" [The SNC documents prepared for the counselors, gentries, and the board members of the offices in the Little Luzon and Thailand]. In Zhaoshangju dang'an [The archive of the China Merchants Steam Navigation Co.]. Beijing Number Two Archive, *zong* 468(2), *juan* 34.

Zheng Guanying. [1894] 2002. *Shengshi weiyan* [Disaster warning in the prosperous era]. Repr., Beijing: Huaxia chubanshe.

———. [1905] 1982. "Ai huang ren" [A sad song for the people of yellow skin]. Reprinted in *Dizhi huagong jinyue wenxueji* [Literary anthology of resistance to Chinese exclusion in the United States], 6–7. Taipei: Guangya chubanshe.

Zheng Xuepu and Guo Jingkun. 1986. "Ningbo kunju xingshuai jihue" [The rise and fall of the Kun opera in Ningbo]. In *Yishu yanjiu ziliao* [Documents for the studies of art], comp. Zhejiang sheng yuishu yanjiusuo [Institute of Art Studies, Zhejiang Province], 3:70–93. Hangzhou: Zhejiang yishu yanjiusuo.

Zheng Yimei, 1992. *Haishang chunqiu* [Springs and autumns in Shanghai]. Shanghai: Shanghai shudian.

———. 1996. "Hongdong yishi de youxi chang" [The playgrounds that made a stir in Shanghai]. In *Yi hai yi shao xu bian* [Continued notes from the ocean of arts], 192–97. Tianjin: Tianjin guji chubanshe.

Zheng Zhenduo, Feng Cixing, Zhang Xichen, Hu Yuzhi, Zhou Yutong, Wu Juenong, and Li Shicen. [1927] 1980. "Jiu Si Yi'er can' an dui Guomindang de kanji shu" [Letter of objection to GMD, regarding the massacre on April 12]. Reprinted in *Wenshi ziliao xuanji* [Materials for historical and cultural studies], 70:1–2. Beijing: Zhonghua shuju.

Zheng Zhicheng. 1996. *Gudong suojji quanbian* [Complete collection of annotated records of antiques]. Beijing: Beijing chubanshe.

Zheng Zu'an. [1870] 1989. "Ti Ji" [Editor's note]. Reprinted in *Yingruan zazhi* [Miscellaneous notes in the city by the sea], by Wang Tao, 1–5. Shanghai: Shanghai renmin chubanshe.

Zhongguo shixue hui [Chinese Historical Society], comp. 1995 *Jiawu zhanzheng yu Weng Tonghe* [The Sino-Japanese War and Weng Tonghe]. Beijing: Zhongguo renmin daxue.

Zhongwai ribao [China and world daily]. [1905] 1962. "Lun zai Shanghai zhi Min Yue shangren jiyi shi" [On the meetings organized by Fujian and Guangdong merchants in Shanghai], April 13. Reprinted in *Fan Mei huagong jinyue wenxue ji* [Literary anthology of opposition to Chinese exclusion in the United States], comp. Ah Ying, 597. Beijing: Zhonghua shuju.

Zhou Zhifu. 1951. *Jingxi jin bainian suoji (Daoxian yilai liyuan xinian xiaolu)* [Peking opera in the past hundred years]. Repr., Hong Kong: Commercial Press.

Zhu Dongan. 1994. *Zeng Guofan mufu yanjiu* [A study on the private secretariat of Zeng Guofan]. Chongqing: Sichuan renmin chubanshe.

Zhu Kebao. [1844] 1962. *Chouren zhuan sanbian* [Biographies of mathematicians and astronomers, vol. 3]. Shanghai: Shijie shuju.

Zhu Shuangyün. 1914. *Xin ju shi* [The history of new drama]. China: N.p.

Zhu Wenwei. 1978. "Zhu Zhiyao" [Biography of Zhu Zhiyao]. In *Minguo renwu zhuan* [Biographies of figures in the Republican period], comp. Li Xin and Sun Sibai, 4:236–42. Beijing: Zhunghua shuju.

Zhu Zongyuan and Gu Xiguang. [1904] 1954. "Yishu jingyan lu xuli" [Prefaces and forewords to Records of the translated books]. In *Zhongguo jindai chuban shiliao* [The second compilation of documents on modern Chinese printing and publishing], comp. Zhang Jinglu, 95–101. Shanghai: Qunlian chubanshe.

Zhuang Shi. 1987. "Zhuang Yu jiazhuan" [A biography of Zhuang Yu]. In *Shangwu yinshuguan jiushi nian* [Ninety years of the Commercial Press], 73–75. Beijing: Shangwu yinshuguan.

Zhuang Yu. 1931. "Zuijin sanshiwu nian zhi Shangwu yinshuguan" [The Commercial Press in the past thirty-five years]. In *Zuijin sanshiwu nian zhi Zhungguo jiaoyu* [Education in China in the past thirty-five years], comp. Zhuang Yu and He Shengding, 46–47. Shanghai: Commercial Press.

———. 1987a. "Tan tan woguan bianji jiaoke shu de bianqian" [The history of the compilation of textbooks in the Commercial Press]. In *Shangwu yinshuguan jiushi nian* [Ninety years of the Commercial Press], 62–72. Beijing: Shangwu yinshuguan.

————. 1987b. "Bao Xianchang xiansheng shilue" [The life and work of Mr. Bao Xian-chang]. In *Shangwu yinshuguan jiushi nian* [Ninety years of the Commercial Press], 6–8. Beijing: Shangwu yinshuguan.

Zhuang Yu and He Shengding, comps. 1931. *Zuijin sanshiwu nian zhi Zhongguo jiaoyu* [Education in China in the past thirty-five years]. Shanghai: Commercial Press.

Zou Yiren. 1980. *Jiu Shanghai renkou bianqian de yanjiu* [A study of the population changes in old Shanghai]. Shanghai: Shanghai renmin chubanshe.

Index

Meng Yue is associate professor of Chinese literature and culture at the Tsinghua University, China. She is the author of *History and Narrative on Contemporary Chinese Literature* and a coauthor of *Breaking the Surface of History: Women Writers in Modern China, 1917–1949.*